Divine Violence

Divine Violence

SPECTACLE, PSYCHOSEXUALITY,

& RADICAL CHRISTIANITY IN THE

ARGENTINE "DIRTY WAR"

FRANK GRAZIANO

Westview Press
BOULDER • SAN FRANCISCO • OXFORD

Copyright © 1992 by Westview Press, Inc.

Published in 1992 in the United States of America by Westview Press, Inc., 5500 Central Avenue, Boulder, Colorado 80301-2847, and in the United Kingdom by Westview Press, 36 Lonsdale Road, Summertown, Oxford OX2 7EW

Library of Congress Cataloging-in-Publication Data
Graziano, Frank, 1955–
    Divine violence : spectacle, psychosexuality, and radical
Christianity in the Argentine "dirty war" / Frank Graziano.
    p. cm.
    Includes index.
    ISBN 0-8133-8231-9 (hc.)   ISBN 0-8133-8232-7 (pb.)
    1. State-sponsored terrorism—Argentina—History—20th century.
2. Violence—Argentina—History—20th century.   3. Torture—
Argentina—History—20th century.   4. Social psychology—Argentina.
5. Argentina—Politics and government—1955-1983.   I. Title.
HV6322.3.A7G7   1992
323'.044'0982—dc20   91-42871
                                                                                          CIP

Printed and bound in the United States of America

The paper used in this publication meets the requirements
of the American National Standard for Permanence of Paper
for Printed Library Materials Z39.48-1984.

10   9   8   7   6   5   4   3   2   1

For Joanne

America is ungovernable. Those who have served the Revolution have plowed the sea. The only thing one can do in America is emigrate. These countries will infallibly fall into the hands of uncontrollable masses and then pass to petty, almost imperceptible tyrants of all colors and races, devoured by crimes and exterminated by ferocity. . . . Where has anyone ever imagined that an entire world would fall into frenzy and devour its own race like cannibals? . . . If it were possible for one part of the world to return to primitive chaos, this would be the final period of America.

—Simón Bolívar

Contents

Preface

THE PRINCIPAL THEMATIC LOCUS of *Divine Violence* lies at the intersection of religion, violence, and psychosexuality. The study is centrally concerned with the Argentine "dirty war" insofar as the discourse and deeds constituting that historical episode occupy its focus, but it is also concerned with the religion-violence-psychosexuality nexus as it relates to the desire for power and to myths and rituals manifesting that desire, all matters well beyond the Argentine case study used to explore them.

The highly ritualized atrocity and symbolically freighted discourse of the "dirty war," documented extensively and uniquely in a body of testimony generated by President Raúl Alfonsín's commission of inquiry in 1983–1984 and by the Junta members' trials in 1985, make the "dirty war" a model case for pursuing the source of political violence in complexities that are generally dismissed by disciplinary analyses. The eradication of terrorism and the violent restructuring of an economy are one matter, any observer must recognize, while application of the *picana eléctrica* to the genitalia of thousands of citizens whose enmity is mythologically constructed (to the degree of stylizing them as the Antichrist, for example) is quite another. And yet both agendas, compounded by others, are manifest in the same overdetermined "dirty war," are implemented by the same polysemous form of violence. I am not convinced by the tradition disregarding the nature and function of that form as an insignificant peculiarity subordinate to a dominant politico-economic agenda. What "dirty war" violence and discourse yield when their peculiarities are called to task rather than dismissed is what this study has to offer.

I hold as self-evident that the institution of "disappearance" (abduction, torture, execution) as a political strategy constitutes a blatant and grotesque breach of domestic Argentine law, of international human rights conventions, of ethics by any rendering, and of the fundamental values on which civilization is founded. But this is not my subject matter. The intent of *Divine Violence* is not to demonstrate guilt, to express moral or political indignation, to editorialize on the banality of evil, or to add a voice to the discourse of political activism, all of which have adequate representation elsewhere. I propose to explore the "dirty war" from within rather than to debate its advocates. I seek to establish a cultural base for analyzing political violence, but my understanding of Junta atrocity in spectacular theatrics, in myth and ritual, and in psychodynamics is by no means a justification or rationale for the atrocity; an understanding is not a condonation, an explanation not a pardon. Nor are they academic exercises. My inquiry is grounded in the romantic belief that we can erode the viability of State violence by exposing the psychosexual structures perpetuating it and by demythologizing the politico-religious masquerade that endows it with eschatological necessity.

*   *   *

A number of concepts central to this study appear throughout the text in quotation marks or italics. Those in the former category include "dirty war," "subversive," and "disappear" in their various forms. Although the repetition of quotation marks is stylistically cumbersome, I felt that the subtle mockery they imply prevents each term's euphemistic gloss from obscuring the original concept that the term politicizes. Subversives seek to destabilize the State; "subversives" are individuals whose seditious identities have been projected onto them.

Signifiers appearing in italics are key Spanish terms defined once but then repeated in the text untranslated: for example, *picana*, *desaparecido*, *quirófano*, and *chupado*. Finally, appearing occasionally in the notes are two acronyms: APDH, representing the Asamblea Permanente por los Derechos Humanos, and CELS, representing the Centro de Estudios Legales y Sociales. The appearance of the acronyms identifies material cited from these organizations' respective archives in Buenos Aires.

Frank Graziano

Acknowledgments

MY GREATEST SINGLE DEBT is to the Latin American Institute at the University of New Mexico, which supported my early research and writing with two Title VI fellowships and a Tinker field research grant. Of considerable help at later stages of the manuscript's development were a research fellowship at the John Carter Brown Library, Brown University; a visiting fellowship in the Program in Atlantic History, Culture, and Society at The Johns Hopkins University; and a Fulbright research fellowship. I acknowledge them all most gratefully.

Americas Watch in Washington, D.C., kindly provided access to its Argentina files, which included the *Diario del Juicio* that was essential to my research. The archives of the Asamblea Permanente por los Derechos Humanos and the Centro de Estudios Legales y Sociales, both in Buenos Aires, were also invaluable. I extend my sincere thanks to these organizations' generous, dedicated staffs and, for related assistance, to Ernesto Sábato and Graciela Fernández Meijide.

I am also deeply indebted to my student research assistant, Erica Hauver, and to Professors Peter Bakewell, Rudolph Binion, Dick Gerdes, and Gilbert Merkx, all of whom provided useful comments for the manuscript's revision.

F.G.

A Note on Method

Texts, yes: but there are human texts. Texts,
undoubtedly: but all texts. . . . Texts, of course:
but not nothing but texts.

—Lucien Febvre

I

THERE HAS BEEN a great deal of concern in recent scholarship about the relationship between history (often denominated "fact") and literary fiction, a matter instigated above all by the nineteenth century's insistence of "fact" as the principal category of reality and by the accompanying departure that history made from literature in pursuit of autonomous status as a more scientific discipline.[1] One result of the recent theoretical inquiries has been a reendorsement—in a higher register—of the affinity between literary and historical discourse, a position grounded in the recognition that history consists not of events per se but rather of events under description, events that either come to us in narrative form or are elaborated through narrative as a means of cognition. But the evidence on which historical narrative is based does not dictate which of the infinite possible competing versions is to be constructed, and no architectural model is inherent in the events themselves. Consequently the "factual" accounts resulting from any events' narration (and in this I include above all their analytical narration) amount to so many interpretations for want of the definitive version, the objective meaning, the moralizable conclusions absent from evidence and events themselves.[2]

That observation was already taking shape in the traditions that underpin contemporary textual theory, traditions that were troubled, as

1

Edward Said summarized it, by "the inevitable contamination of what is supposedly solid positive knowledge by human interpretation, vagaries, willfulness, biases, grounding in personality, radically human circumstantiality, worldliness." Said went on to point out that Friedrich Nietzsche, Karl Marx, and Sigmund Freud each in his own way recognized

> that such apparently safe steps in the production of knowledge as the collecting and disposing of evidence, or the reading and understanding of a text, all involve a very high degree of interpretive leeway, subject not so much to rationality and scientific control as to the assertion of will, arbitrary speculation, repressive (and repressing) judgement.[3]

The subjective influences folded into purportedly cold, hard data, the nonneutral frames of analysis, the determination of what is relevant and what is not, of what constitutes an ensemble of interrelations, of what shall be stressed and what implied, all engender a certain similitude between texts presented as matters of fact and others authored and acknowledged as fiction. Once one has stigmatized what is taken for granted by raising epistemological questions regarding the organization of "facts" in their relation to structures of inference, one is led rather directly to the form in which events are represented, to "a discourse that feigns to make the world speak itself and speak itself *as a story*"[4] and as a story that could be encoded quite differently under an alternative paradigm (or "metaphysics"). Narrative structure, context, moral, truth, and meaning are not metaphysical realities with a priori, Platonic existence independent of human cognition, of course, but are rather constructs produced by the performative properties of discourse that bring human reality into being.

The unlikelihood that the world would present itself in coherent stories endowed naturally with central subjects, highly organized plot structures, thematic integrity, and moralizable conclusions thus fostered the realization that historical events that seem to "tell themselves" are actually authored constructs with distended and complex connections to their sources of production. In other words a virtual chaos of worldly events (which are highly sorted by even the most casual observer) can in itself claim no formal structure whatsoever, much less the narrative coherence that we associate with well-constructed "stories." When such structure is imposed on unordered events to give them coherence, it narrates those events in accordance with a privileged paradigm, never neutral, under whose aegis they are organized and moralized, thereby generating a correspondingly nonneutral type of meaning, of history, of truth.

Even reluctance to accede to events as *entirely* random, as *only* passive recipients of externally imposed formal coherence, leads one finally to recognize that the causality apparent in historical narrative is supplied at least complementarily by some implied (and thus interpreted) structure in the events themselves—the meaningful actions of men and women, for example—and by the sociolect that "coauthors" the narrative and then absorbs it into a society's conceptual framework, the relation between the events' and the sociolect's contributions being inversely proportional. This "balancing operation," adapting Wolfgang Iser's phrase, is sufficient in any case to carry the argument, because even the capacity to envision a set of events as belonging to the same order requires a guiding paradigm under which the cohesion that historical narrative claims as inherent is produced rather than discovered. In this way discourse is generated and incorporated into a grand body of self-congratulating ideas—in the present case "dirty war" ideas—contributing further to the retroactive and tautological substantiation of the paradigm that governed the narrativization in the first place.

II

A shift of the focus from what is traditionally understood as historical content to the discursive forms that produce rather than represent an order of past events calls for a methodology sensitive to textual strategies and properties but at once sufficiently broad viewed to avoid the hermeticism that results when nontextual reference drifts out of range. I have accordingly adopted Gérard Genette's expansive definition of "analysis of narrative" as "the study of a totality of actions and situations taken in themselves, without regard to medium, linguistic or other, through which knowledge of a totality comes to us."[5] I likewise subscribe to Tzvetan Todorov's suggestion that "there is no longer any reason to confine to literature alone the type of studies crystalized in poetics: We must know 'as such' not only literary texts but *all* texts, not only verbal production but *all* symbolism."[6] In the following chapters I will approach the "dirty war" narrative as a "totality" in conformance with Genette's description, taking into account the figurative as well as the literal aspects of acts and discourse, and in particular the relation of acts and discourse in both these registers as they jointly constitute a single cultural artifact. Prominent among the theoretical concerns guiding the analysis are those summarized in the pages that follow. Their brief enumeration here is intended not as a comprehensive methodological systematization by any means but rather as the suggestion of a theoretical position insofar as such a position is separable from the analysis (in Chapters 2 through 5) that manifests and constitutes it as "a language in the process of formation."[7]

1. History is lived forward but read backward. What the actors in any given historical sequence live as an "open work" characterized by unexpected turns of events and unforeseeable conclusions (who will win the war, what will happen when the car turns the corner, how the events will be affected by the elimination of this or that actor) is later read retrospectively by interpreters who apprehend the emplotment of those events with the unknowns eliminated, with narrative closure, with sediments of previous interpretations already embedded.

The openness of lived experience in contrast with the closure of the historical narrative representing it are paralleled on textual terrain by two stages of reading, one heuristic and the other retroactive. During the former a reader's understanding and expectations are guided by the text's syntagmatic unfolding as, for example, a novel's plot and thematics are gradually revealed. One remains unaware in this first reading of how his perceptions will be altered or even undermined by developments forthcoming in the narrative. In the subsequent retroactive stage, once the reader has progressed through the narrative and is cognizant of those new developments, he then "remembers what he has just read and modifies his understanding of it in the light of what he is now decoding . . . reviewing, revising, comparing backwards,"[8] recontextualizing all parts of the text in light of one another and of the whole. Just as one lived event impacts those that precede and follow it, "each intentional sentence correlative opens up a particular horizon, which is modified, if not completely changed, by succeeding sentences."[9] The revision of those sentences—or of narrativized historical events—is then further compounded as the syntagmatic sequence is read backward "through" later developments that perpetually contribute their respective, retroactive gloss on the discourse that preceded them.

The tensions generated by juxtaposing heuristic and retroactive readings in literary texts are most forcefully concentrated by means of enjambment, particularly those uses of the technique in which the second verse of an enjambed couplet alters the meaning established by the first. Though the line "You will sit listening till I am gone" presents one meaning in the heuristic pass, for example, ambiguity and polysemy are generated when it is enjambed and then read retroactively (as the historian reads) with the phrase's two lines in combination: "You will sit listening till I am gone / To seed among the pear trees." The first line suggests death and absence until that reading is retroactively revised as the second line clashes into it the thematics of rejuvenation and fruition.[10] Dominating the passage, finally, is not one meaning or the other but rather a third produced in the space opened by their dynamic interaction and overshadowed by the tension that they generate when they are thus engaged.

In the following lines from Sophocles's *Oedipus the King*, this compounding effect of competing heuristic/retroactive readings is expressed in a manner more directly relevant to my purpose. Speaking of Oedipus, the Leader says: "But here is his queen, his wife and mother / of his children."[11] The first line verifies what the Athenian public already knows from the traditions on which the play is based: Jocasta is Oedipus's wife *and* mother. The second line, however, undermines that knowledge ("mother / of his children," divesting "mother" of its parental relation to Oedipus) because the audience of the play is not to know *yet* what Oedipus does not yet know (that his wife is his mother).

The audience's knowing/not-knowing is analogous to the position in which historians find themselves, as they are first provided sociocultural frames of reference and varying measures of narrative closure but then forbidden "the projection of [their] past into a discourse in the process of becoming."[12] If what historians believe they know with certainty (Oedipus married his mother) excludes from their consideration the significance of multiple representations by which that knowledge is communicated to them (*Oedipus the King* as a polysemous variation on the traditional theme, crystalized in the enjambment), then the meanings generated by nuance are lost with the exclusions. In the process the uniquely revelatory value of a specific text before historians is muddled in a reductionist haste or simply overlooked as the historians' knowledge impedes and oversimplifies understanding rather than enhancing it.

2. A text conceals as much as it reveals. "A text is not a text," in Jacques Derrida's celebrated formula, "unless it hides from the first comer, from the first glance, the laws of its composition and the rules of its game."[13] This doctrine of a text that conceals as much as it reveals, that strategically displaces its focus, is of course indebted to psychoanalysis ("One of the prime functions of speech . . . is not to reveal thoughts, but to conceal them, especially from ourselves"[14]) as well as to Nietzsche, who knew to "recognize in what has been written so far a symptom of what has so far been kept silent" and who stressed on more than one occasion that "every philosophy also *conceals* a philosophy; every opinion is also a hideout, every word also a mask."[15]

Just as a subject often harbors one opinion or emotion while expressing another and just as one's physiognomy often betrays one when what is thought and said are at odds, so too a text is layered in strata of revelation and disguise, each providing index and entry to the other, the meaning in one register often in conflict with the meaning in another. Derrida's concept of *différance*, as Christopher Norris well clarified, suggests that "meaning is nowhere punctually *present* in language, that it is always subject to a kind of semantic slippage (or deferral) which prevents the sign from ever . . . coinciding with itself in a moment of perfect, remainderless grasp."[16] Deconstruction thus intends to avoid the "Platonizing drift that would restore interpretation to a quest for self-present meaning and truth."[17] It seeks out the "blindspots or moments of self-contradiction where a text involuntarily betrays the tension between rhetoric and logic, between what it manifestly *means to say* and what it is nonetheless *constrained to mean*."[18] Aspects of a text—often seemingly irrelevant details passed over by interpreters of more orthodox persuasions[19]—necessarily *stress* the undisclosed laws of composition and rules of the game as they disguise them. As a result a text itself traces out the grammar of the paradigm to which it adheres and under which its seeming inconsistencies are ultimately reconciled. A primary strategy of a reading sensitive to such encoded revelation (in one way Derrida's and in another Michel Foucault's) therefore explores the "silent complicity between the superstructural pressure of a metaphysics and an author's ambiguous innocence about a detail at base level."[20] As I will argue in subsequent chapters, the only authentic truth of the Argentine Junta's discourse emerged by default when the "silent complicity" gained expression without intent.

If the world, as Martin Heidegger aptly observed, "is that whereby human reality discloses to itself what it is,"[21] then what is manifest in that disclosure is more significant than what was intended, and no detail is insignificant or neutral. What a narrative, a ritual, a method of torture signifies through enmeshed strata of the manifest form—always a palimp-sest—that constitute it is of greater interest in this analysis than what it was meant to signify. I therefore will want to explore the nexus delineated by the intersection of an intent and the results it actualizes. The implied author of discourse and deeds—at once speaking and spoken, acting and acted—is Derrida's "first comer."

As far as discrepancies between an intention and its manifestation are concerned, Jacques Lacan summarized the psychoanalytical position de-veloped initially in Freud's *Psychopathology of Everyday Life* with the phrase "every parapraxis is a successful discourse."[22] Pursuant to that position I shall pay careful attention to the relation between what was said and what was meant in military discourse, understanding that this relation—like that between the enjambed couplets discussed earlier—establishes the field in which the juxtaposition signifies. The bungled act that manifests and betrays an intention—particularly because it is stressed by its counterproductivity in relation to that intention—will similarly be deemed a successful discourse and treated as such. And by extending parapraxes as successful discourse to the history under analysis as a whole, in the following chapters I will gradually demonstrate that the "dirty war" (as accented by its predominantly tragic plot structure) "does not just contain or perform a self-deconstruction, but that it is about self-deconstruction, has it as its theme."[23]

One stress point of contradiction that suggested initial access to the "dirty war's" "self-deconstruction" was patent in the discrepancy be-tween the messianic, Christian discourse of the Junta on the one hand and on the other the violent repressive agenda—denied systematically in official proclamations—that implemented the regime's lofty ideals. Casual observers, human rights defenders, historians, and social scientists have tended to qualify that discrepancy in terms of hypocrisy and contemp-tuous cynicism: The Junta established detention centers, sanctioned tor-ture, and standardized "disappearance" as a strategy, this line of reasoning argues, while at the same time it hypocritically and contemptuously denied these methods, displaced the responsibility for "excesses" onto the rank and file, and whitewashed its barbarism with sanctimonious discourse championing the virtues of "Western and Christian civiliza-tion."[24]

There is of course a fair measure of commonsense truth to a reading grounded in the presumption of hypocrisy, but such an interpretation, in the last analysis, dismisses the problem rather than elucidating it. As I will argue in the following chapters, the atrocities committed during the "dirty war" and the sanctified discourse that glossed them with eschato-logical purpose finally constitute not a contradiction or an expression of contemptuous hypocrisy and cynicism, not a proliferation of political rhetoric attempting to justify an incompatible proliferation of barbarous deeds, but rather a kind of rearranged truth, a mythologized reality in which the Junta's words and deeds were integrated components of a single, coherent agenda. I will direct much of the focus in the following analysis to the paradigm under whose aegis this reconciliation was made possible. By exploring the "master fictions" of the "dirty war" via the ideological lineaments of the authority they produce, I will collapse the hierarchical separation that assigned discourse to the Junta and atrocity to the task forces on grounds more viable than hypocrisy, demonstrating how the one interlocks with and is mutually interdependent with the other and how the Junta (for which the "dirty war" was essentially a politico-religious experience) and the torturers (for whom the "dirty war" was essentially a psychosexual experience) shared a common nexus in which the discourse and the deeds were synchronized. And in passing I will pause at stress points signaling other contradictions that may similarly be reconciled, among them how selection of the *desaparecidos* (the "disap-peared") could be both systematic and arbitrary; why destruction of the victims was accompanied—until the final execution—with a persistent effort to keep the victims alive; and how the "dirty war" atrocities, ostensibly clandestine, functioned as spectacular rituals of power that engaged the Argentine public as audience.

   3. *Social actions symbolically recycle what they con-ceal.* Following Freud, who recognized that symbols and symbolic action result from the simultaneous desire to repress and fulfill an impulse, Derrida noted that "coherence in contradiction expresses the force of a desire."[25] Analysis of symbolic distortions and displacements (often ef-fected by means of denial and projection) will thus contribute to my exploration of the paradigmatic coherence in which "dirty war" contra-dictions are reconciled. That coherence will in turn afford access to "the force of a desire" that shaped Argentine violence into the particular ritual form that it assumed and that similarly generated "dirty war" mythology as a recontextualizing agent to imbue atrocity with political and eschato-logical purpose. "It is the effectiveness of symbols which guarantees the harmonious parallel development of myth and action,"[26] Claude Lévi-

Strauss observed, but as I pursue that parallel development, I will proceed cautiously in analyzing symbols and other tropes, avoiding the "simplistic, non-dialectical analogical interpretation" of the "monotonously unilluminating" fixed symbolism of some classical psychoanalysis (a penis here, a mother there) or of the mechanistic morphologizing to which structuralism at its worst succumbs. Both are instances in which effective interpretation is disrupted by closed-system reductionism that translates the free play of one structure into the rigidity of another.[27]

Lévi-Strauss (and, by a different approach, Marcel Mauss before him) recognized that social reality is fundamentally symbolic and is expressed as such in its belief systems, its customs, its monuments, its institutions. Ritual is the paradigm of symbolic social expression, responding as it does to social problems by "reorganizing"—to use the term chosen by the Argentine Junta—the reality associated with the problem, by displacing efficacious, solution-oriented action with symbolic drama that, as a byproduct, indexes the desire behind such displacement. Once symbolic displacement has been effected, ritual as "a form of nonverbal communication, analogous to language at least to some extent"[28] assumes the complex relation with its audience that will be discussed in Chapter 2.

Walter Burkert observed that the communicative function of ritual is the dominant one, gaining a measure of autonomy from the pragmatic situation that called it forth.[29] With the message of symbolic acts preempting the efficacy of pragmatic ones, with the discursive agenda dominating, ritual communication contributes to the mentioned "reorganization": Spectacular violence in Argentina "not only transports information, but often directly affects the addressee and possibly the 'sender' as well."[30] In the analysis of "dirty war" communication (including rituals), one must keep in mind the concern Burkert shares with Lacan regarding who is speaking and to whom, remembering that "if the discourse is played out, it is on a stage implying the presence not only of the chorus, but also of spectators."[31]

Ritual that says by doing, and that in the process effects a change in its actors and audience, provides an inverted complement for those illocutionary speech acts referred to as "performative" that do by saying. Performative statements (the textbook example being "I now pronounce you man and wife") do not describe an act but actually constitute it, provided that the context in which they are uttered is "felicitous" (the priest, rabbi, or justice of the peace is appropriately empowered, the couple consenting, and so forth).[32] As will become most apparent in my later analysis of the military's denial of responsibility for the *desapareci-dos*, performative speech acts supported by rituals themselves assuming performative discursive functions contributed substantially to the Junta's violent "reorganization" of Argentine social reality.

4. All discourse is overdetermined and intertextual. A text is "a braid of different voices, of many codes, at once interlaced and incomplete."[33] "If one grants that every signifying practice is a field of transpositions of various signifying systems (an inter-textuality)," wrote Julia Kristeva, who follows Mikhail Bakhtin as the most important proponent of the concept of intertextuality, "one then understands that its 'place' of enunciation and its denoted 'object' are never single, complete, and identical to themselves but always plural, shattered, capable of being tabulated. In this way polysemy can also be seen as the result of semiotic polyvalence—an adherence to different sign systems."[34] Intertextuality is brought into play through the use of a common language ("the word arrives in [one's] context from another context which is saturated with other people's interpretations"[35]) and through direct quotations, unquoted borrowings, allusions to other discourse, acknowledged and unacknowledged influences, and any of the other various forms by which what Bakhtin called "alien discourse" enters one's "complex choir of other voices." The concept also refers back to "the superstructural pressure of a metaphysics" summarized earlier, which functions as an implied, regulating intertext that is present at the level of discourse in the same way that grammar is present at the level of the sentence.

Intertextuality is paralleled in psychoanalytical terms by Lacan's conception of an unconscious "structured like a language" (a language, as I have suggested following Bakhtin, "inhabited," "saturated by other people's interpretations," and "permeated with intentions").[36] The Lacanian principle of the unconscious as "discourse of the Other" moots one's pseudosingularity partially because "the allocution of the subject entails an allocutor—in other words, that the locutor is constituted in it as an intersubjectivity."[37] "It is not only man who speaks," Lacan added, now grounding that intersubjectivity in language, "but . . . in man and by man it [id] speaks . . . his nature becomes woven by the effects where the structure of language, whose material he becomes, is recovered."[38] When one unravels the "braid of different voices" in analysis of "dirty war" discourse, it is important to identify in the choir not only the voices of intertexts that evidence the "superstructural presence of a metaphysics" but also the "discourse of the Other" that dialogues with that metaphysics within the speaking subject. And one must also keep in mind that separation of one voice from another is a convenience of exposition rather than a strategy of surgical hermeneutics, for intertexts assume their full signification only after all of their strands have been reintegrated into the textual "braid" that they together constitute.

III

Among the tenets of the theory of monarchy during the Middle Ages was an apostolic motif: Christian kings were expected to convert heathens. Paradoxically, however, the "salvation" of populations targeted for characteristically messianic politico-ecclesiastical programs was often accompanied by a catalog of atrocities seemingly inconsistent with the religious agenda generating them.[39] The recipients of salvation crusades were—and are—generally exploited, incapacitated, or destroyed, while the benefits of messianism tend, at least temporarily, to fall back on the messiahs themselves, on regimes pursuing their own glorified salvation by means of a projection and a roundabout masquerade that stylizes them as donor rather than beneficiary.

In the early modern period the medieval notion of missionary king or Messiah-Emperor was carried forward and propagated on this side of the Atlantic by the Franciscans. Fray Gerónimo de Mendieta—to cite one example—construed the Spanish crown apocalyptically as the agent that would reduce "all the visible hosts that Lucifer has in this world" to the obedience of the conquerors' Church.[40] As Mendieta envisioned it the spiritual unity of mankind would be forged—conforming to medieval apocalyptic and messianic-emperor myths—with the Spanish sword; an eschatological king would eradicate politico-religious opposition, secure world unity, and thereby usher in the millennial kingdom.[41] But here again, as Mendieta's rhetoric forecasts and as misapplication of the European crusade model to a "new" world implies, the Native Americans who were claimed to be the beneficiaries of the Messiah-Emperor's apostolic zeal suffered the consequences of salvation—their induction into the Church was brutal, and their lot in Christ less than glorious.

In more recent Latin American history political messianism structured on the Christian apocalyptic model resurfaced dramatically under the Argentine military Junta that assumed power in March 1976. Conspicuous during the Junta's Process of National Reorganization and the "dirty war" that implemented it were predominant medieval images, among them the Natural Order, the Antichrist, the depiction of society as a living organism, and the *corpus mysticum* adapted from ecclesiastical to political application.[42] Similarly in a medieval mode the Junta's cognition tended toward synthesis rather than analysis, reducing complex social realities to binary, archetypal oppositions that were antithetically at odds: Good and Evil, Order and Chaos, Christ and Antichrist. The Junta also, like the medievals, "inhabited a world filled with references, reminders and overtones of Divinity," displaying in its interpretations "a prolongation of the mythopoeic dimension of the Classical period," a "propensity for myth and symbol as a flight from reality," and an imagination inclined to respond to crisis "by developing bodies of symbols."[43] Boundaries between religious and secular agendas during the "dirty war" were likewise as vague as they were in the Middle Ages. The Junta regarded terror, blind faith, and absolute authority as its inherent, inalienable prerogatives (as did medieval monarchs) and presumed for itself a divine right as Christ's vicar "reorganizing" Argentina in order to fulfill a grand eschatological design, greater than man but implemented through his agency.

As Junta member Admiral Emilio E. Massera saw it, "God has decided that we [the Junta] should have the responsibility of designing the future."[44] A typically medieval osmosis merging earthly realities with politicized celestial fantasies led the Junta to characterize that future in terms of a restored Christian Natural Order. Internal, invisible enemies—for the medievals heretics, witches, and epidemics, and for the Junta "subversion" stylized similarly—would have to be purged from the social body before the new age could be ushered in.

A primitive medieval mentality thus predisposed the "dirty war" to an offensive that would preempt "the brief reign of the Antichrist of Apocalypse."[45] Mundane concerns such as due process and human rights were subordinate to the military's eschatological agenda that "does not recognize moral or natural limits, that is realized beyond good and evil, that transcends the human level."[46] Like the medieval Church, which freed itself from moral obligation when it felt its existence to be threatened, the Junta processed social reality with a mytho-logic of sufficient elaborative capacity to reconcile its messianism with the violent repression used to implement the "reorganization" of Argentina around the tenets of "Western and Christian civilization."

The *desaparecidos* were construed as mythically guilty of having sinned against God—via the detour of having sinned against the Junta as vicars of Christ—and therefore became worthy recipients of the most horrific penal measures meted out in symmetry with the gravity of their mythic transgressions. Following Augustinian interpretations inherited by medieval lawyers and theologians alike, just war, even if it is "dirty," is an expression of divine will neutralizing sin and crime.[47] Punishment must be overdetermined to redress the damage done in this- and otherworldly registers. When the naked Argentine victim was bound to the torture table and subjected to electrical discharge on his or her gums, genitals, and nipples, the magnitude of the offense was symbolically avenged. Here the medieval view of the body as a microcosm where cosmic struggles between Good and Evil, between Christ and Antichrist, are battled out is apparent: Each victim's body tortured in the Argentine detention center localized, rehearsed, and ritually mirrored the grand eschatological battle that the just war, the "dirty war," represented in the grand view of the military perpetrators.[48] The cosmic battle waged in miniature on the tortured body was similarly stylized in a parallel metaphorical depiction—again typically medieval—whereby the State was conceived as a living organism, a politicized *corpus mysticum*, on whose body the apocalyptic struggle was likewise rehearsed.

As these and other Junta constructs that will concern us evidence, military narrativization of the "dirty war" adhered to a (medieval) mythologic but, like any fiction, disengaged from the reality of its initial reference. Once politico-religious myths were instituted in the Junta agenda *as though* they were real, however, they left behind tests of verisimilitude, *became real* in a mythological register militarily imposed on the subject population, and generated further mythological constructs and symbolic actions doubling back in affirmation and defense of their reality.

1

The "Dirty War" in Thematic Context

I

ON DECEMBER 7, 1941, Field Marshal Wilhelm Keitel, chief of the German High Command, issued the first of a series of directives implementing Hitler's "Night and Fog" decree. "The decree introduces a fundamental innovation," Keitel wrote, in that offenses against the German state in the occupied countries would now be prosecuted by local military courts only in those cases where unmitigated guilt could be established and the death sentence pronounced within eight days of a prisoner's arrest. Because imprisonment "even with hard labor for life" might be looked on "as a sign of [Nazi] weakness," the directives clarified that in principle "the punishment for offenses committed against the German state is the death penalty." But in those cases in which guilt could not be readily established—clearly the majority—the application of this "death penalty" would be shrouded in night and fog, pursuant to the fuehrer's "innovation": Prisoners were transferred *secretly* (the italics are Keitel's) from their occupied country to Germany. These undisclosed transfers would, the fuehrer believed, achieve "the necessary deterrent effect" because "the prisoners will vanish without a trace" and "no information will be given as to their whereabouts or their fate." "Efficient and enduring intimidation," Keitel concluded following the fuehrer's decree, could only be generated through this combinative strategy of local execution for

15

those readily proven guilty and of transfer measures "by which the relatives of the criminal and the population do not know the fate of the criminal."[1] That these "criminals" of the latter category were not proven guilty and, further, were secretly deported under cover of "night and fog" *precisely because their guilt could not be proven*, and that this "transfer" was invariably a euphemism for extrajudicial execution in Germany, were implications barely veiled by the rhetoric of the field marshal's directives. What dominated the "innovation" was the intent to punish the suspicious with the same penalty—death—as the guilty and to do so in such a way that the eerie absence of these victims would generate sufficient terror to paralyze resistance within the occupied country.

Some thirty years after the seven thousand "disappearances" resulting from the Night and Fog decree, "vanish without a trace" tactics were introduced into repressive strategies in several Latin American regions, most notably in the Southern Cone, Brazil, and Guatemala. In Argentina a Process of National Reorganization, instituted by the military Junta that deposed Isabel Perón on March 24, 1976,[2] was implemented in a program of repression characterized by "disappearances" entailing abduction, torture, and execution.

Analysis of the Junta's repressive methodology will be a direct concern in the chapters that follow, but I may presently note the more immediate, pragmatic advantages of State violence deployed in Argentina as a matter of policy. The first recalls Keitel's term "efficient": By skirting the time-consuming niceties of due process, the Argentine Junta endeavored to hasten the purge of "subversives" through illegal measures that condemned all *desaparecidos* to the same fate—regardless of the offense, regardless of the evidence. As the Inter-American Commission on Human Rights recognized in its 1976 report, "the 'disappearance' seems to be a comfortable expedient to avoid application of the legal provisions established for the defense of personal freedom, physical security, dignity and human life itself."[3] Much the same was expressed in political rhetoric by Junta member Admiral Emilio Massera, who remarked in 1977 that he and his colleagues believed in a justice that was "rapid and efficacious, without legal fissures through which the guilty can slip away."[4] "Justice" by violence further exploited "disappearance" strategies to the Junta's political advantage, because the absence of victims' bodies implied the absence of crimes and, in judicial terms, the absence of evidence essential to prosecution. The frequent use of civilian-dressed paramilitary abduction forces similarly reinforced the regime's systematic evasion of responsibility for the disappearances. Official denial then combined with the lofty objectives of the Junta in a discourse that displaced the source of violence onto the "subversives," while at the same time it emphasized the military's heroism and the responsibility of the citizens to lend full support to the eradication of their common adversary.[5]

The domestic front was thus temporarily calmed. In a similar fashion "disappearance" proved more efficacious before international opinion than the scandals of openly violent politics as conducted, for example, in Chile under General Augusto Pinochet. Before the United Nations, before the Carter administration, before human rights and ecclesiastical bodies formally presenting protests, the military Junta maintained the strategic denial that complemented the physical disappearance of the victim with a conceptual disappearance of the guilty party. Even when all evidence unambiguously implicated the military in massive and systematic human rights violations—as was the case on release of the OAS Commission report, on publication of voluminous testimony in Nunca más, and again on initiation of the 1985 trials—the Junta members believed these accusations verified "infiltration" at the highest levels and consequently reaffirmed their denial with renewed vehemence and indignation, deriving from the experience a more passionate dedication to their ideological convictions. This dogmatic rigor contributed to the last pragmatic advantage afforded by "disappearance" and summary execution as a matter of policy, namely, an attempt to find a "final solution" to Argentine "subversion." Execution in place of incarceration and elimination of even those suspected of "future subversion" was intended to leave no opportunity for a later democracy's acts of amnesty (such as the release of political prisoners that the military commanders witnessed when the Peronist government returned to office in 1973) or for corrupted youth to come indecorously of age.[6]

Violent measures accompanying politico-economic and social-restructuring agendas were by no means new to Argentina when the 1976 Junta overthrew Isabel Perón. Juan Manuel Rosas, to cite the paradigm of the early republican period, ruled with a bloody hand for twenty years until 1852; his portrait—captioned "Restorer of the Laws"—was hanging beside the crucifix in Buenos Aires churches while his goon squads slit the throats of the opposition.[7] Years later, during the "Tragic Week" of 1919, the conservative elite indexed its evolving xenophobia in another register when security forces violently quashed a strike and working-class revolt;

the reactionaries most fearful of "Communist" immigration interpreted the events as the Russian Revolution's local repercussion.[8]

In more recent history the Prussia-inspired José Uriburu—who was trained in the kaiser's guard, nicknamed "von Pepe," and insistent that his aides be "unswervingly Germanic in bearing and public utterances"[9]— deposed the Radical Civic Union party government of Hipólito Yrigoyen in a 1930 coup d'état, becoming the first military president of modern Argentina. Traditionalists behind Uriburu were alarmed by the political power of immigrant-origin urban sectors; the popular vote would be overturned by force. Uriburu's attempt to establish a semi-Fascist corporate state inaugurated a model of repression that would later be rehearsed and revised by the succession of de facto regimes (with coups in 1943, 1955, 1962, 1966, and 1976) that have dominated politics in modern Argentina. Paramilitary forces targeting the Left and labor unions were reminiscent of the strike-breaking goon squads of the Liga Patriótica Argentina (Argentine Patriotic League) that was active from 1919 to 1921, but under Uriburu the role of violent repression as such became more integral to governance, more tightly interwoven with the political program as a whole.

The evolving name of Uriburu's brutal and arbitrary paramilitary force is in itself significant in the context of that transition, for as it progressed from the specific Sección Especial de Represión del Comunismo (Special Section for the Repression of Communism) to the more general División de Informaciones Políticas Antidemocráticas (Division of Anti-Democratic Political Information, referred to as DIPA), it left behind traces of an ideological evolution. The "Special Section"—the unique cellular entity set apart from regular government functions by the extremity of its mandate and its specific constitution—lost its special and autonomous qualities as it assumed a normalized bureaucratic status, becoming a division of the government itself.

Similarly the explicit task of "repression," linked in the transformation of the force's name with "political information" in the new title, was now encompassed in a general program of intelligence. That this transition from "repression" to "political information" denoted a shift in strategy rather than veiling of an unpleasant term with a polite euphemism was retroactively substantiated in later Argentine history, through the untenable but insistent torture-information dyad that placed what the 1976 Junta deemed "political information" at the forefront of the "dirty war."[10] Paramilitary violence unleased in the name of "repression" had as its guiding purpose not quashing a strike or eliminating "red" activists but rather exploiting torture victims as embodiments of "political information," the battleground having shifted from the field to the body as agency of discourse.

And finally, the specific concept of "communism" as employed in the Uriburu force's first denomination was similarly broadened to include all political positions that the armed forces deemed "anti-democratic"; the dragnet's cast was widened. In addition to encompassing the very dictatorship that employed it, the term "anti-democratic" attests to the ideological distance traveled from a real inimical fear of (largely imaginary) "Communist subversion" to a xenophobic stance—aggravated by heavy immigration of activist European labor—that tolerated only homogeneity and was capable of recognizing any Other only through the adversarial negation implied by the prefix *anti*.[11] Indeed the undesired immigrants, who would constitute the majority of Argentina's population, were stigmatized in extreme cases as "debris rejected by other countries, who take refuge in our bosom but constitute an exotic factor, not assimilable to our sociability."[12]

The military ideology by which political plurality and passive dissent were construed as subversive acts against the State was further elaborated and integrated into authoritarian rule in Argentina by General Juan Carlos Onganía. Shortly before the coup d'état that interrupted the presidency of Arturo Illia and brought the military to power again on June 28, 1966, Onganía posited the doctrine of "ideological borders." According to this doctrine the armed forces' responsibility for protecting the republic's geopolitical borders from outside invasion was complemented with the task of protecting public consciousness from the infiltration of "exotic ideologies."[13] The military's new role as the preserver of "the moral and spiritual values of Western and Christian civilization," reminiscent of medieval authorities' dominance of morality, quickly yielded to a rather bizarre (but also brutal) policing of public conduct at even the most trivial levels.[14] The Onganía government's zealous pursuit as the self-appointed ultimate arbiter of morality often led it—to borrow a few examples from former military president Alejandro Lanusse—"to measure [everything] from the behavior of people on the street to the dimensions of women's clothing and the characteristics of bathing suits," concerns more appropriate to the jittery parents of teenage daughters than to executives of national administration.[15]

Now war had two fronts: one in opposition to the external enemy who might violate Argentine sovereignty in an armed attack and the other combatting an internal enemy armed with "exotic ideology" that was deemed dangerous to national security, if only because it was dangerous to national morality. By the time Onganía's "mysticism of redemption" was buttressed with the full mythological substantiation it assumed in the "dirty war" beginning in 1976, the military's role as preserver of the moral and ideological wholesomeness of the people almost entirely displaced the conventional military mandate of protecting sovereignty from outside invasion.[16] The enemy of compelling concern had become internal and "ideological."

Nowhere is that shift from external to internal, from armed to ideological, from real to predominantly imaginary enmity so evident as it is when later Argentine military performance in the Falkland/Malvinas is contrasted with the "dirty war." In the latter (a campaign to eradicate a predominantly unarmed, internal, ideological enemy), the military command generated for itself the illusion of victory, of glory, and of omnipotence, but in the former (a confrontation with an armed, legitimate, external adversary in dispute over an actual question of sovereignty) it could only manage a humiliating display of incompetence, impotence, and ruthless deployment of unprepared troops. When we consider further that war in the Falkland/Malvinas was instigated largely to stimulate diversionary rally around the military flaunting its conventional function against an external adversary, and that this desperate ploy was necessitated by the Junta's crumbling illusion of legitimacy in the aftermath of the "dirty war," it therefore comes as no surprise that in pragmatic terms the manipulation of the concept of enmity—now internal, now external—followed the laws of political ambition and messianism far more stringently than it did the purported defense of national security.[17]

Tensions mounting in reaction to repression during Onganía's regime erupted into violence in May 1969, when riots broke out in several Argentine cities. Government propaganda failed to convince the citizens that the events were instigated by extremists manipulated by foreign Communist agitators.[18] Violent clashes with security forces in Corrientes (which included the killing of a student protesting price increases in the university cafeteria) triggered open rebellion nationwide and, with it, an intensification of the State's repressive violence. The most serious of these events, in the industrial city of Córdoba, was comparable to the Tragic Week in its magnitude and intensity, leaving dozens of people dead after a worker and student demonstration with broad popular support ended in days of armed confrontation between revolutionary and government forces. The *Cordobazo*, as the event came to be known, was followed by a similar uprising in Rosario and by a period of political instability in which bombings, assassinations, and other terrorist acts evidenced a circular phenomenon that is identifiable in retrospect: The military government's attempt to violently restructure society from above contributed decisively to creating the object of its phobic obsession—an "internal enemy"—in the lower strata. Once sociopolitical turmoil and terrorism were patently manifest, they provided ample evidence to verify retroactively the illusion of "subversion," minimal at the start, by which the dictatorship had justified its large-scale repression from the outset. "Heresy," Clifford Geertz observed, "is as much a child of orthodoxy in politics as it is in religion."[19]

The *Cordobazo* and events around it thus contributed to the antirevolutionary regime's consolidation of heterodoxy, social protest, and armed terrorism into a single construct: Communist or Marxist "subversion." Military ideology was thus predisposed to elaborate the inimical illusions on which the forthcoming "dirty war" would be based. As one sociologist explained the transition,

> Forced exclusion led to the formation, in the early seventies, of a mass radical movement, which ranged from guerrilla groups to mass organizations with a middle-class and labor base. The revolutionary threat that did not exist at the inception of the [Onganía] regime was clearly present at its conclusion, when mass mobilization forced the military to step down, and the stage was set for the wave of terrorism from below and of massive terrorism from above, which rocked the country in the late seventies.[20]

In June 1970 the "dirty war" to follow was symbolically inaugurated by the abduction and execution of Pedro Eugenio Aramburu, the general who had led the 1955 coup d'état that deposed Juan Perón and who subsequently served as de facto president of Argentina.[21] The leftist militant group responsible for these acts, the Montoneros, was one of three Peronist revolutionary movements "ready to fight with gun in hand for the seizure of power for Perón and his People." The other two were the Fuerzas Armadas Peronistas (Peronist Armed Forces) and the Fuerzas Armadas Revolucionarias (Revolutionary Armed Forces).[22] Also engaged in armed revolution at the time was the non-Peronist Ejército Revolucionario del Pueblo (People's Revolutionary Army, referred to as the ERP). During the early 1970s these four revolutionary factions (the first three of which consolidated under the Montoneros in 1973) staged bank robberies, assassinations of senior army or police personnel, and Robin Hood–type escapades by which multinationals were coerced into making charitable contributions as ransom for the release of individuals abducted by the revolutionaries. In 1973 alone the ERP extorted $1 million from the Ford Motor Company, $2 million from Acrow Steel, $3 million from Firestone Tire and Rubber, and $14.2 million from Exxon Oil. The Montoneros were yet more dramatic in their demands, collecting $60 million in cash and more than $1 million in food and clothing distributed to the poor in exchange for the release of two abducted Argentine businessmen.[23]

The official and quasi-official response to leftist terrorism in Argentina was formidable.[24] In April 1970 an extremist right-wing organization, reputedly composed of off-duty policemen, made its debut by attacking the Soviet ambassador to Argentina. The counterterrorism of Mano (Hand), as the group called itself, dramatically escalated the use of abduction, a tactic that the militant Right had brought into play earlier. Most of Mano's victims simply "disappeared without a trace," as historian David Rock wrote, his phrasing matching that of Field Marshal Keitel almost verbatim, "and the few to reappear spoke of torture. By the early months of 1971 one such 'disappearance' occurred on average each eighteen days."[25] Other right-wing terrorist groups operative in the years preceding the "dirty war" proper included the enduring and imposing Alianza Anti-Comunista Argentina (Argentine Anti-Communist Alliance, referred to as the AAA or Triple A), which functioned as an officially unauthorized extension of repressive forces of the State. Testimony before a U.S. congressional committee of inquiry in February 1976 revealed that José López Rega—the former minister of social welfare, an intimate of the Perón regime, and the legendarily eccentric astrologer and occultist guiding Isabel Perón—was a founding member of the Triple A and utilized the ministry's press attaché as a liaison with the group.[26] (More informal discourse and public opinion recognize López Rega unambiguously as the Triple A's leader.) A report from the U.S. Department of State to congressional committees on foreign affairs and relations further noted that the Triple A was responsible for two thousand political assassinations between 1973 and 1977.[27]

The confusion of a country embroiled in terrorism from the Left and the Right was further aggravated when Juan Domingo Perón, the most imposing figure in modern Argentine politics, was permitted to return to Argentina after eighteen years of exile in Europe, primarily under General Francisco Franco's protection in Spain. Prior to his deposition by the 1955 coup d'état, Perón and his first wife, "Evita," were paradigms of populist nationalism and played a messianic role for the previously marginalized laboring masses (referred to as the *descamisados,* or "shirtless ones"), whom they incorporated as a force into Argentine politics.[28] Perón's homecoming to Buenos Aires was called "el retorno"—with all of its religious implications intact—by his more devout followers, and the aging caudillo was welcomed as something of a last hope by a half million well-wishers gathered at Ezeiza airport on June 20, 1973. Perón's shifting political position had not yet been clearly deciphered, however, and the resulting confusion disrupted the festivities of "el retorno" when militant Peronists from the Left and from the Right opened fire on one another before the plane landed.[29]

The Peronist party subsequently commanded a huge percentage of the 1973 vote and installed Perón, at the age of 78, to his third term as president of Argentina. The revolutionary "soldiers of Perón," which had contributed significantly to the circumstances resulting in Perón's return, found their initial delight in the new administration short lived, however, for Perón's political shift to an ultraconservative persuasion was accompanied by the rejection of the Montoneros, the new president referring to them as "germs" that were "contaminating" the movement.[30] Such was dramatically revealed when the Montoneros attempted to transform a Peronist May Day jamboree into a popular assembly by which "the People" would engage in "dialogue" with their president. Perón responded by publicly ostracizing the Montoneros, echoing a theme from earlier Argentine history by referring to the party's so-called Revolutionary Tendency as "infiltrators who work within and who in terms of treachery are more dangerous than those who work outside." He also called for internal war against the Montoneros "if the pernicious elements don't give way."[31]

But the reactionary Perón, too, was short lived, his death on July 1, 1974, coming as the fatal blow to whatever "el retorno" had to offer Argentina's fragile new democracy. Perón's widow, María Estela Martínez de Perón, commonly referred to as Isabel, succeeded him as president. Having failed to gain a voice in the Peronist government with which they had identified, the Montoneros denounced what seemed to many the illegitimacy of Isabel's corrupt government, which was increasingly dominated by "El Brujo," José López Rega. In a secret press conference on September 6, 1974, the Montoneros announced their "return to the resistance."[32] The ERP, meanwhile, was staging its revolution in the mountains of Tucumán. Terrorism from the Right, too, was escalated mimetically, its association with the State becoming more and more apparent. The Triple A—"that terrorist group specializing in the repression of certain citizens who committed the crime of thinking," as the prosecution would put it during the 1985 trials of the post-Perón Junta members—was particularly active, by early 1975 eliminating prominent intellectuals and lawyers at the rate of fifty per week.[33] And the economy, finally, was in a state of rampant disarray, the 1975 inflation rate at nearly 350 percent.[34]

On November 4, 1974, the administration of Isabel Perón declared a state of siege and reintroduced most of the "antisubversive" legislation that had been repealed in May 1973. Three months later, under the military pressures of what one observer has called a "coup by quotas,"[35] the military was authorized to assist the police in fighting terrorism in Tucumán. Five thousand troops were mobilized in Operation Independence to quash the one hundred twenty guerrillas of the ERP, this disproportionate display of force providing an index to the repression forthcoming under the dictatorship to follow. In addition to its campaign against the armed enemy, Operation Independence (with the assistance of the Triple A) actively eliminated "ideological subversives" and Argentines suspected of sympathizing with the ERP. In Tucumán and Santiago del Estero it also implemented a pilot project—apparently regarded as a success, to judge by the breadth of its later expansion—of clandestine torture and detention centers under the jurisdiction of the Third Army Corps.

By October 1975 nationwide terrorism had worsened, and the armed forces' authorization to combat the "internal enemy" was expanded beyond the specific Tucumán operation. Among the new measures that escalated military involvement was one generically phrased decree that granted the armed forces liberty to implement the "military and security operations they deem necessary to annihilate subversive elements throughout the country."[36] The army was charged with supervising military and security forces; the role of the navy and air force at this point was limited to complementary operations as requested by the army.

A subsequent order issued by Lieutenant General Jorge Rafael Videla, then commanding general of the army and shortly after de facto president of the republic, gave the army operational control over the Argentine Federal Police Force, the National Penitentiary System, and the Provincial Penitentiary and Police Forces.[37] Intelligence networks and clandestine operational units reminiscent of the DIPA were formed, and the methods of repression that would later characterize the postcoup "dirty war"— "disappearance" and torture prominent among them—were increasingly in evidence.

In Buenos Aires a political power struggle was simultaneously under way and would reach its peak in February and March of 1976. Facing Isabel Perón's refusal to resign the presidency and the failure of impeachment proceedings against her in congress, the military commanders settled their internal differences, reached an agreement to overthrow her government, and strategically procrastinated until the grim scenario collapsed into a desperate state that they could exploit to their own advantage.[38] At approximately the same time the minister of economics, Emilio Mondelli, announced his austerity plan in an attempt to redeem the economy, calling for an 82 percent devaluation of the peso and price increases of between 50 and 150 percent for basic foodstuffs, gasoline, and public transportation fares. By mid-March the public response included retail shutdowns and an industrial workers' strike that idled 70 percent of the major cities' productive capacity, along with a corresponding police reaction enforcing the austerity plan. There was "virtually no sector of Argentine society that had not escalated its organized opposition to the government."[39] The crumbling economic and political situations constituted the classical scenario for a military coup d'état, which came during Carnival week, welcomed by most.

II

On March 24, 1976, a military Junta composed of the commanders in chief of the three armed forces deposed Isabel Perón and assumed control of the government.[40] Lieutenant General Videla was appointed president, the tenth in Argentina imposed by a coup d'état since General Uriburu's overthrow of Yrigoyen in 1930, and remained in office until March 1981. In his first presidential address to the Argentine public, Videla inaugurated the lofty official discourse that throughout the years of the dictatorship engaged in a complex and paradoxical relationship with unofficial remarks, proclamations by lower-ranking officers, and a barbarous repressive policy implemented through disappearance, torture, and summary execution. The coup d'état of March 24, Videla proclaimed, represented not the mere overthrow of a government but rather "the final closing of a historical cycle and the opening of a new one" in which "respect for human rights is not only borne out by the rule of law and of international declarations, but is also the result of our [the Junta's] profound and Christian belief in the preeminent dignity of man as a fundamental value." And though it would require "trust and sacrifice," Videla stressed that "this immense task which we have undertaken has only one beneficiary: the Argentine people."[41] Just months prior to the coup d'état, General Videla spoke more candidly before the eleventh Conference of American Armies convening in Montevideo, stating that "as many people will die in Argentina as is necessary to restore order."[42]

Already in these few shreds of rhetoric some of the major themes that would dominate the mytho-logic of the "dirty war" are evident: a "final solution" to "subversion" in order to firmly found a "reorganized" Argentina on the values of what the Junta termed "Western and Christian civilization," "eradicating, once and for all, the vices which afflict the nation";[43] the paradoxical coupling of the "profound Christian belief in the preeminent dignity of man" and "respect for human rights" with the systematic abduction, torture, and execution of "as many people as necessary"; the presence of sacrifice as a military and political concept lined with Christian connotations; and the messianic posture apparent in the Junta's self-perception as the model of such sacrifice, assuming the "immense task" or the "unrenounceable obligation"[44] to redeem the Argentine people construed as needy beneficiaries.

Following Videla's inaugural speech a proliferation of proclamations elaborated on these thematics and complemented them with others that pieced together the coherent—if only coherently arational—worldview in which the Junta contextualized its "dirty war." A few of the prominent features may be mentioned here, reserving discussion for Chapter 3. The Junta subscribed to a national security doctrine of the cold war variety (as developed in the U.S. document commonly referred to as NSC-68), but it did so with a medieval religiosity, burdening these political interpretations with otherworldly obligations. As the Junta saw it, the world was divided into two antithetical camps, organized around the United States (West) and the Soviet Union (East). God's will required that the military preserve the "natural order" manifest in the Western and Christian civilization to which Argentina is integral, but the East had organized a massive international conspiracy to subvert that civilization by restructuring society in accordance with the seditious and atheistic doctrine of communism. Stress was placed on the imminent doom of "our way of being Christian" under the assault of "subversion," this eschatological crisis tending to overshadow other problems and the contradictions through which they were dismissed.[45] Even in the less bombastic legislative and political registers, preoccupation with "subversion" and attempts at establishing legal grounds for its definition (and annihilation) often revealed—despite the formal, bureaucratic nature of such documents— something of the mythological and religious paradigm that they served. With the Institutional Act of June 18, 1976, for example, the Junta assumed the judicial "power and responsibility to consider the actions of those individuals who have injured the national interest," but this on grounds as generic and suggestive as "failure to observe basic moral principles in the exercise of public, political, or union offices or activities that involve the public interest."[46] That bureaucratically restricted attempt to define the enemy gained clarification in the more candid observation offered by General Videla in response to the inquiries of British reporters who were curious to know how the *desaparecida* Claudia Inés Grumper, who was crippled, could be a terrorist. "A terrorist," Videla explained, "is not just someone with a gun or a bomb but also someone who spreads ideas which are contrary to Western and Christian civilization."[47]

Videla's definition of a "terrorist" (or "subversive," as the unarmed opposition was generally called) was the paradigm of many military statements that, in a simple trope, conformed to a tip-of-the-iceberg model. Limiting oneself to the eradication of armed insurrection at the tip, the military argued, was the error that had prevented Argentina from closing one historical cycle and opening a new one firmly grounded in "the Christian principles of Truth, Love, Justice and Liberty." The situation called for a "global strategy against subversion."[48] An Argentine handbook of ethics for military personnel stressed *"that the action be directed toward the causes of subversion and not only at its effects."* The same author added that "there is no justice in pursuing the guerrillas— the armed component of subversion, but not subversion itself—if we maintain the freedoms of opinion, of university education, and of the press [enjoyed by] the ideologues who intellectually poison our youth."

He then went on to argue that the armed forces would be not merely imprudent but actually criminal not to utilize "all of the recourses—military, political, cultural, etc.—necessary to counteract the subversive aggression which, beginning with the spirit, spills over into all areas, sectors and members of the national body."[49]

Although the same punishment (abduction, torture, execution) was meted out to most of these "subversives" regardless of the severity of their real or imaginary transgressions, there seemed to be a priority by which they were categorized in the repressors' mentality. General Ibérico Manuel Saint-Jean, then governor of Buenos Aires province, explained a strategy based on that implied hierarchy: "First, we are going to kill all of the subversives; then their collaborators; then their sympathizers; then the indifferent; and finally, the timid."[50] The last two categories enumerated in this self-satisfied litany—the "indifferent" and the "timid"—were "useful idiots" in passive compliance, "converted into automatons" because subversive ideology was "clouding their understanding and automatizing them like mechanical parts."[51] These categories underscored the means by which the Argentine public was transformed from the population saved to the victim of salvation; Søren Kierkegaard's "idle onlooker" was conspicuously absent.

The process by which military aggression properly directed toward armed insurrection finally resulted in victimizing the population it was purportedly defending was illustrated by prosecutor Julio Strassera in his closing summary at the 1985 trials. Strassera responded to an analogy that General Albano Jorge Harguindeguy offered in justification to Monseñor Miguel Hesayne when the latter questioned the correctness of the State's use of torture. Suppose, Harguindeguy argued, that a terrorist had placed a bomb in an apartment building and that within ten or twenty minutes the bomb was going to explode, killing the two hundred Argentines residing there. Was torture not then justifiable to determine the bomb's whereabouts in order to save so many lives?[52] Strassera's treatment of the analogy exemplified precisely how those to be saved from a pending threat of doom were punished as its imaginary cause. Harguindeguy intended

> to justify the idea that it was necessary to arrest people and torture them as a method of investigation to see if they knew anything. [But if the military] were unable to identify who planted the bomb, we would have to arrive at the conclusion that the inhabitants of the building could be

tortured, since they could be suspected of having planted the bomb; in this way, the people in 3H, those in 4D, pass from their status as possible victims of the bomb to possible victims of torture. Argentine citizens passed from being possible targets of terrorism to becoming possible targets of an investigation method that began with torture and ended with death.[53]

These remarks advance an initial suggestion of how the Junta constructed the object of its aggression, how the "subversives" were inimical more by measure against precepts mobilized by "interrogation" methods than by any actual or potential threats or transgressions.[54] As the prosecution further recognized in its summary at the trials, "dirty war" tactics inverted causality: "The arrest turned a person into a subversive."[55] Mythopoesis created the potential for "subversion" everywhere, and the Junta brought forth its mythologized reality by responding to an inimical illusion with real, armed "retaliation." The armed terrorism that was nearly eradicated at the time of Isabel Perón's deposition and certainly annihilated shortly thereafter served as a basis to justify expansion of the "dirty war" against a largely imaginary enemy whose existence was necessary to fulfill specific functions—in political as well as mythological terms—for the repressors.[56] During the six years prior to the March 1976 coup d'état, the victims of leftist terrorism numbered approximately two hundred; the number that the dictatorship exacted in retaliation during the "dirty war" is estimated at twelve thousand,[57] fewer than 20 percent of whom were armed terrorists.[58] Others encompassed by the Junta's broadened definition of subversion and executed after having been tortured in detention centers consisted primarily of blue-collar workers (30.2 percent), students (21 percent), white-collar workers (17.9 percent), and professionals (10.7 percent). The tally included professors, psychiatrists, housewives, dissenting or "infiltrated" military personnel, reporters, attorneys, nuns and priests, government workers, teenagers, pregnant women, the elderly, farmers, actors, artists, and, in short, any "citizen who had by word or deed revealed a sympathy for social change of any sort."[59]

Most prominent among social expressions perceived as "subversive" by the military were the customary actions of organized labor (the "industrial front") and the equally nonviolent "activism" of high school and university students ("subversion in the educational field").[60] In regard to the latter, one of the purposes and pragmatic advantages of "disappearance" as a political strategy, mentioned earlier, was its contribution to the "final closing of a historical cycle and the opening of a new one," that first cycle ended by "eradicating, once and for all, the vices which afflict the nation."[61] "The political objective of the Armed Forces in this third world war," General Luciano Benjamín Menéndez explained, "is to annihilate Marxism in our country and to close off all possibility of its future resurgence."[62] "The weakness of even one generation of Argentines is sufficient to turn our common destiny into an ill-fated failure." That was "the crude reality," and as such it had to be confronted "crudely and boldly."[63]

As Admiral Massera saw it, a weak generation undermining the grandeur of common Argentine destiny was evidenced in students "who are disoriented and gloomy."[64] In offering his insights on the corruption of Argentine youth, Massera explained that as a subculture the young indulged in the unhealthy hermeticism of a secret society, celebrating their "rites" (music, dress) "with total indifference." A subsecretary of culture held similar views: Avenues for "infiltration of extremist ideologies" included "protest songs, exaltation of extremist artists and texts, avant-garde theatre . . . putting music to poems [and] café concert performances through which the 'message,' placed in the most innocent manner possible, always appears."[65]

> Afterwards, some of them exchanged their neutrality, their weak-willed pacifism, for the tremor of terrorist faith, the foreseeable derivation of a sensory escalation with a clear itinerary that begins with such an arbitrarily sacred conception of love that for them it almost ceases to be a private ceremony. It continues with promiscuous love, it extends into hallucinogenic drugs, and with the rupture of the last ties to objective reality it flows finally into death, one's own and others', it makes little difference, since the destruction will be justified as social redemption.[66]

The preempting of future subversion required decisive action in the present—"the transformation of the educational and cultural systems"— lest the subversive ideology of "infiltrated" Argentine youth later manifest itself in a new wave of social resistance and terrorism.[67] The Junta thus complemented its vindication of the past and its disinfection of the present with a massive assault at a projected front: future terrorism. "It would have been useless," as Mark Osiel pointed out following the opinions voiced with regularity in the far-right Argentine publications

Cabildo, Digo, and Proyección estratégica, "to kill only the insects that had already hatched, while still more germinated freely in the nest."[68]

Such a philosophy was most dramatically borne out in State action on the so-called "night of pencils," when sixteen students between the ages of fourteen and eighteen were abducted, tortured, and—with the exception of three—executed, their "subversive" act having been participation in a campaign favoring discounted bus tickets for students.[69] In another case a parent in search of his "disappeared" children was told, "We consider your sons subversives because after strumming on their guitars they go out and paint [graffiti on] walls."[70] From the detention centers themselves survivors reported the repressors' initial hesitation and guilt in regard to torturing and executing teenagers, but these feelings were always allayed in the "final solution" context ("it's better not to let those with this social restlessness grow up") or by direct resort to the underlying mythological infrastructure of the "dirty war." One victim was told, for example, "You are our best young people . . . valuable people, but . . . this is a holy war and you want to disrupt the natural order . . . you are the Antichrist . . . I'm not a torturer, I'm an inquisitor."[71]

The military's direct assault at what it perceived to be a virulent "grave moral sickness" of "infiltrated" youth impeding "the positive action to construct the future" was also evidenced statistically.[72] Approximately 44.3 percent of the desaparecidos were under the age of twenty-five, that figure increasing to 70.2 percent when those between twenty-five and thirty years of age are added.[73]

Action on the "industrial front" attested to the pragmatic, politico-economic motivations that fused with military mythology in perpetuating the "dirty war."[74] The labor movement that developed in Argentina in the late nineteenth century and gained a significant political voice during the Perón administration of 1946–1955 was a prominent force in shaping Argentine history. National labor strikes and union mobilization of the masses in demonstrations destabilized more than one de facto Argentine regime, the military government of General Onganía being a case in point that was menacingly fresh in the memory of the 1976 Junta. The mobilization of the working class in the early 1970s and the inclination to bypass the bureaucratized and often corrupt unions was particularly threatening to the Process of National Reorganization ideals. In addition to whatever political disturbance organized labor could mount, effective unions by their very nature were troublesome to the profoundly conservative and unpopular program of Minister of Economy Alfredo Martínez de Hoz, which looked after the interests of Argentina's economic elite and its international partners. To attract multinational investment and accelerate the rate of economic growth, a docile and inexpensive labor force was required; at the same time the freezing of wages to control inflation and to better compete for foreign investment agitated labor. Abduction proved a handy expedient to remedy the tension generated by the Junta's economic policy within the social group (labor) that bore its cost: The problem would "disappear."[75]

One should not be surprised, then, to discover that blue- and white-collar workers figured prominently in *desaparecido* demographics, accounting jointly for 48 percent of the *desaparecidos* reported to the Comisión Nacional Sobre la Desaparición de Personas (National Commission on the Disappearance of Persons, CONADEP).[76] A 1977 proclamation by General Horacio Tomás Liendo, then minister of labor, made clear the need for "the annihilation of this *enemy of us all.*" Liendo went on to point out that those who proved wayward in the "normal development" of the Process of National Reorganization by seeking "individual or sector benefits" (by challenging a pay cut, for example, in the context of three-digit inflation) "*become accomplices of the subversion we must destroy.*"[77] Immediately following the 1976 coup d'état the principal leaders of the General Confederation of Labor (CGT) and the "Sixty-two Organizations" were imprisoned. The CGT was closed and its funds frozen, strikes and collective bargaining were declared illegal, and wage increases were enacted at the exclusive pleasure of the dictatorship.[78] With the legal apparatus for repression of labor thus in place, the Junta ignored—as was its tendency—the laws that it had itself promulgated, opting rather to enforce its economic policies by "disappearance" and intimidation tactics.

Even beyond the rampant invention of "subversion" in a "night of pencils" or a union roundup, the Junta further increased its victimage by allowing the paramilitary operations a 25 percent margin of error. The fate of these erroneously abducted and detained victims, like the fate of those deemed "subversive" due merely to their possession of the wrong books or to their inclusion in another victim's appointment calendar, entailed torture in most cases and both torture and execution in others. One error of this nature was reported to CONADEP in the testimony of Raúl Romero, who was arrested and tortured, as was his wife, for having the misfortune of bearing the same surname and living in the residence previously occupied by Victor Hugo Romero, whom the task force intended to abduct.[79] Other cases of error included one victim abducted for affiliation with the FAP (Fuerzas Armadas Peronistas, Peronist Armed Forces) when in fact he was a member of a distinct organization using the same acronym (Federación Argentina de Psiquiatras, Argentine Federation of Psychiatrists).[80]

The process by which "subversion" was multiplied by a military purporting to eradicate it went beyond errors resulting from carelessness and indiscrimination on the part of insufficiently supervised subordinates. The task forces' crude intelligence tactics—which should have been directed, one presumes, at the identification and arrest of terrorists dangerous to national security—tended rather to generate more "subversives" from within the population at large, to add players rather than eliminate them. In one case, for example, "the children, the mother-in-law, and the wife of Ramón Miralles were detained in order to be able to detain Ramón Miralles, and Ramón Miralles was detained and tortured so that he would explain or invent some economic crime of Victorio Calabro."[81] Apprehension of one possible "subversive" (Victorio Calabro) thus resulted in the abduction of at least six persons. The "immense task" that the military took on itself was expanding exponentially by the very means deployed to accomplish it.

III

Domestic and international political realities require that the executives of national administrations present their programs in discursive registers other than mytho-logical ones. A president cannot, for example, introduce and effectively defend legislation to dissolve labor unions on the grounds that these unions have fallen under the sway of the Antichrist. The Argentine Junta, like bureaucratic authoritarian regimes generally, never lacked a coterie of technocrats to tend to the administration's discourse in political and legal registers. But discourse from the March coup d'état forward was consistently characterized by a *translation* quality that suggested the transposition of mythological discourse into politically acceptable registers. Residuals in the texts of Junta political and legal documents attest to a mythological source language translated into a technocratic target language (the rhetoric of political and legal documents), indexing a paradigm that was dominantly religious and psychosexual rather than political, legal, or economic in nature. Official Junta documents were often little more than pro forma instruments adapting "dirty war" mythology to contexts that demanded formal propriety. They were the necessary incursions into a troublesome reality that politics required of the military before it could retreat and entrench in the mythological system that granted "dirty war" violence unmitigated righteousness, that entrusted the Junta with a messianic mission in a world where all the complexities were simplified and clarified, where everything made sense in relation to one cosmic Whole, where delineations between good and evil were absolute, and where divinely sanctioned annihilation of the latter gave Argentina's "reorganization" eschatological significance.

Perhaps the most apt illustration of the Junta's pro forma attendance to legal and political formalities is in the Acts and Statutes of the Process of National Reorganization. This comprehensive political plan, adopted on the day of the coup d'état and published five days later, provided for the following: establishing a military junta that assumed political control of Argentina; declaring null and void the terms of office of the president and the provincial governors and vice governors; dissolving the National Congress and other representative bodies; removing from office the attorney general and members of the Supreme Court and higher provincial courts; and appointing the citizen—General Videla—who would serve as president.[82] Other provisions later adopted included measures that suspended the constitutional right to leave the country during a state of siege; declared null and void all pending applications to leave Argentina; called for a trial by court martial for civilians accused of offenses involving subversion or sabotage; established the death penalty and unspecified prison sentences for acts of terrorism; and revoked several union, political party, civil, and university liberties.[83]

The legal apparatus set in motion with the coup d'état also subordinated the Argentine constitution to the Process of National Reorganization, as article 14 of the statute provided that "the national and provincial governments shall conform their actions to the basic objectives outlined by the Military Junta, to this Statute, and to the national and provincial constitutions, to the extent that these [the constitutions] are not opposed to them [the Junta's objectives and the statute]."[84]

In evidence, then, is a regime whose debut was accompanied by de facto legal gestures and performative discourse designed to establish whatever authenticity the usurpation of supreme power in all branches of government could claim. Thereafter the crystalline military tidiness of the arrangement becomes muddled. The Acts and Statutes of the Process of National Reorganization are first called into question as translations from the Junta's mythological justification of the "dirty war" by a passage that itemized the "basic objectives" on which the Process was founded: "Christian morals, national tradition, and dignity of the Argentine being," presumably given in their order of priority.[85] Although one would suppose that technocratic discourse subordinating the Argentine constitution (to cite one example) would properly be based on the objectives of a political philosophy as manifest in a program of governance, one rather discovers that the Process was founded on abstractions indexing the mythological preoccupation with a decline of Christian morals, of traditional values, and of dignity.

The extremity of "dirty war" repression calls into focus the juxtaposition of "Christian morals, national tradition, and the dignity of the Argentine being" on the one hand and abduction, torture, and execution on the other. In this light the Process documents are troublesome on two levels: first because the concepts propagated as the "basic objectives" would require redefinition in order to signify amidst the brutal repression used to implement them, and second because, despite all the legal machinery set into motion to eradicate "subversion"—from the decrees of Isabel Perón's government to the Acts and Statutes of the Process—the Junta proceeded systematically, as a matter of implied policy subordinating even the seemingly sacrosanct Process decrees, by the illegal means of abduction, torture, and execution. It is precisely for this second reason that much of the Process of National Reorganization legislation is characteristically pro forma: With the exception of those passages functioning performatively to set the process in motion, the legislation regarding the offensive against "subversion" was for the most part promulgated and ignored. Thousands of Argentines were tortured and executed within a mythologically constructed milieu endowing those barbarities with significance in relation to the "basic objectives," but during the years of the Process not a single "subversive" was successfully prosecuted in either military or civilian courts.[86]

IV

The Junta's methodology of repression was standardized throughout Argentina. A "disappearance" consisted of abduction, torture in a clandestine detention center, and summary execution.[87] The abductions were carried out by task forces (*grupos de tarea*, or GTs), in most cases com-prising six to ten heavily armed men in civilian dress. Characteristic of these *patotas*, as they were known in the repressors' vernacular, was a spectacle of force that was "absolutely disproportional"[88] to any possible danger posed by the "subversive" being abducted. Something of the theatrical nature of the task forces' operations is apparent in the following passage, in which the testifier described the abduction of his brother:

> At two in the morning they [the brother, his wife, and his son] were awakened by a loud explosion. My brother got up, opened the door, and saw four men jumping over the fence.
> They were dressed as civilians, one with a moustache and a turban (a sweater wrapped around his head), and were all carrying rifles. Three of them entered the apartment and ordered my sister-in-law to cover her eyes and the boy to close his. The neighbors say that my brother was dragged out by two of the men and put into a Ford Falcon. . . . They also say that there were several cars and a truck on the scene, and a lot of men with rifles behind trees. The traffic had been blocked off, and a helicopter was circling over the house.[89]

The abducted victims' arms were handcuffed or tied behind their backs, their eyes were blindfolded or their heads covered with *capuchas* (hoods), and they were transported either in the trunk or on the floor of a task force vehicle (often Ford Falcons, as mentioned above), many of which were stolen and without license plates. The denigration and abuse of the "subversive" began immediately. Whether the victim was an armed terrorist or a pregnant housewife made little difference: One's induction into the physical and psychological violence began with beatings and insults as part of the abduction itself, some victims tortured in their homes or in vehicles specially equipped for the purpose. It was made clear to the prisoners either explicitly or by violent implication that they had been *chupado*—the slang designation of abduction, literally meaning "sucked" up or in and connoting, as I will discuss in subsequent chapters, the absorption of the prisoner into the body of repression. The procedure entailed the victims' abrupt dissociation from the world as they knew it, sealing them inside another reality—brutal by design in every particu-lar—that was controlled arbitrarily but absolutely at the local level by task force personnel. As it was simply stated in the sentence handed down following the 1985 Junta members' trial, "The fate of the victims was decided by their captors"—low-ranking officers who were given the broadest discretion regarding the duration and intensity of torture and the decision as to whether a given prisoner would ultimately be executed or liberated.[90] Like medieval and early modern inquisitors, the task forces proceeded against "subversives" ex officio, by virtue of their office, without having to wait for formal accusations to be brought against the desaparecidos.

Plunder of the homes of the victims, either during the abduction or following it, was also characteristic of the repressors' method. One victim observed that "they carried off all of our goods and belongings, the house left without a trace that anyone had lived there."[91] Military ideology provided that as victors the task forces and their superiors were entitled to botín de guerra ("spoils of war"), including not only household possessions looted by the task forces but also the spoils of extortions (often under torture) by which desaparecidos or their relatives were compelled to transfer real estate and automobile titles to officers, some of whom became millionaires through this process.[92]

Also among the spoils of war were infants. The justifying rationale for separating a child from its natural family resorted to the messianic sense of responsibility, which in this application provided that the newborn children of "subversives" would be more appropriately reared in the values of "Western and Christian civilization" if they were adopted by a childless couple affiliated with the repressors. Such adoptions were most frequent with babies born to mothers in captivity; the mothers were executed after giving birth. Testimony by survivors of the Escuela de Mecánica de la Armada (ESMA) detention center revealed that "in the Naval Hospital there was a list of Navy couples who could not have children and were prepared to adopt children of the desaparecidos."[93]

Following their abduction the victims were taken to one or more of the three hundred forty clandestine detention centers established throughout Argentina, the larger centers—such as ESMA in Buenos Aires and La Perla in Córdoba—located near major cities where "subversives" were concentrated. The detention centers were ostensibly established, in part, to institute torture as a means of interrogation, but the following chapters will demonstrate that this purported intelligence function of torture (the generation of information useful to national security) is untenable, and I will consequently posit other motives that more satisfactorily explain why torture is often the centerpiece of de facto regimes. One immediately troublesome inadequacy of the torture/intelligence argument is apparent in the very nature of the victims, 80 percent of whom had no relation to terrorism. Whatever information a nonmilitant factory worker or journalist or university student could scream out during interrogation under torture was of little importance to national security, as were the names of whatever other Argentines a torture victim might implicate dimly through his or her pain when the electrical currents applied to the body were no longer bearable. The names of innocent Argentines, the dates of insignificant meetings, the confessions of trivial deeds—such useless data was what the torture of "subversives" could generate. It was not the information itself but rather manipulation of the concept of usefulness that made "dirty war" torture efficacious. The torturers, again like the medieval inquisitors, altered "the very fabric of reality" by scripting roles and making those summoned before them "play these pre-assigned and largely pre-written parts."[94]

The predominant method of torture in the Argentine detention centers involved discharging electric current on a victim's body using the *picana eléctrica*, a kind of prod attached to a voltage regulator with which the shock's intensity was adjusted. A medical doctor was generally in attendance to diagnose the victim's ability to endure without cardiac arrest. The intent during torture was not to kill the victim—that would be accomplished without ceremony afterward—and the death of a victim on the torture table was deemed an error in the process, a failure on the part of the torturer. Torture rather endeavored to break down the victims physically and psychologically, keeping them alive so that they could be repeatedly and ceremoniously undone. The eroticism of torture with the *picana*—beyond the general sexuality of violence as registered in the definition of "sadism"[95]—was emphasized in the detention centers by application of the phallic-like instrument as a matter of preference (or even of policy) to the genitals, anus, breasts, and mouth. The naked bodies of the victims were usually wetted to better conduct the electrical discharge, and application of the *picana* was often complemented by various forms of beatings devised scientifically to create the greatest sensation of pain. Young children were tortured in front of their parents,[96] parents in front of their children,[97] husbands in front of wives, and wives in front of husbands, the torture in these last cases often accompanied by rape.[98] Pregnant women were tortured (and raped),[99] elderly men and women were tortured, and in at least one case an infant was tortured after the torturer consulted an attending physician to determine what voltage could be endured by a child of that young age.

In addition to the *picana*, other methods of torture used frequently in the Argentine detention centers included the "submarine" (dunking the victim's head, sometimes hooded, into a vat of putrid water, urine, excrement, or other such substance until "the last bubbles come up," then releasing the victim long enough for a gasp of air before resubmerging); the "dry submarine" (a waterless technique of strangulation/suffocation); the hanging of victims by their arms handcuffed behind them (sometimes in combination with electric shock);[100] the infliction of cigarette burns (often on the breasts); and the throwing of boiling water on the anus and genitals.[101] Mock executions were also frequent, their impact on the victims well illustrated by the following passage from the trial testimony of survivor Pablo A. Díaz, who was sixteen years of age at the time of the incident:

> They put me against a wall . . . there were other people there . . . they told me "We're going to shoot you," one said "Where you're going you'll be better off"; I heard the girls crying, people fainted, I don't know why I reacted this way but I was suddenly mute, I heard the order to get ready, I heard one man shout "Long live the Montoneros," another "Long live Argentina," girls saying "Mom, they're going to kill me." I was crying, mute, they fired, I could hear the guns, I believed it, I was waiting for blood to pour out of me somewhere, I'm dead, I'm not dead, it's a second but that second is eternal.

Díaz then reemphasized: "I didn't know whether or not I was dead."[102]

Also prevalent in the detention centers were unofficial, extracurricular tortures that the guards devised to entertain themselves. These included the "human pyramid" (under which the victims at the bottom were sometimes crushed to death)[103] and drunken bouts in which prisoners were beaten by guards until they performed some humiliating act or recited some debasing litany composed for the occasion. The festive nature of these informal, ludic entertainments is evident in the following passage from testimony presented to the OAS Commission in 1979:

> They called one of the prisoners "peg-leg." . . . One night the guards got drunk and began to bet that they could make him stand on his peg-leg. They brought him into the middle of the room and ordered him to do it. He begged them, said that it was impossible, that he was going to fall. Then they began to kick him, punch him, and they stood him up. Of course, he fell. They stood him up again, he fell again, and so on, throughout the night. It was a most macabre spectacle. The guards went

crazy, they beat him without interruption and the poor man was begging them to stop. There was the sound of blows to the lungs, the abdomen, the noise of broken bones. They stopped when he fell unconscious.[104]

Following their formal sessions of torture, some prisoners were released, either because they were *perejiles* (individuals with no conceivable involvement in "subversion," such as the neighbors or relatives abducted along with a targeted victim) or because they had been arrested erroneously. Other prisoners remained incarcerated for protracted and unspecified tenures, often performing maintenance or quasi-intelligence services (clipping articles on the "dirty war" from foreign periodicals, for example). Near the end of their arbitrarily designated sentence, some of these detainees were permitted weekend leaves from the detention centers during a transition period apparently designed to serve a halfway-house function between the hermetic penal milieu and the world at large. Still other prisoners, in this case mostly high-ranking Montoneros, were afforded elite status with considerable material and psychological benefits, first in the ESMA detention center and later in a low-security facility. By virtue of actual or feigned compliance with a "resocialization" program that put them in the service of Admiral Massera, these members of the Montonero leadership—to a great degree responsible for the insurrection that triggered the indiscriminate State offensive against civilians—suffered less severe punishment than the thousands of *desaparecidos* with no involvement in militancy whatsoever.[105] The fact that privileged status was granted to the legitimate enemy while innocent civilians were arbitrarily annihilated is a paradox I will unravel subsequently.

With the exception of the small percentage of victims included in these categories of liberation or extended incarceration, the *desaparecidos* were executed shortly after their torture. The methods of elimination varied. In some areas the victims were shot at the edge of massive graves, their bodies incinerated and then covered over. The prisoners at ESMA suffered a more Kafkaesque fate: They were sedated to a lethargic state in the detention center, loaded onto an airplane destined to a specific seaward location where the currents led away from the continent, and thrown alive into the ocean. On one of those daily flights were the French nuns Sister Léonie Duquet and Sister Alice Domon, subsequently referred to by the repressors as "the flying nuns."[106] In that same vernacular the other victims were referred to more generically as "fish food."[107]

V

Official denial of responsibility for "dirty war" abductions functioned as a performative speech act that transformed arrests into "disappearances." If all factors (the abduction, the torture, the execution) remained constant but were accompanied by the government's affirmation of responsibility (X is in cell number five; Y has been executed) rather than by denial, there would have been an arrest and a barbarous flaunting of power, but not a "disappearance." A "disappearance" occurs when the acts of abduction, torture, and execution are complemented by the speech act of denial. The mixed message of the said and the done, the internal contradiction, the spectacularly violent reality clouded by the discourse negating it ensnares the public in a double bind, in a paralyzing uncertainty and terror.

Denial during the "dirty war" was maintained on two tiers: officially by the Junta (and the high command), which disclaimed responsibility for the "disappearances" and sought to annul the reality of their occurrence,[108] and unofficially by the low-ranking personnel who came into direct contact with the relatives of *desaparecidos*. One mother of a seventeen-year-old *desaparecido*, to cite an example of denial as expressed in the rank and file, was informed that the police had nothing to do with her son's abduction because police officers wear uniforms and the abductors were dressed as civilians.[109] In the context of the Junta's official denial of responsibility, such informal remarks signified beyond their apparent worthlessness as arrogant stupidities; they added a voice at the local level to the performative discourse by which abductions were being transformed into "disappearances." One "vanished without a trace" only because systematic denial obscured the traces.[110]

Denial of responsibility by lower-ranking officers and security personnel was often antagonistic, contributing further to the terrorization and paralyzation of Argentines acting on a *desaparecido's* behalf. One could never distinguish between what constituted effective and prudent action in petitioning for a *desaparecido's* release and what counterproductively aggravated the victim's situation and perhaps even contributed to his or her execution or to other "disappearances." Family members were thus in a double bind, not knowing whether a persistent search for the *desaparecido* was beneficial or detrimental. The psychological effects of that situation became apparent after the "dirty war," when group sessions for family members of *desaparecidos* revealed that, although some mothers pursued one course of action on the *desaparecido's* behalf and other mothers pursued the opposite one, most came away with "the omnipotent idea that they could have prevented the disappearance if they would have done precisely the opposite of what they did."[111] The cruel dynamics of "disappearance" provided that all efforts made on the *desaparecidos'* behalf were wrong. The victims were subjected to torture and execution despite intervention, and the relatives suffered a wrenching angst, compounded with uncertainty, incapacitation, terror, and loss.

When reports of a "disappearance" to police and military authorities brought little result, the families of many victims filed writs of habeas corpus. These, too, proved fruitless in the overwhelming majority of cases for the courts were subordinated to the Junta's governance as provided in the Acts and Statutes of the Process, as well as by changes in personnel. "The writ of *habeas corpus* became a useless formality, totally ineffective as a means of restraining the policy of forcible abduction espoused by the military,"[112] this precisely because denial—whether at the local police station or in the Supreme Court—was integral to "disappearance." Habeas corpus (from Latin: [that] you have the body) petitions for an individual's physical appearance and is therefore obviously in direct conflict with a strategy adopted to make that individual "disappear." The military explained that

> there are legal rules and standards which do not apply in this instance [the "dirty war"]—the writ of *habeas corpus*, for example. In this type of struggle the inherent secrecy with which our special operations must be conducted requires that we do not divulge whom we have captured and whom we want to capture; everything has to be enveloped in a cloud of silence.[113]

Between the March 1976 coup d'état and the substantial reduction of State terrorism in the early 1980s, only two writs of habeas corpus—one prompted by unappeasable international pressure—are known to have resulted in release of their beneficiaries. The first case was that of journalist Jacobo Timerman, owner/editor of the outspoken Buenos Aires newspaper *La Opinión*. After having been incarcerated and tortured under the supervision of General Ramón J. Camps, Timerman was released by order of the Supreme Court but deprived of his citizenship by executive power and expelled from Argentina.[114] The second case, that of Benito Moya, resulted in Moya's "conditional release" under house arrest.[115] Of the thousands of other Argentines named in the habeas corpus writs nothing was disclosed. The *desaparecidos* would remain, as Lieutenant General Roberto E. Viola put it on Soldier's Day in May 1979, "absent forever."[116]

In addition to the role played by denial in effecting a "disappearance," the proliferation of official Junta statements constantly reelaborating, recontextualizing, and challenging the apparent reality of State-generated violence fostered public disavowal of the "dirty war." Government lies were comforting; the official discourse of denial strengthened each individual's tendency to privately deny the unthinkable. The verisimilitude of direct negation of the facts—such as General Videla's "I categorically deny that there exist in Argentina any concentration camps"[117] (there were three hundred forty detention centers)—was simultaneously reinforced by the suppression of venues for opposing data. Publications were carefully censored, the veracity of contrary reports was undermined, suggestion of the detention centers or *desaparecidos* was tainted as politicized hearsay, so that "there [were] only subjective, uncontrollable, unreliable reports about the places of the living dead" on one side, while a barrage of widely disseminated official statements on the other side stimulated the public's "common sense disinclination to believe the monstrous."[118] The "dirty war" refrains *Por algo será* ("It must be for something") and *Algo habrá[n] hecho* ("He/she/they must have done something")—mumbled by witnesses who saw a neighbor or coworker abducted for reasons no one could ascertain—emerged from this desire to normalize the tragic by way of dismissal, to endow senseless brutality with meaning by supposing that the authorities had privileged access to the unknown "something" that established a victim's guilt.

Although the Junta policy to deny responsibility and to withhold information regarding the *desaparecidos* was applied in the vast majority of cases, there were also several instances in which international pressure compelled the Junta to provide information (generally untrue) about the fate of a given prisoner. Perhaps the most baroque and revealing example of such official statements is found in the case of Rosa Ana Frigerio, a nineteen-year-old girl who was abducted while immobilized in a cast from her waist to her calves as the result of a spinal operation. Following her abduction the girl's parents made repeated inquiries to determine their daughter's whereabouts and were finally told that she was being held in the naval base at Mar del Plata. This was later denied. Subsequently, after having filed a writ of habeas corpus, the parents received a letter explaining that their daughter was being held at the discretion of the executive power for "subversive activities." In March 1977, a month after receiving that letter, the parents were summoned before a naval officer who clarified that Rosa Ana—though at the time presumably still in or in need of the cast—had been "killed by her comrades" during a confrontation with antisubversive forces. When the family demanded a death certificate, the authorities then claimed therein that the cause of death was "cardiac arrest, cardiothoracic traumatism," a cause completely inconsistent with the original claims.[119] In its April 1980 document contesting the OAS Commission's report in which the case of Rosa Ana Frigerio was included, the Junta continued its policy of denial despite the evidence, remarking that "the Argentine government cannot accept the judgement that its responses [in regard to the *desaparecidos*] are negative, unsatisfactory, and even contradictory."[120]

As the content and tone of this passage suggest, the Junta's denial of responsibility for "dirty war" atrocities also served to reinforce the mythological premises on which policy and strategy were based. When "dirty war" mythology and the regime dependent on it were threatened by incursions from external realities—as they were with the challenge to the Junta's denial of responsibility posed by the OAS Commission's report—the result was a reaction formation, a retrenching in mythological precepts that became all the more sacrosanct and hermetic. Rather than yielding in some politically redeemable manner to the incontestability of evidence accumulated against it, the Junta reacted by withdrawing more deeply into the delusional mythology that protected it. It rearranged reality to transform all opposition into a guaranty of the mythology's veracity, all repudiation into avowal.

One precise demonstration of this phenomenon was apparent in a passage from the above-mentioned document that the Junta published in response to the OAS Commission's report. Having prepared for the commission's 1979 in situ investigation by propagating the slogan *Los Argentinos somos derechos y humanos*[121] and expecting the best, the Junta reacted to the report with indignation in the wake of what it deemed a betrayal. The report, the Junta argued, evidenced "infiltration" at even the highest levels: "It seems to have been written following presumptions defined in advance." The response continues:

> The painful experience accumulated by the free world in its struggle against Marxist subversion has demonstrated, indubitably, that the enemy

has not and will not hesitate in calling upon the most absurd means of propaganda, discrediting governments and men in order to gain support for its effort to dominate the West under the slavery of Bolshevism.[122]

Mytho-logic seals and protects itself, it recasts all incriminating data that penetrates it into evidence in the myth's favor, thereby strengthening its hermetic closure and correctness. As the prosecution observed during the 1985 trials, "General Videla's empty references affirming that he takes full responsibility but that nothing happened expose a primary thought process which, giving magical power to words, tries through them to make reality disappear because one wishes to deny it."[123] Just as victims of the repression "disappeared" by means of denial functioning performatively, so the "magical power" of speech acts shift register from facts to myth through a similar mechanism of "disappearance."

VI

In September 1979, just a few months after General Viola's "absent forever" remark, the Junta promulgated the Law of Presumption of Death Because of Disappearance in an effort to regularize the legal status of the *desaparecidos*. This law, which met with severe domestic and international criticism for failing to clarify the *desaparecidos'* fate, was one of the Junta's first attempts to efface its deplorable human rights record through legislation.[124] A communication that accompanied the law as it went from the minister of the interior to the president enumerated the official grounds on which the Junta denied responsibility for the *desaparecidos*.[125] These grounds had similarly been alluded to in other statements made by the Junta when the OAS Commission made its visit and report, when an Episcopal declaration was issued protesting violent repression in Argentina, and during a television interview with General Videla in the United States.[126] On this last occasion Videla summarized the Junta's accounting for the *desaparecidos'* absence:

> They have disappeared to go underground and participate in subversion; they have disappeared because other subversives considered them traitors to the cause and eliminated them; they have disappeared in confrontations [with security forces] in which there were fires and explosions, the cadavers being mutilated beyond recognition; and I accept that they could have disappeared due to excesses committed in the repression.[127]

Videla was quick to clarify that he claimed responsibility only in those few cases occasioned by the "excesses" of lower-ranking servicemen and in closing assured the audience that his government was doing everything in its power to prevent the repetition of such cases. Other Junta reckonings added suicide and surreptitious flight from Argentina to the list of probable causes for absences perceived as "disappearances."

Even before the massive body of evidence disproving these accounts regarding the *desaparecidos*' fate was revealed in the OAS Commission's report, the CONADEP investigation, and the trial proceedings, a glance at the Junta's arguments themselves suggests their untenability. If the greatest percentage of fallen soldiers throughout the history of warfare have been identifiable, what sort of war was this in which there were primarily mutilated, unidentifiable, or missing corpses? And how is it that unidentifiability was characteristic only of the fallen enemy soldiers, while the State forces killed in combat were ceremoniously recognized? And if "subversives" had committed suicide or were living in exile or "underground" in Argentina, would their parents or wives or friends not have been apprised of this status rather than being doomed by such oversight to the traumatic charade of visiting police stations and military bases and filing writs of habeas corpus? And did not most family members or acquaintances of the *desaparecidos* witness their abduction, thus mooting the remaining arguments of flight or execution by the terrorist movements to which these individuals allegedly belonged?

Although the arguments of denial were at best questionable, the fact that the Junta maintained its insistent pro forma denial at all levels was, as I have suggested, essential; the pragmatics of "disappearance" required it. Before both domestic and international opinion, too, denial of responsibility had a clear diplomatic function, calling into play a strategy which first reduced the index of responsibility by attributing most "disappearances" to a catalog of pretexts that pardoned the Junta and then claimed responsibility for the leftovers only as isolated instances of "excesses" committed by the rank and file. With this second tactic, which would surface again in defense arguments at the 1985 trials, the Junta sought to exculpate itself by displacing responsibility onto the subordinates who implemented the violent policies that the commanders themselves had ordered.

By 1981 the faltering stability of the Junta's administration demanded decisive action. The Law of Presumption of Death generated widespread domestic and international demands for a less cryptic clarification of the *desaparecidos*' fate. The credibility of Junta propaganda had eroded over the years of repression, and the absence of armed insurrection called into question the legitimacy (even if only de facto legitimacy) of a military regime. Severe economic crisis under the burden of inflation and foreign debt service was also generating open protest, and the mobilization of opposing political parties likewise demonstrated a decline in the level of acquiescence that the Junta had maintained through the late 1970s.

The search for a political solution in 1982 (like that in 1976) took the form of a military campaign, the offensive this time redirected from an internal to an external adversary. The social and symbolizing function that wars serve by uniting populations and subordinating individual interests to national identity was exploited—just a few days after the largest antigovernment demonstration since the inception of the Process—when the Junta diverted hostilities outward, onto the British, with the hope of unifying Argentines and reaffirming the validity of military rule. As de facto president at the time, General Leopoldo Galtieri propagated the Malvinas as the "common denominator" of all Argentines, this rhetoric reinforced by a national campaign marketing the slogan, "United it's easier." When thousands celebrated the victorious "recapture" of the Malvinas in the Plaza de Mayo on April 10, 1982, the press echoed the unification theme with these words: "This time the plaza was everyone's. . . . It wasn't a demonstration of one sector, it wasn't a march of one group against another. [It was the] testimony of a people reuniting again after so much time."[128] Were Galtieri's "malvinization"[129] of the dictatorship's politics to succeed, the Junta might effectively divert attention from its human rights and socioeconomic woes, promote a nationalistic rally around the defeat of an external adversary, and regain something of the messianic reception it catered to on deposing Isabel Perón. Its failure, however, would carry political consequences that the destabilized regime would be unable to endure.

On April 2, 1982, the Argentine military invaded the Falkland/Malvinas Islands off the southeast coast of Argentina.[130] A British task force recaptured the islands on June 14, 1982, after more than a thousand men had died. The Junta's war with the British displayed in the most humiliating terms the Argentine military's incapacity in true war (as opposed to "dirty war") against an armed adversary. Argentine soldiers who returned alive from this tour de force of military incompetence reported "a spectacle of corruption, incapacity, and tragedy" in which some officers commanded their troops and others fled or stood paralyzed with fear; in which food supplies did not reach the front and rotted in storehouses a few kilometers away; in which starving soldiers were savagely punished for stealing sheep; and in which General Menéndez, one of the more fanatical veterans of the "dirty war," lined his office with furs while inadequately protected troops literally died of exposure and had their frostbitten limbs amputated.[131]

Defeat in the Falkland/Malvinas war, combined with an economy in near collapse and increasing political pressure regarding the *desaparecidos*, so discredited the Junta that it was compelled to announce the return of democratic rule in Argentina. De facto president Galtieri, largely responsible for the islands' invasion, was forced to resign and was replaced by an interim president, General Cristino Nicolaides, a representative of the authoritarian tendency within the army. The navy and the air force withdrew from the Junta, and Nicolaides appointed General Reynaldo Bignone to the presidency on July 1, 1982, for the eighteen-month period of transition to civilian rule.

In April 1983, shortly before the elections to be held that same year, the Junta published and broadcast on national radio and television networks its Final Document on the War Against Subversion and Terrorism. With this proclamation and the accompanying Institutional Act the military attempted to formalize and elaborate some of the arguments outlined earlier in this chapter: that all of the operations against subversion and terrorism "were executed in conformity with plans approved and supervised" by the Junta but that any transgressions beyond "the limits of fundamental human rights" were errors and excesses rather than policy.[132] The Final Document also specifically reiterated official denial of responsibility for the *desaparecidos*, on the same grounds listed previously. In reference to the accusation that the military held prisoners in clandestine detention centers, the Final Document clarified that "all of this is nothing other than a falsehood utilized for political purposes, since there are no secret places of detention in the Republic, nor are there persons secretly detained in the prisons."[133]

That statement was not without its cynical truth, for by 1983 all of the *desaparecidos* once detained in the clandestine detention centers had been either executed, released, or transferred to legal incarceration. The document accordingly reiterated the presumption of death ("for all legal and administrative purposes") of the *desaparecidos*, excepting those individuals living in exile or clandestinely within Argentina. Presented in its introduction as "a message of faith and recognition of the struggle for freedom, for justice, and for the right to life," the Final Document rounded out the Junta's position by concluding with the self-congratulatory reminder that "those who gave their lives to combat the scourge of terrorism deserve eternal homage of respect and gratitude."[134] Three weeks before the October 1983 elections that would return Argentina to civilian rule, the Junta promulgated a second law that anticipated the possibility of human rights litigation under the forthcoming democracy. The Law of National Pacification, often referred to as the Amnesty Law, granted impunity for all crimes committed by the armed forces during the "dirty war." As a gesture of "national pacification," the military attempted to balance its autoamnesty by extending pardons to incarcerated "subversives," who were urged "to leave the confrontations behind and pardon our mutual grievances."[135] The law also explained to the "mourning Argentine family" (appealed to as though a third party rather than as the victim of the repression that occasioned its "mourning") that "man's dignity" was the banner under which the Junta fought amidst "the severity and irrationality of the subversive and terrorist phenomena." It further stated that "the cruel and cunning way in which terrorist subversion initiated the battle" may have resulted in military deeds incompatible with the Junta's honorable intention.[136]

The immunity from prosecution that the military granted itself in the national pacification law was followed by a more direct measure to muddle accountability for the *desaparecidos*. As a safeguard in the event that the autoamnesty failed and litigation came to pass, a late 1983 Junta decree ordered the destruction of documents relating to the "dirty war."

VII

In December 1983 Raúl Alfonsín, candidate of the same Radical Civic Union party that was deposed by General Uriburu's coup d'état in 1930, was inaugurated as constitutional president of Argentina. After only three days in office, on December 13, Alfonsín announced in an address to the Argentine public that he was repealing "the de facto law 'of pacification' or 'amnesty,'" and at the same time he issued a decree ordering the arrest and prosecution of the nine officers constituting the three military Juntas of the Process of National Reorganization.[137] Two days later the National Commission on the Disappearance of Persons was created by decree, with Alfonsín appointing the thirteen-member body that elected novelist Ernesto Sábato as its president at its first meeting.[138] CONADEP conducted an extensive nine-month investigation that included interviews with thousands of witnesses (primarily released prisoners and relatives of *desaparecidos*, as well as reluctant, largely uncooperative members of military and security forces) and the inspection of former centers of torture and detention. The investigation resulted in fifty thousand pages of documentation, a five-hundred-page summary of which was presented to Alfonsín on September 20, 1984. That report was then published in Argentina by the University of Buenos Aires Press (EUDEBA) as *Nunca más* in November and was subsequently released in English under the same title.[139]

Despite the gruesome testimonial descriptions of torture that would seem to distance *Nunca más* from an audience of casual readers, the book quickly became a best-seller; sales figures during the first months of its release alone exceeded one hundred thousand copies. Popular dissemination of *Nunca más* contributed most significantly to a new Argentine consensus recognizing the scale and aberrant character of "dirty war" violence, but it also had consequences that were "sometimes disconcerting": "This overwhelmingly monotonous tale of systematic cruelty became the favorite reading of hordes of [Argentine] tourists who converged on Mar del Plata during the summer, making copies of the *Informe* [*Nunca más*] as much a part of the beach scene as bottles of suntan lotion."[140] "This trivialization of a horrible past" as "the most paradoxical consequence of the success of the *Informe* in exorcising the experience"[141] is a post–"dirty war" example of an issue that I will address in the following chapter, which considers the role of the public as audience of the violent spectacles through which political power is generated.

For the first time in Latin American history a civilian government would now try former military rulers for atrocities committed during their de facto regime. The legislation ordering these trials provided that all military crimes committed since 1973 were to be first tried in camera by the Supreme Council of the Armed Forces, but it also provided a time limitation for the completion of the trials, after which the Federal Appeals Courts would be specifically empowered to assume jurisdiction.[142] Having delayed the court-martial with some indignation and nearing the end of a ninety-day extension of its period of jurisdiction, the Supreme Council dismissed the case, issuing a statement that declared its unwillingness and inability to complete the proceedings. It found that the decrees and directives implementing the antisubversive operations were "unobjectionable" in both form and content.[143]

The Federal Appeals Court thus assumed jurisdiction and placed five of the former leaders under "rigorous preventative detention," requiring the other four to remain at the court's disposal. During seventeen weeks of testimony that virtually monopolized the political attention of Argentina, the court heard over eight hundred witnesses in nearly five hundred hours of public testimony.[144] General Videla, de facto president of Argentina during the most intensive years of repression, "spent a good deal of the sessions reading religious tracts, looking up occasionally to stare at a cross behind the judges' bench."[145] Though the quasi-mystical posture of the messianic Right was otherwise more subdued during the trial, the secular ideology that translated it into policy and juridical discourse was expressly evident.

The Junta members' defense counsel gave voice to that ideology by calling upon familiar arguments. The military government's official involvement in or responsibility for "disappearances" was formally denied. The "dirty war" discourse on the international conspiracy of "subversives" was expanded to discredit testimony against the officers on trial; the defense referred to prosecution witnesses as losers of the armed battle who were now retaliating in an insidious unarmed campaign on the "psychological front," "conquering hearts and minds" through the trial's publicity. Exemplary in that position was Dr. Jaime Prats Cardona, attorney for Admiral Massera, who prefaced his defense by pointing out that "under the title of human rights defenders" were diverse groups "perfectly identifiable by their political and ideological orientation" who were "orchestrating a campaign of psychological action, using the most diverse, underhanded, treacherous means to undermine the prestige of the Armed Forces."[146] Admiral Massera also spoke for himself: "We are here because we won the armed war but lost the psychological war." He went on to explain that the Junta underestimated "the enemy's exceptional propaganda resources," which by mobilizing "an extremely efficient system of international persuasion began to throw the most sinister and deformed shadows over our reality."[147]

Elsewhere the defense arguments were less bombastic and more specifically directed to the legal validity of the trial and the credibility of specific testimonies. But always explicit was the defense's suspicion that a villainous conspiracy had scripted the testimony in advance. Too many details coincided, recollections seemed too precise, repetition of the same

gruesome story seemed to add up too neatly to a great chorus of perse-
cutory compliance orchestrated against the victors of the "dirty war." In
advancing these perceptions the defendants and their counsel reinvoked
an enemy-generating mechanism used earlier: Just as the victims of repression were transformed into conspiratorial "subversives" during the "dirty
war" by virtue of having been abducted into a mythological system, so
now these victims—here witnesses for the prosecution—were rendered
insidious and conspiratorial by testifying to what they suffered. In the
following passage Assistant Prosecutor Moreno Ocampo effectively con-
tested the defense arguments that attempted to discredit testimony by
raising the conspiracy issue:

> I have made a tally of the first 240 cases presented by the Prosecution; in
> 172 of them at least one writ of habeas corpus was filed in which the
> narration of the events coincides with what the witnesses have testified
> here. Is it possible that some diabolical organization exists with sufficient
> power to achieve, during those years when Argentina was governed by
> the defendants with all-embracing power, that university professors from
> Bahía Blanca and Cordoban peasants, bankers from the Capital and
> workers from the Tucumán sugarcane fields, lawyers from Mendoza and
> employees from Chaco, Tucumán teachers and doctors from Buenos Aires
> province, psychologists from Neuquen, industrialists, diplomats, land-
> scape painters, priests, housewives, sixteen-year-old teenagers—could all
> of these people have come to an agreement to denounce false facts? Is
> there an organization capable of making this sampling across Argentine
> society coincide in narrating facts that are false?[148]

The prosecution then added this observation: "If all of this is a
conspiracy, we would have to consider that the defense attorneys are part
of it too, since many of the witnesses they offered confirmed the facts
presented by prosecution witnesses."[149]

Most of the other defense arguments implicitly contradicted the defendants' official denial of responsibility for using illegal tactics in the
"dirty war." One of those arguments contended that the Junta acted "in
compliance with a legal duty" because the "dirty war" was initiated by
decrees issued by the constitutional government of Isabel Perón. Although that indeed was so, former President Italo Luder, who signed the
decrees (under military manipulation) during Isabel Perón's extended
leave, clarified at the trial that their purpose was to incorporate the armed
forces into the fight against subversion, not to effect a change in the

juridical structure of the rule of law or in penal legislation. The prosecution added to Luder's testimony the observation that the decree gave the armed forces the opportunity to fulfill its mandate by defending the community from those attacking it, rather than attacking that community itself.[150] The prosecution also found it peculiar that the military Junta could propose the legitimization of its actions by resort to the decrees of a government that it had itself deposed on grounds of corruption, ineptitude, and mismanagement.

Other justifications offered to the court by the defense invoked the legal doctrine of "necessity," or the need to commit a lesser evil in order to prevent a greater one (as illustrated earlier in the hidden bomb analogy) and the notion of "self-defense" understood as the military's fulfillment of its role as protector of national sovereignty under attack. The court meticulously addressed these justifications and ruled against them. It also rejected the justification of human rights violations on the basis of the nonjusticiability of acts of war and the defense's contention that such violations were excesses committed by the rank and file and therefore not the legal responsibility of the commanders.[151]

At the conclusion of the trial, Jorge Rafael Videla was sentenced to loss of military rank, to absolute and perpetual disqualification from holding public office, and to life imprisonment for charges including homicide, torture, robbery, and false arrest aggravated by threats and violence. Also sentenced to life imprisonment was Admiral Emilio Massera of the first Junta. General Robert Viola, of the second Junta and president of Argentina following Videla's tenure, received a seventeen-year sentence; Admiral Armando Lambruschini, the naval representative in the second Junta, was sentenced to eight years; and Brigadier General Orlando Agosti, air force representative of the first Junta, received a four-and-a-half-year sentence. The air force commander of the second Junta, Omar Rubens Graffigna, was acquitted, as were the three members of the third Junta: Leopoldo Galtieri (army), Jorge Isaac Anaya (navy), and Basilio Lami Dozo (air force). (These members of the third Junta, however, were later convicted by a military court in separate proceedings based on an eighteen-month military investigation of their "negligence" in conducting the 1982 Falklands/Malvinas war against the British.) On December 30, 1986, the Argentine Supreme Court upheld the judgment of the Federal Appeals Court that convicted the Junta members, making only minor changes in the sentences of Viola and Agosti.[152] A second major trial for crimes committed during the "dirty war" concluded on December 2,

1986, convicting former Buenos Aires province police chief Ramón Camps and five other police officials of human rights abuses and sentencing them to prison terms of between four and twenty-five years.

VIII

In response to pressure from the military and in an effort to lift the cloud "of interminable suspicion" hindering the incorporation of the armed forces into Argentina's new democracy, President Alfonsín proposed a law establishing a deadline after which no further prosecutions for "dirty war" human rights violations could be filed. The "full stop" law, as it was known, was passed by congress on Christmas eve of 1986. The law established a sixty-day period from the date of its promulgation for initiating charges regarding crimes committed before Alfonsín assumed office. The law was met with outcries of protest from human rights and other groups that deemed it a betrayal, particularly because Alfonsín had campaigned on a human rights platform. However, these same groups, along with victims of the repression and their relatives, managed to expeditiously gather sufficient evidence to result in more than three hundred new summonses issued by Argentine courts prior to the February 22, 1987, deadline.[153]

The flurry of new charges, accompanied by budget cuts that significantly reduced wages and curtailed arms purchases, stimulated new resentment within the military. In February and March of 1987, these external factors were compounded by heated internal debates regarding whether the army and navy would attempt to grant asylum to the active-duty officers summoned to court. The military eventually acceded to the court orders, at the same time initiating an aggressive campaign to heighten public opinion of its "dirty war" performance. Speeches, interviews, paid newspaper advertisements, and displays of extreme right-wing civilian support were all intended to dissuade the civilian courts from prosecuting the active-duty officers.

During Easter week the tension of those months came to a climax when Major Ernesto Guillermo Barreiro, the chief torturer at the La Perla detention center during the "dirty war," refused a court summons and barricaded himself in the military barracks of the Fourteenth Airborne Infantry Regiment in Córdoba. The commander of that army unit announced that he would not deliver Barreiro to the court. Several dozen additional military personnel then joined the rebellion, demanding an end to the trials and an ouster of Army Chief of Staff General Hector Erenu (who subsequently resigned).

As commander in chief, Alfonsín ordered military action to quash the rebellion, but the armed forces refused to mobilize against the rebels. Confronted with this breakdown in the chain of military command, Alfonsín utilized a populist tactic reminiscent of Perón's by calling the masses to streets and plazas throughout Argentina to "show their support for peace and this historic pact" and to make clear to the military that it lacked the popular support to successfully stage a coup d'état.[154] Thousands of Argentines responded to the call—one hundred fifty thousand in the Plaza de Mayo alone, where Alfonsín made speeches from the balcony of the Casa Rosada. The mutiny of junior officers in Córdoba was quelled without violence by the afternoon of Good Friday, but earlier that same day another uprising was staged at the Campo de Mayo near Buenos Aires. Rebels led by the messianic fundamentalist Aldo Rico, recognized as one of the few "heroes" of the Falklands/Malvinas war, seized the infantry school until Easter Sunday, accusing the army high command of doing nothing to protect officers who had duly obeyed their orders in a just war against communism. (Somewhere between two hundred and four hundred fifty court cases were pending at the time of the uprising, about a third of which were thought to be against active-duty officers.)[155] After a fiery speech to the masses gathered in the Plaza de Mayo, Alfonsín flew by helicopter to negotiate the rebels' surrender in person. Troops with greasepaint-blackened faces (thus referred to as the *Carapintadas*, Painted Faces) and riot police armed with shotguns kept civilians on the base perimeter while Alfonsín met with the rebelling officers. Within two hours the president had returned to the balcony of the governmental palace to announce the surrender: "Compatriots, Happy Easter."

But that happiness, the compatriots would later learn, was a compromised happiness, for the Semana Santa (Holy Week) uprisings resulted in Alfonsín's acceding to the rebels' demand for an end to the prosecution of officers in active service. General sympathy throughout the armed forces with the rebels' position left Alfonsín little choice—the army had recomposed itself after its post–Falkland/Malvinas disarray and was openly insubordinate, and the fragility and imminent jeopardy of Argentina's democracy was plainly in evidence. But the concessions that Alfonsín made granted virtual amnesty for almost all of the crimes committed by the military during the "dirty war," exonerating more than a thousand soldiers from prosecution. The Law of Due Obedience, which formalized the policy, was passed by congress on June 4, 1987, abolishing liability to prosecution for all middle-ranking, junior, and noncommissioned officers and privates in the armed forces, as well as in the security, police, and prison services. The law resorted to the rationale that lower-ranking servicemen followed orders and were not legally authorized to question the legitimacy of these orders. The Law of Due Obedience was applied automatically to all pending trials for murder, torture, arbitrary arrest, and similar offenses committed by servicemen during the "dirty war," and the courts were required to drop all charges against these defendants—regardless of the stage that the proceedings had reached—within five days of the law's promulgation.[156] Even before the conclusion of that brief period, the due obedience law was judged unconstitutional by a federal district court, a ruling upheld by the federal appeals court to which it passed. But the Argentine Supreme Court had the last word, upholding the law's constitutionality on June 23, 1987.[157]

In some of the more radically discontent quarters of the military, however, the impunity granted by the Law of Due Obedience was not sufficient. There were still about eighty officers facing charges, and the Alfonsín government refused to grant the blanket exoneration that radical factions of the armed forces were demanding. A further point of contention was Army Chief of Staff General José Caridi's position in regard to the trials (which did little, the rebels believed, to defend military honor); the radical factions alleged that Caridi fostered a split in the army and called for his removal.

In mid-January 1988 Lieutenant Colonel Aldo Rico, leader of the Semana Santa uprising in the Campo de Mayo, escaped from custody and staged another rebellion. This Operation Dignity, Rico stated in a video program made earlier to accompany the rebellion, was "a response to the continuous aggression committed against the Argentine Army by those seeking a juridical and moral condemnation of the Armed Forces" that had done nothing other than serve their country in "a just and necessary war." Those worthy of punishment, Rico maintained, were the retired and active-duty generals accountable for the mismanagement of the Falkland/Malvinas war, which resulted in the military's fall from grace after its victory over leftist guerrillas. Rico and a group of less than one hundred rebels dug trenches and set up nests of machine guns, mortars, and light artillery around the town of Monte Caseros, four hundred miles north of Buenos Aires on the Uruguayan and Brazilian borders. They also detonated a bridge and mined the entry roads to deter the approach of loyalist forces. Other isolated rebellions simultaneously occurred in the provinces of Tucumán and Santa Cruz, and the Buenos Aires civil airport was overtaken by some thirty army and air force personnel.

Unlike the Semana Santa uprising, however, in this case the military forces not directly participating in the rebellion were loyal to the senior command and constitutional government, and Alfonsín was therefore able to secure the unconditional surrender of the rebels. Two thousand infantrymen converged upon Monte Caseros in tanks and trucks, some of which were towing heavy artillery, to quell the rebel forces. Army Chief of Staff General Caridi, against whom much of Rico's aggression was directed, personally took command of the loyalist forces in Monte Caseros. A brief battle ensued before the rebels surrendered. More than seventy officers faced charges as a result.

Although Rico's January rebellion was directed more at high military officials than at the constitutional government, it was the second major military crisis in less than a year and as such again emphasized the fragility of Argentina's new democracy.[158] The January uprising was followed by a purge of extremist middle-ranking officers in an effort to secure more trustworthy military support and to foster a new role for the military within Argentine democracy. "Out of the wreckage we are building the foundation of a modern Argentina," Alfonsín had proclaimed earlier at an annual armed forces dinner on July 5, 1985. "And building a modern country also includes reconstructing our armed forces for their specific function and for their definitive placement in the bosom of society."[159]

Be that as it may, there were still currents in the armed forces that favored "legitimization" of the military's performance in the "dirty war." On December 3, 1988, a third rebellion was staged by nine hundred mutinous troops headed by Colonel Mohamed Alí Seineldín just six miles from the Plaza de Mayo.[160] Seineldín, allegedly linked to the Triple A death squads of the 1970s, was discontent with Alfonsín's attempts to "Sovietize our Fatherland" and suggested in a proclamation at the time of the uprising that "society should stop treating illegal repression as a genocide in order to recognize it as a just, necessary and victorious war."[161] Alfonsín's order to quell the rebellion met with conditional compliance in the military, the "loyal" troops agreeing to no more than containment of the rebels. When an attack on the Casa Rosada seemed possible after the "loyal" troops allowed the rebels to move from the Campo de Mayo army base to the Villa Martelli garrison, Alfonsín made contingency plans to escape with his cabinet by helicopter and to reconstitute his government in the interior. Matters never came to that, but the faulty chain of command was again apparent as the army, refusing to attack, negotiated an end to the rebellion, letting all but the rebel leaders escape.

The Villa Martelli mutiny made it clear that in 1988, as in 1976, the Argentine military was far from a depoliticized body loyal to civilian authority. The mutiny also underscored the slim difference between rebel and loyal factions within the military.[162] Many "loyal" soldiers were sympathetic toward Seineldín's demands for a comprehensive amnesty law (beyond the "due obedience" and "full stop" laws passed earlier) that would absolve the convicted, imprisoned officers as well as the forty-some others then facing litigation. Also generating widespread discontent in most quarters of the armed forces was the new democracy's withdrawal of the prerogatives to which the military had become accustomed. Impingement on military autonomy set the mood, and tightened control of the military budget, promotions, and defense industries made the results clear to both officer and soldier.

Alfonsín's refusal to grant comprehensive amnesty and to accede to other demands made by the Villa Martelli rebels was possible only because broad popular opposition to reestablishing military rule counterbalanced the mutiny's strength.[163] The mobilization of the mutinous troops in December 1988 triggered mass popular demonstrations, as well as denunciations of the rebellion by all major (including right-wing) political parties, the business community, and agricultural interests. Such popular support for Argentine democracy also contributed to a most symbolically significant accomplishment on July 8, 1989: For the first time in sixty-one years, the executive power of the republic was transferred between two democratically elected presidents.[164] That transfer was yet more momentous because Alfonsín was succeeded by Carlos Saúl Menem, who initially appeared to be a Left-leaning Peronist populist and as such a target for military antagonism.

Menem's economic "shock treatment," his rapid strides toward the Right, his courtship with the military, and his granting of presidential pardons in October 1989 to most of the "dirty war" and rebellious personnel indicted or convicted under Alfonsín all initially stabilized the military reception of Peronism's return to office.[165] By early 1990, however, the deterioration of the social and economic situation rendered

Argentine democracy extremely precarious, and the resulting desperation again provided a forum for the messianic Right. The Carapintadas began to clearly express political ambitions, with leader Aldo Rico appearing in civilian guise before a popular following in Rosario as "the man who symbolizes national recovery" and making speeches under a banner boasting "Aldo Rico for President." Mohamed Alí Seineldín, who instigated a fourth army revolt in early December 1990, similarly took to speechifying, calling for defense of Argentina's "honor" and—in a written proclamation—observing that in these "black days" the Argentine people were "once again looking to their army as the final guarantee of security and preservation of constitutional order."[166] Other Carapintadas—La Perla torturer Ernesto Barreiro among them—likewise were "increasingly involved in political life" as civilians, their clear military support, allegiance, and ideology most explicit.[167] Whether the Argentine presidency jeopardized by socioeconomic and political woes can resist formal or informal domination by the military remains to be seen. What is certain is the perpetuation within the Carapintadas and the Argentine military of a strong ideological movement that would like to be recognized for self-sacrifice in defense of "our way of being Christian" and would welcome the opportunity to sacrifice itself again.

2

The Strategic Theatrics
of Atrocity

I

DURING THE FIFTH AND SIXTH centuries before the birth of Christ, Greek civilization counted among its accomplishments the birth and development of tragedy. Along with satyr plays and comedies, tragedies were produced as components of annual ceremonies worshipping Dionysus, the god of fertility and wine. Dionysian mythology was based on eternal fecundity as evidenced in the annual cycle of death and rebirth in the vegetable kingdom, that fecundity referring in turn—as we might expect, given the anthropomorphic deity—to human fertility. But the significance of human fertility as represented by the phallus that was omnipresent in ritual (and often theatrical) worship of Dionysus was bound not to human or animal procreation but rather to qualities derived from the god's affinity with wine and intoxication: sexual arousal for its own sake, ecstatic frenzy as an end in itself.[1] That frenzy was as violent as it was erotic, the rituals combining orgiastic sexuality with animal and human sacrifice, sparagmos (tearing apart of bodies), castration, and omophagy (the eating of raw flesh).[2] The worship of Dionysus that evolved into tragedy was also characterized by its interpersonal nature, with the state of ecstasy realized as a mass phenomenon spreading from individual to individual through the dynamics of a group. Masks were frequently instrumental in one's transformation into a frenzied Other capable of behavior beyond daily norms; the subject "disappeared" into the rituals of worship. The poetics of incorporation that were integral to these rituals, most apparent in omophagy, provided further that the god entered the worshipper as did the wine (and frenzy) with which Dionysus was associated and that the internalized god (along with the subjectivity of the votary merged with him) was symbolically destroyed by the rituals exalting him.[3]

The birth of tragedy from its source in choral songs (or dithyrambs) sung in praise to Dionysus thus carries in its history a number of significations implying matters well beyond—or beneath—the "courage and inevitable defeat" characteristic of dramatic tragedy. The sexual and transcendental nature of violence, the intersection of divine and erotic love, the insistent presence of the phallus, the merging of votary and god, the transformation of actors through group dynamics within a ritual context, and the use of metaphoric and literal sacrifice almost as a "standard accompaniment" are characteristics of tragedy's prehistory that obtain in the contemporary offstage tragedy of the Argentine "dirty war."[4]

In the Dionysia of Athens, where the frenzy of cult worship was civilized and Western tragedy was developed during annual competitions, this nexus of religious, sexual, and violent impulses brought to the stage served not solely as an agent of catharsis for the fourteen thousand citizens in attendance but also as a dimension of civic governance, as a means of fostering the ideals of Athenian democracy.[5] Tragedy served, that is to say, a political as well as a religious function. By the time Greek theater degenerated into the gaudy spectacles of the Roman *ludi*, the original religious impetus in combination with the governmental agenda to cultivate a responsible citizenry gave way to spectacular extravaganzas more immediately political in intent, more clearly identifiable as diversions with which the ruling class entertained and placated the masses. Bodies were depersonalized and reduced to instruments of power, objects of lust, or agents of spectacular atrocity. Plays were intermingled with boxing and rope dancing and bloody spectacles until they finally yielded to less sophisticated theatrics—tableaux and lewd dances, for example—laying bare the unrefined human duality of sex and violence that predated Greek tragedy in Dionysian cult observation and that prevails today as popular entertainment's basis and cliché.

This untiring presence of erotic violence prompted Nietzsche to stress that "without cruelty there is no festival . . . and in punishment there is so much that is festive," whether the social context is that of ancient empires or of contemporary Argentina.[6] It is in fact not long, Nietzsche continued, "since princely weddings and public festivals of the magnificent kind were unthinkable without executions, torturings, or perhaps an auto-da-fé."[7] Spain inherited the political celebration of atrocity from the Roman Empire (whose fondness for torture was apparent not only in the ludi but also in interrogatory, juridical, and penal procedures), once again fusing religious and political agendas most notably—leaving the Reconquest aside—in the Inquisition rituals to which Nietzsche made reference.

Following exploration of the New World, European public torture was exported and utilized in Latin America through the decades of conquest and colonization. Noses, hands, and feet were amputated; natives were sliced up the middle with the stroke of a sword; sodomists were thrown to the dogs;[8] feet were fried in oil; caciques were burned alive. Spectacles of atrocity during conquest, installation of the Spanish State, and colonial exploitation of native labor coerced the indigenous populations to submit to political, evangelical, and commercial programs. Execution ceremonies deriving their poetics from religious motifs functioned in service to the State, manifesting in spectacular violence the prevailing partnership of cross and sword: "[The hanging victims'] feet were almost touching the ground, and in groups of 13, in honor of Our Redeemer and his twelve apostles, they piled firewood beneath them, lit it, and burned them alive."[9]

Before reverence for Our Redeemer and his apostles had inspired this variation on a common theme, the indigenous American cultures themselves were fulfilling various penal and politico-religious needs through public spectacles of atrocity. In his *Cartas de relación*, to cite one example, conqueror Hernán Cortés related the following episode, stressing the theatrical setting of the execution and the public announcement of the crime to be punished:

> They took [the prisoner] and made him walk through that great market while making a grand announcement stating his crime, and there they held him at the base of a kind of stage in the middle of the said market, and the announcer climbed onto the stage and in a loud voice again stated the crime, and with everyone watching they clubbed him to death on the head.[10]

Other Native American cultures went well beyond penal spectacles by integrating public torture into the very politico-religious structures of their society. Most noteworthy among these civilizations committed to what Nietzsche termed "the 'deification' of cruelty"[11] were the Aztecs, who in ceremonial centers dominated by imposing structures of cybernetic architecture—huge temples and pyramids designed specifically for the worship of deities through human sacrifice—instituted violent spectacles not accessory or diversionary in nature but rather central to Aztec metaphysics, social structure, and political affairs both within and outside of the empire. Sacrifice will be discussed in Chapter 5, where the relation between atrocity on Aztec pyramids and in "dirty war" detention centers is explored.

As its title implies the present chapter specifically addresses the nature and political function of spectacles of force, with a focus on torture, demonstrating the means by which these "gloomy festivals of punishment"[12] engage a population as audience-guarantor in a system that transforms spectacular atrocity into political power. This analysis of the strategic theatrics of atrocity will also lay the groundwork for discussions in subsequent chapters of themes evolving into and out of tragedy from its source in Dionysus worship—eroticized violence, human sacrifice, and "the 'deification' of cruelty" as they relate to the symbolic punishment of mythologically constructed enemies of the State. A summary of the most prominent surface indications of theatrics that perhaps contributed to CONADEP's description of the "dirty war" as "the greatest tragedy in our history"[13] will establish a basis for analysis of the more intensified but less apparent theatrics integral to rituals in the detention centers.

"Dirty war" theatrics opened with the task forces' flaunting of State power. The paradoxical—but systematic—discrepancy between the force needed and the force deployed in carrying out an abduction calls the "clandestine" nature of the violence into question. Why make a spectacle of an abduction that will later be denied? To abduct a worker, an attorney, a psychiatrist, a teenager, none of whom had any conceivable involvement with armed insurrection, a team of six to twenty (or, in cases regarded as of greater importance or danger, up to fifty) heavily armed special forces arrived in various configurations of official and unmarked vehicles, often closing off streets, blacking out and surrounding the neighborhood, then subjecting the obviously unarmed, obviously passive victim (and often family members or friends found in his or her company) to handcuffs and head covering, to beatings, to a place in the trunk or on the floor of a car en route to the detention center where he or she would be tortured.[14]

The *patotas'* indiscreet displays of force "absolutely disproportional in respect to the supposed danger of their victim"[15] suggest that dramatic action was utilized to accomplish some objective greater than the simple apprehension of an unresisting victim, that the excess was strategic. The abductions, described by the CONADEP report as "the first act of the drama,"[16] were the most visible indication that the "clandestine" or "undercover" pretensions of the "dirty war" veiled a more dominant need for disclosure, that the Junta's encoded repressive agenda was at some level intentionally decipherable.

The absence of sufficient armed terrorism to justify the Junta's violent repression and the regime's simultaneous dependence on the continuation of that repression was a second particularly prolific source of theater. Pseudoterrorist acts were staged by the military and then duly neutralized as though they were real in order to perpetuate the illusion of revolutionary threat (and of competent action eliminating it) that generated whatever legitimacy the Junta could claim. On the "industrial front," for example, the military would "Montonerize" strikes by forging and distributing the "pernicious documents" that on other occasions it ceremoniously burned. "Montonero" flyers calling for strikes were printed in the La Perla detention center, then disseminated in the context of an imminent job action to document subversive "infiltration" and thereby "justify" the violent repression of organized labor. This drama's last act consisted of removing a prisoner from a detention center and executing him or her in, as the government would report it to the press, "a shootout between the forces of order and a militant Montonero instigating a strike." To assist public reception of the staged act of subversion, they put in the dead prisoner's hand "the flyers that the military had previously printed in La Perla."[17]

The military's use of detention center prisoners to stage confrontations with "terrorists" was mentioned frequently in the testimonies gathered by CONADEP following the "dirty war." The commission's report summarized them as follows: "Days before they were to be shot, these prisoners received better food and were cleaned up and obliged to bathe, since it would have been difficult to explain to the public why 'extremists killed in shootouts' turned up with skinny, tortured, bearded, and ragged corpses."[18]

The prisoners were prepared, like actors, for the parts scripted for them. The staged terrorism, choreographed before and marketed after the spectacle, was structured by considerations of public reception rather than by strategies of enemy elimination. The dead "terrorists" generated by mock battles mediated a discourse between the Junta and the public. Here the military's maneuvers were distanced from theater proper only by the forced participation of some of the players and by the use of bullets in place of blanks. The illusion of power generated by the spectacle was dependent on an imaginary enemy whose pain was real. And it was precisely in this forced imposition of the repressors' fiction onto the victims' reality that the essence of the tragedy resided.[19]

II

Until the close of the eighteenth century, on both sides of the Atlantic, torture as a public spectacle was a political ritual that belonged "even in minor cases," as Michel Foucault effectively demonstrated, "to the ceremonies by which power is manifested."[20] Such was the case with Aztec sacrifice, with the Inquisition's auto-da-fé, and with the secular but religiously informed spectacles of atrocity in the colonies. Such was also the case, as will gradually become apparent, with torture as employed by the Argentine military. Ceremonial acts of cruelty, particularly when performed by regimes lacking legitimacy, make clear how a body in the political sphere can be exploited for the generation of power as it can be in the workplace for the generation of wealth. In Foucault's description of such power he identified certain characteristics that can add to an accumulating understanding of the Argentine case at hand, for this was a power that not only did not hesitate to exert itself directly on bodies but that also derived its exaltation and strength from these visible manifestations. It was a power that asserted itself as an armed force whose functions of maintaining order domestically were barely distinguishable from the functions of war; a power that imposed an ideology and obligations as personal bonds, the breach of which constituted an offense (in moral as well as legal terms) and exacted retribution; a power that construed disobedience as hostility, as rebellion, and therefore as indistinguishable in principle from acts of civil war; a power that made apparent not the criteria by which it enforced its law but rather who its enemies were; a power, finally, that endeavored to renew its potency in the spectacle of its individual manifestations, that recharged itself in the ritualistic display of its (illusory) omnipotence.[21]

The violence characteristic of authoritarian governments is integral to the generation and sustenance of these regimes' power, and as such it must be developed and defended. Excess is never incidental, accidental, or supplementary to such violence; it is always central to the regimes that employ it, always strategic, always a renewal of potency. In introducing the gruesome catalog of atrocities to follow in its report, CONADEP alluded to this normalization—or institutionalization—of excess:

> The cases included are not those which constituted excesses since, if we understand by "excess" isolated acts that were particularly aberrant, such excesses did not exist. Rather, the entire system, the entire methodology, right from its conception, constituted a grand excess; the aberrant extended into common practice.[22]

Prior to its semisecret resurgence in recent history, the "grand excess" of violent spectacles as agency of political power was particularly apparent at the beginning of the eighteenth century. A 1701 treatise entitled *Hanging Is Not Enough*, for example, graphically took prudence in punishment to task, calling for a condemned man to be broken on the wheel, flogged until he fainted, hung up with chains, and finally left to die slowly of hunger.[23] Foucault cataloged other spectacles of public execution yet more gory in their poetics, among them a procedure by which careful preservation of the body being destroyed (one of the hallmarks of all torture) was combined with skillful timing to engage the victim as a participant in and witness of his own demise: "The condemned man was dragged along on a hurdle (to prevent his head smashing against the cobble-stones), in which his belly was opened up, his entrails quickly ripped out, so that he had time to see them, with his own eyes, being thrown on the fire; in which he was finally decapitated and his body quartered."[24]

If during the elaborate acting out of these "thousand deaths" the torture victim wailed in agony, it was seen not as an unfortunate side effect of the execution but rather as the voice of the State's triumph, as "the very ceremonial of justice being expressed in all of its force."[25] The logic of the penal spectacle has always been one of excess rather than measure, its aim here (as in Argentina) not so much to reestablish the balance disrupted by a real or imaginary transgression as "to bring into play, at its extreme point, the dissymmetry between the subject who has dared to violate the law and the all-powerful sovereign who displays his strength."[26] There would afterward be no mistake about the unrestrained presence of the sovereign, even in his absence.

That is why the penal ceremony is performed in public: to make visible for all the truth of the crime that was established beforehand, privately, in judicial proceedings. That truth, to be sure, was the absolute right of the regime that had also defined the offense. But afterward the criminal's body was brought from the chambers of whatever judicial system had condemned him or her and was exhibited, paraded, disfigured, so that the people might participate in the enactment of the truth to which they, too, were both party and subject.[27] This ritualistic enactment of the sentence defined a continuum of decipherable relations between torture as a public spectacle, the crime itself, and the public that guaranteed the propriety of violent restitution and the inalienability of the social and moral tenets offended by the transgression. It dramatized, as Michel de Certeau put it, "the triumph of royalty over criminals whose crimes had particular symbolic value."[28]

Decipherability was often aided by punishments that carried a direct symbolic relation to their crimes: The tongues of blasphemers were pierced, the impure were burned (pursuant to the poetics of hellfire), the violating hand was amputated, the breasts of libidinous women were mutilated, the homosexuals were hung upside-down and sawn in half, beginning with the crotch.[29] The intent—reminiscent of the early modern "scientific" belief that a wound could be healed at a distance by treatment to the *weapon*[30]—was to neutralize the offense by implied appeal to sympathetic magic. The practice has its dramatic complement in the reenactment of crimes—the symbolic appropriation and *repetition* of crimes—as a component of the penal rituals neutralizing them. "There were even some cases of an almost theatrical reproduction of the crime in the execution of the guilty man—with the same instruments, the same gestures," wrote Foucault. "Thus justice had the crime reenacted before the eyes of all, publishing it in its truth and at the same time annulling it in the death of the guilty man."[31] In the same horror the crime was inscribed on the visible body of the condemned man and erased with his execution; the public was bound as witness of the spectacle to the truth of the crime, the justice of its punishment, and the power of the regime that brought them to bear on the criminal.

The symbolics of power rituals are also evident beyond the specific confines of crime/punishment spectacles, notably—to cite an example from the Americas—in the ceremonial means by which Spanish conquerors subjugated the native Latin American populations. Francisco Pizarro's conquest of the Incan empire had as its first symbolic climax the garroting of the Inca Atahualpa.[32] The poetics were simple enough: separation of the head of state from its body—which resonated with corpus mysticum overtones left over from the Middle Ages—served as paradigm for a military-political strategy that entailed replacing the high-level Incan administration with Spaniards while maintaining the lower-level bureaucracy that the conquerors, given their limited numbers, needed. One political head was chopped off and another grafted on, the political body left more or less intact presumably expected to continue the routine of its functions. When the Spanish garroting of Atahualpa gravitated toward the Incan myth of Incarrí and was expressed in Guamán Poma de Ayala's Nueva crónica y buen gobierno, Atahualpa's execution—faithful to the mentioned trope—was represented as a decapitation.[33] Later in the Incan conquest, at its symbolic conclusion in the execution of Tupac Amaru, the Spanish followed suit, reinforcing the one trope (severence of the head of state from the political body) by demetaphorizing the other: "Taking the hair in his left hand, [the executioner] severed the head with a cutlass at one blow, and held it high for all to see."[34] The same poetics then gained architectural expression in the city of Cuzco (navel of the Incas' cosmos, as well as their empire), where the Spanish razed Incan edifices and erected religious and governmental structures on the stonework foundations of the conquered capital. Such symbolic layering of the conquerors' civilization on the destruction of the natives' own had an even more significant precedent earlier in the conquest, when the very viceroyalty of New Spain—most important in the empire—was seated on the ruins of the Aztec's Tenochtitlán.[35] One of the matters of concern in the Argentine case at hand is the relation between the "conquerors" (Junta/military) and the "conquered" (desaparecidos representing Argentine population) as this gains symbolic expression in the forms of violence instituted to penalize mythologically construed offenses. The symbolic value of that punishment's most common instrument—the picana—will be of central concern in this regard.[36]

By the end of the eighteenth century, the propriety of ceremonies "concluding the crime" with penal methods more grotesque than the crime itself was called into question. The decline of atrocity in penal theatrics was notably signaled in Europe by the third article of the 1791 French code, which—in sharp contrast with the logic of Hanging Is Not Enough a century earlier—established that "every man condemned to death will have his head cut off" by "a machine that beheads painlessly."[37] Thus the "thousand deaths" began their descent into an execution of more restrained and equitable measure: one criminal, one death. The new penal code and its guillotine that took life "almost without touching the body" redirected punishment toward the condemned person's *being* rather than his or her *body*, applying the law "not so much to a real body capable of feeling pain as to a juridical subject, the possessor, among other rights, of the right to exist."[38]

This downgrading of torture as a public spectacle at the turn of the nineteenth century initially put the State a bit ahead of the people. The public square had become a theater, and spectacular atrocity—particularly when directed toward a renowned criminal—was the occasion for a festive gathering. "Peddlers and hawkers moved among the crowd awaiting the execution, shouting their wares, selling refreshments and ballads about the condemned man. Householders around the square rented out their windows"; "all around, it was like a fair . . . filled with smiling, laughing people."[39] In the New World violent spectacles similarly attracted their crowds. The number of people who turned out to see a 1639 auto-da-fé celebrated in Lima was so great "that it was impossible to calculate it. . . . Suffice it to say that five days beforehand benches were put out, and behind them platforms on both sides of the street, where the said people were, as well as on balconies and in windows and on rooftops, and in many places there were two levels of platforms, and in the plaza three."[40]

The masses were entertained by the State's ad nauseam reiteration of its authority on criminal bodies, to be sure, but beyond entertainment the public's presence, emotion, interaction with, and guardianship as witness of violent spectacles had also evolved into a function of social involvement, of social responsibility. One simple manifestation of that sense of public duty involved the executioner: "He had to deliver the death blow according to the rules, otherwise the crowd might turn against him." Executioners practicing their office improperly were often stoned, and on at least one occasion the audience "finally rushed on to the scaffold, killing the executioner with the axe which he had used so badly."[41] In this direct sense and in more pertinent implied ones, the masses were the spectacle's guarantors and were therefore the guarantors of its efficacy and truth; that responsibility was distributed among them as a corporate whole. The public's collective body, united by and meaningful in relation to the body being brutalized, constituted the agency by which the macabre display was transformed into a ceremonial strengthening of the institutions in which all were now participating. The public endowed the torture/execution victims with political worth beyond (but based in) the shock, the immediacy, of their agony and their howls, beyond their transient value as the centerpieces of a brutal circus, because the public's engaged presence and its cohesion as a group, as an audience, as a body of guarantors, generated the illusion (an illusion accepted as a reality) that it shared in the State's power and truth because it shared in the spectacle that manifested them.

It comes as no surprise, then, that the first use of the guillotine in France disappointed its audience. The head plopped off too quickly, the elaborate and redundant agony of power rejuvenating itself (and the audience) through its application to a body was eliminated. "The machine," as Camus's Meursault put it, "dominated everything."[42] The spectacle took place with the audience's role already written out, and consequently the onlookers were inspired to script for themselves a line that implied a desire to have their ritual function restored: "Give us back our gallows!"[43]

Soon, however, the transition from spectacular penal procedures to more subdued ones resulted in a public consensus to abolish penal rituals that concluded crimes with barbarities more excessive than these crimes themselves. Rather than inspiring shivers and cheers for the truth of the crime that was barbarously manifested and annulled before the eyes of all, it seemed now that during spectacular executions the roles were reversed, that the judges and the executioner (and, by extension, the State) became the murderers, and that the tortured victim was transformed by the unjustifiable excess into an object of pity and admiration, into a martyr. If the State executed its criminals under this new, more humane public consensus it would need to do so (as it does in capital punishment today) "not as a glorification of its strength, but as an element of itself that it is obliged to tolerate, that it finds difficult to account for."[44] Execution governed by that logic would be swift, anesthetized, untheatrical, and without formal public audience; it would be directed at the being rather than the body of the condemned. Justice would become abstracted rather than exacted on the flesh, and publicity and audience functions would shift accordingly from the execution to the trial preceding it.[45]

Such would be the history we might idealize for ourselves if experience did not demonstrate that something of the passion for spectacular violence survives. Foucault cited by way of example the theatrical ritual that the French Revolution rallied around the guillotine, observing in regard to more recent history that "capital punishment remains, even today, a spectacle that must actually be forbidden."[46] On that last account the self-generating spectacle of executions conducted *outside of public view* was quite apparent when serial murderer Theodore Bundy was electrocuted by the state of Florida in January 1989. The official audience of that capital punishment consisted of two dozen witnesses separated from the execution chamber by a window, but some two hundred others gathered of their own accord outside the Florida State Prison and "cheered lustily and whooped" when a signal indicating Bundy's execution was relayed from the cellblock.[47] The self-appointed audience responded not to visual access to the execution itself—they were looking only at a wall—but rather to abstraction, to representation. The group also prepared to celebrate the event beforehand, their placards, banners, and T-shirts boasting slogans that reflected the range of emotional involvement: "Burn, Bundy, Burn" made its point directly; "Buckle Up Bundy, It's the Law" lined the morbid with a gallows humor; and "Chi-O, Chi-O, It's off to Hell I Go!" (in reference to the two Chi Omega sorority girls killed by Bundy) introduced a bit of melody to the festivities. That these two hundred individuals in attendance were representatives of a larger, implied audience was evident by the extent of news coverage and by informal comments circulating throughout the public. Radio announcers, to cite one example, were reputed to have facetiously encouraged their listeners to refrain from using appliances at the hour of Bundy's execution so that the electric chair would have plenty of "juice." The humor carried the message from previous centuries that I have underscored: The public audience *participates* in the restoration of truth and justice, in this case by "redirecting" electricity from domestic use to the execution chair.

The involvement of the public audience in the Bundy case is not exceptional. On April 8, 1990, the *Washington Post* ran an article in its "Style" section entitled "Death Row's Macabre Death Watch," which pointed out that "California has a waiting list—plus alternates—for viewing executions." The article also noted that a predawn hour was chosen for the executions "to avoid a traffic tie-up outside the prison" caused by those who were "gathering in throngs."[48] This remarkable turnout for spectacles hidden from public view followed a pattern begun a century ago with the first electric chair execution. On that occasion, despite the fact that the prison warden did not disclose the date and hour of the execution as required by law, an audience began gathering outside the prison at four o'clock in the morning. By seven o'clock, one newspaper reported, "it seemed as if all Auburn had congregated in the immediate neighborhood of the prison." Later, when electrocutions were resumed in New York after a controversial lapse, Ossining (Sing Sing) Prison scheduled four men for execution in a single day. "A system of flag signals was set up—with each man designated by a different color" to apprise the crowd gathered outside of the events progressing beyond its field of vision. Lewis E. Lawes, the prison warden, implicitly noted the audience's involvement: "Sing Sing's first electrocution required, on average, a half hour per man, including the raising of the flag."[49]

Although the disappearance of torture as a public spectacle constituted "the end of a certain kind of tragedy,"[50] the needs that made it manifest in the first place were not erased but rather were displaced by social pressures onto a new kind of tragedy—like that of the Greek stage—that depended on violence but kept it out of sight, produced it offstage. Such was the tragedy of the Argentine "dirty war": The violent spectacle hidden from sight, enacted behind the closed doors of the detention centers, was projected to its audience, its guarantors, as representation, "with the same imprecision of dreams, but also with the same potency."[51] What I shall refer to as the *abstract* spectacle of atrocity as evidenced in the Argentine "dirty war" differs from spectacles staged in public view in that the rituals of torture, the doing and undoing of the crime on the victim's body, the cries of agony attesting to the generation of power and the restoration of truth, were all brought to bear without direct public witness and therefore engage their participant-observer audience not through graphic displays of atrocity but rather through *representation* of an absence (indexed by *desaparecidos*) whose presence was at once insisted and denied. The eerie, overwhelming silence of the victims—tortured but absent—was paralleled by that of the audience, terrorized by having "witnessed" the abstract spectacle that the Junta at once staged and forebade.

Instead of cheering or gasping or screaming beside the gallows, the public voice reached only a hushed whisper risked in the shadows, a mumble of rumors diffusing the spectacle by word of mouth through a population that was itself diffused, confused, frightened, forced into the guarantor's role that it was simultaneously forbidden. The abstracted spectacle, like the *desaparecidos* themselves, was ever present in its absence, vague but insistent, never completed nor resolved, an endless, ephemeral, undefinable, uncertain torture. The disappeared body was no longer alive but never dead, never buried, never fully spoken, and consequently never fully silenced.[52] On the model of Seneca's classical Roman plays and of contemporary suspense and horror drama, the "empty grave" effects of "disappearance" generated by jamming certainty with unverifiability "provoke strong feelings without resolution, leaving the audience stranded . . . with feelings of anxiety, fear and grief."[53] The "ominous silence" policed by "a dementedly generalized repression" ensured that this resolution would be perpetually postponed at the same time that the abstract spectacle was made perpetually present because a population "is more securely held together through the common experience of a secret ritual than by the common sharing of the secret itself."[54] The precise nature of that secret was always suggested but never revealed: Its enactment *as* a secret assured the abstract spectacles' efficacy.

III

"Dirty war" torture was displaced into the ritual context of detention centers that were at once integral to and insulated from the sociopolitical context that produced them. "What is otherwise forbidden becomes legitimate in, and only in, the sacred ritual context."[55] Symbolic acts, assignment of roles, inverted hierarchies, "reorganized" morality, and politico-religious mythology give the "forbidden" act its semisecret forum; they construct the milieu in which an elite carries out the dirty, sacred task, in which atrocity is not merely possible but also essential and meaningful.

Elaine Scarry elucidated the process by which attributes of pain generated during torture "can be severed from the pain itself and conferred upon a political construct."[56] Torture as a "grotesque piece of compensatory drama" first makes visible "the structure and enormity" of the pain usually contained incommunicably within the sufferer's body.[57]

> It then goes on to deny, to falsify, the reality of the very thing it has itself objectified by a perceptual shift which converts the vision of suffering into the wholly illusory but, to the torturers and the regime they represent, wholly convincing spectacle of power. The physical pain is so uncontestably real that it seems to confer its quality of "uncontestable reality" on the power that has brought it into being. It is, of course, precisely because the reality of that power is so highly contestable, the regime so unstable, that torture is being used.[58]

Spectacles of atrocity generate power, in part, by dramatizing the dissymmetry between the omnipotent regime and the suffering subject, this power brokered by the body in pain in its relation to the direct or implied audience witnessing the spectacle. On the one side is untempered, boundless liberty, and on the other, the subjugation of an *object* "soft-ened" by torture, made malleable and shaped; on the one side absolute domination and on the other absolute servitude.[59] The Junta's sustenance of the (illusory) power it generated through torture rituals was contin-gent—first on a continual supply of bodies and second on the public audience that was engaged as guarantor of the abstract spectacle's ritual efficacy. The Junta's exploitation of its population as the source of both torture victims and of audience-guarantors was characterized, borrowing a phrase from Nazi recruitment, by "the unrelenting necessity of selection that knows neither extenuating circumstances nor clemency."[60] No Ar-gentine was exempt from one participation or another in this drama that posed the individual against his or her own interest and will. "Today," as Admiral Massera put it, "no one has the right to not rise to the heights of the burning demands of the moment."[61]

The less fortunate rose to Admiral Massera's occasion as victims in the detention centers, positioned there—like the prisoner on the scaf-fold—as intermediaries between the Junta's discourse and the public's reception of it. The *desaparecidos* were deprived of the voices tortured out of them and were bespoken then by the discourse of the State. They were made to emit signs designated by the Junta; they were transformed into signifiers in a chain of communication, and a chain of repressive command, that broke down without them, without their absence: ghost-writers. The public outside of the detention centers was then imbued with this message of terror generated by the abstract spectacle celebrated on the *desaparecido's* body. The message disseminated from its distended source of production anonymously, endowed with haunting immediacy and emotional charge because it seemed to speak itself, because it was spoken through the *desaparecidos*, through absence.[62] When Argentines outside of the detention centers received the inescapable imposition of the message, it "invests them, is transmitted by them and through them; it exerts pressure on them"[63] and forged them into the audience-guarantor that the system required, just as torture forged the victim's body into the locus of the spectacle and his or her pain into the agency of Junta discourse and power. That *forgery* engaged public participation in the perceptual shift by which the ritual translated the torture victim's pain into the Junta's power; the public's fear, like its silence, was used against it.

The Argentine public aware even nebulously, even against the insistence of government and intrapsychic denial, of the "grotesque piece of compensatory drama" under way in the detention centers thereby fulfilled a role as "neither actor nor bystander" similar to that played by the chorus of Greek tragedy.[64] Bernard Knox noted that the chorus, as "an anonymous crowd with only a group identity," creates a peculiar sensation "as if the audience itself were part of the acting."[65] That last quoted phrase describes precisely the role of a population under repression: The public is "audience" because it "witnesses" the abstract spectacle of the detention centers and is "actor" because its status as audience—however passive it may appear—is a *function* integral to the efficacy of the spectacle by which power is being generated.[66]

On another level the population of a country under totalitarian rule is also "neither actor nor bystander" because it is reluctant to fully realize one position or the other, because it generally vacillates between competing positions and therefore is never situated effectively in either. The public's avoidance of commitment and recognition predisposes it to further manipulation by the repressive system that flourishes in an ambience of nonresolution. As Hannah Arendt pointed out in reference to Nazi Germany, the public of course knows the general facts—"that concentration camps exist, that people disappear, that innocent persons are arrested"—but at the same time it resorts to "the common-sense disinclination to believe the monstrous."[67] It takes a step forward and a step backward. The message of terror permeating society reinforces this disinclination to believe: "It is the greatest crime ever to talk about these 'secrets.' "[68] The silenced knowledge, deformed by terror and battled on all fronts by denial, eventually "loses its quality of reality and assumes the nature of a mere nightmare." The dreaminess of this horrific reality facilitates efforts to dismiss the events as unreal, but the luxury of that dismissal then exacts in exchange an inescapable, nightmarish milieu, as imprecise as it is implacable. The repressors "alone are in a position to believe in what they know to be true"; they constitute a privileged elite exclusively empowered to acknowledge and access "what actually constitutes the reality for all."[69]

Identification with this aggressive elite was perhaps the most prominent mechanism by which the Argentine public feigned an escape from its eerie uncertainty and attempted to restore "the quality of reality" to its knowledge and its truth.[70] This efficacious sleight of hand provided that individuals could participate in the truth that terrorized them by allying themselves psychologically with the secret elite, by situating themselves tacitly but symbolically in the aggressor's camp and by then communicating their introjection of the military reality insofar as they were permitted to speak. Those dynamics were nowhere as apparent as in the refrains *Por algo será* ("It must be for something") and *Algo habrá[n] hecho* ("He/she/they must have done something") that were repeated by witnesses of abductions ("as though trying to propitiate awesome and inscrutable gods, regarding the children or the parents of the *desaparecidos* as plague-bearers")[71] who sought to make sense of the apparently senseless violence acted out before their eyes. Acknowledgment of the "secret" truth (the "something" of the refrains) momentarily halted their vacillation between the roles of actor and bystander by situating them psychologically in the former position, exploiting their "sympathy through the use of inside views."[72] The public audience served itself an implied share of the elite truth at the expense of disavowing its falsity. And although public identification with the repressors as manifest in *Por algo será* or *Algo habrá[n] hecho* afforded the psychological comfort of deterrorizing and reinstating meaning to the confused context in which Argentines were made to live, although it fabricated for the indiscriminate violence the legitimate purpose and omniscience of command patently lacking in the "dirty war," and although it allowed the Argentines not directly affected by "disappearances" to continue their daily lives without radical interruption,[73] the public attitude as evidenced in these refrains was profoundly counterproductive because it strengthened the arbitrary repression by glossing it with a consensus of purpose and implied compliance and because it engaged the public-as-audience with the spectacle staged to repress it. As the victim of that spectacle was silenced and then bespoken through torture as a mouthpiece of Junta discourse, so too was the public's silence politicized until it spoke the discourse of its aggressor: *Por algo será, Algo habrá[n] hecho*. The refrains were an informal rite of obeisance; they deferred to the military; they conceded in bad faith that the military knew the "something" that the public did not know, the "something" that made atrocity just and necessary.

IV

The eighteenth-century ceremonies of public execution required an audience to generate State power, and in much the same way, as I have suggested, the efficacy of torture in the Argentine detention centers required an audience population as participant-observer and guarantor. The apparent difference in visibility between a town square execution intentionally staged before the eyes of all and a detention center torture session intentionally hidden from public view then suggests problematics that must be addressed. How does a population serve as participant-observer of an unseen spectacle performed in a clandestine detention center?

The initial response to that question is implicit in the first act of the drama, the abductions. During these the task forces flaunted an excess of power and made their indiscretions quite visible to the public. The hiddenness of the repression was thereby compromised and the sensitive information leaked from the start; the "secret" maneuvers in public view (in combination with rumor and terror) suggested to their audience the violent nature of the "clandestine" acts to follow in the detention centers. With that suggestion clearly made, decorum relegated the more intensified atrocity to an arena behind closed doors: The spectacle went underground. Propriety before domestic and international opinion required that the spectacle (torture) be hidden, but at the same time the repressive system on which the Junta's political power depended required that violence retain its spectacular properties. From those conflicting demands an abstracted spectacle of atrocity resulted, engendering corresponding abstraction of the key concepts of the "audience" and how it "sees."

The abstract spectacle has as its audience not a specific subject who necessarily witnesses a specific act of atrocity but rather an *implied audience* that functions as an integral component of the spectacle itself in the same way that an implied reader functions in a text. The implied audience in the present case was composed of the Argentine population that at some level of cognizance knew how the "dirty war" was being fought, even though that knowledge may have been denied, ignored, or elaborated by mechanisms of defense, such as the one engendering the refrains mentioned earlier. The implied audience derived that knowledge from— in tropes that I will consider momentarily—the projection of the abstract spectacle into its field of perception or from windows that opened into the hidden spectacle so that it could "see" the atrocity staged for it. As Luis Armando Rebura, a regional associate of CONADEP, put it during the trials, the term "clandestine center" was a euphemism. "All of Córdoba," he testified, knew of the existence of the La Perla detention center located there, "except those who preferred to ignore it."[74] But to ignore—

like to deny or to negate—requires that one first recognize what is then wiped from consciousness: Those who ignored also knew. One can contend with relative certainty that the implied audience of the abstract spectacle—despite claims of being unaware during and after the "dirty war"—encompassed the majority of Argentines.

The metaphors by which torture centers are represented in the vernacular lexicons from various countries register the concern to bring abstract spectacles within the range of their implied audience. One finds, for example, "the production room" in the Philippines, the "cinema room" in South Vietnam, "the blue lit stage" in Chile, all euphemisms suggesting theatrics and their projection.[75] In "dirty war" Argentina the torture rooms were denominated quirófanos, which translates to the English words "operating theater."[76] In addition to the metaphor's suggestion of surgical warfare (the removal of subversion as a disease in the political body) as I will discuss in the following chapter, and beyond the reference to the mock-surgical nature of torture (with its operating instruments—among them the scalpel—and its attending physician), inverting the terms presents a common concept of military discourse: theater of operations. Under the aegis of that inversion, the activities in the torture center take form as rehearsals in miniature of the "dirty war," as microcosmic wars battled out (one-sidedly, to be sure) between the torturer and the victim. But this "war"—like the spectacle that goes unseen and the audience that is implied—is an abstracted one, a conceptual one that is parallel to but fundamentally distinct from the destructive magnitude characteristic of real war. Torture "imitates the destructive power of war: Rather than destroying the concrete physical fact of streets, houses, factories, and schools, it destroys them as they exist in the mind of the prisoner"; it destroys them miming war as it obliterates conceptual reality, as it crushes everything in the victim's consciousness that is not pain.[77] One survivor of the La Perla camp described forced (and mock) reconnaissance outings into that obliterated reality as comparable to being "in a tentacle of the camp, in a tube that was extended." Nothing existed outside of the hermetic enclosure sealed by torture in the detention centers, regardless of excursions testing its elasticity. The testimony continued to describe the experience of looking through the car windows at the world beyond La Perla: "When we saw life, on the other side of the window, it was hard for us to believe what we were seeing, that life went on and we returned to torture and death. Life came to be something belonging to others that had nothing to do with us."[78]

Also suggested by the concept *quirófano* and most important in the present context of an abstract spectacle received by an implied audience are the metaphorical significations generated by a torture center as a "theater." The dictionary of the Royal Spanish Academy elaborates on the definition of *quirófano* by pointing out that the "operating theater" is so designed that "the operations can be seen without being in the same room" in which they are performed. The signifier *quirófano* assigned by the repressors to the "clandestine" torture rooms thus contributed to the poetics of the hidden spectacle's disclosure: A window—such as those along the ceilings of operating theaters—opened into the "clandestine" torture sessions to make them accessible to the implied audience. Those poetics were also reinforced by the boasts of personnel who attempted to impress Jacobo Timerman with fabricated detention center embellishments: "They spoke of the mirrored rooms where the electric shocks were applied and of the numerous observers who witnessed the episode from the other side."[79] Borrowing from the international, cinematographic tropes noted above, the audience's access was also facilitated and its expansion assured because the "operation" performed in this theater was not limited to those metaphorically gathered around a window or one-way mirror but was also "projected" to more broadly disseminate a representation of the spectacle staged behind closed doors.[80]

Reinforcing the "visibility" of the abstract spectacle as suggested by vernacular tropes were other "dirty war" practices that made the "hidden" violence indirectly accessible to its audience. Most prominent among these were the various means by which the *desaparecidos* were made to reappear among the public. Like the overacted abductions, the fostering of public contact with torture victims seems inconsistent with the Junta's overriding program of denied violence until one understands that the efficacy of that program depended on the strategic revelation of its secrets. Affirmations of a violent authoritarian presence (the spectacular abductions, the abstract torture spectacle into which a "window" opened, the rumors rippling outward from these violent impacts) created fear and the illusion of power, and at the same time a series of negations paired with them (the use of paramilitary and quasi-military forces in visible spectacles, a general clouding of State affiliation, official denial foreclosing verifiability of the "secret," censorship paralyzing opposition press) generated the requisite mixed message. By staging limited but direct contact of prisoners furloughed from "the place of the living dead" with the public and by releasing *perejiles*[81] (abduction victims whom the detention center personnel deemed "innocent" or useless in intelligence terms), but only after these prisoners were tortured, the repressors multiplied the "windows," the modes of public access, into the "clandestine" violence. The visibility of detention center atrocity afforded by victim/public contacts was consolidated with the blatant abduction spectacles, with the eerie absence of the *desaparecidos*, with the informal discourse of military officers and of detention center personnel, and with the obstinate official denial that—on one level—was so obviously mendacious that it constituted a kind of inverted affirmation, all to project a nebulous image of the certain but unverifiable atrocity that engaged the implied audience in its roles as participant-observer. The abstract spectacle of detention center torture could thereby fulfill its function of generating State power without leaving the closed quarters to which less subliminal politics relegated it. For torture "must create fear without creating a scandal, legitimize the system without toppling it."[82] The Argentine public, like the Athenian audience of tragedies derived from narratives of popular currency, knew the "dirty war" plot in advance but was nevertheless engaged by the theatrics and afterward "surprised by what it had foreseen."

The Argentine system of repression, then, allowed the public to "see" into the "clandestine" events of the *quirófano* but only to the extent that the sight could be used against its subjects and guaranteed the abstract spectacle's objectives. When the signs scarred onto the torture victim's body are seen and deciphered by the public, they must always read: Power. In the same way that the attributes of pain—as Scarry recognized—are broken away from the torture victim's body and conferred to the State, so too is the audience's perception of this spectacle of power appropriated and reversed. The public that was engaged as witness of the "dirty war" spectacles soon found itself caught in a mechanism that transposed it from seer into the object seen, into another guilty party under surveillance. When it looked into the *quirófano*, its own vision turned back on it, turned against it, but its attendance at the spectacle was mandatory: "In this decisive moment no one has the right to be absent."[83]

The public looked into the abstracted spectacle as though—reversing the repressor's trope mentioned above—into the reflecting surface of a one-way mirror that returned its gaze absorbed within the gaze of an Other, as intangible as it was hostile and omniscient. From this reflection-projection each Argentine received his or her own sight disappropriated and alien, tangled in a network of public gazes interwoven with the repressive gaze of the State. The one-way mirror of the metaphor was strategically imperfect: Citizens outside the detention centers were terrorized because they saw through the mirror before it reflected back to them, because their insight made the faces disfigured by torture their own, because the fusion of a penetrating gaze and a reflecting one made it clear that being inside the *quirófano* or outside of it was a matter of perspective, of chance, or of luck. "We lived in constant tension," testified one Argentine who "looked into" the abstract spectacle under way in a detention center in his neighborhood, "as if we ourselves were also prisoners."[84] In a closed system without exits, public knowledge terrorizes as much as public ignorance. The boundaries between knowing and supposing, between knowing and denying, fade. The same totalizing repression that prohibited sight through the use of head coverings in the detention centers employed the reverse of that tactic for the public at large: Sight of the abstract spectacle was permitted, was mandatory, but the act of seeing and knowledge of what had been seen were used to terrorize and repress the seers.

What Tulio Halperin Donghi described as "the overwhelming monotony of living with fear"[85] in Argentina captures the tenor of this culture engendered by torture and terror. The monotonously homogenous and closed culture of fear provided that all public acts, seeing and knowing among them, contributed to the same drab congratulation of the tautology that—in its most overwhelming application—made its victims guilty by virtue of having been abducted. Monotony serviced that tautology through isolation as well, for the Argentine dictatorship—no less than any illegitimate regime—depended on the destruction of public bonds to cripple the political capacity of its potential adversaries. But totalitarian domination, as Hannah Arendt well observed, "is not content with this isolation and destroys private life as well. It bases itself on loneliness," on the experience of not belonging to any community at all, on the sensation of being in jeopardy even among one's peers, on an implied condemnation to solipsism.[86]

The isolation of individuals in both public and private realms and the destruction of social bonds at their most fundamental level are stages in the process by which a totalitarian State "transforms the whole society into a field of perception."[87] The process calls precisely for the installation of a self-perpetuating and generalized function carried out and multiplied by the repressed public itself (the implied audience) but simultaneously amplified and regulated from a central source (the Junta) to induce a state of consciousness (or a culture of fear) that sets in motion the dynamics by which the illusion of power is generated. By focusing on the moment in the history of repression where it became, "according to the economy of power, more efficacious and more profitable to watch than to punish," Foucault described the disciplinary society as an extension or generalized function modeled on the Panopticon.[88] This architectural structure, designed by Jeremy Bentham, has all cells of a prison laid out in such a way that they can be viewed from a guard tower centrally positioned in the courtyard of a circular edifice.[89] The ingenuity of the Panopticon is in the efficiency of the illusion it creates: an abstract surveillance, a "faceless gaze" always imperceptible within the tower and thus always constant, generates a power far more imposing than any that could be maintained by the proportionately few guards on a prison's staff or—by extension—the few soldiers policing a population. Bentham had in mind a power, like the power exploited by the Argentine Junta, that was at once visible and unverifiable. "Visible: the inmate will constantly have before his eyes the tall outline of the central tower from which he is spied on. Unverifiable: the inmate must never know whether he is being looked at at any one moment; but he must be sure that he may always be so."[90]

A theater of surveillance, an illusion of authoritarian omnipresence, is called into play and compounded by systematic denial to foster a subjugation founded on unverifiability. Fictions are deployed to generate real subjugation, real pain. And here the totality of the repressive program is highlighted: The regime's appropriation of *certainty* and *incontestability* attributes from the torture victims' pain, as Scarry observed, is now complemented in panopticism with a parceling out among the repressed public of these attributes' antithetical counterpart, *doubt*.

Everyone outside an Argentine's intimate circle of relatives and friends became suspect, not of "subversion" (as he or she would be before the State) but rather of suspicion itself, of surveillance, of using one's sight and knowledge against one's neighbor, one's classmate, one's coworker. Because "it is impossible ever to know beyond doubt another man's heart," the suspicion generated by panoptic repression "permeates all social relationships in totalitarian countries and creates an all-pervasive atmosphere even outside the special purview of the secret police."[91] Arendt went on to observe that

in a system of ubiquitous spying, where everybody may be a police agent and each individual feels himself under constant surveillance; under circumstances, moreover, where careers are extremely insecure and where the most spectacular ascents and falls have become everyday occurrences, every word becomes equivocal and subject to retrospective "interpretation."[92]

There are "thousands of eyes posted everywhere,"[93] or, as the Junta put it on taking control of Argentina, "there is a battle post for every citizen."[94] Individuals begin to retreat, to guard their silence, to modify their behavior, to recode their perceptions, and, at the same time, without intention and perhaps even against their will, to function solely by virtue of their presence in the panoptic system as agents causing the same reaction in others. "Perception" of the abstract spectacle in the detention centers was thus interwoven into the fabric of society, multiplying the Junta's illusion of power by first engaging the repressed population as participant-observer of the "grotesque piece of compensatory drama" and by then utilizing cognizance of that abstract spectacle as a means to paralyze an alienated, suspicious, and terrorized population. The spectacle was generalized into a theater of surveillance. "There is no well-founded division between those who perform and those who are spectators, between the subjects and the objects of communicative sight: As one performs before another, she or he is at once regarded by a third, and so on throughout a network of asymmetrical observations patterning the entire space of being."[95]

V

In most narratives, be they historical, theatrical, fictional, cinematographic, or otherwise, time and space are divested of their respective linear and geographic constraints and are altered to suit the demands of thematics and emplotment. A century of conquests might be represented in a textbook by a single paragraph; several years of travel might pass on the stage in the course of a single hour that the viewers experience without leaving their seats; a novel might juxtapose the linearity of reading time—several days or weeks—with the single day in which its narrative unfolds; or a film might engage in temporal and spatial rearrangements by flashing backward and forward, transporting the viewers through the narrative that unifies its improvisations.

Emotional distance can also be manipulated to elicit a desired response from the viewer of—for example—a theatrical production. Among the common techniques used to broaden the emotional distance between an audience and potentially traumatic material are those "which remind the audience that the action is not real," this accomplished on stage by three techniques also evident in the abstract spectacle of "dirty war" repression: "Plots which give the characters mythic or fictional dimensions" (as discussed in the following chapter), "disruption of the time frame," and "the classic device of having violence occur offstage" (in the detention centers) and then representing it abstractly for the audience.[96]

Emotional distancing during the "dirty war" regulated the violent spectacle's intensity and thus kept its gruesomeness from overwhelming (and thus losing) its audience. Mythologization, manipulation of temporal representation, and abstraction of the violence all helped maintain the audience's oscillation within the bounds of its participant-observer function, allowing for respite (though never exit) through emotional disengagement as a viewer's psychic equilibrium required. The emotional distance between the *quirófano* and the public maintained a certain flexibility, elongating and contracting as the pressure demanded, perpetually readjusting the threshold of the audience's ability to cope. In "dirty war" Argentina, as in medieval Europe, "measures of time and space were an exceptionally important instrument of social domination. Whoever was master of them enjoyed peculiar power over society."[97]

Within the *quirófanos* themselves the paradigm of emotional distancing was rehearsed in extremity by the relation of the torturer to the victim.

> The pain is hugely present to the prisoner and absent to the torturer; the question is, within the political fiction, hugely significant to the torturer and insignificant to the prisoner; for the prisoner, the body and its pain are overwhelmingly present and the voice, world and self are absent; for the torturer, voice, world and self are overwhelmingly present and the body and pain are absent. These multiple sets of oppositions at every moment announce and magnify the distance between the torturer and prisoner and thereby dramatize the former's power, for power is in its fraudulent as in its legitimate forms always based on distance from the body.[98]

For these reasons, Scarry argued, there is no greater human distance than that between torturer and victim. Scarry also recognized that "it is only the prisoner's steadily shrinking ground that wins for the torturer his swelling sense of territory."[99] Against the total debasement of the victim the Junta's domain burst forth, the magnitude of its sovereignty directly proportionate to the servitude that it exacted.[100] Separate consideration of spatial and then temporal manipulations in the detention centers will illustrate the means by which this relation was enforced.

SPACE

The Argentine detention center was a microcosm sealed unto itself, the prisoner's space within that enclosure further reduced by head coverings that denied visual access even to the small square of reality to which he or she was confined. The prisoners were sealed inside their bodies in pain. Their gestures outward, their attempts at orientation, were handicapped by the imposed blindness, terrorized by the seeming omnipresence of the hostility surrounding them, and beat back as their efforts to grope forth were met with punches or kicks or club thrusts that penetrated their darkness unannounced.[101] Blinding compounded by constant physical intimidation accentuated the prisoner's absolute helplessness and the conceptual destruction of reality beyond the detention center microcosm, beyond the wounded body. "With the 'hood' [*capucha*] on I became plainly aware that contact with the outside world was nonexistent. . . . One experiences total solitude."[102] The structure of social isolation imposed on the population at large under the vigilance of panopticism was thereby intensified in the detention center by props (the hood) and by direct rather than abstract intimidation of the subjects (the beatings). Within the closed, controlled, laboratory-like quarters of the detention center, the repressive techniques meted out to the population at large were concentrated and concretized to a totalitarian degree; the ritual context hyperbolically "perfected" the repressive agenda.[103]

The sense of terrorized alienation brought about by the capucha was further compounded by spatial disorientation tactics that the repressors systematically utilized. To confound nonvisual attempts at orientation, the detention center personnel walked the prisoners in circles; made them walk while squatting, like circus clowns, to boggle mental measurement of distance; and, during transports, drove them to their destinations by indirect routes.[104] The calculation of whereabouts was similarly impeded by beating (and thus distracting) the hooded prisoners en route to bathrooms. Detention center tactics further muddled the victims' attempts to orient themselves in relation to their repressors by altering rhythms of personnel arrivals and departures. The usefulness and trustworthiness of auditory orientation was similarly debilitated by interchanging real screams from the torture rooms with recorded screams and by playing music at a painfully high volume.[105] The effect of such assaults on the psychological stability of a subject who was already tortured, already terrorized and reduced to a vulnerability without recourse, was predictably profound. One survivor's testimony illustrated the magnitude of disorientation and the consequent threat to sanity that many *desaparecidos* suffered: "I remember holding onto the mattress as hard as I could so I wouldn't fall off, even though I knew it was on the floor."[106]

Thus the sight-deprived victim in the detention center was confined to his or her body in pain by the capucha, and that body itself was confined in what the victim perceived as a hostile, spatially indecipherable environment. The use of abstract, mapless space against the prisoners' psychological stability was then complemented by converting the physical place—the detention center and the objects furnishing it—into an arsenal implementing the prisoners' destruction and the conceptual obliteration of social reality beyond the ritual context. "Made to participate in the annihilation of the prisoners, made to demonstrate that everything is a weapon, the objects themselves, and with them the fact of civilization, are annihilated":[107] The cold floor on which one slept, the pipe with which one was beaten or sodomized, the wall against which one's head was pounded lost their attributes as floor, pipe, and wall through their reconceptualization as weaponry, as more instruments in the repressors' arsenal. "That is, in the conversion of a refrigerator into a bludgeon, the refrigerator disappears; its disappearance objectifies the disappearance of the world . . . experienced by a person in great pain; and it is the very fact of its disappearance, its transition from a refrigerator into a bludgeon, that inflicts the pain."[108]

"Civilization," Scarry summarized, "is brought to the prisoner and in his presence annihilated in the very process by which it is being made to annihilate him."[109] The simultaneous destruction of the prisoner and of the civilization into which his identity extends is etymologically predisposed by the signifier *world*, the root of which, *wer*, means "man."[110] Scarry traced a separate fragment of etymology that from another direction recorded

the path that torture in its unconscious miming of the deconstruction of civilization follows in reverse: The protective, healing, expansive acts implicit in "host" and "hostel" and "hospitable" and "hospital" all converge back in "hospes," which in turn moves back to the root "hos" meaning house, shelter, or refuge; but once back at "hos," its generosity can be undone by an alternative movement forward into "hostis," the source of "hostility" and "hostage" and "host"—not the host that willfully abandons the ground of his power in acts of reciprocity and equality but the "host" deprived of all ground, the host of the eucharist, the sacrificial victim.[111]

In Argentina the path traced by that etymology was discernible in the vernacular denominations for the detention centers. As is frequently the case in the discourse of summary justice, the detention center names in dialectic with their function rehearse the making/unmaking of the world and of the victim to which Scarry referred. Although the intent of the detention centers was of course destructive ("unmaking"), the constructive function of "making" was generally stressed in the names of the Argentine centers. Recuperative, re-creational, and educational motifs were most in evidence. There were, for example, many names falling directly under the rubric of *hospes*—La Casona (The Big House), El Motel, Sheraton, La Casita (The Little House), El Refugio (The Refuge)—as well as others implying much the same—El Jardín (The Garden), La Huerta (The Orchard), El Descanso (The Rest/Resting Place), Sala de Felicidad (The Room of Happiness), El Chalecito (The Little Chalet), Quinta de Seré (The Villa/Country House of Seré). Regarding this last entry, *Seré* was most likely a place or surname, but its literal meaning—"I will be"— implies the reconstitution of the victim who was first violently unmade: The tortured *desaparecido* "will be" what the State makes him. "Quinta de Seré" bridges the distance between the home/hostel and the hospital/ healing content of *hospes*; the names of other centers fall directly within this latter class of restoration, recuperation, re-creation: Hospital Posadas, Hospital Militar de Campo de Mayo, Club Atlético (Athletic Club). In addition, as discussed above, there was within each detention center a torture facility denominated *quirófano* ("operating theater"), complete with its attending physician and its "surgical" apparatus but divested of healing qualities and reciprocally loaded with the pain-related attributes of surgery. Ambulances were sometimes used as "dirty war" abduction vehicles, a La Perla torture room was referred to as a *sala de terapia intensiva* (combining the medical trope with a psychiatric-ideological one—the victim's ideas would be reoriented in this "intensive therapy" room), and scalpels were occasionally used as torture instruments.[112]

These tropes of physical remaking were complemented by other denominations suggesting the victims' psychological adjustment (via "electroshock therapy" with the *picana*) or ideological adjustment under torture, with educational motifs being the most prominent. Escuelita Para Mudos (The Little School for Mutes—the victims' discourse muted by the State, which then instructed a new language) and El Reformatorio (The Reformatory) were particularly suggestive, although there was also La Universidad (The University) and several other detention centers with *escuela* ("school") in their names.[113]

Elsewhere in the language of the repressors, tropes corroborating the present theme were also strongly in evidence. The concept of a prisoner sealed by deprivation of sight into a body that, in turn, was locked inside a detention center gains metaphoric expression in the repressors' use of the terms *capucha* and *tabique* ("a thin wall or partition"). In the vernacular of the detention centers, these terms signified the blinding devices worn by prisoners, conceptually reinforcing the actual covering over and walling up of victims inside the shrinking radius of their incarceration. The more telling use of capucha and tabique, however, was found in their extension (which mimed in reverse the extension beyond the body that was denied to the prisoners) into a second usage intermingling literal and figurative meanings. In the ESMA detention center, for example, the large room in which the prisoners were housed was named *Capucha* with the initial letter capitalized, and the wooden partitions situated therein between one prisoner and the next were termed *tabiques*. Poeticized through this use of the same signifiers to denote the blindfolds and the makeshift cell walls (*tabiques*) and to denote the head coverings and the room where prisoners were imprisoned (*capucha*) was a layer of coverings between the incarcerated prisoner and the world at large from which he or she was separated: a self inside a body inside a cell inside a room. The extension from *capucha* as hood to *Capucha* as cellblock carried the further metaphoric implication that the sealing of prisoners inside themselves was a model in miniature of a greater, collective blinding and closure: one head covering for each individual prisoner, and then another larger one for all detainees as a corporate whole. Unification through *blinding* of profoundly alienated prisoners into a collectively repressed community was the inverted equivalent of a phenomenon discussed earlier: the use of *sight* to entangle the isolated citizens-at-large in a "network of gazes" that they collectively constituted but that contributed to their own repression. The common context shared by public sight and prisoner blinding was recognized in the prosecuting attorneys' extension of the conceit at the 1985 trials: The *capucha* blinding each prisoner individually and the *Capucha* blinding all prisoners collectively were themselves concentric within "a great *capucha* over society as a whole."[114] At the same time another spatial distortion recalling *tabique* was called into play. Though the prisoners were crowded in their *Capucha*, one separated from the next only by the few inches of "a thin partition," the compound enclosure of prisoners within one literal *tabique* (a wall) and another figurative *tabique* (a blindfold) opened an unbridgeable psychological abyss between one prisoner and the next. Isolation within that elongated repressive space was then reinforced by the unverifiable—and for that reason seemingly panoptic—vigil of guards who brutally punished attempts to communicate or to remove a head covering.

In the Argentine detention centers, then, space was manipulated to maximize the alienation and psychological destruction of the victims, and place (the detention center and its furnishings) was converted into an arsenal of weaponry assaulting the victims' bodies. The detention center prisoners were permitted to extend beyond their bodies in pain only insofar as that extension resituated them in the hostile, hermetic ambience that further contributed to their destruction. Punishment was the systematic compensation for gestures away from the self. The prisoners were always beaten back deeper into their pain, always made to retreat into their shrinking territory, "curled up into a ball like a fetus."[115]

Within the detention centers enforcing a prone or seated position for the prisoners was also significant in the symbolics of subjugation. "Upright, man is ready to act. Space opens out before him and is immediately differentiated into front-back and right-left axes in conformity with the structure of his body."[116] The prisoners were largely denied upright posture, one of the attributes that distinguishes man from animals, at the same time that their spatial orientation was confounded by deprivation of sight. "The standing posture" denied to the prisoner "is assertive, solemn, aloof. The prone posture is submissive. . . . A person assumes his full human stature when he is upright."[117] The very word *exist* has its root in the Latin *existere*, meaning to stand forth, to arise, to set out, to stand out. That fragment of etymology modulates into the denial of upright posture as another index of the program that was designed to annihilate the victims' existence conceptually before they were destroyed physically, to make their world and their subjectivity "disappear."

TIME

"When a society breaks down, time sequences shorten." Repression in "dirty war" Argentina illustrated René Girard's contention that "institutional collapse obliterates or telescopes hierarchical and functional differences, so that everything has the same monotonous and monstrous aspect."[118] All of the *desaparecidos* were abducted for the same mythological crime, were tautologically guilty by virtue of that abduction, and were sentenced to the same punishment. By totally bypassing the lengthy formalities of due process (warrants, formal charges, documentation of evidence, trial by jury—all mooted by the collapsed linearity between the imaginary transgression and its summary punishment), the time required to eliminate the "subversives" was telescoped. The lumping of complex differentiation into similitude "so that everything has the same monotonous and monstrous effect" was most apparent at the torture table. There the generation of "evidence," the judgment, and the punishment became indistinguishable constituents of the single pseudo-interrogatory/judicial/penal expedient (torture) in which these formal distinctions collapsed and fused. Layered within that collapse in strata prior to the fusion, torture's manipulation of time sequences manifests a reversal of cause and effect: The function of a trial is to generate and evaluate evidence that may lead to punishment, but torture uses punishment to generate "evidence."[119]

Nowhere, however, was the linearity of time so profoundly distorted as in the experience of the detention center victims themselves. Here Girard's term "obliteration" is exact. Fifteen seconds of voltage applied to the genitals or gums is indistinguishable from fifteen minutes or from any allotted measure of time conceived in terms of linear progression. "I had no sense of time," testified one torture victim. Another stated that during torture "one loses all sense of formal time," and a third victim extended the concept to encompass her entire tenure in the detention center, where "time didn't exist."[120] Regarding mock execution another victim observed: "It's only a second but that second is eternal."[121]

After sessions in which a prisoner was electroshocked senseless, his or her residual ability to normalize the passage of time was eroded by the detention center's general assault on temporal orientation. By linear measure the victim's history and fate were played out at an extremely accelerated pace—one was transformed from a worker or student or lawyer into a *desaparecido* moving through collapsed due process toward death with astonishing rapidity. But the victims themselves experienced time as halted, frozen, with their temporal faculties as incapacitated as their spatial ones.[122] The victims separated from time; they moved from time into pain. They sat or lay in their assigned spots through an interminable present of sightless, muted, frightened, and resigned stasis in which one moment was the same as the next, painful, and in which rather than time pain passed and was measured while beyond them the swift linearity of their fates blew by. The sharp juxtaposition of the prisoner's obliterated notion of time with the telescoped sequences processing the *desaparecido* expeditiously through a repressive system recalls another affinity that the Argentine theater of cruelty shared with the source of tragedy in Athens: Like the "dirty war," "Greek tragedy described an acute crisis of a temporal nature belonging to a world which, in many ways, remained nontemporal."[123]

VI

In additon to spatiotemporal distortions, torture rituals in the Argentine detention centers share with theatrics proper an implied casting of roles and the scripting of discourse appropriate to those roles. Jean-Paul Sartre sharpened the focus on offstage role-playing as it pertains to the workplace, directing our attention to the dialectics between the job and the man, each producing the other. Sartre recognized play in observing a café waiter "trying to imitate in his walk the inflexible stiffness of some kind of automaton while carrying his tray with the recklessness of a tight-rope-walker by putting it in a perpetually unstable, perpetually broken equilibrium which he perpetually re-establishes by a light movement of his hand."[124]

At what is this waiter playing? "We need not watch long before we can explain it: He is playing at *being* a waiter in a café." Like children who play with their bodies in order to explore and take inventory of them, "the waiter in the cafe plays with his condition in order to *realize* it." The waiter's playful fulfillment of the demands that his profession and the public it serves make of him is "wholly one of ceremony," as it is in any profession: "There is the dance of the grocer, of the tailor, of the auctioneer, by which they endeavor to persuade that they are nothing but a grocer, an auctioneer, a tailor."[125]

Or a torturer. The role-playing identifiable in normal social functions of the *teatrum mundi* was more plainly visible in the extreme case of the detention centers, where the acting out of primitive instincts contrasted rather than blended with the social backdrop against which it was performed. Before analyzing the roles assigned to "dirty war" victims, it is helpful to understand the repressors as *actors*, broadening the theatrical sense of the term to encompass Sartre's observations and to echo social science usage that might refer, for example, to actors in a war's theater of operations.

Suggestions of the repressors' role-playing are first evident on the surface of "dirty war" events. In the provinces the costuming during abductions with "balaclavas, hoods, wigs, false moustaches, glasses, and so on"[126] was as central to the task forces' playing with their condition in order to realize it as the Junta's pomp of military formality was in Buenos Aires, with its ceremonial uniforms and its celebrations of mass. In the context of such pomp and of a generally accentuated military presence throughout the Process years, the absence of uniforms during abductions implied a double costuming: the first a direct one (military personnel wear uniforms) and the second its negation (the uniforms are "covered" in the "undercover" operations by plain clothes). Expressions of repressor costuming and role-playing also surfaced more spontaneously. One junior officer dressed up "as an ice cream man. He stole a 'Frigor'-brand ice cream pushcart and liked to show himself off in 'the ward' [of La Perla], going around yelling 'Frigor, Frigor' so the prisoners could see how clever he was."[127] There also were, of course, the overt theatrics of staged confrontations with "armed terrorists," as discussed earlier.

Such surface indices of the presence and potential significance of dramatization are brought to fruition by investigation of the most extreme repressive role, the torturers', as it related to the roles assigned the victims. The training of torturers consisted of a violent program in which the trainees were required to torture others and to be tortured themselves, to perform self-debasing acts before their fellow recruits, and to accept as given the necessity of violence and unquestioning conformance to the ideology of their superiors.[128] They were shaped by both coercion (including "disappearance" and execution, death threats, lowering of rank, and so forth) as well as reward. The latter was provided materially in the form of the "spoils of war" that the task forces looted from homes of abducted victims and psychologically through the sexual gratification that torture afforded and the emotional reinforcement derived from the domination of subordinates (*desaparecidos*) by right of membership in an elite society carrying out an eschatological mission.[129]

As evidenced in almost all detention center personnel testimony presented to CONADEP, torturers were integrated at a very young age into extremist right-wing organizations and indoctrinated into "a fabricated political reality in which their victims have been set outside the pale of humanity."[130] The "subversive" was depersonalized; the *desaparecido* on the torture table was stripped of human attributes and tortured as the embodiment of an evil (Marxism, the Antichrist) that had endeavored to "destroy [the country], by destroying the army"[131] and that therefore must be annihilated without remorse. At an age when violence as a solution has its strongest appeal, the recruits identified with leaders who, in moral indignation, confronted a mythologized threat that was imagined to be so imminently catastrophic that the ethical norms of society had to be altered to combat it. The ideological hermeticism within which the recruits mutually reinforced one another's aberrant violence provided a context for normalizing the pathological position that each trainee adopted under a leader's tutelage. In psychoanalytic terms identification with the leader replaced the group members' ego ideal and consequently led each trainee to identify with the others, and with the victim, on the basis of the ideal represented by the leader.[132] One moral structure was dismantled, and another more suited to the "immense task" was constructed. The ritual context of the detention centers—within Argentine society but insulated from it—reinforced that exchange and the hierarchical relations facilitating it, resulting in the normalization of pathological violence.[133] The mythology of the "dirty war" infused the torture recruits, their "blood pact" binded them to their leaders within a culture of torture, while the same mythology was manifested inversely, divisively, among the general population that was alienated in a culture of fear.[134]

As Jacobo Timerman observed from his contact with detention center personnel, the leaders catalyzed fantasies that endowed the culture of torture with an elevated status; the detention center personnel were encouraged to perceive the gloomy detention centers as examples of institutional beauty utilizing state-of-the-art methods, equipment, and techniques, thereby adding "a touch of distinction and legitimacy" to the underworld they inhabited.[135] On some occasions the pride implicit in such perceptions and in the ideal represented by "dirty war" leaders gained expression in tragicomic gestures. One testimony related that "the tub [for 'submarine' torture] was full of putrid water, vomit, blood, etc. One day when General Luciano Benjamín Menéndez was coming to La Perla the sergeant Alberto Vega, not knowing what else to do to receive 'the General' . . . changed the tub's water and sprayed deodorant in the torture room."[136]

Despite the absurdity of their beliefs and related behavior, the detention center personnel "felt themselves to be masters of the force required to alter reality."[137] By defending the Junta's mission and the ritual context in which it was rehearsed, in which it was possible, the torturers insulated themselves with benefits that the myth afforded them and consequently experienced a sense of omnipotence and an immunity to pain and guilt. The interdependence of Junta and torturer was reciprocally beneficial: The Junta's detention centers provided the "reorganized" moral structure in which the torturers' aberrations were legitimized and granted ample forum, while the torturers' exercise of destigmatized aberrations in those centers sustained the Junta that institutionalized atrocity precisely because its power depended on it.

But just as the victims of torture were "set outside of the pale of humanity" (thereby providing the mytho-logic for their deprivation of *human* rights) in the same gesture by which they were set outside of Argentine nationality as *apátridas* ("countryless"), so too were the torturers socially ostracized and "dehumanized" once they had been "deprived of their personalities" through training.[138] Torturers were also victims of the repressive system of which they were at once the supreme expression.[139] Their deviance was exploited, and when the ritual context legitimating their actions collapsed, society (including their officers) stigmatized and disowned them.

By virtue of their training, then, the torturers came to the detention center theater of cruelty *in media res*, their formation having preceded the spectacle enacted through their agency in the detention center. The dramatic focus of the *quirófano* (like that of the torturers' cruelty and the implied audience's gaze) was therefore concentrated on the victims, who were violently obliged to play the scripts assigned them.

The initial role in which the victim was cast was that of the guilty party. The abduction itself, as discussed earlier, transformed a person into a "subversive,"[140] with the public-as-audience implicitly endorsing that transition through discourse crystalized in refrains such as *Por algo será* and *Algo habrá[n] hecho*. The repressors who transformed innocent Argentines into guilty *desaparecidos* "do not realize that they chose their victim for inadequate reasons, or perhaps for no reason at all, more or less at random." Rather one could "expect the victim to be seen as guilty and therefore to *be* mythically guilty" in the "reorganized" reality being instituted by the Junta; one could expect the repressors to be incognizant of the vicarious nature of their victims.[141] Anybody would do—any *body.* The repressors were satisfied a priori with their victims' guilt, the public contributed its implied consent to the sentence by default, and it remained only for torture to ground these convictions retroactively in the "facts" of confession (or even in refusal to "confess"), to coerce the victim into corroboration of his or her own mythological guilt. That is one reason why torture, rather than rapid-extermination, summary execution, was prominent in the "dirty war": It forged the opposition's (even if only imaginary opposition's) verification of a mythological truth being brought into existence. The "confession" wrenched from a *desaparecido,* regardless of its content, was a performative discourse: It transformed the prisoner into "a witness for the prosecution." The torture victim, "who serves as a witness, gives the group the satisfaction of truth, which is infinitely greater and richer than the satisfaction of justice that would have been achieved by his [immediate] execution."[142]

The truth of "dirty war" ideology was first established conceptually via mythological elaborations and was then "proven" retrospectively, tautologically, by reiteration, by inscription of this truth on the tortured body where its verification was celebrated. As the officer in Franz Kafka's *Penal Colony* put it: "My guiding principle is this: Guilt is never to be doubted."[143] The victims were guilty because they were abducted; the "dirty war" mythology was verified because they were guilty; and the extreme measures (torture) called into play were justified because the very presence of victims (now *proven* "subversives") in the detention center demonstrated and reaffirmed the veracity of the repressors' ideology. This circular logic was the guaranty of the repressive system's self-perpetuation; the victims themselves were the verification of the system's righteousness in destroying them. As long as there are bodies and a felicitous ritual context for their destruction, there will be a Junta celebrating the violent hermeticism that guarantees its truth. "Power," as Scarry put it, "is cautious. It covers itself. It bases itself in another's pain and prevents all recognition that there is 'another' by looped circles that ensure its own solipsism."[144]

But as I have suggested in passing, the implied establishment of guilt grounded in the victim's presence was in itself insufficient. "No victory is complete," as Claudius wrote, "which the conquered do not admit to be so."[145] The *desaparecido* "must give up his desire and satisfy the desire of the other; he must 'recognize' the other without being 'recognized' by him"; he must subordinate himself to the Junta's sovereignty and truth.[146] The victims' role in the "dirty war" drama required that they actively participate in the guilt assigned to them, that they announce it as it has been announced throughout the history of spectacles of power, that they scream out their endorsement of the repressors' mythology and of the public's tacit vote of confidence. Just as the Soviet secret police was "eager to convince its victims of their guilt for crimes they never committed" and just as the Nazis managed to brutalize the Warsaw ghetto Jews to the point where they themselves considered (and created eschatological justification for) the propriety of their own punishment,[147] so the repressors in Argentina tortured in order to generate a victim discourse that—regardless of what it said or did not say—would mythologically constitute a confession and generate an overwhelmingly painful confusion in which the prisoners themselves would entertain the possibility of their own guilt. The victims' discourse was silenced, even though they spoke; the *desaparecidos* had no say. The Junta made its victims' version of the events a "sub-version," a version subordinated to the military truth.

Having fulfilled their role as bodies and having had their discourse used against them as a contribution to the edification of their guilt and the mythology sustaining it, the *desaparecidos*' role was now precisely to perform the function explicit in their denomination: to disappear. In the most literal sense that role was fulfilled as individuals with social identity were converted into anonymous corpses with no graves—their existence as well as their lives were erased, they "disappeared." The repressors, as Hannah Arendt observed in a separate context, "took away the individual's own death, proving that henceforth nothing belonged to him and he belonged to no one. His death merely set a seal on the fact that he had never really existed."[148] That view of the prisoner's fate as perceived from outside of the repression was played out most ritualistically within the detention centers themselves, where physical and psychological torture had as their primary objective the destruction of the prisoner's attributes as a human being. By crushing the prisoner's body, psychological integrity, values, subjectivity, and discourse, the repressors effected a "disappearance." CONADEP recognized the Junta's repressive program as "a meticulous and deliberate stripping of all human attributes" and that incarceration in a detention center "in all cases meant *to cease to exist*" because the torturers intended "to destroy the captives' identity."[149] Testimonies of survivors themselves were replete with passages from the repressors' discourse that make this objective immediately apparent: "Since we abducted you you're nothing. . . . You don't exist."[150] Another survivor added that "the first thing they told me was to forget who I was, that from then on I would be known only by a number, that for me the outside world ended there."[151] Music played at high volume similarly contributed to this chorus of obliterating indoctrination, one survivor reporting repetition of lyrics along these lines: "And now what are they? Where are they? What are their ideals?"[152]

Also common in the survivor testimonies were descriptions of attempts to resist the imposed role as "disappeared," of psychological defenses summoned to protect one's individual integrity against the comprehensive agenda of destruction to which it was subjected. Something of the complexity of such resistance against all odds is apparent in the following passage, where the struggle for preservation of psychic integrity alternates with the desire for a speedy death. The latter alternative was inviting not only as liberation from pain but also as removal of oneself (albeit by default) from the system whose efficacy was contingent on the presence of one's living body. "My mind struggled constantly. On the one hand: 'I must regain clarity and not let them rearrange my ideas,' and on the other: 'I hope they finish me off right away.' "[153]

Other attempts to resist the imposed role as *desaparecido* included the conceptual divorce of the self from the body, that split acknowledging that the body had been overpowered and defeated by the State but that the mind, as locus of the essentials that constitute subjectivity, could by momentous acts of will deny the repressors the total destruction they sought through inflicting pain. "I knew they were destroying my body," one victim testified, "but they didn't have *me*." Others added that "they were destroying my body, but my mind continued working" and that "I was not going to sing, regardless of what they did to my body."[154]

The system running smoothly rather called for victims resigned to the role that the Junta's mytho-logic violently imposed, victims who spoke up only to speak against themselves. Eradication of the self ("all I wanted was to erase myself," one survivor remarked)[155] and participation of the residuals in the repressors' agenda of total destruction was apparent in one testimony, in which a prisoner was so psychologically devastated that he called out during a selection for "transfer": "Take me . . . take me . . . 571." The phrase is doubly significant, first because it voiced a desire for execution but also because the prisoner's "disappearance" was patent in reference to himself as "571" not as a matter of subordinate courtesy but rather as an expression of his "disappeared" identity as such. The torturers' methods had achieved their goal, he explained, because "I was no longer Lisando Raúl Cubas, I was a number."[156] Another prisoner's fulfillment of the "disappearance" required of her was even more complete: After being liberated, after the guard had taken the pistol away from her head and driven away, the woman literally believed she was dead and remained several moments in a kind of paralyzed catatonia, absent to herself, "disappeared."[157]

In the Argentina detention centers, to take stock, the torturers reduced their subjects to imaginary objects made to fulfill specific functions that the myths and rituals of the "dirty war" assigned to them. The victim's role until he or she was executed was to be in the process of disappearing, to be present but absent, to be dying but not dead, to be among the "walking dead" or, as another torturer put it, "neither with the living nor with the dead."[158] As the detention center and its furnishings were incorporated—along with manipulations of time and space—into an arsenal of weaponry to destroy the victim, likewise the victim's body and discourse were, as Scarry succinctly stated it, "made to be the enemy."[159] "The goal of torture is to make the one, the body, emphatically and crushingly *present* by destroying it, and to make the other, the voice, *absent* by destroying it."[160] The body was politicized; the unnegotiably imposing presence of the tortured body made an access to the victim's discourse tangible. The body's sentience gave the power destroying the victim a theater of operations.

VII

Judicial torture in the Roman Empire and in subsequent Western polities from medieval Europe to contemporary Argentina claimed interrogation and the extraction of truth as its justification. The Roman *Digest* of 534, which synthesized earlier imperial jurisprudence, argued characteristically that "it is customary for torture to be applied for the purpose of detecting crime."[161] The medieval view was much the same: "What is called Torture is distress of the body devised for exacting truth."[162] But already in late antiquity attentive observers were recognizing that the extraction of reliable information as the motive for torture was untenable.

Augustine, to cite a thinker whose formulations were otherwise championed by the Argentine Junta, recognized that a victim often "declares that he has committed the crime which in fact he has not committed"; the victim resigns himself to capital punishment resulting from his "guilt" admission "rather than endure any longer such tortures."

> And when he has been condemned and put to death, the judge is still in ignorance whether he has put to death an innocent or guilty person, though he put the accused to the torture for the very purpose of saving himself from condemning the innocent; and consequently he has both tortured an innocent man to discover his innocence, and has put him to death without discovering it.[163]

During the Enlightenment the same recognition led to more developed analysis: "The impression of pain may become so great that, filling the entire sensory capacity of the tortured person, it leaves him free only to choose what for the moment is the shortest way of escape from pain." In his influential treatise *On Crimes and Punishments*, Cesare Beccaria further observed that "the examination of an accused person is undertaken to ascertain the truth. But if the truth is difficult to discover in the air, gesture and countenance of a man at ease, much more difficult will its discovery be when the convulsions of pain have distorted all the signs by which truth reveals itself." Torture then results in a "strange consequence" that transforms the innocent victim's disadvantage into an advantage for the guilty. The innocent victim either confesses to the crime that he did not commit and is condemned, "or he is declared innocent and has suffered a punishment he did not deserve." The victim of judicial torture who is guilty of a crime, conversely, finds himself in a favorable position: "If, as a consequence of having firmly resisted the torture, he is absolved as innocent, he will have escaped a greater punishment by enduring a lesser one." Beccaria thus concluded that even on its own terrain torture is defeated because "the innocent cannot but lose, whereas the guilty may gain."[164]

The untenability of interrogation or "intelligence" as the primary motive for torture was also recognized by survivors of the "dirty war" detention centers. One testimony dismissed the interrogatory justification and suggested the pro forma application of torture: "It doesn't happen because of what one thinks but rather because one is there, in that place, in that situation."[165] Another victim was startled that the repressors tortured him "without asking me a single question" before finally, formally, interrogating him about irrelevant matters.[166] A third victim elaborated the theme by illustration:

> The idea was to leave the victim without any type of psychological resistance, to put him at the mercy of the interrogator and thus obtain any type of response that this interrogator wanted, even if it was entirely absurd. If they wanted someone to reply that he had seen [independence hero] San Martín on horseback the previous day, they succeeded. Then they would tell us that we were liars, which we also came to really believe, and they kept on torturing.[167]

In a context in which the motive for one's arrest was mythologically determined and inadequate on any real grounds (one Argentine, for example, was abducted for having been seen dancing at a party with an "extremist"),[168] it remains consistent that the motive for torture was something other than the interrogatory one that "dirty war" mythology claimed for it.[169] The few prisoners who in fact had information of use to Argentine national security (such as Montonero or ERP guerrillas) could resist through lying or silence; the overwhelming majority of others who—outside of the mythology—had nothing of value to offer State intelligence could improvise to extinguish their agony ("broken by torture, crying out in agony, they were saying yes to everything they were asked"[170]) or, amounting to much the same, could respond to the irrelevant inquiries as though they were of substance. The presumption that one tortured "subversive" would confess the names and whereabouts of his or her "subversive" accomplices was prevalent in the detention centers, "as if a man who [falsely] accuses himself would not more readily accuse others."[171] The torturers whose interpretations purported to sift the truth from the fabrications and to base efficient State action on the fruits of one interrogation rather than another thus established (by appeal to pseudoscience, chance, and folly) a hierarchy of the largely meaningless data, instituting a criterion of verisimilitude that mocked tests of truth as much as it mimed them. It is for this reason that Foucault referred to torture as always "a torture of the truth."[172] "This inversion of the situation," one survivor testified, "in which victims were made guilty and those thought to be dead were alive, constituted the context in which torture in the strict sense [the torture of truth] was put into practice by means of direct physical aggression."[173] The concept did not escape expression in the repressors' vernacular poetics, in which an electrified torture device was referred to as "the truth machine."[174] In the course of torture, like most rituals, "the truth is declared; it is not proven. It is used as proof but cannot itself be proven."[175]

Rather than a means of interrogation, torture is the ritual by which a reorganized truth is instituted and the power to defend that truth generated. Among the spoils of the victor are definitions. It is not that the torturers get no information from their interrogation of a nonmilitant *desaparecido*; it is rather that the useless information they generate is rendered useful tautologically by being used *as though* it were valuable. The mock dialogue of interrogation pieces together a truth based on the coerced participation of the victim whose word—regardless, again, of its content—is brought to bear in the torturer's favor. The useless is made mythologically useful by tracking down the leads, by abducting the grocer or mother-in-law or professor implicated by a torture victim who through his or her absurd agony responded to devastatingly irrelevant questions by conceding that so-and-so also danced with an extremist or attended a meeting or spoke in favor of bus ticket subsidies for school children. The circular system provided, as discussed earlier, that the grocer, the mother-in-law, the professor were then converted into subversives merely by virtue of having been "denounced" and abducted, the mytho-logic thereby looping back to congratulate itself for the useful information generated by the original interrogation, to reinforce its conviction in torture as an effective means of intelligence, and to exploit the new mine of information strapped to the table before it.

If the rituals manifesting State power require victims, and if terrorists deemed legitimate victims for those rituals are not available in sufficient numbers, then the State will generate more victims so that it can then ceremoniously glorify itself and its truth in their undoing. That process was suggested in the first chapter, where an expansive definition of "subversion," a broad margin of error, and abduction of some victims to entrap others increased the "immense task" exponentially. The creation of enemies with the express purpose of ritually destroying them is then intensified by localizing the process on the body of a specific victim. The following passage, recited by Vietnamese torturers to victims doomed regardless of their political persuasion, gave voice to what Scarry termed "the making and unmaking of the world": "If you are not a Vietcong, we will beat you until you admit you are; and if you admit you are, we will beat you until you no longer dare to be one."[176]

In Argentina the repressors likewise "torture you because you are guilty, because you may be guilty, because I insist that you be guilty":[177]

If the victim denied knowing anything, they would continue torturing him based on the idea that he was a "tough" case, that he was holding out so as not to tell them what they wanted [to know]. If, on the other hand, the victim opted to invent something to satisfy his torturers so they would leave him alone or, for the same reason, claimed some responsibility, then the torture would be intensified, based now on the supposition that the victim had more information.[178]

The circularity of the logic ensured continuation of the torture in all cases, regardless of the victims' replies. Because the interrogation was primarily formal, an acting out of the torturer's dominance and a recitation of discourse contributing to the remaking of the *desaparecidos* as ritual objects, the specific content of the victims' responses to questions under interrogation was less significant than the fact that *they were being made to respond*. The destruction of the victims' bodies had to be paralleled by the destruction of their voices. In accordance with the role assigned to them, the victims' broken speech on the torture table was prelinguistic: The first response was a scream. It was then not what the victims being interrogated said that motivated the continuation of torture but rather that they were being made to use their speech against themselves, that their voices were being appropriated and translated into the power that destroyed them. The torturer's remaking of his victims mimed the textbook fundamentals of behavior modification, with a twist: The "wrong" answer was punished with a shock, but all answers were "wrong." The circuit was closed and inescapable. The victims were engaged in a formal rehearsal of questions that, "no matter how contemptuously irrelevant their content, are announced, delivered, *as though* they motivated the cruelty, *as if* the answers to them were crucial."[179]

The formal *as if* with which the questions were delivered predetermined the content and reception of any response; a monologue masqueraded as a dialogue. Whatever was said, the regime was speaking. Whatever response the victims managed to articulate was subordinated before it was uttered. The victims could only announce their absorption into a monologue that edified the State. They were, adapting Claude Lévi-Strauss's formulation, subjects spoken by a myth. Their role, scripted by the repressors, was to assume "the position of the subject upon whom the theatre of identity is being performed" and to then disappear from the spectacle by saying their lines.[180]

VIII

Once the victim's voice had been appropriated, his or her silence was enforced: "We couldn't say a single word."[181] The *desaparecido's* role now was to be a body without a voice, a body emptied of identity. Stress accordingly fell on the violated flesh costumed for the part with its nakedness, with its pain, with the crust of its excrement, with its disfigured features, its open infections, its bruises, its limps, its blood. Once the voice was tortured out of the body meticulously kept alive in order to prolong the ceremony of its destruction, once the *desaparecido* fulfilled his or her function as an agent in the abstract spectacle by which truth is reorganized, power generated, and enmity multiplied, the victim was then exhausted as a ritual object and, useless to the State, discarded unceremoniously. The subject reduced by torture to an object exploited by State rituals thus underwent a second and final denigration: The human-object of the torture session ("human" because still exploited for the voice "extracted" by torture) was afterward divested of all human attributes, of all subjectivity, and the *desaparecido's* role was now reduced to assuming the lumpish posture of a piece of troublesome trash to be disposed of. Once the victim became "a subjugated thing (or dead body), the goal then evaporates, and the master is left with only the shadow of his coveted prey." An "object that is conquered and possessed, by the very fact that it is conquered and possessed, becomes property and as such can no longer be an object of [Junta] desire."[182]

"Dirty war" vernacular registered this final dehumanization of the ritually exhausted *desaparecido* by referring to prisoners selected for execution as "packages." In further development of "package" poetics, detention center personnel sometimes tied red ribbons around prisoners' necks to identify them for the task forces that carried out their "transfer" (execution). Other victims had a number from one to five painted in yellow on the chests of their naked bodies, as if they were "bundles, things, or animals, or garbage thrown into a dump."[183]

The unceremonious means by which the bodies of the *desaparecidos* were "disposed of like garbage"[184] included mass execution by gunshot at the edge of huge graves and the dumping of bodies into the sea. The stark contrast between such wholesale elimination of "packages" and the slow, individualized destruction-preservation of victims during torture reveals a structure also evident in rituals of many primitive cultures, where highly prized and ceremoniously guarded ritual objects were likewise rendered worthless once their ritual charge was exhausted.

One most appropriate illustration similarly concerning the acquistion of power through destruction and absorption of an enemy is found in the *tsantsa* or headshrinking rituals practiced until the nineteenth century by the Aguarunas of the upper Marañón River in Peru.[185] These rituals, much the same as those in the Argentine detention centers (although the contemporary ritual expended half its ceremony in disguising its intent), were undertaken to strengthen, protect, and cleanse the warriors (or task forces/Junta) who had killed their enemies in battle. By shrinking the head of a defeated adversary, the Aguaruna warrior obliged his victim's spirit to occupy the tsantsa; should the Aguaruna fail to do so, the enemy would roam freely to menace him and his people. Sewing the shrunken head's lips closed and blackening the skin with coal were intended to confine the enemy's spirit to the place created to dominate it and to prevent it from seeing beyond its confinement, much the same as the detention center confined the *desaparecido* to the ritual space in which his or her "spirit" (voice) was exploited, likewise impeding vision through the literal and metaphorical head coverings (the capuchas).

Once the shrunken heads were prepared for the Aguaruna ceremonies, the tsantsa rituals neutralized the destructive power of the enemy (the body and voice of the *desaparecido* destroyed under torture), channeled the enemy's strength into the Aguaruna warrior who had killed him (torture as the ritual through which power is manifested), and cleansed the warrior of impurities associated with killing (by endowing atrocity with mythological justification and eschatological purpose), these ritual accomplishments paralleled in the "dirty war" as indicated parenthetically. When, after a ten-day ordeal, the Aguaruna rituals were duly concluded and their objectives realized, the shrunken head was ritually exhausted and, of no further value to the Aguarunas, was tossed away in the trash.[186] In both the tsantsa and the Argentine detention center cases, the emphasis of the ritual was on the *function* that the object (tsantsa, tortured body) fulfilled rather than on the object itself. The next head, the next body available for torture was of far greater interest than ceremonious disposition of an exhausted agent, of a spent object that had already fulfilled its ritual function. The only defect in the symmetry of this comparison comes after the ritual itself, when in the Argentine case the exhausted object (the *desaparecido*) again assumed communicative functions. While the Aguarunas trashed their tsantsa and left the rest to the imagination of enemies who knew, as a matter of tradition, what their fallen fate would entail, the Argentine repressors disposed of their "garbage" with strategic carelessness, tortured bodies turning up among the public in numbers that were scant but sufficient to infuse a terrorizing dread through the absence of others who had "disappeared."

3

The Mythological
Structure
of the Imaginary

I

"THE DISAPPEARED"—that euphemism in itself conjures up the magical possibilities that distance myths and folktales from positive empiricism. One of the Argentine detention centers, El Casco, was indeed referred to in the repressors' vernacular as "La Cacha," the name alluding to a television character, "The Cachavacha Witch," who made people disappear.[1] As a complement to these poetics of fantastic vanishing, one finds in the "dirty war" other motifs also prevalent in folklore and, notably, in the religious tales of the Middle Ages: an enemy-as-monster; a diabolical, invisible force of evil; an Antichrist; a society cast into chaos by its own sins; a legend-laden Hero—courageous, self-sacrificing, divinely guided and empowered—assuming the immense messianic task and struggling, prevailing, restoring happy order for the People. One finds, in addition, a proliferation of fantastic images (people "vanishing without a trace," bodies streaming through the air above the sea, flying nuns, intelligence operatives clipping newspapers in a "fishbowl"), as well as the transformation of identities through the use of "magical" (torture) instruments, the distortion of spatiotemporal constants, and the normalization of the "unthinkable." Mythopoesis "as a process of symbolization through which

107

the catastrophic event [the 'dirty war'] is submitted to the symbolic order"[2] is similarly suggested in the discourse of the traumatized population. The Mothers of the Plaza de Mayo, for example, still demanded the *desaparecidos'* "appearance alive" more than ten years after their execution, and at the same time they magically annulled the "disappearances" by sensing "the live presence" of the *desaparecidos* in the Plaza de Mayo.[3] The insistence of an underlying aura of irreality when confronting the "dirty war" is also suggested by the refrain *¿Será cierto?* ("Could it be true?") that circulated through the public, by CONADEP's assertion— even after fifty thousand pages of "dirty war" testimony—that "it's hard to believe," and by a general resonance in the Argentine public of the "common-sense disinclination to believe the monstrous," the incomprehensibility of a reality overwhelmed by atrocity that is at once affirmed and denied.[4] The very process that situated the *desaparecidos* between life and death—dead and not-yet-dead—and utilized them in that suspended animation to transmit a message to the population finds in myth its perfect textual parallel because "myth . . . is a language which does not want to die: it wrests from the meanings which give it its sustenance an insidious, degraded survival, it provokes in them an artificial reprieve in which it settles comfortably, it turns them into speaking corpses."[5]

Mytho-logic that transforms meanings, like *desaparecidos*, into "speaking corpses" accomplishes this metamorphosis in part through a rejection of complexity and an incapacity to recognize nuances of differentiation. Its nature is reductionist, and its disdain for the texture of reality is conspicuous; it demands the "reorganization" of reality in formal conformity with its binary block-logic and in conceptual conformity with the precepts that sustain it; it exploits stereotypes as its foremost discursive strategy; it lumps all gradations of distinction into polarized extremes, into binary oppositions modeled finally on the Self and Other, on a theatrically pronounced opposition between presence (Junta) and absence (*desaparecidos*).[6]

At the end of the Middle Ages, when intolerance of ambiguity and heterodoxy was more blatantly prevalent, Ignacio de Loyola illustrated the essence of the Christian revisionist block-logic that would later dominate Junta cognition when he declared that if the Church "defines as black what appears to us as white, we must clarify that it is black."[7] Apparent here is a mind that is not only insistent on an authoritarian imposition of truth but also incapable of envisioning shades of gray: Reality will be rearranged according to the Church's desire that white be black and that the distinction between the two be absolute. Dissenting perceptions, of course, will be punished severely—with an auto-da-fé, with a *picana.* Once politico-religious myths (Marxists are omnipresent, dissent is pure evil) were incorporated into the Junta agenda *as though* they were real, they displaced reality and tests of verisimilitude, *became real* in a mytho-logical register that was militarily imposed on the subject population, and generated further mythological constructs attesting to and defending their reality. To this degree myth, like all fantasy and delusion, is in essence narcissistic. Rather than revising the premises it derived from (mis)reading the events before it, the Junta attempted to "reorganize" reality to conform with its mythology.

Arthur Miller once observed that the McCarthy era in the United States (like medieval church dominance in Europe and the Process of National Reorganization in Argentina) involved "a political, objective, knowledgeable campaign from the far Right . . . capable of creating not only terror, but a new subjective reality, a veritable mystique which was gradually assuming even a holy resonance."[8] The efficacy of the myth requires belief in it, this belief itself requiring a psychological apparatus that is capable of sufficiently stifling critical rationality among the myth's faithful while, less subliminally but more violently, a repressive campaign restructures human reality among nonbelievers. An appeal to that psychological apparatus does not, however, imply irrationality: "The kind of logic in mythical thought is as rigorous as that of modern science," Lévi-Strauss recognized, "the difference lies, not in the quality of the intellectual process, but in the nature of the things to which it is applied."[9] Mytho-logic is similar in this regard to the pseudologic apparent in the paranoid psychoses, where the highly sophisticated dexterity and precision of analytical constructions wrought to perfection are undermined only by the inclusion of one or more absurd premises. One of the predominant functions of any myth is to provide a symbolic reply—by displacing the issue from real to symbolic grounds—to something in reality that society cannot fully comprehend or master. Myth then legitimates the social institutions (the Junta, the "dirty war," the detention centers) called into play by this displacement.

The Junta's unwavering faith in its mythologized world instituted a truth that gradually neutralized the political content of the Process of National Reorganization, gradually detached from its referent in socio-political reality and grounded finally in the medieval concept of what the Junta termed the Natural Order. "A conjuring trick has taken place; it has turned reality inside out, it has emptied it of history and has filled it with nature." The grotesque, violent aberrations celebrating that truth in the detention centers were refabricated as myth "purifies them, it makes them innocent, it gives them a natural and eternal justification, it gives them a clarity which is not that of an explanation but that of a statement of fact."[10] The Junta's "matters of fact," or what Clifford Geertz referred to as "master fictions" (under whose aegis discourse and ritual are generated), operated as the unchallenged, irreducible constants reordering reality.[11] Already in the nineteenth century the prevalence of such master fictions led to the observation that "the Argentine army is a mythological fantasy." That fantasy was later extended to engulf the Argentine sociopolitical milieu as a whole: "The nation is a military reality."[12]

Like many tenets of Junta ideology, the concept of Natural Order belongs to a long tradition in the history of Christian ideas. The medieval mind in particular set the Whole before the parts, revered totalities (most of which were imaginary), and viewed the absence of unity as a defect in need of correction.[13] A preoccupation with order permeated Augustine's thought and was closely associated therein with other concepts fundamental to Christian doctrine, among them Love, Harmony, Obedience, and Peace. Augustine and the Argentine military deeply influenced by his tradition posed order in antonymous relation with perversion, and peace was understood as the tranquility of order, the "natural" result of things in their proper place. For medieval Christianity as much as for the military Junta, God's creation was the manifestation of order as He willed it, and the source of any disorder (such as "subversion") was sinful disruption of His design.[14] The world was "like a book written by the finger of God."[15]

Thomas Aquinas, to whom Argentine military ideology was also deeply indebted, was another of the great proponents of the "natural" doctrine, his contention that "participation of the eternal law in the rational creature is called the natural law" opening the door to dictatorship by divine right. Before Aquinas, Aristotle justified slavery on the grounds of its propriety within "natural" hierarchies, and the stoic emperor Marcus Aurelius, not unlike the Junta, similarly governed with the belief that "nothing is evil which is in accord with nature."[16] During the Spanish conquest of the New World, just-war theory was similarly manipulated to the extreme, with the pope and the crown often described as *obliged*—under "penalty of mortal sin"—to subject by force those "who by invincible ignorance sin mortally and are perpetually in a state

of condemnation."[17] The Junta's political theology modernized these formulations, and preservation of the natural order by eliminating "subversion" was firmly established as the armed forces' religious responsibility.
All concerns of ethics, of human rights, of due process, of constitutional
hierarchies, and of division of power were subordinated to this urgent
eschatological crusade.

Witness, by way of example, the following observations from Marcial
Castro Castillo's handbook of military ethics "directed to the Official
combatant" to help him "be a perfect Crusading Knight for God and
Fatherland."[18] Departing from an interpretation of Aquinas as applied to
Argentina, Castro Castillo postulated: "When the natural order . . . of
civilization is being altered by the attack of corrupting subversion . . .
sometimes there is no temporal remedy other than to restore it by orderly
force in fulfillment of the Will of God."[19] Such force was seen as a
dimension of that same Order, a "natural" function by which the peace-
able kingdom self-regulates and restores itself. From the military's "dirty
war" efforts, "peace will naturally result."[20]

Because violations against the Natural Order are sins, punishment
was required to vindicate them, for "without justice, peace is dirty." The
military therefore imposed penance on the "subversives" because "the
cleaning begins by punishing the guilty."[21] Central to the Junta's attitude,
as to Augustine's, was "the conviction that war was both a consequence
of sin and a remedy for it."[22] Despite the fact that it may have taken the
form of "disappearance" and torture as a matter of policy, "the punishment of the guilty is not an evil, but rather an act of goodness" that
counted among its beneficiaries the victims—the penitants—themselves.[23]
Here the Junta again followed Augustine, who believed that the "just
warrior restrained sinners from evil, thus acting against their will but in
their own best interest."[24] The authority for the "dirty war," like any just
war, came from God, and its punitive Christian wrath was therefore "a
sign of love and mercy in imitation of Christ . . . to force heretics
['subversives'] from the path of error for their own benefit, compelling
them to goodness."[25]

The interchangeability of the Lord's Natural Order and the Junta's
public order—of religion and politics—was characteristic of Junta discourse. Because the legitimacy of military authority was based in delegated
divine will rather than, say, in the Argentine constitution, civilian governments would also be punished when their policies disrupted the
Natural Order. If a government "protected" subversives (by honoring due

process or human rights, for example), then this "tyrannical usurper of authority . . . is itself the enemy of order and the Nation."[26] Constitutional governments that had fallen into military disfavor thus became fair prey, with the military claiming final arbitration of what constituted order and what did not. Castro Castillo's inversion of the common notion of political legitimacy is also noteworthy: Civilian government was the tyrannical usurper of "legitimate" (though de facto) military authority because the military was divinely sanctioned to crusade against "enemies of order" in all quarters.

The severity of punishment expiating "subversive" sins against the Natural Order and the Nation had to be meted out in symmetry with the gravity of their mythic transgressions. It had to be sufficiently excessive to redress the damage done in all registers overdetermining the crime. "It is evident that the subversive is guilty of the most serious crime against the Common Good," and therefore "the magnitude of the punishment must correspond proportionately to the magnitude of the good against which he has committed an offense."[27] The Junta claimed legitimacy for its total and unlimited use of violence because its "dirty war" avenged transgressions not only against the sociopolitical order but also against the moral order offended by "subversion." From this view "any violation of God's laws, and, by easy extension, any violation of Christian doctrine, could be seen as an injustice warranting unlimited violent punishment."[28] In the early modern period Francisco de Vitoria similarly called for total just war because "shame and dishonor of the republic are not erased" unless the guilty are afflicted with "the severity of punishments."[29] The Junta followed suit, arguing that the nature of the Enemy and the magnitude of the offense rendered violence "necessarily" and "naturally" as just as it was total. The Enemy's means and ends were "antinatural and anti-Christian, which is more than sufficient cause for total war to secure the Peace of Christ in our Fatherland."[30]

The Junta viewed military atrocities so naturally with such righteous, religious conviction and sustained appeal to Christian canon, that the barbarities committed and the sanctified discourse glossing them with eschatology finally constitute not a contradiction or an expression of contemptuous cynicism but rather a kind of "reorganized" truth, a mythologized reality in which the Junta's words and deeds are integrated components of a single, coherent agenda. By resort to mythopoesis, the military situated atrocity in a realm "beyond good and evil,"[31] where abduction, torture, and execution—all "naturalized" by the mythology—

were as ethically neutral and exempt from tests of morality as the sun setting, a big fish eating a little fish, or any natural matter of fact. In this mythologized context all repudiation of the Junta's acts was metamorphosed into an avowal of its ideology. Nothing escaped absorption. "Tragedy ['dirty war'] does not evade; it negates."[32] The vacuum opened by the "disappearance" of objective reality was filled by the mythologized reality in which the Junta and its "dirty war" made supreme sense.

A determination "to ignore the complexities of reality, or even eliminate reality, and instead establish a simple goal and a simple means of attaining that goal"[33] precisely characterized the driving impetus behind the Junta's mythopoetic "reorganization" of Argentina. Incapable of distinguishing between an armed terrorist and his defense attorney, between passive dissent or political plurality and subversion, between politics and eschatology, the Junta's ideology polarized the complexities and ambiguities of reality into simple, dichotomous antitheses, into binary oppositions mapping out the absolute positions of actors in a mythological struggle.[34] Umberto Eco's morphology of the James Bond novels commented directly on such reductionism in this way:

> Fleming [Junta] is not a reactionary because he fills the "evil" slot in his scheme with a Russian or a Jew; he is a reactionary because he proceeds schematically. Schematic construction, Manichean bipartition, is always dogmatic, intolerant. A democrat rejects schemes and recognizes nuances and distinctions. . . . Fleming [Junta] is a reactionary as is the fable in its origin, any fable. The conservative, ancestral spirit, dogmatic and static, of fables and myths transmit an elemental knowledge, constructed and transmitted by a play of lights that does not permit any criticism. If Fleming [Junta] is a fascist, he is because characteristic of fascism is its incapacity to move from mythology to reason, its tendency to govern utilizing myths and fetishes.[35]

Because one pole of a binary opposition is dependent for its existence on the symmetry of the antithetical counterpart that defines and guarantees it, the Junta was well disposed to a "reorganization" of reality to generate imaginary enmity making possible or reinforcing this or that attribute that it desired for itself. Without its Enemy, and without this process of reciprocal reloading, the reactionary difference in which the Junta founded its identity would have broken down. In Hegelian terms, "The Master can never detach himself from the World in which he lives, and if this World perishes, he perishes with it."[36] Developments following

Hegel's understanding of the simultaneous rejection of and dependence on the Enemy (for our purposes the Junta's enemy) have stressed the eroticized, symbolic inclusion of the subordinated group in the subordinating authority's constitution: "The result is a mobile, conflictual fusion of power, fear and desire in the construction of subjectivity: a psychological dependence upon precisely those Others which are being rigorously opposed and excluded at the social level."[37] Torture surfaces as the ideal drama in which to act out those conflicting needs because it kills and keeps alive, dominates the enemy but postpones his elimination. In his elucidation of Hegel, Alexandre Kojève made specific reference to that point: "It does the man of the Fight no good to kill his adversary. He must overcome him 'dialectically.' That is, he must leave him life and consciousness, and destroy only his autonomy."[38]

Once Hegel filtered through Kojève into Lacanian psychoanalysis, these master/slave dynamics became central to the theory of desire: "The subject-object pair is formed in a single development: the object as that through which need comes to be satisfied; the subject as that which knows desire and feels alive as the seat of desire." Serge Viderman added that the subject (Junta) "has taken form in a constituent relationship to the object ['subversive']: The latter is part of the subject himself." It is not the "subversive" whose presence frustrates the Junta, but rather "it is the subject who frustrates himself by means of an object he has determined through projection." Finally "the object exists in terms of two essential modalities: as a reality belonging to the world of things [the lawyer, the student, the union worker], and as a purely inner reality projected by the subject ['subversives']."[39] Jean-Paul Sartre arrived at much the same conclusion from another direction, pointing out that the passion for antagonism of individuals or regimes that thrive on opposition "precedes the facts that are supposed to call it forth; it seeks them out to nourish itself upon them; it must even interpret them in a special way so that they may become truly offensive."[40]

In the previous chapters I discussed the Junta's seeking out of enemies for its own "nourishment," *creating* "subversives" through strategies ostensibly designed to *eliminate* them. In the following list of the oppositions most prominent in Argentine military discourse, an antithetical "straw man" is similarly created in the "Subversives" column. This mythopoetic inimical composite—"the stereotype of the fanatical and half-mad guerrilla"[41]—is of course well beyond the confines of probability and based on the Junta's manipulation of empirical evidence. The mythological construction of "subversives" with extremely negative attributes reciprocated inversely to glorify the antithetical counterpart, the Junta, in extremely positive terms. The Junta constructed its own identity as it constructed the Enemy's.

Junta	"Subversives"
West	East ("Marxist")
Christian	Atheist
Good	Evil
Christ	Antichrist
Natural Order	Anarchy/Disorder
Argentine (*patria*)	Alien (*apátridas*)
Freedom	Enslavement
Soul/Spirit	Flesh/Matter
Peacelovers	Warmongers
Life	Death
Love	Hate/Lust
Truth	Lies/Deceit
Protect	Destroy
Home/Family	Communal binds/Party
Mature	Immature
Political Right	Political Left

The last two entries introduce concerns resonating through many of the others and are therefore worthy of comment. The Mature/Immature dichotomy draws on "the antique idea that when the roles of life are assumed by the improperly initiated, chaos supervenes."[42] The Argentine population was ill prepared for democracy, the Junta argued, because its "immaturity" engendered the political disarray from which the messianic military was now redeeming it. A 1977 military course on counterrevolutionary warfare explained: "Democracy is government by the people, but if the people are not mature enough to govern, then democracy turns them into the author of their own misfortune."[43] Democracy was seen as an agent of anarchy and a prologue to communism. The Junta therefore had to guard ideological borders until the public matured sufficiently to distinguish the "exotic ideologies" that democracy allows to flourish from the "natural" values of "Western and Christian civilization."

The perception of a population as naive children who require constant tutelage is colonial in essence. In the early stages of colonialism proper, such as those realized in Spanish America early in the sixteenth century, the conquerors' ethnocentrism denied the validity of the subjected populations' societies and imposed on them the empire's "naturally" superior order. A paternal attitude grounded ultimately in the Aristotelian doctrine of natural slavery and sanctified with a religious gloss through Augustine (who "compared the punishment of unwilling souls to that dealt a child by a loving father") often provided the ethical smoothing for an authoritarian "outsider" to exploit and violently abuse a colonized society.[44] The motif most dear to the Franciscan Gerónimo de Mendieta, for example, speaks directly to the point: the childlike innocence of the Indians. Francisco de Vitoria argued in 1532 that the governance of the American Indians "should be entrusted to people of intelligence and experience as though they [the Indians] were children."[45] Juan Ginés de Sepúlveda, more directly ethnocentric in his rhetoric, shared the belief that the indigenous population was a ward in need of a guardian: "The Indians are as inferior to the Spaniards as children are to adults." The issue in Sepúlveda's mind was very clear: "The man rules over the woman, the adult over the child, the father over his children. . . . That is, the perfect should command and rule over the imperfect, the excellent over its opposite."[46] In these cases, as in the case of the Junta patronizing its "immature" population, "the chivalrous principle of the strong protecting the weak and the Christian idea of charity were both invoked."[47]

Despite this invocation in the conquerors' mythology, despite this conception of nations as enormous orphanages, the benefits of messianism tend to fall back on the messiahs themselves, on regimes pursuing their own glorification by means of a roundabout masquerade that stylizes them as donors rather than beneficiaries. In the Junta's case, a neocolonial one, a force that arose from within the "colony" but resembled an external occupying army took control of its own country to exploit the population (as inferior to the Junta as children are to adults) for the benefit of an elite minority. The Junta's insistence on "subversives" as *apátridas* who infiltrated the country and then functioned as an armed presence inside it can here be understood as an attribute proper to the Junta itself, denied and projected onto the antithetical counterpart, the "subversive," that the Junta constructed and restricted by this means. "An important feature of colonial discourse is its dependence on the concept of 'fixity' in the ideological construction of otherness."[48]

Like all mythological concepts the "immaturity" trope that the Junta adapted from personality development was an oversimplification and an imaginative distortion of the empirical data from which it was derived, and the "reorganization" it effected was self-serving. In fact the dictatorship created an antithetically "immature" population (much the same as it created "subversives" to increase the victimage on which it depended) in order to fortify its self-image and its self-assigned role in the mythology as paternal, as powerful, as necessary, as omniscient. It enforced its imposition of mythology on social reality through terror that reduced the public to a childlike helplessness, that made the citizens beg for permission, that made it clear that a higher (and mythologically wiser)[49] authority was defining the rules verifiable only through its totalitarian authority ("Because I said so," dominating parents are fond of repeating) and that differences of opinion ("mature," rational response) would be construed as belligerent defiance requiring punitive action. "The privatization generated by fear triggers a process of de-enlightenment," Juan Corradi summarized, "a regression on the part of citizens to minority status [status as minors], to a sort of political infancy in quest of authority figures."[50] A "trusteeship" was established ("And this—understand it well—is an obligation, not an option"), guarded by a paternal Junta that had matured beyond "childish fits of rage."[51]

The poetics of punishment within the detention centers themselves more dramatically illustrated the creation of a "political infancy" archetype that the military myth required. Prisoners wet their beds and defecated in their pants.[52] They were entitled to nothing. They were not to speak unless spoken to. And when they were spoken to, in torture interrogation, they were reduced, in the image of infants, to a state anterior to language (prelinguistic screams) and to begs and whimpers before they were allowed to respond with a few "mature" words that were continually punished until the victims retreated to a childlike submission.[53] They were denied an upright posture, as though, like babies, they were incapable of it, and when they were permitted to stand, it was to punish them with their own uprightness through endless deprivation of movement, to punish them for being adults, for standing up and forth, and to compel them to find relief in the submissive posture forced on them as "immature": They curled up on the floor like babies. "The word 'stand' is the root for a large cluster of related words which include 'status,' 'stature,' 'statute,' 'estate,' and 'institute.' They all imply achievement and order,"[54] and they all were denied to the prisoners who, in circular fashion steering all positive attributes back to the Junta, were charged with lack of order and had their achievements in life annulled with their "disappearance."

The second set of oppositions under consideration, Political Right/ Political Left, incorporates a number of corroborating intertexts into "dirty war" mythology.

> In nearly all cultures for which information is available the right side is regarded as far superior to the left. . . . In essence, the right is perceived to signify sacred power, the principle of all effective activity, and the source of everything that is good and legitimate. The left is its antithesis; it signifies the profane, the impure, the ambivalent and the feeble, which is maleficent and to be dreaded. . . . Christ, in pictures of the Last Judgement, has his right hand raised toward the bright region of Heaven, and his left hand pointing downward to dark Hell.[55]

Opposition of right and left survived from Indo-European traditions into the Middle Ages, especially in representations of the Last Judgment, in which the sacred are at the right hand of God and the damned at the left. In his earliest known portrayal the Devil is seated at Christ's left hand as the sheep are separated from the goats.[56] When the "leftists" were detained in the "dark Hell" of the detention center they were, in effect, being returned by His soldiers of the "sacred power" to the punitive milieu Christ assigned to them. They were being put where they belonged in accordance with the divine plan. Having fulfilled its restitution mission within the Natural Order, the Junta on and in the Right reaped the reciprocal benefits: reinforcement of its mythopoetic self-conception as "the source of everything that is good and legitimate."

Rejection of the complexities of reality by processing historical events through a simplifying system of antithetical opposition created a "*very truthful fictitious structure*," a "reorganized" Argentina as a "military reality" that—mythologized, natural—verified the Junta ideology in every particular.[57] Mythological constructs of enmity then doubled back tautologically to reinforce the messianic attributes of their antithetical counterpart: The Junta disavowed itself as their source of production, responded to the manifestations of its inimical mythopoesis as realities rather than as ideations that it preceded, and then exploited the discovery of what it itself had projected onto the world in order to validate its ideology and the righteousness of its messianic quest.

Imaginary constructs were read as matters of fact; the Enemy was "both the cause and the effect of the system, imprisoned in the circle of interpretation."[58] And insofar as entanglement of the Argentine public in these circular wefts of mythopoesis was concerned, the question was not, of course, whether the "dirty war" was real but rather "whether the traumatizing power of these situations is not the result of the fact that at the moment when they present themselves, the subject experiences them immediately in the form of a lived myth."[59]

II

The "dirty war" as a lived myth is structured on a hybrid literary model consolidating elements of romance and tragedy. Romance dominates initially, the quest of the Hero (Junta) being the foremost characteristic of the narrative, but tragic motifs gradually emerge and overpower the denouement as the Hero's means of fulfilling his quest result in his self-destruction. In a myth, properly speaking, the Hero is endowed with divine attributes; in a romance or tragedy he is simply human. The "dirty war" accommodates both readings: the supernatural provided by the military's mythopoetic self-perception as a holy order divinely guided in an eschatological mission, and the mundane romantic and tragic motifs by returning to the (demythologized) historical narrative more rationally representing the events under consideration. My use of the term "myth" shall encompass both the divine and the mundane as composite parts of a single whole: the "dirty war" narrative emplotted as a tragic myth with romantic traits.

The final dominance of tragic over romantic structure is brought about by these same shifts between the divine and the mundane. A romantic Hero generally receives supernatural assistance to realize the goal of his quest (in the "dirty war" that help came in the form of both Christian deity and the *picana* as what Vladimir Propp called a "magical object," as I will discuss presently). But outside of the romance, in the historical register, these supernatural means are illusory, and the "dirty war" narrative is therefore left with a tragic Hero who "cannot simply rub a lamp and summon a genie to get him out of his trouble."[60] The source of "magical power" (torture) that seemed to deliver the Junta through its romantic quest, I will argue, turns out to be the metonymy of its tragic flaw; the Hero's agenda self-deconstructs by the same quotas with which it realizes his goals.

A quest involves an obstacle situated between a given state of affairs and an ideal, and its narrative is generated through conflictive interaction between two primary characters: a Hero, whose intentions create the axis of the narrative, and an Enemy.[61] Because "dirty war" mythology is a creation of the repressors, they likewise enjoy the prerogative of assigning roles: The Hero represents the military, and the Enemy "subversion." "A text structured by some kind of collective victimage will reflect the view of the victimizers and therefore will not advertise itself for what it is," René Girard wrote.[62] Later, when the romantic structure yields to the tragic as the mythology is applied back to the historical events, one must abandon the victimizer's perspective and recognize that "each agent is his own hero."[63] For the moment, however, the Junta's polarizing logic reviewed above provides very neatly that the two opposing camps of the "dirty war" romance present themselves "like black and white pieces in a chess game,"[64] with their respective roles parceled out by the Junta.

THE HERO AND HIS MESSIANIC QUEST

The Hero (Junta) regards himself as the creative agent of historical destiny. Analogous to the mythic Messiah who appears when a series of woes require his properties of salvation ("We have faced a tremendous political vacuum capable of sinking us into anarchy and dissolution"),[65] the Hero arrives to "put an end to the situation which has burdened the nation,"[66] his struggle signifying "the final closing of a historical cycle and the opening of a new one."[67] The Hero defends "the most sacred interests" by assuming the "unrenounceable," "indispensable," "immense," and "rigorous task of eradicating, once and for all, the vices which afflict the nation."[68] He makes the world habitable and safe for "the honest and exemplary citizen." He finds the People "engulfed . . . in an atmosphere of insecurity and overwhelming fear" and redeems them from "corruption," from "deterioration," from "anguish and desperation," from "the corrupting effect of demagoguery," from "the scourge of subversion," and from "the total absence of ethical and moral examples which the directors of the state should exhibit"—"all of which translates to an irreparable loss of greatness and faith," a "grave crisis."[69] The Hero cleanses the land of impurities, he conquers chaos by restoring the Natural Order, in righteous abnegation he deploys the force with which he alone is endowed ("not motivated by an interest in or desire for power") in order to realize his "specific mission to safeguard the highest interests," "the traditional values of Family, Fatherland, and God."[70] For when "the very foundations" are being destroyed by "the forces of subversion and chaos," the Hero must assume "the mission to defend essence," "to rescue the Republic from so much insult and affliction."[71]

The quest of the Junta-Hero took the form of a mythologized war narrative that, for expository convenience, can be divided into three substructures: The Myth of International Conspiracy, The Myth of the Metaphysical Enemy, and The Myth of the Holy War. Ultimately these will need to be rewoven into the textual fabric they together constitute, but for the moment considering them separately will assist in understanding dimensions of the "dirty war" master myth.

In the Myth of International Conspiracy, the Junta's inimical constructs were formulated by resort to predominantly political rather than religious motifs, to just war rather than holy war. The domestic struggle against "subversion" was couched in a global context: "World War III had begun; the enemy was left-wing terrorism; and Argentina was the initial battleground chosen by the enemy."[72] Although bilateral international influence was as much in evidence in the "dirty war" as it is in any political struggle, the World War III concept—developed explicitly by the Junta in two official declarations[73]—was grounded more firmly in the military's desire to depict its adversary hyperbolically, to justify the extremity of its repression, and to endow its barbarities with central importance in world affairs, than in any reasonable interpretation of the events. "International conspiracy" launched the Hero's quest, it gave Argentina the opportunity "to play the leading role" rather than be "the stage for someone else's battle."[74]

Echoing cold war national security doctrine, the Argentine military argued that local subversion, "no matter how seemingly insignificant, is always part of a homogenous, global whole centrally directed by the leading Marxist-Leninist countries, which have made ideology the principal means of domination."[75] Distorted as its representation of Argentine sociopolitical reality may have been, the Myth of International Conspiracy was the least delusional of the three subplots structuring "dirty war" mythology because it still depicted the Enemy in this-worldly terms rather than in the diffuse metaphysics or the apocalyptic Christianity of the Junta's other mythopoetic constructs. Here the romantic quest of the

Hero was to shape Western historical destiny by preempting a global struggle through decisive victory in its first battle. It would thereby redeem Western and Christian civilization worldwide from the protracted international hostilities associated with world war and—should that war be lost—from domination by the evil Enemy, "communism." The questing Hero would "show the world—even the most powerful nations—the miraculous energy contained by a people *moved into action by faith.*"[76] When Admiral Massera explained further that Argentina was "of great geopolitical importance to the West" and implied that without the Junta's "dirty war" efforts the United States "would have had to fight for the first time in its own continent," he underscored a more general Argentine preoccupation with being—in Videla's words—"the focus of world attention."[77] Through the "dirty war" Argentina would assume new status as the stronghold of Western and Christian civilization, as the reserve of power and purity, superseding Europe and the United States that—as evidenced in vice, corruption, the decadence of tradition, and sexual promiscuity—were sinister in their "denaturalizing" of the sacred principles on which Western grandeur was based.[78]

This preoccupation with being the "focus of world attention" suggests the Myth of International Conspiracy's interrelation with another Junta penchant: the spectacle. As was apparent in the ceremonious Argentine sponsorship of the 1978 World Cup Soccer championship (on which the Junta spent $700 million—10 percent of that year's national budget),[79] in the post-Junta publication of *Nunca más* (which referred to the *desaparecidos* as having made Argentines "tragically famous"), and in the spectacular nature of the 1985 trials, the authors of events in and around the "dirty war" were acutely cognizant of outside observation. By depicting "dirty war" Argentina as the geographic theater in which Western and Christian civilization's climactic offensive unfolded and by propagating the international and conspiratorial nature of the Enemy in a domestic struggle that drew the attention of a considerable foreign audience, the Junta's World War III discourse contributed to generalization and internationalization of the spectacle of atrocity reviewed in the previous chapter, broadening its audience, repackaging it for export.

And it also provided grounds for the Junta's insistence that its repression was *war*, colored by the "good war" sentiments sometimes associated with World War II. The sanctioning of violence that was better characterized, as one survivor put it, by "dirty" than by "war" exploited the international conspiracy motif to process out the "dirtiness" as it empha-

sized the single heading under which modern civilization condones atrocity, "war." General Menéndez remarked that all of the subversive talk
about excessive violence—as if the "dirty war" were the "persecution of
innocents opposed to a supposedly military government"—missed the
point because "the entire problem of subversion and countersubversion
constituted a war."[80]

The Junta's mytho-logic ascended into a higher delusional register in
a second conception of the "dirty war," wherein motifs of enmity gradually disengaged from politics and gained representation in archetypes of
evil. That shift of register was one expression of the more general Junta
tendency to abstract empirical sociopolitical reality, to perceive the world
in metaphysical terms. In Chapter 2 I noted that, according to the Junta,
"the first World War was a confrontation of armies, the second of nations,
and the third of ideologies," the agency of antagonism becoming progressively more abstract, moving from armies to nations and from nations to
ideologies.[81] "During the last thirty years a true world war has been
developing," Admiral Massera explained, "a war that has man's spirit as
its preferred battleground."[82] Massera's metaphysical urge further assisted
in the transition from World War III to the Myth of the Metaphysical
Enemy by abstracting the term "Western," freeing it from its geopolitical
referent, and glossing it with religious overtones: "The West today is a
state of the soul, no longer tied to geography."[83]

The diffusion of international conspirators into a more ominous and
omnipresent metaphysical Enemy accompanied this tendency to detach
concepts from their concrete and this-worldly meanings. Máximo Gainza
Castro, for example, argued that the absence of terrorism signaled not
the absence of the Enemy—let us not be fooled—but rather the more
diabolical and invisible means by which the Enemy was realizing his
insidious goals.[84] In Gainza Castro's expression of the myth, the inimical
threat was abstracted so thoroughly that it rendered the absence of
political violence a greater danger than its presence. The concern that
was earlier focused on armed international conspirators was now concentrating on "the dark forces" and "the forces of evil."[85]

What survived the transition from one myth to the other was the
Argentine Enemy's relation to a larger inimical body. The Myth of the
Metaphysical Enemy left the domestic and international theaters behind
as the struggle assumed cosmic proportions: "What we are seeing is the
'present act' of that constant war between good and evil."[86] As explained
by the military's archbishop Adolfo Tortolo shortly before the 1976 coup

d'état, God permits evil because in adversarial response to it "latent forces" of goodness surge forth from "profound reserves" with "decisiveness, courage, ingenuity and holiness" to initiate a "process of purification."[87] Here the Hero fights a mighty battle with suggestions of apocalyptic conflagration against the forces of an invisible Enemy, perceived either through signs that the Hero wisely interprets or else through evil's highly concentrated embodiment in archetypes such as "the monster of Marxism," which "since 500 years before Christ" (and two millennia before Marx put pen to paper) has been lumbering toward Argentina.[88] Concretization of metaphysical evil in a tangible enemy (accomplished in the myth by archetypes and in the "dirty war" itself by creating "subversives") provided access to the invisible Enemy in the same way that during torture the body provided access to the victim's voice. The myth's concentration of evil in destructible beings is replete with eschatological overtones, implying ultimately that the Hero's elimination of these embodiments would constitute utter annihilation of evil not only in Argentina or on earth but cosmically—a final solution.

Once the metaphysically conceived "dirty war" was permeated by the Junta's Christian canon, by "our way of being Christian," it assumed more specific apocalyptic and eschatological value as the Myth of the Holy War. Despite the fact that since the third-century writings of Origen the predominant Christian interpretation of the *Civitas Dei* battling the *Civitas Diaboli* has been metaphoric, staged not on battlegrounds but in the believer's soul,[89] and despite the fact that the Junta itself had propagated its crusade as "a conflict inside each one of us,"[90] the holy war trope was demetaphorized in Argentina, the allegory lived, as the myth and figurative models were imposed on the sociopolitical reality that experienced them as "dirty war." Similarly the apocalyptic tradition in the Middle Ages, based in Revelation and foretelling a glorious kingdom of Christian unity—a New Jerusalem—on earth, was extremely suitable to political adaptation and dynastic agendas; eschatological emperors crusading to unite a Christian world enjoyed along the way the expansion of their empires and a secular apotheosis. A shift to a higher register, like that of the Argentine Junta, was also evident: "Medieval World Unity was a part of the Christian eschatology and therefore does not refer to this earth and its surface alone; it embraces the whole depth of Space and is in fact a Unity of the Universe."[91] In the "dirty war," as in medieval crusades and Iberian expansion during the Renaissance, this- and otherworldly referents became indistinguishable as they fused (with "the one referring to the other, reflecting the other and flowing over into the other") in a single politico-eschatological program to unify world Christendom (or "Western and Christian civilization") in accord with the Natural Order. The violence that apocalyptic politics could inspire, to cite one early modern example, was apparent in the opinions of Portuguese Antonio Vieira, who saw his small nation as that of the Chosen Race elected by God to spread the True Faith across the globe. The Portuguese, Vieira envisioned, would bathe their swords "in the blood of heretics in Europe and the blood of Muslims in Africa, the blood of the heathen in Asia and in America, conquering and subjugating all the regions of the earth under one sole empire so that they may come under the aegis of one crown and gloriously be placed beneath the feet of St. Peter."[92]

As in the medieval apocalyptic tradition, the Myth of the Holy War mobilized a Hero as warrior-savior, as a "modern crusader fighting for God and freedom," called into action by "signs" that heralded the coming of the Antichrist.[93] Many such medieval signs—"bad rulers, civil discord, war . . . sudden death of prominent persons and an increase in general sinfulness"[94]—were interpreted by the Junta in the historical events precipitating the "dirty war," providing the myth with a point of departure. Because "the political triumph of atheistic communism through the International Power of Money" would bring upon Argentina "the kingdom of the Antichrist of Apocalypse," decisive action was necessary to preempt one reign and usher in another.[95] "An antisubversive war begun under these conditions cannot legitimately and reasonably be waged toward any end other than the establishment of a new natural order for renovation in Christ, which offers the inhabitants of the Fatherland an authentic opportunity for temporal perfection."[96]

"The antichrist and the antinational being," "pagan agents of the Antichrist,"[97] and other such constructions evidenced the synthesis that the Junta's two key concepts, "Western" and "Christian," were undergoing as elaborated in the Myth of the Holy War. Depiction of the Enemy as Antichrist endowed the "dirty war" with eschatological purpose and—by reverberating off the binary opposition—strengthened the Junta's self-image as Christ's vicar, as crusading defender of Christendom's Natural Order, as heir of "the heavenly militias of Genesis," a host of saints, and "the Virgen General."[98] Such megalomania by divine right was not without ample precedent in the Argentine military, which in 1940 was already congratulating itself for its "historical and spiritual grandeur" as a "holy order" comparable to the crusaders of the Iberian Reconquest.[99] "The military profession," as the episcopate affiliated with the Junta put it, "is a profession of religiosity."[100]

THE ENEMY

The representation of "subversives" in "dirty war" mythology predictably assumed archetypes of enmity relating them antithetically to the Hero. "The enemy may be an ordinary human being, but the nearer the romance is to myth, the more attributes of divinity will cling to the hero and the more the enemy will take on demonic mythical qualities."[101] Prior to this supernaturalization of the "dirty war" narrative as the romance approached myth, the Hero's adversary was an essentially ideological enemy, the this-worldly, political enemy of the Myth of International Conspiracy. "A terrorist is not just someone with a gun or a bomb," recalling General Videla's definition, "but also someone who spreads ideas which are contrary to Western and Christian civilization."[102] Castro Castillo expounded on the point:

> The enemy is not "the guerrilla": the enemy is Communism and the materialist Liberalism which leads to it; it is the Anti-Christian Revolution in all of its facets: religious (anti-Catholicism or pseudo-Catholicism, such as progressivism); philosophical (nominalism, idealism, positivism, materialism, existentialism, etc., etc.); political (populist democracy or universal suffrage); social (egalitarianism, proletarianization, and massification); economic (liberal capitalism and state capitalism, developmentism, usury, etc.).[103]

The Junta's sweeping conception of opposition tested the limits of what constituted an assault on "Western and Christian civilization," and the elasticity of these terms was exploited to reinforce the righteousness of the questing Hero who found "invisible" adversaries in all quarters. As in medieval just-war theory following Augustine, "guilt of the enemy merited punishment of the enemy population without regard to the distinction between soldiers and civilians."[104] Junta mytho-logic provided that U.S. Secretary of State Cyrus Vance was no less an Enemy of the Junta than Montonero leader Mario Firmenich.[105] Students favoring modest school or university benefits, workers protesting pay cuts in the context of three-digit inflation, priests working among the poor (guilty of "cunningly distorted interpretation of Christian doctrine"),[106] and medical doctors giving appointments to the relatives of *desaparecidos* were all the Enemy as much as the armed terrorists were, that equation of culpability forged by the common punishment meted out equitably to all: abduction, torture, execution. "Motivated by a righteous wrath, the just warriors could kill with impunity even those who were morally innocent. Objective determination of personal guilt was not only unnecessary but irrelevant."[107] The guilt of "subversives," again, was ratified by the "disappearance" itself. "The word 'subversive' thus became a magical word, implying that the citizen to whom it was applied was automatically degraded [and] lost all of his rights."[108] The word was "magical," or performative, beyond that by effecting a reversal of roles between the innocent and guilty parties: The Junta as victimizer of the "subversives" it created viewed itself as the victim of its own victims, of these Enemies seeking to destroy Argentina "by destroying the army."[109]

In mythopoetic elaborations following that reversal, the Enemy became increasingly "invisible," perhaps in subliminal homage to the fact that his existence was largely a mythological construct, his ranks insufficient outside of the myth that multiplied them. A shift away from a concrete Enemy and toward inimical abstractions began, as I have suggested, with ideations of international conspiracy. An antinational being believed to have penetrated Argentine political and ideological borders imperceptibly infiltrated citizens who, in turn, were recruited to the "forces of evil," disseminating their invisible enmity everywhere. In the Myth of the Metaphysical Enemy, cosmic evil was then localized and concentrated; it was made visible. The more the Hero's slaying of "subversion" metonymized in the "monster of Marxism" was rehearsed, the more the Enemy was abstracted and described within an eschatological framework as pure, metaphysical Evil. When the metaphysics were finally elaborated with the gloss of Christian canon, apocalyptic imagery recast the incarnation of Evil, with the legendary archetype ("monster of Marxism") displaced by a Christian one, the Antichrist (described in Revelation as a "beast," following similar imagery from the Book of Daniel). In the Myth of the Holy War, "everything opposed to the Kingdom of Christ and to the natural order is the enemy."[110] Here the military said aloud, as Roland Barthes put it in a separate context, "what the unconscious of powers only whispers: *I am sacred and anyone who contests me is a blasphemer.*"[111] The Enemy's "transgressions" correspondingly left behind their political and social nature to assume the religious gloss more appropriate to the role myth assigned them. The Enemy sought "to dominate the spirit," to deprive Argentines of "entrance into the kingdom of Christ"[112] by "implanting the Kingdom of the Antichrist and enslaving all men and all nations, separating us from our only Savior."[113]

In medieval theological usage the Antichrist was antithetical to Christ in relation to the *corpus mysticum*: Just as Christ was the mystical head of His body, the Church, the Antichrist (not a devil but under Satan's sway) was fashioned the mystical head of the body of Evil. More informal usage, which tended to coalesce religious and secular agendas by applying the term to political leaders, viewed many evil men—antichrists with the initial letter lowercased—as forerunners who were gradually instituting the reign of the Antichrist. Similarly in "dirty war" mythology each individual "subversive" filled the role of antichrist, while the collective body of "subversives" as a whole, the corporate abstraction, constituted the Antichrist. (The myth, however, tended to embody the totality of that corporate whole in each individual "subversive" punished in the detention centers.) Medieval commentators believed that the Antichrist would deceive men by performing "great wonders,"[114] that his deluded followers would worship him sacrilegiously, and that he would keep them enthralled by performing false miracles. Deception as a predominant attribute also characterized the Antichrist of the "dirty war," who seduced "useful idiots" and Argentine "automatons"[115] into his evil ways. The deceiving Antichrist of "subversion" entrapped the weak and desperate with the false hope of "exotic ideologies," then turned them against their own interests to destabilize the Natural Order and its mundane counterpart, the Process of National Reorganization. The myth held a happy ending in store for its authors, however, because the Antichrist would ultimately be defeated either by Christ directly or by Christ's power exercised through His vicars.

The medieval motif depicting the Antichrist as death, in contradistinction to the life-giving force of Christ, was also adapted in the Junta's Myth of the Holy War. In a 1976 speech broadcast nationally from the ESMA detention center, Admiral Massera opened by taking the trope quite seriously: "We are not going to tolerate death walking about freely in Argentina."[116] Later in the same speech he utilized the death/"subversion" equation in the polarizing structure characteristic of Junta thought: "What is certain, absolutely certain, is that here and throughout the world . . . those who are in favor of death fight against those in favor of life." The "nihilists," the "delirious destroyers," "will not only be considered guilty of high treason against the Fatherland, but also guilty of high treason against life."[117] In Argentina, Massera exclaimed elsewhere, "death will not win!"[118]

The concept of "infiltration" ubiquitous in Argentine military discourse also resonated in the context of the Antichrist, accommodating the biblical notion of diabolical possession: The Enemy's "ideological borders" were penetrated by the devil. In the New Testament "infiltration" by demonic forces often endowed the possessed ("subversive") with supernatural strength or knowledge, calling all the more for special resources (the *picana*) and decisive, innovative action on the part of Christ's vicars struggling to exorcise the evil. The Junta took its cue from Christ Himself, who "went about doing good and healing all who were in the power of the devil." "Come out of the man, thou unclean spirit," Jesus said in one case, which turned out to be plural: "My name is Legion: for we are many."[119] When torture rituals in the Argentine detention centers exorcised the "unclean spirit" from each infiltrated "subversive" with the touch of the *picana*, the many-in-one poetics obtained. Cleansing of not only the specific victim (antichrist) at hand but beyond him two corporate entities to which he was integral was suggested: the Antichrist with the capital letter was assaulted through each embodiment representing him on the torture table, and in the process the *corpus mysticum* of Argentina, the social body to which the victim belonged and which he defiled with his demonic possession, was ritually purified via the casting out of the "unclean spirit." "For as by one man's disobedience many were made sinners, so by the obedience of one shall many be made righteous."[120] In the mythology sanctioning Argentine torture the medieval view of the body as a microcosm where cosmic struggles (between Heaven and Hell, Order and Disorder, Christ and Antichrist) are battled out was thus apparent; torture cleansed out "the abnormalities that afflict the spiritual body of Argentina."[121] Casting out of the "unclean spirit" during torture adapted the Catholic model for forgiveness of sins, first by making the victims, like the penitents, bear witness against themselves, and then by telescoping the chronological progression from confession to the penance resulting in expiation: A victim's coerced "confession" and the penance that neutralized the "sin" collapsed during torture into one and the same.[122] In the broader perspective the torturer's domination of each victim's body localized, ritually mirrored, and rehearsed victory in the grand eschatological battle that was under way mythologically through the Junta's crusade against the Antichrist.[123]

III

The cosmic battle localized in the tortured body as microcosm gained similar expression in "dirty war" mythology through metaphoric depictions—again typically medieval—of the State as a living organism. In medieval Church history prior to the mid-twelfth century, the concept *corpus mysticum* referred to the mystical body of Christ—as opposed to His natural body as man—that the consecration of the eucharist made present. The *corpus mysticum* as eucharist then evolved into a corporational Church doctrine, dogmatized by a papal bull in 1302, by which the many faithful together constituted one mystical body of the Church, the head of which was Christ.[124] As Thomas Aquinas explained it, "Just as the whole Church is styled one mystical body for its similarity to man's natural body and for the diversity of actions corresponding to the diversity of limbs, so Christ is called the 'head' of the Church."[125] Aquinas frequently employed the term *corpus Ecclesiae mysticum* (the mystical body of the Church), in place of the customary *corpus Christi mysticum* (mystical body of Christ) that had predominated in reference to the concept. That change in terminology, Ernst Kantorowicz recognized, indexed an initial secularization of the "mystical body." The original sacramental meaning of *corpus mysticum* was gradually displaced by a sociological function, thus establishing the groundwork for a mystery governed more on earth than in heaven.

The secularization of the *corpus mysticum* was increasingly in evidence as the Middle Ages progressed, the roles of Church and State moving closer together. Laymen would proclaim that "the Church compares with a political congregation of men, and the pope is like to a king in his realm on account of his plenitude of power."[126] Christ as "head," too, would be relegated to the background as he was replaced on earth by His vicar: "Just as all the limbs in the body natural refer to the head, so do all the faithful in the mystical body *of the Church* refer to the head of the Church, the Roman Pontiff."[127]

By the thirteenth century the *corpus mysticum* had become a corporational, nonchristological concept represented by what Kantorowicz calls the Two Bodies of Christ: one the *corpus naturale*, the natural body of Christ as man (developing a tradition of its own, with something of the initial mystical qualities surviving in the eucharist), and the other the

Church as *corpus mysticum*, "a super-individual body politic and collective," which became progressively more secular and less mystical. The Church displaced the eucharist as *corpus mysticum* at a time when "the doctrines of corporational and organic structure of society began to pervade anew the political theories of the West."[128] In reciprocal fashion the *corpus mysticum* began its transfer from the Church to the State and found a role in medieval political theory. While the Church was emphasizing political corporation through self-declaration as the *corpus mysticum*, the secular world authorities were propagating their domain as a "holy empire." By the middle of the thirteenth century, the State was designating its body politic a *corpus reipublicae mysticum* (mystical body of the republic); the State was transcendentalized as political theorists envisioned "a perfect kingdom directed by the king as the vicar of Christ and guided by the ministers of the Church."[129] The Two Bodies of Christ thus provided the ecclesiastical model adopted by medieval jurists and applied to the State: the King's Two Bodies. In addition to possessing his *corpus naturale*, "the Prince is the head of the realm, and the realm the body of the Prince," the original sacramental meaning of *corpus mysticum* now seemingly displaced entirely by a secular political function. "Nevertheless, the designation of *corpus mysticum* brought to the secular polity, as it were, a whiff of incense from another world."[130]

When an act of "subversion" was committed within the Argentine State depicted as the living *corpus mysticum*, the offense was not simply against person or property but rather against "a perfect kingdom directed by the king as the vicar of Christ" and against the Junta's mystical body. Punishment of "subversion" therefore "requires redress for the injury that has been done to his kingdom," as Foucault observed, ". . . but it also requires that the king [Junta] take revenge for an affront to his very person."[131] It is perhaps for this reason that in premodern Europe castration of the testicles, extirpation of the penis, and the two combined were inflicted as punishments not—as might be expected—for sexual crimes but rather for violence, attempted violence, or conspiracy to commit violence against a ruler or prince.[132] In the Argentine case, when the psychosexuality I will later analyze subsided, the "whiff of incense from another world" resumed, and the affront of "subversion" was ultimately held to be an assault against Christ himself. As Castro Castillo explained to the Argentine soldiers, "*Subversion is a crime against God: God is the author of the natural order, which is in the image of the Creator of the* universe; to try to subvert, or to invert, this order is to make a direct assault against the will and creative intelligence of God."[133]

When the *corpus mysticum* of the many incorporated into the One constituted the Junta's body and, beyond it, Christ's, the punishment of an offense against these bodies would be overdetermined to redress the damage done in all registers. Excess made a blunt but symbolic contribution in that regard, and spectacular atrocity arose as a particularly apt form for excessive punishment of crimes against the *corpus mysticum* because—as noted in the previous chapter—"in these rituals in which blood flowed society found new vigour and formed for a moment a simple great body."[134]

One of the most loaded images of enmity in the mythology of the "dirty war" depicted "subversion" as a disease inside an Argentina conceived as a living organism. The disease trope, adapted to a variety of sociopolitical contexts in the modern era, was a favorite of Adolf Hitler, who depicted the Jews as an "alien racial poison in our bodies" while Marxism was "eating deeply into the national body like a pestilence."[135] "What we long for outwardly," the fuehrer reasoned, "can be won only through prior inner cleansing" that required "a bloodiest tribunal to punish our people's poisoners."[136] In the Americas, similarly, Guatemalan reformist governments of the 1950s were referred to in cold war rhetoric as the "Guatemalan Cancer," and this small country was seen as a "malignant growth" of the "Soviet menace in the Western Hemisphere."[137] Following the 1959 Cuban revolution disease tropes proliferated, one succinct example—beyond the ubiquitous "cancer"—referring to post-revolutionary Cuba as an "infection."[138] Likewise in Argentina the inner corrosion metaphor has ample history, notably in the discourse of Juan Domingo Perón.[139] During the "dirty war" itself pathology tropes were frequently deployed to propagate the presence of an invisible "enemy who assaults us from within."[140] Admiral Massera described the Enemy's "will to kill" as an "epidemic," comparing it to "plagues that scourged the world" in previous centuries.[141]

Figurative discourse utilizing body tropes to establish a need for cure or purification gained particularly vivid expression in a speech by Admiral César A. Guzzetti, then minister of foreign relations: "The social body of the country is contaminated by a disease that corrodes its insides and forms antibodies. These antibodies must not be considered in the same way that one considers a germ. In proportion to the government's control and destruction of guerrilla warfare, the action of the antibodies is going to disappear."[142]

Guzzetti asserted that right-wing terrorist acts were only "a natural reaction of a sick body," a matter expressed as well in a military training document: "When the Nation is sick . . . the nationalist reaction emerges almost like something natural."[143] In defining this natural reaction of right-wing violence, Guzzetti further stated that "subversion or terrorism from the right is not such."

Immediately apparent among the many thematic threads and intertexts woven into Guzzetti's figurative passage is the reintroduction of the prefix *anti* (antibodies), occasioning another binary opposition: Disease (or germs) ◄——► Antibody or, more broadly, Poison ◄——► Remedy.[144] This pair of oppositions is particularly significant because, as Guzzetti developed it, the repressive forces' dependence on subversion for their existence was explicit: "The action of the antibodies is going to disappear" in proportion to the subversives' disappearance.[145] Here, then, is another expression of the Process's self-deconstruction through the same acts by which it achieved its goal: The "antibodies" eliminated *themselves* as they eliminated the "germs" that—in the myth's version—brought them into being. (Outside of the myth, however, the process was inverted: The Junta preceded the "germs" or "subversives" that it brought into being.) Guzzetti's passage then went further to solidify the military's self-elimination by reassigning the subject of the verb "disappear": With each *desaparecido*, in effect, one of the repressors "disappeared." Were the Junta to neglect the constant invention of its Enemy, it too would soon be "absent forever." The Hero thus found himself "in the unhappy position of having a vital need for the very enemy he wishes to destroy."[146] Synthesizing the germ conceit and the Christian model discussed earlier, the Junta as vicar of Christ might have expressed itself well in His words: "Behold, I cast out devils and perform cures today and tomorrow, and the third day I am to end my course."[147]

The Junta's method of repressing "subversion" stylized as a disease inside the *corpus mysticum* of Argentina was not unlike the measures taken—according to an order published at the end of the seventeenth century—when the plague hit a European town.[148] Among those measures were the prohibition of emigration (under penalty of death), of leaving one's home (under penalty of death), and of any form of communication with others. Systematized and omnipresent surveillance controlled movement, a task that was undertaken by "a considerable body of militia, commanded by good officers and men of substance." Syndics assigned to each street went from house to house daily, to inform themselves of the occupants' state and to "observe their actions." The occupants were required "to speak the truth under the pain of death." Many other tactics common with authoritarian repression—constant registration, State control of personal and domestic matters, the imposition of military order in an attempt to solve a nonmilitary problem—were present in the plague town as well, a matter that led Michel Foucault to conclude that "the plague gave rise to disciplinary projects" in the same way that the leper gave rise to rituals of exclusion.[149]

Posing the depiction of "subversion" as a disease against the repression of a plague-stricken town's inhabitants highlights the germ trope's expression of a mythological tenet discussed above: the necessity of repression for the common good. Argentines living through the years of the "dirty war" were expected to accept the eminent necessity of repression for their common well-being as a social body, in the same way that the inhabitants of the plague-stricken town were obliged to understand that they were locked inside their houses (from the outside, the syndics carrying the keys) not because the State was evil but because the authorities were safeguarding their best interest. The repression was thereby naturalized as the unfortunate but necessary means to cleanse the social body of the contaminant destroying it from within. In the Argentine case the plague model was particularly apt because—as I shall develop in the following chapter—the Oedipal structure of detention center violence recalls that the Junta, like Oedipus, turned out to be the *cause* of the plague rather than its cure. Once the "dirty war" methodology has been revealed, it becomes clear that the Junta "passed a poison off as a remedy."[150]

The insistence on the bond between the repressors and their victims was also implied, now by negation, in Guzzetti's statement, "Subversion or terrorism from the right is not such." Patent in this phrase is the simultaneity of contradictory meanings on the model of the paradox "this statement is false." The mixed message, characteristic of Junta discourse, resulted in an inescapable double bind. In order to express what he meant to say, Guzzetti's phrase must read: "There is no such thing as right-wing subversion or terrorism," or "What the right-wing extremists do cannot [by definition—they are acts of the Right] be considered subversion or terrorism." What Guzzetti said, however, affirmed what it also negated: "Right-wing subversion or terrorism" was first established, and then it was taken away ("is not such"). One recalls Roland Barthes's observation that in speech one can only erase what he or she has said by adding to it, by "showing the eraser itself."[151] What "subversion or terrorism from the right is not such" accomplishes, well beyond its intentions, is first the equation of the repressors with their victims (we are subversives and terrorists/they are subversives and terrorists) and then the denial of that equation in a gesture of undoing. The retroactive reading (we are not subversives and terrorists) clashes the negation into the heuristic reading (we are subversives and terrorists), creating two conflicting meanings, both obtaining, that generate through their juxtaposition a third meaning that sheds its absurdity only within the myth: We are the same as them, but different. Violence from the Left is the evil infliction of suffering. Military violence, however, is emptied of its evil content, is neutralized. As the euphemism *quirófano* implies, some instances of causing pain—such as that pain caused by the surgeon's scalpel—fall outside of violence because their intent is to heal rather than to inflict suffering. This is how the Argentine military saw its role: The pain it caused was virtuous, not violent, because its intent was to heal the sick body of the *patria*.

The myth from which Guzzetti spoke accounts for part of that difference by naturalizing the propriety of military action. As the military saw it terrorism from the Right (which was not such) was a natural function of the diseased body of Argentina; it was a spontaneous, self-generating reaction, a biological matter of fact. That the germs were "natural" too, however, that social unrest was also the effect of a "diseased" sociopolitical body and not its cause, is conspicuously absent in the trope. In Plato's *Timaeus* natural disease was compared to a living organism that must be left to develop in accordance with its own norms and rhythms; remedies—in the present case, the one described by Guzzetti—were thought to perturb the natural progression of the illness and thus were considered "the enemy of the living in general, whether healthy or sick."[152] "Dirty war" mythology, in contrast, held the opposite view: Right-wing "terrorism and subversion" were integral to the political *corpus mysticum* that they protected, while the same acts from the Left were alien contaminants that infiltrated the body, disrupting its nature. The germs' proliferation therefore had to be preempted.

Metaphorical depiction of subversive germs infiltrating the State's "living organism" was an extreme expression of the discourse of exclusion by which the Enemy was separated from Argentina's sociopolitical body. Even though the victims of Junta violence were Argentine rather than international conspirators, these victims were conceptually ostracized from their national identity when the myth qualified them as "infiltrators," *apátridas* ("countryless"), or "antinational." Isolation from but at the same time constituency within the Argentine social body would seem to imply the possibility of removing "subversives" by surgical warfare, as expressed metaphorically in the torture centers' vernacular signifier, *quirófano*: "Just as a surgeon cuts and mutilates a limb to save the whole body when there is no other efficacious remedy," so the military amputated "subversion" from the social body.[153] In a similar fashion selective and remedial destruction was expressed in the biophysical trope: The germs ("subversion") would be engulfed and destroyed by (military) antibodies that distinguished between the disease and the organism it was afflicting, eliminating the former to protect the latter.

Rituals of cure and of cleansing integral to the psychic economies of many cultures often function in much the same way as they are represented in "dirty war" mythology: An illness or evil is concentrated into a scapegoat either alien to, separated from, or disposable within a particular social context, and the suffering patient or population is then symbolically purged of the illness or evil by the ritual destruction of that scapegoat. The *curanderos* in Peru, to cite an example from the folk cures that manifest externalizing cleansing metaphors most visibly, rub a patient's body with a guinea pig that is believed to absorb the illness. The transfer of the illness from the patient's body to the animal's purifies the former as it objectifies and concentrates the illness outside of the patient's body. The guinea pig is then killed, and the disease "dies" with it. Residuals of the disease that resisted externalization by absorption into the guinea pig are similarly expelled metaphorically through the ritualized vomiting that completes the cure.[154] Thus an "infiltrating" illness/evil is concentrated into and objectified by a scapegoat (the guinea pig, the "subversive"), and destruction of this scapegoat cleanses the body of the patient or the sociopolitical body of Argentina that was depicted as a living organism.

Such is the structure of Guzzetti's germ/antibody conceit, but it is undermined by the manner in which the "dirty war"—a war "without quarter," as the Junta made clear from the start—was fought.[155] The task forces as "antibodies" attacked the Argentine social body far more than they did the "germs" that were ostensibly targeted. An apt pathological metaphor to represent the "dirty war" outside of Junta mythology would have to be based on lupus, a disease that turns the body's own antibodies (military) against the tissue and vital organs (Argentine population and corporate entities) that these antibodies are designed to protect.[156] Alternatively, emphasizing the "external" nature of the military as a corporate entity separate from the civilian population and stressing the neocolonial aspects of the "dirty war" (the Junta as an army occupying its own country), the lupus trope could be replaced with one of chemotherapy as an oncological remedy. In this case an "outside" agent (chemicals/military) assault the entire body indiscriminately to eliminate the cancer cells ("subversion") that are "hidden" inside the healthy tissue. In both the lupus and chemotherapy tropes, the social body suffers a grand assault "without quarter," with the antibodies or chemicals annihilating undesirable elements while bringing the entire body to the verge of destruction.[157]

Outside of military mythology the "subversives" were not sufficiently distinguished and separated from the social body to have their elimination purge rather than traumatize Argentina. Guzzetti's conceit, in combination with the repression it misrepresented, thus manifests a *peripeteia*, a reversal: The remedy turns out to be the disease.[158] The Junta was the predominant cause of the woes for which it believed itself the solution, and it therefore, like Oedipus, had to be driven from the State before "health" could be restored.

Whether depicted as a germ, an archetype of monstrosity, an invisible force, or an Antichrist, the Enemy was established in hostile polarization to the Hero whose quest was to purge, to cleanse, to slay, to restore "health" and Natural Order. Once the attributes of defilement were consolidated in the Enemy, each victim absorbed into Junta mythology "obviously appears as the all-powerful cause of all the trouble in a community that is itself nothing but trouble. The roles are reversed. The victimizers see themselves as the passive victims of their own victim, and they see their victim as supremely active, eminently capable of destroying them." René Girard also pointed out that

At the time of the Black Death, foreigners were killed, and Jews were massacred, and a century or two later, "witches" were burned, for reasons strictly identical to the ones we found [and we presently find] in our myths. All these unfortunates were the indirect victims of internal tensions brought about by epidemics of plagues and other social disasters for which their persecutors held them responsible. The imaginary crimes and real punishments of these victims are the crimes and punishments we find in mythology. Why should we have to believe, in the case of mythology only, that if the crimes are imaginary, the punishments and the victims themselves cannot be real?[159]

IV

Interactions between the Hero and Enemy as described above are divisible into a series of narrative functions that constitute a generic myth of the "dirty war," itself created by reintegrating the three submyths (International Conspiracy, Metaphysical Enemy, and Holy War) into the single narrative structure from which I have extracted them. My use of the term "function" is broadened from its strictly morphological usage as introduced by Vladimir Propp; the narrative units discussed here in some cases represent sequences, clusters of functions, and they go beyond strictly morphological concerns to incorporate commentary into enumeration of the "dirty war's" syntagmatic structure. This departure reflects my intent in the following discussion not to offer a morphological analysis of the myth for its own sake but rather to explore the narrative structure of "dirty war" mythology insofar as identification and discussion of the narrative components contribute beyond formalism to the overriding thematic concerns of my inquiry.[160]

ABSENCE AROUSES THE HERO

"In terms of narrative, myth is the imitation of actions near or at the conceivable limits of desire."[161] Because desire always has its object, is desire *for something*, or, as Kojève put it, is "the presence of an absence," what-is-missing engenders and engages the desire of the Hero, predisposing him to the quest by which he will recompense the lack.[162] "In contrast to the knowledge that keeps man in a passive quietude, Desire dis-quiets him and moves him to action."[163] Absence of Western and Christian values and other intrinsic components of the Natural Order arouse the Hero's desire to act. That absence was occasioned by others (either explicitly or by implication in the death of Juan Perón, the incompetence and corruption of Isabel Perón's administration, and the lack of civilian "maturity" for self-government), and it indexed the gravity of sociopolitical problems that were manifesting the lack of order ("subversion" and armed "Marxist" insurrection). These lacks (along with the Junta's lack of and desire for power, as discussed later) motivated the Hero, who responded mimetically by creating other lacks (*desaparecidos*) and by terrorizing the public through violence lacking reason (a void in which the refrains *Por algo será* and *Algo habrá[n] hecho* echoed).

Chaos reigned in Argentina, but the Hero was stirred by his recognition that beyond the lack of social and political stability there was an Order that—were he to have the courage, the vision, and the power—he could restore to the *patria*. In the Catholic traditions informing Junta mythopoesis, that Order was metonymized in Christ. Civilization as an extension of man's desire, as an ordering and humanizing of natural chaos under the aegis of a God whose apotheosis was deeply (and circularly) indebted to that same Order, was apparent in the apocalyptic imagery that permeated the mission of the "dirty war" at all levels. In the following schematization prepared by Northrop Frye, another many-into-One reduction is evident as one moves from the left-hand to the right-hand columns. This system of simplification and urge toward homogeneity provides a religious paradigm for the reductionism discussed earlier as a central characteristic of Junta mytho-logic.

divine world	=	society of gods	=	One God
human world	=	society of men	=	One Man
animal world	=	sheepfold	=	One Lamb
vegetable world	=	garden or park	=	One Tree (of Life)
mineral world	=	city	=	One Building, Temple, Stone[164]

The concept "Christ" is the nexus in which all categories of worldly and cosmic reality fuse: Christ is the one God and the one Man, the Lamb of God, the tree of life (also depicted as a vine), and the rebuilt temple (metaphorically equated with the risen body). If He were absent from Argentina, then the Natural Order that consolidates all of the parts, in which everything integrates into the significant whole, would likewise be lacking: Chaos and meaninglessness would reign. For that reason evil was equated as much in the Argentine military mentality as in Christian canon with disorder. The ultimate remedy for disorder was seen as the ultimate internal source of cosmic perfection, Christ, in whom the creation (including the Hero's Argentina) was joined to the divine person as His own in perfection and unity. Christ, the Hero reasoned, must therefore be restored at any cost. But because Christ indeed was physically absent from the world and acted only through His faithful, that restoration would require a vicar to fulfill His will on earth: the messianic Hero.[165] The purported agenda of Christ's restoration thus occasioned the displacement from *corpus mysticum* to *corpus reipublicae mysticum*, after which politico-religious agendas and their accompanying atrocities were sanctioned in His name. Not Christ's will but the Hero's, not the Word but its interpretation, not the Natural Order but the Process of National Reorganization, not Christianity per se but "our way of being Christian" were what the Junta achieved empirically, while in the mythology the "not but" construction was erased, the juxtaposing elements made congruous, the "dirty" war made "holy."

The mythopoesis elaborating Junta violence called the concept of absence into play on the most fundamental level, where myth displaced reality—absented it through negation—in order to make the "dirty war" possible. It then denied its own negation by setting the Hero loose to fight his battles against *real* Argentines, outside of the myth, whose tortured bodies became the ritual objects on which reality was unmade and the truth of the myth was celebrated. "The function of myth is to empty reality: It is, literally, a ceaseless flowing out, a hemorrhage, or perhaps an evaporation, in short a perceptible absence."[166] The Junta emptied the "dirty war" of its real content as it mythologized it. In doing so it created "a perceptible absence," was aroused by a desire to rectify this absence that it had itself created (an autoerotic arousal), and then acted mythologically, *but within the reality it emptied of meaning,* by imagining that paramilitary operations were appropriate solutions for social, political, and economic problems. The mythology of the Hero created the lack that brought the Hero into being. "Rupture, cleavage . . . make absence emerge—just as the cry does not stand out against a background of silence, but on the contrary makes silence emerge as silence."[167]

THE HERO IS CALLED INTO ACTION

In this function the desire of the Hero to rectify the Absence is made manifest in specific actions, and the quest is thereby initiated. The Enemy assassinated; he assaulted soldiers, police, security personnel, citizens; he blew up buildings, abducted people, robbed banks; he spread evil doctrines; he undermined the infrastructure of Western and Christian civilization; he disrupted the Natural Order. Apprised of these misfortunes, the Hero's call to adventure was "like a spontaneous reaction" for he had to restore "the empire of virtue, well-being and grandeur."[168] The Hero was drawn spontaneously, naturally, into "a tremendous political vacuum capable of sinking us into anarchy and dissolution,"[169] into the void created by the absences that now called him to task as Hero, as Messiah, delivering the People because they were incapable of delivering themselves.

AN INTERDICTION IS ADDRESSED TO THE HERO

A discourse implied by the values of "Western and Christian civilization" warned the Hero to avoid the violent repressive methods that, should he employ them, would constitute a violation of his own doctrine and purpose, of his essence as Hero and defender of the Natural Order. This discourse was on occasion also made specific: in international human rights conventions to which Argentina was a party, in formal actions by the Jimmy Carter administration and the Organization of American States in response to Junta human rights violations, in ecclesiastical declarations, and in other domestic and international protests against "disappearances." The interdiction argued: "Do not abuse your Power. Do not become a terrorist to fight terrorism. Do not violate the international human rights accords to which you are party.[170] Do not violate the values of Western and Christian civilization that you uphold or the spirit of the Natural Order that you defend." But as a lack initially motivated the Hero, now "the law that forbade gave rise to a desire for what was forbidden"—to be like the Enemy. "Transgression of the law is the goal of the struggle against the prohibition: *The obstacle is the essence of desire*."[171]

THE HERO GOES TO WAR/
THE DONOR PROVIDES THE HERO WITH THE MAGICAL OBJECT
WITH WHICH HE WILL DEFEAT THE ENEMY

The Hero was tested and attacked by an armed Enemy (Montoneros, ERP) but also, and most overwhelmingly, by an invisible Enemy ("subversion") who was not readily identifiable, who was as elusive as he was evil. In order to win his struggle to restore the Natural Order, the Hero needed a means to make the Enemy visible, a "magical object" (in Propp's term) that would empower the Hero to *locate* the Enemy as well as destroy him. In the myth of the "dirty war," the *picana* as used during torture fulfilled this role of the magical object.[172] The functions of the Donor, responsible in the narrative for providing the Hero with the means by which he realizes his quest, were in the "dirty war" myth assumed by the Enemy himself because he (as torture victim) endowed the object (*picana*) with the "magical" properties that empowered the Hero. Torture rituals, discussed in Chapter 2, translated the victim's pain into the illusion of the Junta's power. "Subversives" became Victim-Donors at the torture table because their bodies charged the *picana* with this "magical" power by which the Hero fulfilled his quest.

Application of the magical object (*picana*) to the Victim-Donor's body first dismantled the Enemy's "invisibility"—the victim became visibly, undeniably (and tautologically) the Enemy by virtue of having been abducted and tortured, and similarly the magical object in combination with "interrogation" resulted in "confessions" that made other "subversives" visible. What outside of the myth constituted a "disappearance" was thus inverted within the myth: Abduction and torture demanded the *appearance* of the Enemy, they were the Hero's means of *making the Enemy visible*. The priest, the barber, the psychiatrist "disappeared" from the social register precisely because they were being made to appear as Enemy in the mythological register.

Once the *aparecido* is apprehended, applying the *picana* to his body (as Victim-Donor) empowered the Hero to realize the objectives of his quest. The "magic" of that process was well illustrated by Elaine Scarry:

> As an actual physical fact, a weapon [*picana*] is an object that goes into the body and produces pain. As a perceptual fact [within the myth, for our purposes], it lifts the pain out of the body and makes it visible or, more precisely, it acts as a bridge or mechanism across which some of pain's attributes—its incontestable reality, its totality, its ability to eclipse all else, its power of dramatic alteration and world dissolution—can be lifted away from their source, can be separated from the sufferer and referred to power, broken off from the body and attached instead to the regime.[173]

The *picana* as a magical object "lifted" the pain out of the Victim-Donor's body and transferred its attributes to the Hero as power. Among those transposed and transferred attributes was one at the center of the mythopoesis that fabricated the context justifying the "dirty war" in its perpetrators' consciousness: "Dramatic alteration and world dissolution." The Junta annulled sociopolitical realities, made them "disappear," and filled the vacuum created by their absence with its "reorganizing" mythology.

Though the *picana* had its own power (its electrical discharge), in the myth of the "dirty war" it represented the greater Power by which the Hero realized his quest, the Power that the de facto Junta lacked legitimately but exercised through violent repression. The *picana* in itself had no direct access to Power; it could only tap into it when applied to the Enemy's body. The Hero was powerful only insofar as he tortured.

THE HERO VIOLATES THE INTERDICTION
AS HE DEFEATS HIS ENEMY

"We have used against the terrorists the same drastic methods that they have employed." "As legal forces we adapted many of our combat procedures to those used by subversion."[174] In these and many similar passages the Hero expressed the mimetic structure of his mission against the Enemy. By using "the same drastic methods" of terrorism to fight terrorism—these methods metonymized in the use of the magical object, the *picana* generating Power to defeat the Enemy—the Hero violated the interdiction in the second function above. There is a directly proportional relation between the Hero's acquisition of Power (through use of the magical object) to defeat the Enemy and the extent to which he undermined his own agenda by violating the interdiction and the principles he purported to defend. The Victim-Donor whose body endowed the *picana* with Power was ultimately the agent through which the Hero acted against his own interest, the agent who drew from the Hero his tragic flaw, because the only power the Victim-Donor contributed to the Hero was a power whose positive attributes were negated and channeled toward the Hero's self-destruction. The *picana* applied to the Victim-Donor's body afforded only an illusory power whose reality was defensible within the myth but not outside of it. It was a power that could only be exercised and abused—like the electric charge of the *picana* itself—but not legitimately possessed. It was a contingent power, a power detachable from its subject.

When the mythological struggle subsided with the Enemy's defeat, the myth then disclosed that the means of the Hero's victory (torture with the *picana*) were more "magical" than one had supposed: The Hero was transformed into the Enemy as one form of terrorism (Montoneros, ERP) was displaced by another (Junta). What the Hero assumed to be the virtuous realization of his messianic quest turned out to be the exercise of his tragic flaw. The Hero thus suffered the consequences of his mis-guided means, and the romantic narrative yielded to tragedy accord-ingly.[175] Because he became the Enemy as he defeated him, the Hero's final victory was in defeat of himself.

THE TRAGIC HERO'S VICTORY
IS ALSO HIS DEFEAT

The progression of the romantic myth of the "dirty war" toward the peripeteia that recast the Hero in the image of the Enemy illustrates Lévi-Strauss's observation that "mythical thought always progresses from the awareness of oppositions toward their resolution."[176] Although the Junta anticipated that resolution of oppositions would be realized in restored homogeneity via the annihilation of the Enemy, the narrative took a tragic turn instead as the Hero "disappeared" into the image of his antagonist. "Here we see the tragic hero as disturbing a balance in nature, nature being conceived as an order stretching over the two kingdoms of the visible and the invisible, a balance which sooner or later *must* right itself."[177] If the Enemy was he who violated the values of "Western and Christian civilization," then the Junta, by virtue of its violent methodol-ogy, was that Enemy par excellence.[178] And because the Hero's quest in Argentina was undertaken in the name of the kingdom in Heaven, because the Hero was called into action as the vicar of Christ, his fusion with the diabolically construed Enemy concluded the myth with a Hero built on the model of Algernon Swinburne's apocalyptic and oxymoronic concept: the "supreme evil, God."

V

The absence in Argentina of the Natural Order (consolidated by biblical imagery and medieval traditions into the mystical body of Christ) aroused in the Junta a desire to restore Order by annihilating the Enemy in whom evil and chaos were embodied. An implied and explicit interdiction forbade the Junta from using methods that violated human rights and fundamental values of the "Western and Christian civilization" under whose banner it crusaded. When the Junta responded and went to battle with messianic zeal, it violated that interdiction not simply because it resorted to political violence and terrorism as a means of repression, but also because these methods served as the quintessential function of its regime—as the purpose of its regime—and at once the means by which the political power of that regime was sustained. As General Albano Harguindeguy, then minister of the interior, put it, "The struggle against subversion characterizes and conditions each and every measure that the government adopts at all levels."[179] Within an enclosure of concentric circles representing the Process of National Reorganization, the inner-most circle was occupied by "the annihilation of subversion, in all of its manifestations" or, in other words, by torture and execution of "subversives." Occupying the privileged central point within that circle of tor-ture/execution, the point from which all others on the outer rings' circumferences had their reference, was the "magical object" empowering the repressors, the *picana*, as the metonymy of the Junta-in-Power. The Junta's entire political orientation—precisely because it was de facto and illegitimate—emanated outward from that locus. The detention center rituals implemented the Junta's agenda, legitimated it by creating the "subversives" who constantly reaffirmed the need for it, and generated the power that sustained the regime's ongoing "reorganization."[180]

These observations will gradually accumulate substantiation in the following chapters, particularly the last, in which Argentine torture and execution are considered in the context of human sacrifice as instituted in pre-Columbian Mesoamerica. In reviewing Aztec violence one readily recognizes that the mythological tenet necessitating human sacrifice—the sustenance of the Sun by nourishing it with victims' blood—is absolutely untenable, that the desire or need to institutionalize violence *precedes* the mythological system called forth to justify it. Mythology—in the Aztec case, in the Argentine case, and as a metacultural model applicable almost universally—arrives late to the scene in order to justify, by appeal to the symbolic order, the ritual violence that comes before it. "Ideas do not produce ritual; rather, ritual itself produces and shapes ideas, or even experiences and emotions."[181] The mythology of "dirty war" Argentina or Aztec Mesoamerica tidied up atrocity by depicting an authoritarian regime's acts as eschatological necessities (eliminating the Antichrist, restoring the Natural Order, sustaining the Sun), but the absurdity of these justifications in empirical terms—accompanied by the insistence of myths diverting that absurdity—reveal that the a priori institution of torture and execution services the generation of power, the ritual rehearsal of a "reorganized" truth, and the psychosexual dynamics that I shall review presently.

In the mythological narrative of the "dirty war," the torture victim's body provided access to power as the attributes of his or her pain were "lifted" and transferred to the repressing regime, but that power in real terms—outside of the myth—was only illusory. The power generated by the *picana* as it touched the body of a victim was not real beyond the immediate theater of domination in which it functioned (although the illusion of power was effectively exploited politically). What seemed advantageous in the "dirty war" narrative as a romance (torture as the Hero's means to fulfill his quest) proved outside of it to be counterproductive and to turn the Hero's destructive agenda against himself. My understanding of the *picana* as metonymy of the Junta-in-Power therefore requires greater precision: Because the *picana* was a symbolic representation of imaginary power, was dependent on an Other (the torture victim) to realize its function, resulted in the Junta's remaking of itself in the likeness of this adversarial Other, and represented a power that the de facto Junta could exploit but never legitimately possess, the *picana*, the "magical object," must be perceived as a metonymy representing the Junta's *desire* for power. It was ultimately this desire beneath all others that aroused the Hero's action in the first narrative function discussed earlier.

As Bernadette Bucher observed in discussing the relation of ritual symbolism (Junta mythology and detention center rituals) to the meaning of historical events (the "dirty war" outside of Junta mythology),

> The functions of this symbolism, which longs to accomplish in fact what it signifies [in myth and ritual], are not simply "magical" and thus "null," as one might be tempted to believe. They also serve to detach and reenforce systems of classification linking the cosmic order to the social and political order, and . . . governing the behavior and actions of a social group toward the new event it must confront.[182]

My task now will be to explore the Junta's desire to accomplish in fact what its myth signifies and to do so by focusing on the central lack into which the *picana* rises.

4

In the Name
of the Father

CREON: *Laius—what did* he *do?*
OEDIPUS: *Vanished,*
swept from sight, murdered in his tracks.

—*Sophocles,* Oedipus the King

I

THE TENDENCY IN "Western and Christian civilization" to repress human sexuality and to divert its insistent resurgence into religious violence gained abundant expression in the early Middle Ages. When Palladius's *Lausiac History* was being translated from Greek to Latin for use by Western monks—to cite one subtle but telling example—a religious tale devoid of erotic content was overhauled by the translators to stress the sinfulness of sexual desire.[1] As the Greek text related the particular episode in question, Marcarius of Alexandria was weaving a basket and praying when a mosquito bit his leg. Marcarius angrily crushed the mosquito with a spontaneous, reactive swat of his hand, but he then repented the outburst of violence and recognized the need to repent his sinfulness in kind. A swamp infested with insects provided the agency of retribution. Marcarius dived in naked, wallowed in his penance, and reemerged six months later, unrecognizable but atoned.

147

In the Latin translation of this episode, however, the mosquito was deleted from the narrative completely, despite its centrality to the thematic integrity forged in the original by linking the punishment (insect bites) to the transgression (killing an insect that bites). The Latin translation enacted its displacement by substituting the mosquito as instigator of sin with Christianity's abiding preoccupation: sexual desire. A lustful fantasy was what motivated Marcarius's penance in the swamp in the Western, Latin version, and a repressed sexual impulse was thus metamorphosed into a religious expression with this transition, this translation, brokered through corporal punishment. The eroticism absent from the Greek narrative was supplied by translation into a tradition obsessed with repressing it and was then duly neutralized with violence. Indeed, if the mosquito's replacement—sexual desire—is projected backward into the original Greek text, that modification yields representation of sexuality itself violently destroyed, crushed by Marcarius's hand falling on it.[2]

The diversion of sexual desire into religious violence is a reappearing motif of considerable currency in the episodes of radical Christianity, ranging from the self-castration of extremists (like Origen and the many other eunuchs) to the ascetics who compensated in perseverance what they lacked in drama, searching for God in the desert often only to discover their own bodies.[3] Pope Gregory the Great's saintly anecdotes of those religious few who turned away from "the changes of chance of this fleeting world" include one notable narrative relating directly to the point. Having overcome great sexual temptation earlier in his ascetic life, Saint Benedict was suddenly overwhelmed by the image of "a certain woman," to such a degree that "the holy man was assaulted with such a terrible temptation of the flesh, as he never felt the like in all his life."[4] Thoughts of the woman "so mightily inflamed with concupiscence the soul of God's servant" that he was "almost overcome with pleasure, he was of a mind to forsake the wilderness."

> But, suddenly assisted with God's grace, he came to himself, and seeing many thick briers and nettle-bushes to grow hard by, off he cast his apparel, and threw himself into the midst of them, and there wallowed so long that, when he rose up, all his flesh was pitifully torn; and so by the wounds of his body, he cured the wounds of his soul, in that he turned pleasure into pain.[5]

Whether the phrase "to grow hard by" is a vernacular expression or a translation error, it well illustrates the point: "Off he cast his apparel" and Benedict goes down on nettles that replaced the woman as the agent "to grow hard by."[6] Pleasure was detached from the sexual fantasy, negated, and diverted through the nettles to revised expression as a celebration of religious agony, with the eroticism resurfacing symbolically. Gregory explained further that the "outward burning" of Benedict's torn flesh extinguished the evil "carnal cogitations, [which] did inwardly burn in his soul." It was by the exchange of one burning passion (sexuality) for another (religious agony) that Benedict accomplished his diversion, "because he made a change of the fire."

Legends that later accumulated around this episode of erotic diversion further poeticized Benedict's mortification, contributing additional tropes to the sexualization of the nettles as substitute for the "certain woman." The thorns that tore the saint's flesh were said to have turned into roses, thus enhancing the symbolic representation of this- and otherworldly love by calling into play the rose's two-tiered tradition of symbolism.[7] The rose's representation of completion, perfection, beauty, and other concepts of religiosity and purity was no doubt the intent here, but rose symbolism, like Benedict's piety, is never free of its carnal lining, carrying specific reference to the female genitalia and, by brief extension, to the echo of virgin fornication as "deflowering." The trope was complete with blood flowing in one direction toward Benedict's wounds and in the other toward the rose's color. Rather than deflowering the woman, Benedict "flowered" the nettles.

Christianity's obsessive interrelation of sin, the flesh, and violent atonement later gained more sustained expression in the hagiography of another manifestation of flower poetics, Rosa de Lima, who occupies a privileged position in Christendom as first saint of the New World and patron saint of the Americas.[8] Born into the baroque era's "veritable corpus of macabre eroticism,"[9] Rosa de Lima maintained a rigor of mortifications that render Benedict's naked wallow in the bramble bed modest. Like Catherine of Siena preceding her, Rosa engaged in a voluptuous, cruel agenda of self-torture inextricably linked to her mystical preparation for Christ the Bridegroom, who sanctioned and encouraged her mortifications, planning later to "enjoy her as his Wife eternally."[10] When one recalls that the speaking subject of Christ's discourse is Rosa herself, Rosa's discourse of the Other, and when we view the drama with the Bridegroom's presence restored to the imaginary realm that brought it forth, it then becomes especially evident that Rosa's mortifications served an agenda other than the purported Divine one, that a rationale was invented to sanction the desire for the suffering that preceded it. For Rosa, as for Benedict in his brambles, the transformation of sexual pleasure into self-inflicted pain was accompanied by its inversion: Pain became pleasure, as eroticized as it was sanctified. In 1671, the same year Rosa de Lima was canonized, the Dominican priest Juan Meléndez explained that Rosa's "greatest pleasure and consolation was to open up her flesh"; forbidding Rosa self-torture, he concluded, would therefore be "to deprive her the opportunity for so much pleasure."[11] Erotic pleasure returned to Rosa after having made its detour through pain endowed with transcendental purpose.

Rosa de Lima's mortifications as acts of mystical love, as preparations for union with the heavenly Bridegroom, are further revealed as diversions of normal sexuality when the this-worldly factors precipitating specific episodes of asceticism and self-inflicted pain are considered. When Rosa was five, to cite one cornerstone in her deification of diverted sexuality, she chopped off her hair (believing its beauty might lead men to sinful thoughts) and took a lifetime vow of virginity. Later many of Rosa's self-tortures (lime rubbed onto her hands and *ají* onto her eyelids, a heavy stovepot dropped onto her foot, a hatpin jammed into her scalp) were designed to preempt the social outings arranged by her mother to expose the girl to appropriate suitors. On one occasion, when Rosa's mother began arrangements for her daughter's ideal marriage, Rosa rejected the possibility by resort to her presumed status as Christ's wife, asking if she was expected to abandon God for a man.[12] Rather than courting, Rosa withdrew to the tiny hermitage in which "my Husband and I fit well," and the ceremony of erotic torture ensued.[13] On another occasion the "devil" appeared at that same hermitage in the guise of a handsome man who "sent her lascivious signs with his eyes and mouth." Rosa responded by running inside her house and locking the door; she then "undressed, and with an iron chain . . . gave herself so many and such bloody lashes that the blood flowed down to the floor."[14] Rosa's repertory of austerities on earth in preparation for matrimony with Christ hereafter was gruesome, including a daily schedule of ten hours of work, twelve hours of mortification and prayer (the latter often recited while hanging by her hair from a peg in the wall), and two hours of sleep (on a bed made of "three of the most knotty and crooked willow trunks," the cracks between them filled with "pieces of rooftiles and broken plates and bowls").[15] Her diet's staple was ashes mixed with bitter herbs. Flagellation was routine (but augmented in response to particularly "sinful" occasions), as was the wearing of a silver crown of thorns with ninety-nine barbs rotated regularly to keep all parts of the scalp perpetually wounded. No part of Rosa's body could be spared the glorified pain. When it once occurred to her that the bottoms of her feet remained untortured, she compensated for the oversight by walking barefooted across the iron of a hot stove. "Lord, increase my sufferings," Rosa prayed at the hour of her death, making the agenda explicit, "and with them increase thy love in my heart."

As Rosa de Lima's deathbed supplication illustrates, Christian mortification agendas often establish a proportional relation between pain and love. There are, however, more factors at play than Rosa's simple relation accounts for. The concept of "love" signifies simultaneously in two registers: The mortifications are set in motion by denial of carnal love, of sexuality, but this flesh-bound love is then disembodied through mortifications penalizing the body, symbolically mutilating the body that experiences it. Love is then transcendentalized, either by stylizing the carnal model into mystical love for an imaginary deity (as in Rosa's case) or more generally by desexualizing it into the Platonic love propagated in the New Testament. What mediates that transition from human sexuality to divine love in the extreme cases—and even in the paradigmatic case, if we recall Christ-the-man's crucifixion in relation to Adam's sin—is the interposition of violence between them. A diversion through pain consecrates the denial of sexuality and transforms the one love into the other; the ascetic, the self-mortifier, makes a "change of fire." The "sin" of the flame's heat is neutralized by the penance of its burn. The more psychosexual demands on the subject are denied and diverted, the more pathological their symbolic expression in the subject's behavior; Rosa's proportional relation of love and suffering is salvaged in this balancing operation of psychic pressure and the deformation of normal sexual expression.

It is at this juncture of psychosexuality and Christianity that the Junta's discourse on love assumes its full signification by calling "love's" two meanings into relation. Like Rosa de Lima, the Argentine military believed that "love can be the motive for an act of force, for a punishment that helps to perfect the sinner."[16] The detention center victims were "perfected" at the torture table. General Ramón Camps further contributed to the just-war discourse of Christian charity by giving love the privileged position:

It is love that prioritizes and legitimates the actions of soldiers.

The use of force to put an end to violence does not imply hate since it is nothing other than the difficult search for the restoration of love.

In the ["dirty"] war we are fighting, love of the social body that we want to protect is what comes first in all of our actions.[17]

Admiral Massera concurred ("our work began with love"), and General Videla, for his part, later described the Final Document on the Disappeared—which sought to justify the violence—as an "act of love."[18] The Junta's insistence of love was intended to evoke not the sexual act, of course, but rather the Christian ideal, the "corrective" love propounded by Augustine and rehearsed throughout the Middle Ages. This was "a love for one's enemies that did not preclude a benevolent severity."[19] Such love as upheld by Thomas Aquinas provided further that "officials in authority could legitimately kill evil-doers when they were motivated by charity."[20] In this context of crusading Christianity, the Junta maintained that the torture it inflicted had transcendental value, that the pain it exacted was constructive rather than destructive, or, more accurately, was constructive *insofar as it destroyed*. The pain, as Rosa de Lima would have it, was the measure of the love. Rosa mutilated her own body and the Junta mutilated the bodies of others in accordance with their respective Christian agendas: Rosa's to perfect herself for the heavenly Bridegroom, and the Junta's to restore the Natural Order to Argentina as rehearsed in "perfecting" the *desaparecidos*. "The redeemed person was a tiny microcosm of a universe that had begun to undergo a gigantic mutation."[21]

The Junta's "dirty war" love was, however, more complex than the ambiguous naiveté of its Christian discourse suggested. As expressed through the task forces deploying Junta policy in the detention centers, the "act of love" at the torture table was not of the metaphysical, Christian variety but was rather sexual love aberrantly redirected (again like Rosa de Lima's) through violence. The eroticism of Argentine torture that I shall review presently cast a blatantly sexual gloss on the "dirty war's" "difficult search for the restoration of love." The torturers brought the "act of love" to bear down brutally on the social body metonymized in each victim.[22]

The concept of "love" in "dirty war" discourse thus signifies in two registers: metaphysical, Christian love on the one hand and perverse sexual love on the other. In the "dirty war," as in the autoassault of Rosa de Lima, eroticism *preceded* Christian love; psychosexual impulses were denied, diverted through torture, and transcendentalized into Christian canon. It was not in the first instance Christianity that repressed sexuality; denied sexuality rather summoned Christianity forth as the rationale to fortify denial and to congratulate sexuality's diversion through aberration (in this case eroticized torture) by endowing that detour with transcendental meaning. The Junta's Christian discourse doubled back retroactively to sanctify torture, while the diversion of sexuality was enforced by the same torture rituals that lent it symbolic representation. The detour from sexual to metaphysical love left behind discernible traces that related erotic violence both to the psychosexual crisis (on an Oedipal model, as I shall discuss) rehearsed in "dirty war" aberrations and to the canon of "our way of being Christian" that sanctified it. The prime mover of the "dirty war," the common denominator that reconciled the Christian myth with the torture rituals and impelled the two forward in tandem, was in the last analysis a psychosexual paradigm thrown into motion by the "act of love" clashing its one signification into the other.

II

Torture merges the carnal act of love with violence. The eroticism of torture is first suggested by the ritual form—as inefficient as it is dramatic—that "executions" often assume. As discussed in Chapter 2, the bloody, eighteenth-century spectacles of atrocity that brought real and mythic dissenters to their demise were, like the religious mortifications preceding them, directed at the body rather than the being of the victim. The "thousand deaths" celebrated a prolonged mutilation of the flesh rather than an expeditious elimination of an adversary. Torture spectacles in these, as well as in the abstracted Argentina instances, mimed the sexual act in their structure of graduated intensity, in their fascination with the multiplicity of responses made possible through exploration of a body's diverse sensitivities, and in their climactic denouement of explicit or contained Dionysian frenzy. At the same time, however, they mocked the act of love by reversing its intent, emptying the sexual structure of affection and filling it with brutality, annulling reciprocity and replacing it with unilateral domination, and refining technique to maximize ecstatic pain rather than ecstatic pleasure. From the opposite direction this mock morphological similitude of torture and lovemaking was given canonical support as Christianity's early theologians depicted copulation in terms of violence rather than affection. In *The City of God* and later in *Contra Julian*, for example, Augustine described copulation so horrifically that it seemed an act of torture, the entire body lurching into a kind of spasm, overtaken (like the body tortured with the *picana*) by terrible jerks.[23] Tertullian concurred: "The whole human frame is shaken," while it also "foams with semen."[24]

The derivation of pleasure from another's pain also contributes substantially to the bond forged between eroticism and violence. Spectacles of atrocity—at once irresistible and grotesque, erotic and disgusting, absolutely necessary and absolutely unthinkable—aroused in their public a *sensual* experience redoubled in intensity by virtue of the ambivalence it generated. The ritual had sufficient free play to accommodate morbid pleasure during the spectacle's prolongation before finally quelling emotional and cognitive ambivalence by "killing" one of the dichotomous counterparts (the disgust of one's pleasure as voyeur in the orgy of violence, the guilt of one's joy) with the victim. The ritual accent thus fell on the other, heavily stressed counterpart that reaffirmed the truth of the spectacle and the propriety of the crowd's climaxing together in an exultant celebration of unity. The baker dusted to numbness in his flour, the farmer holding a cow by a rope, the parish priest steeped in the monotony of venial confessions were all retrieved from their daily drabness and awakened suddenly by this explosion of blood at the limits of conceivable experience, the spectacle impacting their entire instinctual constitution, be the victim a flayed Saint Bartholomew (undressed twice, once of clothes, once of skin) or the common criminal whose real or mythic transgressions earned his body the privilege of serving as agency of eroticized violence and as object of the sensual gaze.

The greatest measure of erotic satisfaction derived from the agony of a dominated Other, however, is of course allotted to the torturers themselves. An SS guard at a Nazi concentration camp, to cite one succinct example that makes the point directly, testified, "Usually I keep on hitting [the prisoner] until I ejaculate."[25] Sexual perversion bound to violence is also frequently evidenced outside of penal contexts in eroticized executions that tend, like institutionalized torture proper, to ritualize and prolong the victim's destruction (in some cases providing, through documentation and preservation, for its later repetition). Again like institutionalized torture, sexually motivated murders often recontextualize atrocity within a mythology that—together with its rituals—establishes a delusional justification, providing symbolic access to the psychopathology expressed in the aberration. Sessions of "foreplay" preceding a victim's execution introduce the eroticism of violence at its extreme. These events recently have included—beyond rape, sodomy, and other forms of sexual assault—the production of pornographic movies and audio recordings of victims pleading for mercy; biting (particularly of the breasts, with a nipple bitten off in one case); knife slashes; strangulation; and sexual arousal by cutting open women's abdomens to produce a flow of blood. Necrophilia is prevalent, as are mutilation, decapitation, cannibalism, positioning of corpses in sexual postures, castration (one woman was stabbed to death because she refused to chew off the penis of a man also held at gunpoint by a perpetrator "on a mission to kill by removing genitals"), and the storage of corpses for later rituals. One perpetrator highlighted the onanistic nature of eroticized torture—the victims reduced to objects, props, in the perpetrator's autoerotic theater—by default when he described the pleasures of throttling, mutilating, disemboweling, and eating his victims as "much greater than I experience while masturbating."[26]

Rather than cataloging extraneous horrors ad nauseam, I will assume that the erotic dimension of torture is sufficiently introduced and turn to "lustful murderous drives" in the specific Argentine events under analysis. My immediate concern is to present "dirty war" violence as the "emotional and erotic expression of a [militarized] nation," gradually folding in the Christian constituents of the psychosexuality-violence-religion nexus as the discussion progresses.[27]

The following testimony relates abuses suffered by a victim in the city of Rosario four years prior to the 1976 coup d'état that inaugurated the "dirty war" as an official government program.

> They tie me down by my ankles and wrists and begin to torture me with the *picana*, especially on my breasts, genitals and armpits. They alternate the *picana* with feeling me and masturbating, insulting me the entire time and saying the most disgusting vulgarities. . . . The torturer insisted that I insult him, provoking me by saying that I surely thought he was a sadist and that I would describe what he was doing as "feeling me up." But I was wrong: He was a scientist, that's why he accompanied all of his actions by explications concerning my physique, my tolerance, [and] the fundamentals of his different methods, especially those he called "sexual techniques."[28]

Readily apparent in the passage is the genital and erogenous organization of Argentine torture. Following the 1976 coup d'état use of the *picana* described here was standardized in detention centers throughout Argentina, its application focused on the male and female genitalia, the breasts and nipples, the anus, and the mouth.[29] The cited passage also well illustrates the masturbatory nature of eroticized violence, with the torturer alternating between the injuring and caressing that jointly aroused an autoerotic experience through exploitation of the *objectified* victim. On other occasions the violent and autoerotic agendas totally fused: One naked torturer of a female victim masturbated as "he stuck an instrument called 'the expander' in her anus" while another torturer at the victim's head "slashed her superficially with a scalpel."[30]

The detour by which the torturer returned to his autoarousal through domination of an objectified victim was also expressed in the mock dialogue, in the coerced insults, through which the torturer *speaks to himself* by making the victim ape his discourse. As discussed in Chapter 2, one of the primary functions of torture is to access the victim's discourse through the sentience of his or her body, to destroy that discourse, and to replace it with the discourse of the State. In the instance cited above this procedure was primitively rehearsed as the torturer insisted that the victim mime his discourse: He insulted her, and therefore she must insult him. The torturer crushed the victim's "wrong" discourse—incorrect in generic terms because it is not his and then specifically because she "mistakes" his "scientific" technique for aberrant sexuality[31]—and continued to sexually brutalize her until she "understood," until she conformed her perception to his truth. The torturer thus violently coerced his victim to engage in his autoerotic drama and compelled her to *participate* not only in her own undoing but also in the sexual aberration he celebrated in word and deed. His violence transformed her into the partner (a partner-object, a subject objectified) of the love he made to himself, and he became increasingly excited by her resistance (which in his drama equates with her engagement, her feistiness) before the climax of her final succumbing, her delivery.[32]

Coerced discourse in its relation to eroticized violence also rehearses in miniature another aspect of the drama played out more grandly in torture as a political strategy. In the political view torture obliges the victim to participate in rituals by which the State generates power through destruction of "subversives." Similarly at the local, erotic level between a specific victim and his or her torturer, the victim is obliged to engage in a theater of brutal sexuality that empowers and gratifies the torturer, again, only because the dominated victim is being destroyed. For the victims the common denominator is destruction. For the perpetrators the process in all cases is reflexive, with the State and the torturer both directing their actions toward themselves via the agency of a subject made into an object. Sexual pleasure and the allied power manifested via dominance are generated by the torturer who exploits the victim as a fetish in his autoerotic drama. The torturer and this sexuality are then repressed out of the scheme in the larger, political view as the power is transcendentalized and conferred upon the State.

The detention centers' institution of sadism in the strict sense of the term, as "desire to inflict pain upon the sexual object," provided ample forum in "dirty war" Argentina for proliferation of the most severe perversions.[33] One repressor "tortured the prisoners viciously while he talked to them in a low voice, almost sweetly, enjoying this situation enormously."[34] A trial testimony similarly made reference to a torturer with "a very special, very sensual voice," who would say to his victims, "Now we're going to give you a little *picana* to see if you enjoy it."[35] Another torturer, referred to as the "feminine voice," began his auto-erotic ritual of torture by "caressing one's testicles, anticipating the pleasure that his work must have given him," and a third twisted the victim's testicles as a means of torture, each expressing in his own way the erotic impetus of his violence.[36] Rape, gang rape, and the two in combination with beatings or *picana* discharges also gave frequent expression to that impetus. One victim testified, "I was raped and beat on the bottoms of my feet with a hammer for three hours"; another more generically related that she suffered "every type of rape"; and in a third case rape was repeated so insistently that it resulted in the victim hemorrhaging from the vagina.[37] "They untied my legs," another survivor related during the trials, "and they lifted my blindfold a little so I could see a man, very close to me, exposing his genitals." The exhibitioning torturer then told the victim that he and his cohorts would rape her one after the other.[38]

The penis on display here as an object of domination was often substituted in symbolic rapes and sodomies by phallic objects, notably the *picana* itself.[39] As noted earlier the torturers stressed and exploited the instrument's phallic form by the genital and erogenous organization of its application.[40] One need only imagine the *picana* releasing its discharge (the term's ejaculation connotations intact) in a vagina or anus to conjure a sense of what was acted out brutally at the torture table.[41] The drama becomes yet more explicit when one overlays onto that scene the torturers' caresses of the naked, bound victim; their monologues "in a low voice, almost sweetly"; their masturbations; and their symbolic vernacular expressions laden with sexuality.[42]

III

The centrality of the phallus in Argentine torture had ample precedent in contexts of politico-religious violence. "Whether it be a stick or a club, a spear or a sword, a gun or a cannon, as a symbol of masculinity the weapon has been equivalent to and almost interchangeable with the sexual organs from Stone Age drawings to modern advertising."[43] The phallus similarly served a pivotal role in cult and theatrical veneration of Dionysus, as noted in Chapter 2. The frenzy of cult worship, as violent as it was erotic, resulted in practices anticipating the sexual aberrations cataloged above, these Greek rituals intermingling orgiastic sexuality with sacrifice, dismemberment, castration, and the eating of raw human flesh. At the same time, however, "the erect phallus symbolised sovereign power,"[44] repositing the thematics of Dionysian frenzy within the interests of political agendas. In political contexts the phallus—like Dionysus's insignia, the mask—"is not primarily what it represents, but what it transforms."[45] If the phallus is a signifier (as discussed later), then in the "dirty war" its signification encompassed illocutionary properties: The *picana*-phallus functioned as a *performative* signifier in the symbolic order, transforming erotic violence into political power, aberrant sexuality into Christian love. With its symbolism pulling in one direction toward Dionysian frenzy and in the other toward totalitarian State control, the phallus, again like the mask, "is able to deny what it is affirming while simultaneously remaining affirmative."[46] The mixed message of the phallus consolidates sexuality and power, the one enmeshed in the other, while it simultaneously calls into play the thematics of denial and affirmation, of what is present in its relation to the absence it represents.[47]

In Chapter 3 I then suggested that "dirty war" mythology, not unlike Greek mythology, situated the *picana*, the phallus, in a privileged position as the "magical object" at the center of the narrative and as the instrument empowering the Junta. The power of the *picana*-phallus, however, was a contingent one, because its generation depended on a sentient body whose pain it translated and appropriated. I therefore posited the *picana* as signifier not of the Junta's power per se but more exactly as signifier of the Junta's *desire* for power, with the *picana* functioning as "a lack which is brought into being."[48] The discussion further stressed how the desire for power in the detention centers encompassed sexual desire aberrantly rehearsed through the torture of overpowered and disempowered victims.

One noteworthy historical expression of phallocentric symbolism in its relation to violent manifestations of power is legible in Pedro Berruguete's 1490 painting *St. Dominic Presiding at an Auto-da-fé*. In this work the victims, otherwise naked, have their genitals bound in the likeness of jockstraps, and protruding outward from the posts to which they are bound, just beneath their crotches, are disproportionately large phallic forms provided by the executioners. Later, in colonial America, the rituals and performative discourse creating municipalities and inducting remote New World regions into the Spanish empire centered around the erection of a phallus symbolizing royal power. As one historian observed of Castile, "When her captains founded a city in the New World, they could never forget the royal *rollo* in the plaza as one of the first civic constructions, together with the Town Hall and the Church."[49] In a 1599 handbook for caudillos, Bernardo de Vargas Machuca described this centrality of the *rollo* or *picota* to the act of foundation, specifying the rituals and the performative discourse required to bring the new municipality into being.[50]

As the "most esteemed symbol of the groups in power" and "the very image of the local lord, with all of his power and force," the *picota*-phallus served not only as a passive symbol of sovereignty but also as the site and the insignia of spectacular punishment.[51] "All or almost all of the colonial penal procedures were developed around the *rollo-picota*."[52] The power of the State was deployed against those who came into contact with the *picota* (or, later in Latin American history, the *picana*), and the spectacular value of mutilations and executions was prolonged by exhibiting parts of the victims' bodies on that same phallus. "Whatever the method of execution suffered by the criminal—beheaded, garrotted, hanged—all of their heads were left for long periods tragically exposed on the *rollos-picotas*."[53]

The word *picota* (derived from *pica*, or "lance") and the word *picana* are both rooted in *pic* ("point"). The *picota's* denomination alludes to its form, tapering at the upper end into a point; to the metaphoric "piercing" of its victims; and—through the *picota's* function as the locus "where the heads of the executed were displayed"—to spectacular uses of the lance in advertising decapitation of the Enemy.[54] The word *picana* (derived from *picar*—to prick, puncture—plus the Quechua suffix *na*, which designates an instrument) originally meant "a stick of approximately three meters in length, with a one-centimeter iron barb stuck in the point; it is used to drive or to steer oxen pulling a wagon."[55] On the farm and in the detention center, the *picana*'s point leads one in the proper direction. Figurative uses of *picar* then infuse the *picana* with two meanings that, when considered in combination, speak directly to eroticized violence: "to wound" and, in the sexual sense of the term, "to screw."[56] The English-language vernacular denomination of the penis as "prick" similarly echoes the connotations carried by *picar*, encompassing *picota's* connotations as well through its etymological relation to the lance.

Phallocentric violence was also expressed in the indigenous populations of the colonies (as depicted by the European chroniclers), notably in the rebelling Incas' 1565 execution of Fray Diego Ortiz in Vilcabamba. After a protracted spectacle syncretizing a reenactment of Christ's passion with Incan punishments, Ortiz's martyrdom concluded as "they pierced him through all of his natural parts with a long pole, until it came out the back of his neck."[57] A seventeenth-century engraving entitled "Martyrdom of the Blessed Fray Diego Ortiz in Vilcabamba" depicted the execution, with an enormous phallic pole entering the priest at the crotch and exiting through the top of his head.[58]

Also in subliminal homage to the phallus as a symbol of power, the French colonizers in the Americas erected marker columns, engraved with the king's coat of arms, as monuments of sovereignty over the explored regions. In one of Theodore de Bry's illustrations, "Florida" natives are shown worshipping the column erected by Captain Jean Ribaut in 1562. The occasion was the arrival of a second French voyage in 1564, under René Laudonnière, after Ribaut's failed colonization attempt. The natives brought the soldiers to see the column, now an object of veneration, that was left by the French explorers two years earlier. As the narrative accompanying the illustration dramatized the affair, all approached the column, and the chief "kissed it and the other Indians did likewise." Baskets of fruit, vases of perfumed oils, edible and medicinal roots, and a bow and arrows were placed before the monument, which was wreathed with flowers. But "after watching the rituals of these wretched barbarians," the French gravitated more to the monument's "point": They rejoined their companions to find the most suitable site to

build a fort. The narrative concluded by sounding an Oedipal theme—
absolutely out of context until the phallocentrism of the image is recognized—by relating that the chief who had brought the French to the
worshipped column had "married his mother." The final sentence observed: "It might be added that after he married his mother his father,
Satourioua, ceased to live with her."[59]

IV

What most characterizes the phallus as a symbol of sovereign power "and
reappears in all its figurative embodiments is its status as a detachable and
transformable object,"[60] its transferability from one subject to another.
Whoever has the phallus, whoever wields the *picana* (the "magical object"
of the myth),[61] whoever controls the *picota* exercises the sovereign power
it affords, until he or she in turn is destroyed or the empowering instrument is usurped or neutralized by another. The symbolic function of the
phallus, however, is conveyed more by what the *picana* or the *picota*
represents, by the absence they replace, than it is by their empirical
presence as forms, as objects. The *picana*-phallus metonymically represented the Junta's desire for the power it lacked, a desire that was ritually
satisfied through the repetitive enactment of a psychosexual drama during
torture. Ultimately "the phallus is not a question of a form, or of an
image, or a phantasy, but rather of a signifier, the signifier of desire."[62]

The symbolic struggle for power during torture is waged largely on
discursive grounds, with the *picana* functioning as this signifier. The
Word occupies the same space as the phallus (*picana*) in that struggle;
whoever has the phallus has the Word. The *picana* arose as the Junta's
insignia because a *lack* of legitimate power called it forth as it called forth
torture. Once the lack was satisfied symbolically, once the *picana*-phallus
released the Word that it at once inserted into the torture victim, it
displaced the possibility of restoring the absence (legitimate power on
one level, *desaparecido* on another) that brought it into being. The phallus
"corresponds to the act of symbolization where the thing 'dies' in order
to be reborn with renewed vigor in the network of the laws of language."[63]
Use of the *picana* thus enforced "the absence, the non-being or death, of
the very object it seeks to designate."[64]

Jacques Lacan introduced the phallus as the ideal model for signifiers
because it is "never wholly present there where it is, nor wholly absent

there where it is not."[65] By this description the phallus modulates into the definitions of both the fetish and the *desaparecido*, each in its respective way neither wholly present nor wholly absent. As a demand "that there be something where there is nothing" and as "*the signifier of another signifier, the phallus,*" the fetish is positioned as an intermediary symbol.[66] As far as the aberrant "act of love" in the detention centers is concerned, the fetish had in the *desaparecidos* its perfect embodiment because these subjects were representations of an erotic absence that the ritual, the torture, made present.[67] "Subversives" appeared in response to the torturers' and Junta's demand that there be something (a sexual object, an Enemy) where there was nothing, and when these Enemies "disappeared" they barely veiled the lack that brought them into being: the signifier of desire, the phallus. The fetish was a displacement onto "something insignificant" (a farmer, a lawyer, a factory worker, all insignificant in terms of national security) that was highly meaningful in symbolic terms (the sexual object, the Enemy).[68] If the *desaparecido* was the fetish of the torturer and if the fetish veiled another signifier, the phallus, behind it, then the *desaparecido* was, like the *picana*, linked symbolically to the phallus. The Enemy not only had the phallus, he *was* the phallus.[69] It is for this reason, in part, that the "subversives" were mythically guilty and condemned not for what they did but rather for what they symbolically *were*: a lack brought into being, signifiers in a discourse that "is at once the object of the struggle for domination and the means by which the struggle is waged."[70]

V

"Whosoever looketh on a woman to lust after her hath committed adultery with her already in his heart," Matthew warned Christendom, and therefore "if thy right eye offend thee pluck it out, and cast it from thee. . . . And if thy right hand offend thee, cut it off and cast it from thee." This self-surgical tactic of punishment as salvation is reminiscent of the *quirófano's* intent to remove evil or defiled members from the *corpus mysticum*. "Subversives" were severed from the social body "for it is profitable for thee that one of thy members should perish, and not that thy whole body should be cast into hell."[71] Christianity's abiding denial of the sexual body, the Argentine military's long history of preoccupation with puritanical morality, and the sexuality of torture in the detention centers all signaled the "member" most vulnerable as the target for extirpation in "dirty war" symbolics: not the eye or the hand but the male member, represented symbolically by the phallus.

As discussed earlier the *picana*-phallus was detached from the *desaparecidos* who had it, who were disempowered as the "magical object" passed to the torturers. In ancient history actual (rather than symbolic) castration was used in the warfare of Egypt and Greece as the toll that the victor exacted from his defeated enemy. In these castrations "the victor's main purpose was to gain for himself the masculine power of his victim."[72] Walter Burkert similarly observed that "when stimulated by sexual jealousy, the destructive rage operating in the battle of man against man will turn against the adversary's masculinity: When killed, a warrior is immediately castrated."[73] The desire to assault the enemy's masculinity was expressed more recently in fantasies of the McCarthy era, one report claiming that Manhattan Project spy Klaus Fuchs "had betrayed the secret of a 'hormone ray' that had the potential to 'feminize' enemy troops."[74] In more literal and gruesome expressions of the same phenomenon, castration was one of the prevalent motifs of torture in Guatemala during the early 1980s, and in "dirty war" Argentina (or, at least, in the fantasy of the one torturer who mentioned it) *desaparecidos* were likewise castrated on occasion.[75]

Considered through the Christian overlay, however, the symbolic emphasis of castration stresses not the detachability of the phallus from victims who have it but rather a stylization of victims *as the phallus itself.* The evil ("subversion," sexuality) appended to and defiling the *corpus mysticum* was castrated from the social body during ritual "surgery" in the *quirófano* to prevent "that thy whole body be cast into hell." At the same time, recalling the discussion of the King's Two Bodies in Chapter 3, the *corpus reipublicae mysticum* was the *Junta's* body: When "dirty war" torture castrated the *desaparecidos*-as-phallus from this corpus, it carried the symbolic meaning of the Junta's own self-emasculation, its own disempowering. The "dirty war" castrated its authors, it cut off the signifier of its desired power, it reversed the results it strove for. That process was patent in "dirty war" mythology, where the means by which the Junta empowered itself with the "magical object" (*picana*-phallus) and the means by which it brought on itself a tragic demise were one and the same.

In medieval Europe, where analogical thought like that of the Junta flourished, tales of moral instruction were characterized almost exclusively by a clearly decipherable relationship between transgressions (many of them sexual) and the punishments recompensing them. The roots of this crime/punishment relation lay in antiquity, with Augustine insisting "that the hiatus between will and sexual feeling had been inflicted on Adam and on all his descendants as a *poena reciproca*, a punishment imposed to fit the crime."[76] One medieval tale treated the theme generically, depicting the punishments of hell as varying in accordance with the sins committed.[77] Others were more specific: A blasphemer drowned and was found with a shrivelled tongue; a merchant who swore by the breasts of the Virgin died with his tongue protruding; a rich man choked to death on the meat of a cow he had stolen; a drunkard was allowed no water; a canon who seduced a nun discovered ominous signs on his genitals; a glutton was pierced by a sword until he defecated; a fisherman who committed fornication was burned by a hot iron, and so on.[78] Similarly, as mentioned in Chapter 2, many European punishments were determined by symbolic relation with their crime, and the eighteenth-century public executions as precursors of the abstract spectacles in the Argentine detention centers often accentuated a symbolic bond between crime and punishment. "In the same horror [torture in the Argentine detention centers, for our purposes] the crime had to be manifested and annulled," and further, "There were even some cases of an almost theatrical reproduction of the crime in the execution of the guilty man—with the same instruments, the same gestures."[79]

If torture in the Argentine detention center conforms, as I believe it does, to this model of symbolic consonance between a (mythic) transgression and its punishment, then one must come to understand the crime that the myth attributed to "subversives" in its relation to the eroticized violence that exacted retribution in rituals of torture. What drama was acted out in the Argentine detention centers "with the same instruments, the same gestures" to occasion institutionalized aberration? What was the crime that called forth the ubiquitous *picana*-phallus and the prolonged theater of domination at the torture table?[80]

The phallocentrism of "dirty war" torture and mythology, the "castratability" and transferability of the *picana* (as phallus, Word, power), the dynamics of Junta desire, and the insistent presence of Christian doctrine with its hierarchical relation within a Father-Son deity together suggest an Oedipal structure of "dirty war" violence. My understanding of the term "Oedipal," as will become clear from the discussion, is Lacanian in essence, but it is also indebted to the human sciences' extension of the complex to politico-familiar structures. René Girard's development of mimetic rivalry, as Hegelian as it is Freudian, is one such extension to which I shall owe a debt, for in place of the Oedipal father Girard posited any model-rival; in place of the mother, any object valued by the rival; and in place of the unconscious, mythic mentality.

The officer of Franz Kafka's "In the Penal Colony" who explained to a troubled visitor, "Whatever commandment the prisoner has disobeyed is written upon his body by the Harrow," articulated quite explicitly what "dirty war" torture and discourse only imply: The symbolic relation between the punishment and its crime is "written" on the victim's body, in the Argentine case with the *picana*-phallus. "This prisoner, for instance," Kafka's officer continued, "will have written on his body: HONOR THY SUPERIORS!" The line from the crime to the punishment is unmistakable. When the visitor tried to clarify whether the prisoner knew his sentence (which—as in the "dirty war"—he did not), the officer simply replied, "No . . . there would be no point in telling him. He'll learn it on his body."[81]

When the bodies of Argentine torture victims were carved into what one survivor termed a "map of misfortune,"[82] the linkage of crime and punishment was obviously less direct than that in the inscriptions of Kafka's Harrow, but it was nevertheless legible. Oedipal dynamics were nonconscious on the part of the Junta, the torturers, and other actors, and as such they gained indirect, distorted expression through the myths (reviewed in the previous chapter) layered over them and through the torture rituals that gave them symbolic expression. "Dirty war" myth and the torture generating it were manifest in the specific forms I have reviewed, rather than in any infinite number of other possible forms, because they were overdetermined under the aegis of an Oedipal paradigm that organized diverse pressures (from sexual to political) around desire in its relation to the Other. Once the cryptic code is cracked, once scars on the body are "read," once the "map" is traced back to the *picana*-phallus inscribing it, the Oedipal structure that is revealed reconciles the incompatibility of the torture room's violent sexuality and "dirty war" mythology's loving Christianity, agendas otherwise at odds save in their common and respective obsessions with the flesh. "The denuded body [of the victim] knows not what it says," Michel de Certeau once observed. "It presupposes a reader by whom it allows itself to be read like a hieroglyph that is indecipherable in itself."[83]

VI

The torturer put his Word into the victim's mouth. He did this directly by displacing the victim's discourse with his own (the insults and obscenities that the victim must repeat) and with the State's (the "confession"), thereby coercing the victim's participation in an autoerotic drama and in "recognition" of his own guilt and subjugation. The oral focus at the torture table then made the decisive transition to incorporation "when the mouth's *words* do not succeed in filling the subject's emptiness, so [the torturer] fills it instead with an imaginary *thing*."[84] In addition to putting his Word into the victim's mouth, the torturer filled that same emptiness, the space of that lack, with the *picana*-phallus. Against empirical measure the chronology was linear: The Word went in because the *picana* went in first; the victim recited his lines because he was tortured.[85] On symbolic grounds, however, the distinction between the Word going in and the *picana*-phallus going in is moot because the phallus was itself a signifier, the signifier of the Junta's desire for power. Torture with the *picana* "emptied" the *desaparecido's* mouth, then twice filled the void it created with the Junta's Word: once because the *picana*-phallus embodied the Word, once because it opened the way for it. The victim's mouth was overfilled, the victim's coerced discourse was overdetermined. In the detention centers the Junta's Word forged and filled to Dionysian excess a "community of empty mouths,"[86] the overflow spilling as terror into the Argentine public at large.

Insofar as the victim's coerced utterances are concerned, Lacan's question, "Who is speaking and to whom?" is answered with the ultimate reply: The torturer is speaking, to himself. When the *desaparecido* was made to speak, he announced that "being bespoken is being broken— broken apart by the signifiers whose proper locus is to be found in the Other."[87] Had the Junta and the torturer asked Oedipus's question, "Where's my voice?" the implied response would echo from the victim's mouth filled with the phallus.[88]

The Oedipal vestiges of the victim's coerced discourse come into focus when one considers what specific Word the torturer elected for his victim, what he said to himself through the mouth of the Other. The Oedipal presence became particularly insistent on the occasions when detention center guards tortured prisoners for no purpose other than their own entertainment, often with the objective of making their victims recite some self-debasing obscenity. The following refrain, to use a most telling illustration, was recalled by Jacobo Timerman. For their pleasure the guards on duty obliged a male prisoner to run naked up and down a corridor repeating these lines: "*My mother is a whore.* . . . *The whore who gave birth to me.* . . . *I masturbate.* . . . *I must respect the corporal on duty.* . . . *The police love me.*"[89] Once the victim's role as mouthpiece of the Word imposed on him is underscored, it becomes clear that the first person pronouns here refer to the torturers who invented the lines rather than to the victim coerced to recite them.

Through the first clause, *My mother is a whore*, the authors of the refrain assumed the voice of the dominated subject in the Father-Son hierarchy, while simultaneously they acted out the reverse through domination of the victim. The second clause restated much the same more specifically, stressing the torturers' expression of a fantasy as an *hijo de puta*, the son of a whore, a phrase that when used as a colloquial insult in Spanish translates to the "equivalent" English insult "mother fucker." That transition from the whore's son to the mother's fucker was also suggested by the following phrase, likewise invented by torturers for recitation by a victim. The prisoner in question suffered a lengthy "orgy" of torture that had as its sole objective the coercing of this line: *Me la como doblada y mi madre es una hija de puta.*[90]

When placed "under the surveillance of its mother tongue,"[91] this phrase speaks directly to my point. The first half of the compound—*Me la como doblada*—fuses two vernacular uses: first *comer* ("to eat") here signifying fornication or oral sexual penetration, then this eroticized *comer* extending into *comersela doblada* ("to eat it up doubled over"), which connotes penetration by a penis folded in two, doubled in thickness. When addressed to a female, the intent of the insult is to imply that she is a whore, this connotation coinciding with the direct assertion *My mother is a whore* in the lines recalled by Timerman. The refrain consolidates the "son of a whore" and the "mother fucker" as expressions of a single subject fulfilling the son function: *Me la como doblada y mi madre es una hija de puta*, the term *hija* ("daughter") extracted from the passage (which now reads "my mother is a whore") to return it to the source from which it was feminized and projected: the son (*hijo*) who "fucks his mother the whore." The "equation of the mother with a prostitute" at work here is not uncommon in clinical cases; through Oedipal fantasy "it brings the unattainable within easy reach."[92]

In the original passage cited from Timerman, however, the mother is not yet within easy reach. The refrain places an obstacle between the son and the mother as object of his desire: *I must respect the corporal on duty.* The authority of the corporal (or, in Oedipal terms, the father) lays down the Law that the son must obey. Depicting the mother as a whore in this context stresses not so much the fantasy of access as the son's disapproval of the mother's sexual intimacy with the Other, the father. For want of access to the mother, for want of outlet for his desire, the son resorts to "that dangerous supplement" to compensate for his lack: *I masturbate.*[93] In the detention centers, as discussed earlier, that masturbation assumed the aberrant form of exploiting *desaparecidos* as fetishes in the torturer's theater of autoerotic arousal. The mother was replaced by an onanistic fantasy, the torture victims serving as apt substitutes because, like whores, they were engaged in sexual acts but not party to them, utilized but not present as subjects.

The testimonies taken from detention center personnel following the "dirty war" also evidence mother/son relations as they pertain to Oedipal dynamics. Graciela Fernández Meijide, the CONADEP subsecretary responsible for testimonies, observed that the repressors frequently made voluntary reference to their mothers despite the fact that the questions addressed to them made no inquiry in this direction. "As they related how they had become increasingly involved in the repression and in torture a clear adhesion to their mothers was also surfacing. . . . One very common comment was '. . . because my mother, I don't want anyone touching her.' "[94]

The testimonies left Fernández Meijide with the impression that the torturers were boys "who had not grown up, who were hoping that some day their mothers would love them"; she noted also that one of the torturers was nicknamed "the Baby."[95] Testimony from the victims corroborated that observation, one survivor reporting that a sixteen-year-old torturer (called *Manzanita*—"little apple"—owing to his round and rosy face) would torture throughout the night, then repair to a room where a female prisoner obliged to serve as his confidant (a Platonic prostitution) was detained. The torturer related his troubles, then "ended systematically by crying and calling her 'Mommy, my dear Mommy.' "[96]

Considered jointly, the last two clauses of the cited refrain—*I must respect the corporal on guard* and *The police love me*—complete the Oedipal dynamics by specifically introducing the ambivalence that the son experiences in his relation to the father. The father is at once the son's prohibitive authority and his role model, at once the rival for the mother and the source of identity that makes the son's rivalry a possibility. As it speaks through the cited phrases, ambivalence bows to the Law after an influx of guilt: *I must respect my father* because *he loves me.* Although the son identifies with the father and shares his love, the father also poses a *terrorist* threat (epitomized in the symbolics of castration). The father is *on guard,* he is enforcing the Law that denies the son access to the mother-whore whom he enjoys, the Law that relegates the son to "that dangerous supplement" in the detention center.

Behind all of the paternal masquerading, then, the Junta and the torturer assumed the position of what I shall symbolically call the *Son* in these Oedipal dynamics.[97] That Son rose up (so to speak) to confront the father who had the phallus and was "touching" the mother with it ("because my mother, I don't want anyone touching her!"). To realize the object of his desire, the Son eliminated the authoritative obstacle (the father) that rendered his phallus impotent before the mother. He challenged the father's authority in kind, turned the phallus (*picana*) against him, empowered his phallus by usurping power from the father's. *I tortured because he was touching my mother (with the phallus),* the torturer's ritual reads, *I lifted the power of the phallus out of his body and conferred that power to my own.*[98] The triumphant Son thus exited his rebellion empowered by disempowering the victim, usurping the "mother" and the Word as his spoils.

In opposition to the Junta/torturer's assumption of the Son functions, the Enemy, the "subversives," the *desaparecidos* constitute as a corporate whole what I shall symbolically call the Father. "We got Papa," the "dirty war" task forces reported in code when they had abducted a victim.[99] The repressors' allocation of the conceptual position of Father to their victims reflected "a reality of the external world, whose omnipotence is proportionate to the impotence and dependence of a subject"; the insecurity of the Junta's own position resulted in its aggrandized perception of the Other. The Son authoring the "dirty war" and its myth struggled for "a negation of impotence and its narcissistic reverse, the subject's [Junta's, torturer's] imaginary omnipotence."[100]

Repetition of the reversal whereby the Son became the Father, whereby the Junta usurped power and the Word as it wielded the *picana*-phallus, was the dominating motif of the Oedipal drama rehearsed in the detention centers. The torturers as boys "who have not grown up" and the victims of the "dirty war" as primarily youths[101] pinpoint, at least in metaphorical terms, the pivotal moment of the peripeteia that recast the actors in opposite roles, each assuming the position formerly held by his rival. Focusing on this moment and none before or beyond it, the struggle between the Junta and its Enemy seems a fraternal rivalry, a battle of Son against Son for the position held by the figure of authority, the Father, who was beyond both of them but incapable of effectively exercising the power assigned to him.[102] In that configuration the Father's role was most notably assumed by the paternal Juan Perón (first in physical and then vicarious presence) because the two Sons (terrorists and military) engaged in battle to fill the void created by the impotence of the government bearing Perón's name. As Admiral Massera expressed it, "We learned to fight against an enemy disguised as a brother."[103]

In the broader view, however, what seems here to be fraternal rivalry is rather the moment of transition during which the Son (Junta) dominated the Father (Enemy), replaced him in the empowered position from which he was deposed, and subordinated him to the impotent and subjugated role. The reversal of roles was accomplished by mirror-image permutations on two fronts: the Son remade himself by internalizing the Father through identification and incorporation, as discussed later, while at the same time, in the detention centers, the Son reduced the Father to the inferior, dominated role by turning the *picana*-phallus against him, by *remaking him* (as the Son had been remade inversely) to assume the impotent position.[104]

And the "Mother"? "I would have you fix your eyes every day on the greatness of Athens until you fall in love with her," Pericles preached,[105] this amorous relation with a geopolity similarly patent in "love for the social body" of Argentina. Depicting the *patria* as a body in general terms was a trope of notable currency during the "dirty war." The germ/antibody conceit analyzed in the previous chapter is one case in point, as is the Junta's reference to corporal imagery in tropes such as "the palpitating body" of Argentina.[106] In popular culture much the same gained expression, as exemplified by the following slogan spray-painted on the wall of a morgue in Buenos Aires: "Argentina is the body of the crime."[107] The "disappeared" *cuerpo deleti* that never made it to the morgue resurfaced symbolically as the Argentina-body for which (and, in this image, *on* which) the "dirty war" was waged.

In medieval adaptation of the ecclesiastical *corpus mysticum* to the body politic of the State, the equation of the king's body with the State was complemented by a separate trope—borrowed from the mystical marriage contracted between the bishop and his See—that depicted the State as the ruler's bride. "And the comparison between the corporeal matrimony and the intellectual one is good," Cynus asserted in 1578, "for just as the husband is called the defender of his wife . . . so is the emperor the defender of that *respublica*."[108] Sir John Mandeville went so far as to describe the Holy Land as "mistress over all others."[109] In apocalyptic imagery geopolitical entities were also metaphorically depicted as women, perhaps the most outstanding example found in Revelation's description of the holy city descending from On High not only as a woman, but as "the bride, the Lamb's wife," "prepared as a bride adorned for her husband."[110]

With its roots in Christian Europe, Latin American history is also replete with geopolities styled as women, beginning with the feminizing of Amerigo Vespucci's name in designating the New World "America." Later, during and following the wars of independence, the feminizing of names continued (from *Colombo* to *Colombia*, from *Bolívar* to *Bolivia*), and the country-as-woman trope was politically exploited in—to cite a most outstanding example—the discourse of Simón Bolívar.[111] The etymology of the ubiquitous *patria* of Junta discourse also contributes to the provisional equation I shall establish between Argentina and the Mother function in these Oedipal dynamics, the word being rooted in *pater* ("father") and *terra* ("land"). The Mother-country is the Father's land, the terrain off limits to the Son.[112] The detention center struggle between the usurpatious Son and the dominated Father has, initially, Argentina as its spoils. As the Latin *patrius* indicates, the Mother-country is "property inherited from one's father." If the Son (Junta) is not a legitimate heir to that inheritance, he may covet it through violence that "reorganizes" the roles of the players.

VII

In 1936 Anna Freud isolated and described the defense mechanism known as "identification with the aggressor," which was later qualified by D. Lagache as essentially sadomasochistic. When faced with a threat, typically a threat from an authoritarian figure (in our schema the Father), the subject (the Junta, the torturer) defends himself from the affront by internalizing the aggressor through identification in order to symbolically emulate the threatening power.[113] As Jean Laplanche and Jean-Baptiste

Pontalis have summarized the mechanism, "He may do so either by appropriating the aggression itself [usurping power, taking the offensive in the 'dirty war'], or else by physical or moral emulation of the aggressor [fighting terrorism in kind, turning the *picana*-phallus against the Father], or again by adopting particular symbols of power [*picana*-phallus] by which the aggressor is designated."[114] As Junta policy in relation to these three tactics illustrates, "aggression is intimately linked to identification."[115] This matter was introduced through discussion of the ambivalence generated by the Son's simultaneous reverence of and rivalry with the Father. Aggression's link to identification is also evident (and in this case it is plainly sadomasochistic) in the erotic violence of the detention centers, for though the torturer's "pains are being inflicted on other people, they are enjoyed masochistically . . . as sexual excitation . . . through his identification of himself with the suffering object."[116]

The Junta's identification with its "dirty war" Enemy was directly and symbolically expressed in repressor discourse at all levels. One unique component of this discourse of identification appeared in several official statements that ostensibly had the Enemy as their subject but that more aptly applied to the Junta than to the adversary it endeavored to describe. Consider, for example, the following passage, spoken by Admiral Massera from ESMA in November 1976. Massera's intent, again, was to comment on the Enemy, but his words turned back reflexively as a description of the Junta's own "dirty war" effort: "Slowly . . . a machine of horror was unleashing its wickedness on the innocent and the unprepared . . . [amidst] . . . the incredulity of some, the complicity of others, and the astonishment of most."[117] Elsewhere Admiral Massera well summarized the manifestations of the Junta's messianic mythology by attempting to describe the Enemy: "Explosives became a form of political dialogue. Words, unfaithful to their meanings, disturbed their reason and the murderers even tried to take advantage of the Word of God to invent a justifying theology for their violence. How indifferently and coldly they killed men in order to save humanity!"[118]

In the 1983 Final Document, which sought to legitimate the military's "dirty war" operations, the Junta's autodefinition was yet more specifically compiled by default through reading attributes off of its Enemy. The actions of the leftist terrorists, the document said, "directed at paralyzing the entire population, were characterized by a constant and indiscriminate violation of the most fundamental human rights: Murders, tortures and prolonged abductions are indisputable proofs of their acts and their criminal intentions."[119]

The structure of the Junta's unintended self-expression through description of the Enemy is not unfamiliar, paralleling as it did the torturer's projection of his discourse into the Enemy's mouth. When a torturer obliged his victim to recite My mother is a whore, that torturer lent out his first-person pronoun and spoke through the Other's mouth, but nevertheless remained the subject of the discourse. When the Junta described its Enemy the discourse was similarly rerouted away from its subject and through the Other, a self-description masquerading as an assessment of the Enemy by projecting negative attributes onto him but returning finally to the speaker, the Junta, as subject and "proper locus." The one was spoken by the victim and the other spoken about the victim, but in both cases the victim "disappeared" and was replaced by the repressors.

In addition to these detours through confusions and fusions of speaking subject and the object of discourse, identification with the aggressor was quite explicitly expressed by the military throughout the "dirty war." On some occasions the detention center personnel's identification with the Enemy gained expression in the form of "professional" appreciation, one "soldier" to another. A torturer in the La Perla detention center, for example, repeatedly emphasized that he was fighting a "war of equal to equal," despite the fact that one of the "equals" was bound naked to the torture table.

> He always talked about the "respectable enemy." After torturing he would congratulate the prisoner for "having had himself tortured," as he put it. When I was brought to La Perla he came up to me and shook my hand, saying "I congratulate you, Señora, for having had the courage to jump out of the car, and for the brave way your husband died."[120]

In other instances the expression of identification with the Enemy was yet more direct: "To infiltrate our enemy we have to resemble him."[121]

These rank-and-file expressions of identification solidify into a true mimesis, into the manifestation of military ideology as reactionary in the fullest sense of the term, in Junta and high-ranking military discourse. General Cristino Nicolaides described the military's role in the "dirty war" as a "reaction" to "an international Marxist-communist action," and General Juan Manuel Bayón similarly recorded "a spontaneous reaction" of love for the fatherland in response to shame.[122] In a political plan revealingly titled, in part, "A New Argentine Historical Cycle: From the Process of National Reorganization to the Third Republic," General Ibérico Saint Jean made it clear that Argentina's new era was *founded* on the Junta's response to its Enemy: "The Third Republic assumes a state born in response to subversive aggression."[123] Once the link was that tightly established, the Junta's attachment to its Enemy, the Junta's self-definition in terms of the Enemy, gained abundant expression:

> The subversives are the ones who made it [the "war"] dirty. They chose the form of the struggle and determined our actions.[124]

> —General, what you are saying means that the State acted in the same way as a group of terrorists, with terrorist methods. . . .
> —Yes.[125]

> We have used against the terrorists the same drastic methods that they have employed; . . . we adapted much of our combat procedures to those used by subversion. . . .[126]

The Junta's miming of its Enemy was in fact escalated to such a degree that Assistant Prosecutor Moreno Ocampo would observe during the 1985 trials that "it is impossible to differentiate between [Montonero leader Mario] Fermenich and Videla."[127] In *Nunca más* CONADEP expressed much the same, noting on its opening page and later in the report that the Junta replaced one terrorism with another.[128] And the Junta itself, finally, was not unaware of the concept of mimetic rivalry; Admiral Massera observed—on Navy Day in 1977—that in the contemporary world "enemies reciprocally mime one another until their identities get confused."[129] Massera apparently pardoned himself and his colleagues from that entrapment, though he indeed took mimesis to new and confusing heights when he assigned detained Montonero leaders an elite status as his personal advisers.[130]

During the "dirty war" a variation of identification with the aggressor occasionally assumed the extreme form sometimes referred to as the "Stockholm syndrome," named after a hostage incident that took place in a Stockholm bank in 1973. Because in a hostage situation, as in an Argentine detention center, the victim's life is at the mercy of the captors, the hostages or prisoners are under substantial psychological pressure to empathize, cooperate, and sometimes even love the perpetrators who violently subjugate them. As the six-day Stockholm ordeal progressed, the hostages began to negotiate on behalf of their captors, demonstrating sincere concern for the bank robbers' well-being. When the criminals decided to surrender, the hostages insisted on walking in front of them as they left the bank to prevent them from possibly being shot by the authorities. Following the incident the hostages refused to testify against their former captors, and one woman of the group went the extra distance, divorcing her husband and marrying one of the men who had previously held her hostage.[131]

In the "dirty war," where the terror of captivity and the imminent possibility of execution were compounded by systematic agendas of physical and psychological torture, victims who were not executed (and they were few) were prime candidates for developing an identification with the aggressor of the Stockholm type. One notorious case occurred in the ESMA detention center, where a former terrorist leader, Marta Bazán, engaged in an extended love affair with Rubén Chamorro, then director of the center.[132]

The degree to which mimetic rivalry can confuse the identity of adversaries also was accentuated in post-"dirty war" Argentina, when in January 1989 the Third Infantry Regiment camp at La Tablada was suddenly assaulted. When the incident was announced, it was taken for granted by most Argentines that the barracks disturbance was another military uprising—President Alfonsín's administration had already suffered three. When identification papers found on the first guerrilla killed in battle established a link with the People's Revolutionary Army (ERP) from the 1970s, many Argentines then believed that the military had staged the conflict (as it had staged confrontations with "terrorists" throughout the "dirty war") as a means of cultivating civilian sympathy or that military intelligence officers had catalyzed the attack for the same reason. The left-wing guerrillas actually responsible for the La Tablada incident themselves contributed to the clouding of identities by distributing pamphlets in which they claimed to sympathize with military officers who had rebelled in response to "dirty war" litigation under President Alfonsín. At the same time a communiqué published in Uruguay by these leftists, calling themselves the People's Resistance Front, lugged their heavily freighted assault in the other direction by announcing that their militant action was intended to preempt a plot by dissidents within the army to mount a coup d'état against the constitutional government. Alfonsín himself then got in on the theme, remarking in a speech delivered to the nation after the La Tablada attack, "We are not going to confuse ourselves with our enemy."[133] Perhaps, however, it was already too late.

Complementing internalization of the enemy through identification, military discourse during the "dirty war" revealed a simultaneous, symbolic appeal to a corporal model, the Enemy's *incorporation* into the body of repression. The fantasy of incorporation, like "dirty war" mythology generally, aspired to accomplish its desired goal "magically" through demetaphorization, "carrying out in a literal sense something that has meaning only in a figurative sense."[134] As depicted in the germ/antibody metaphor discussed in the previous chapter, the Enemy was engulfed by the military, sealed inside it, and there destroyed. The fantasy of incorporating the Enemy was also prominent in "dirty war" vernacular, where the repressors' word for abduction was *chupar*, literally meaning "to suck; to absorb, to take in." The verb implied an incorporation that was doubly efficient: The Enemy was internalized (through identification) as the Junta's mimetic model, while that same internalization engulfed the Enemy and destroyed him—as *chupar* connotes—erotically.

When European Christians began graphically portraying their new encounter with pre-Columbian cultures, their fantasies often mingled with the realities before them. In the context of abduction as incorporation, as *chupar*, the early depictions of cannibalism are noteworthy, particularly because they often paired incorporation of the Enemy with sexuality. One of the earliest European ethnographic portrayals depicted a cannibalistic feast in combination with open lovemaking, complete with parts of dismembered bodies dangling from trees—a kind of orgy for all appetites.[135] A suite of woodcuts illustrating a 1509 German translation of Amerigo Vespucci's *Letter* treated the same motif, its narrative in this case attributing the sexuality not to the cannibals themselves but to their victim. These images portrayed a sailor from the Vespucci expedition, chosen for his physical appeal, who was sent ashore to seduce women. Once he was distracted by a coterie of female natives feigning admiration, one woman struck him over the head from behind. The would-be suitor was then dragged inland, where he was slaughtered for a native feast.[136]

As in the case of the *chupados*, the cannibal victim's objectification, incorporation, and decomposition is often celebrated by the victors erotically. One early engraving directly to the point portrayed a soon-to-be-eaten fellow obliged to exclaim, "I am your food."[137] This statement serves as a paradigm for all *desaparecido* discourse coerced under torture, regardless of its specific content, because what the *chupado* announced when bespoken was his absorption into and "digestion" by the repressive body that had "sucked him up." The women who coerced the victim's "I am your food" statement—here again paralleling "dirty war" torturers—pursued an accompanying erotic interest: "One caresses her companion's sexual parts during a ritual dance they perform around the victim . . . another does the same thing to herself, during a cannibal meal."[138] Metaphorical incorporation of the *chupados* followed the corporal model of cannibalism by erotically destroying the object (the Enemy, flesh) that had been internalized. The *chupado* was "digested": His positive attributes (the phallus, power, Word) "nourished" the repressive body into which they were absorbed, and the residual waste was "fecalized" and expelled through execution.[139]

More than one appetite was satisfied by torture of the *chupados*, as the torturer who incorporated also sought "to obtain pleasure by making an object penetrate oneself."[140] Although the *picana*-phallus penetrated the victim and not the torturer, that penetration, as mentioned earlier, was "enjoyed masochistically . . . as sexual excitation . . . through [the torturer's] identification of himself with the suffering object." The subject of the incorporation was split and distributed: The torturer penetrated the victim with what he wished to incorporate into himself (the phallus as locus of the Enemy's power and Word), but by doing so he reaped the positive attributes of the incorporation (phallus) without himself suffering the means (*picana*) that made them possible. One cannot forget, however, that the penetrated victim was already *chupado*, already incorporated inside the repressive body. The reflexive and autoerotic nature of the affair is thus accented once again: If the *chupado* was inside the body of repression, then the *picana*-phallus that penetrated him was there also.

VIII

I have mentioned in passing that the March 24, 1976, coup d'état inaugurating the "dirty war" was staged, after months of "calm meditation," during Carnival week.[141] The Argentine navy had begun specific plans for the coup d'état in November of the previous year, and on February 16, 1976, the army formalized its initiatives at a highly publicized conference attended by Videla and his eight senior generals. The plainly signaled deposing of Isabel Perón was postponed, however, then finally enacted during an occasion freighted with significance.

Carnival was a most appropriate moment for the symbolic inauguration of the "dirty war" for a number of reasons. Historically, to cite the most ancient link to "dirty war" themes, Carnival shares with tragedy a common source in worship of Dionysus. Evolving as it did from the Greek and Roman Bacchanalia (festivities paying homage to Bacchus and Dionysus), the sensuality characteristic of modern Carnival has in its prehistory "libertinism, feast, banquet and orgy."[142] Carnival was introduced to Europe by the Romans and developed in the Middle Ages, after which "certain traces of violence, which were part of the ritual, were gradually dismissed and debauchery was partially replaced by a liking for dismal and macabre sensations."[143] As the violent and libertine features were phased out, masks were phased in, along with an appreciation for the spectacular showiness of balls and parades of floats. Later, under the influence of Christianity, Carnival became associated with Shrove Tuesday (from *shrive*, "to hear confession") and Lent; the word's etymology (from *carnelevamen* and later popularly modified to *carne vale!* or "farewell, meat") suggests a final excessive celebration prior to a period of religious fast.[144] Indeed, as a Catholic dictionary hastens to affirm, during this "time of merrymaking before Lent . . . spent in feasting and noisy unrestrained reveling . . . the Blessed Sacrament is exposed for adoration . . . to expiate the sins of excess committed during these carnival times."[145]

Eroticized violence charged with religious signification is outstanding among the "dirty war" themes echoed by Carnival, as are the literal and metaphoric maskings of the Junta's (violent) licentiousness on the vespers of a new religious era: "the final closing of a historical cycle and the opening of a new one," as Videla described his Carnival coup.[146] The spectacular qualities of Carnival also speak directly to "dirty war" themes: "Because of their obvious sensual character and their strong element of play, carnival images closely resemble . . . the spectacle." Mikhail Bakhtin observed further that "Carnival is not a spectacle seen by the people; they live in it, and everyone participates because its very idea embraces all the people. While carnival lasts, there is no other life outside it,"[147] an observation that applies as well to the panoptic Process of National Reorganization. The abstract spectacle of violence dismantled the distinction between spectacle and audience, as discussed in Chapter 2, and the participation of all Argentines in this "reorganization" was mandatory.

The most relevant aspect of Carnival in the present context, however, coincides with Carnival's most essential characteristic: symbolic inversion.[148] As the pioneering work of Bakhtin and research pursuant to it

have demonstrated, Carnival is based on an inversion of binary oppositions. "As opposed to the official feast [the de jure regime], one might say
that carnival [the Junta regime] celebrates temporary liberation from the
prevailing truth of the established order."[149] During Carnival certain
groups or social categories of people (the military), usually occupying a
subordinate position, "exercise ritual authority over their superior."[150]

The previous chapter detailed the essential role that binary oppositions played in the Junta's mytho-logic, each polarity making the other
possible and necessary. In the context of Oedipal dynamics, that observation accommodates another: By "exercising ritual authority over his
superior," the Son (Junta) exchanged roles with his binary opposite and
assumed the functions of the Father (Enemy). With that transition from
one pole to the other, the Junta acquired—as its "dirty war" abundantly
evidenced—many of the negative attributes that it had designated as
proper to the Enemy.[151] The condemned man of spectacular atrocity,
Foucault noted, was the inverted image of the king.[152] These positions
that king and criminal, Junta and Enemy, assume in a hierarchical arrangement are symbolically volatile, subject to "reorganization."

An understanding of the carnivalesque Junta/Enemy role reversal in
Argentina can perhaps be enhanced by analogy to a similar practice that
is more legibly ritualized in preindustrial culture. On specific occasions
the women of Gogo society (of the Bantu tribes of Tanzania) assume the
role of men and adopt aggressive and obscene behavior that mimes and
mocks the stereotype of masculinity. The men, conversely, assume the
roles generally held by women in that society.[153] Temporary reversal of
sex roles in Gogo society is undertaken as a means to manipulate time.
(Temporal manipulation was integral as well to detention center rituals,
as discussed in Chapter 2; its central function in the Oedipal structure
of torture will be addressed presently.) The Gogo conception of time
alternates between two states posed in binary opposition, one "good"
and the other "evil." When a catastrophic event traumatizes the group (a
famine or livestock disease for the Gogo; terrorism and "subversion" for
the Argentine military), the Gogo say "that the years have turned about."
The rituals responding to these respective traumas reverse the roles
assigned to the sexes in the Gogo case or those assigned to the Son (Junta)
and Father (Enemy) in the Oedipal/Argentine case. By doing so they
enact a symbolic gesture seeking to reestablish the normal flow of time
(in the Gogos' case) or Natural Order (in the Junta's) and to purify their
respective restorations of any evil elements (in both cases).[154]

When Carnival similarly acts out the reversal of roles, its assault at enforced, polarized differentiation "is considered to be an instance of ritual neutralization of semiotically significant oppositions."[155] For Lévi-Strauss the foremost function of ritual and myth is the revelation of an intermediary between polarized opposition and the resolution of antitheses. Structural analysis of the ambivalence inherent in popular culture led Bakhtin independently, and before Lévi-Strauss, to the similar conclusion that the "carnival image strives to embrace and unite in itself both terminal points of the process of becoming or both members of the antithesis."[156] "Dirty war" myths and torture rituals conformed to this carnivalesque model: They strove toward a neutralization, a mediation, of the antithetical opposition of Junta and Enemy, Son and Father, insofar as the author of those myths and rituals, the Junta, could *unite in itself,* could internalize, "both members of the antithesis." One of Anna Freud's most far-reaching realizations regarding identification with the aggressor approached that point from another direction: Internalization of the role model, she argued, results in the subject's symbolical transformation "from the person threatened into the person making the threat."[157] Rather than fearing the Father, by whom he is subjugated and made impotent, the Son defends himself by fantasizing domination and destruction of the Father.

IX

René Girard, broadening the perspective on Oedipal dynamics, described the regulating mechanism by which rivalries engage their parties in mutual mimesis. For our purposes the Junta (Son) began with the mimetic impulse to be like its Enemy (Father), then sought to appropriate the object (Argentina in one register, the phallus in another) that it mimetically desired. "Rivalry does not arise because of the fortuitous convergence of two desires on a single object; rather, *the subject desires the object because the rival desires it.*"[158] The Hegelian understanding of desire here echoed by Girard was yet more heavily stressed in post-Lacanian psychoanalysis: "Truly anthropogenic desire is that alone which bears not on an *object* but on a *desire*—with that fundamental distinction of Hegel's that the object of a desire is desired only because it is the object of desire of the other."[159]

The desire for reconciliation of self and other developed by Hegel (and by Carnival, myth, and ritual) is similarly evident in the second level of Girard's mimesis. Here the Junta lost sight of the initial object of its struggle as its mimetic engagement with the Enemy dominated its attention. As the mimetic fascination between the rivals intensifed, desire broke away from the object (Mother/Argentina) and fixed on the rival protagonist. At the height of the struggle, both rivals abandoned the original object of the struggle altogether, and the conflict became totally mimetic, each rival's desire modeled on and gauged by the other's. Mimetic rivalry thus fueled violence, and violence fueled rivalry, in an intensifying spiral that left behind its original object and progressively unified the miming rivals' identities.[160]

In the case of the "dirty war," which lacked a legitimate rival outside of its mythology, the Junta's mimesis was largely a one-way affair, a sword dance before mirrors. The Junta mimed its projected reflection, aped an Enemy of its own construction, encompassed "both members of the antithesis."[161] Adapting a baroque but efficacious passage from Djelal Kadir, "The trajectory of its [the Junta's] quest is rendered as its own spectral impossibility, moving in a mirror reflection and inverted telos inexorably away from, rather than toward, its longed-for destination."[162] The values of "Western and Christian civilization" were left in the dust. Argentina as the eroticized spoils of the struggle became "the body of the crime." The means of gaining power resulted finally in disempowerment. And the mimesis multiplied rather than annihilated the Enemy.

As Lacan recognized, the Son's rivalry and simultaneous identification with the Father is ultimately explicable by the Oedipal threat (symbolized in castration) only if it is preceded by primary identification in the mirror stage of development, which structures the subject himself as his own rival.[163] As the Junta's battle with its reflection attests, "It is always the mirror image that succeeds in destroying whoever it is who sees himself reflected."[164] The entire psychodrama of mimesis, rehearsed ad nauseam in torture sessions by which the Son transformed himself into the Father, was ultimately another perspective on the Junta's self-defeat in proportionate relation to the accomplishment of its goals. For once the Son had become the Father, once the Junta had become the terrorist, the Junta then had become the Enemy itself and as such the ultimate object of its own destructive agenda. Like Oedipus, the Hero of the "dirty war" drama "is thus his own destroyer; he is the detective who tracks down and identifies the criminal—who turns out to be himself."[165] "*You* are the curse, the corruption of the land!" Tiresias tells Oedipus, "I say you are the murderer you hunt."[166] The Junta as cure, again, turned out to be the disease. Oedipus is "the doctor who speaks of the evil from which the city is suffering in medical terms, but he is also the one who is diseased and the disease itself."[167] The Hero is trapped in carnivalesque oscillation between the opposing poles of the *pharmakon*, a concept whose meanings include both "remedy" and "poison." "The pharmakon [Junta] is that dangerous supplement that breaks into the very thing that would have liked to do without it [Argentina] yet lets itself be breached, roughed up, fulfilled, and replaced, completed by the very trace through which the present increases itself in the act of disappearing."[168]

X

The relation of punishment by *picana* in the detention centers to the mythic transgression calling it forth is now discernible. In Chapter 2 I established torture in the Argentine detention centers as "the ceremonies by which power is generated."[169] I noted that the "thousand deaths" of excessive violence to which each victim was subjected were not incidental or accidental but were rather strategic: Theatrical, overabundant, and gaudily grotesque, the spectacle dramatized the dissymmetry between the power of the State and the impotence of the subject, its efficacy not in expedience but in *prolongation* of the ritual by which power was manifested. In discussing the mythology of the "dirty war" in Chapter 3, I then explored the contingency of the *picana's* power, noting that the *picana*-phallus had no power in itself but only in application to the victim's body. Having the phallus, wielding the *picana*, was in itself insufficient. The generation of power required an adversary (Enemy/ Father) whose torture would endow the *picana*-phallus with its power-generating properties, allowing it to "lift" the desired attributes from the victim's body and confer them to the torturer (Junta/Son) through a mechanism of translation and transferral. For this reason, the Junta's desire for power required the constant generation of enmity, with the offense and nature of the victim subordinated to the necessity that there *be* a victim (Father), a constant supply of victims who engaged in this power-generating ritual, touched by the "magical object." The Son, after all, had the organ (penis) and the Junta had the *picana*; what they lacked was its phallic function, which had to come through its "castratability" from the Father.[170]

Torture was thus recognized as the political ritual by which de facto regimes institute a "reorganized" truth and generate the illusory Power to defend that truth. These rituals require a body, not a specific subject, and therefore readily gravitate toward innocent citizens; any body suitably mythologized will do. A housewife's pain satisfies the ritual as well as a terrorist's. The innocent and arbitrarily selected victim also affords the regime a secondary benefit: Although spectacular atrocity directed toward an acknowledged terrorist momentarily stuns the population, the same directed toward the public at large paralyzes it. The message of terror is dramatically enhanced by the symbolic value of *innocent* victims who seem to have been selected *at random*.

The symbolic relationship between the mythic transgression of the "subversives" and its punishment in the detention centers then becomes clear in the psychoanalytical perspective. Within the Oedipal complex the Father poses a symbolic threat constituted not so much by what he does as by what he *is*: the possessor of the empowered phallus and the obstacle to the Mother. In the Son's perspective this threat of the Other, even when it is exclusively passive, is construed as an aggression, all the more injurious because the Son identifies with this aggressor (Father) who serves as the model of his desire. Because the unconscious "will murder even for trifles," the Junta's ritual at this juncture "knows no other punishment for crime than death . . . for every injury to our almighty and autocratic ego is at bottom a crime of *lèse-majesté*."[171]

When the Junta (Son) launched its offensive against "subversives" (Father), the victims were adversarial not by virtue of what they did (because outside of Junta mythology their actions were not criminal) but rather for what they were: the Other. The very existence of an Other implied a threat to the Junta, which overreacted to the threat it *created* by construing it as an assault and by then *taking the offensive* in retaliation. The Argentine military, as pointed out earlier, tolerated otherness only when it was defined by negation and ossified into binary opposition, only when it was polarized and recast as the Enemy. The Junta qualified all otherness adversarially with the prefix *anti* (antidemocratic, antinational, Antichrist), which is to express by inversion its projected perception of all otherness as *anti-Junta*.

The "crime" of "subversion" was thus inherent in its otherness; the Junta would tolerate only one Version. Difference was criminal. Obstacles between the Junta and its mythology were intolerable. The "subversives" were mythically guilty of this crime-of-the-father, this threat of empowered otherness that the Junta misconstrued as manifestly, overtly, and conspiratorially adversarial. They therefore had as their just punishment a means of retribution, a means of neutralizing what was perceived as empowered otherness, in violence formally faithful to the same psychodynamics that "reorganized" reality to establish their "subversion" to begin with. The crime and its capital punishment were related in a self-congratulating tautology, in a circular structure with no exits.

If the Son (Junta) was to command the power he desired, then the Father (Enemy) would have to be eliminated. As discussed earlier, in torture that goal was realized simultaneously from two directions: the Son (Junta) *became* the Father (Enemy) by a violent "reorganization" of hierarchical roles through the empowerment of the *picana*-phallus, that reversal accomplished at the expense of the Father who was subordinated to the disempowered role held originally by the Son. The symmetry of the inversion was mocked as the Son (Junta) went beyond that reciprocal arrangement's mere subordination by *destroying* the Father (Enemy) whom he had so ceremoniously remade in his image, not once but repeatedly in the "thousand deaths," in thousands of surrogates, in detention centers throughout Argentina. "A father's murder is repressed . . . only to reappear in an orgy of slaughter that banalyzes the event into death's feast."[172] Blood flows in the merriest way, as Dostoevsky once put it, as though it were champagne. And in an orgy indeed, with the struggle for the Father's phallus entailing usurpation not only of its abiding power and authority but also of its *erotic* rights as rehearsed symbolically, and aberrantly, through the "act of love" at the torture table. Sexual desire and violence are both sufficiently adaptable to fasten on surrogates if the object of original attraction is inaccessible. They both accept substitutions with great facility.

The orgy of the Father's vicarious slaughter, however, had to be very carefully, very ritualistically, enacted because it was highly overdetermined and carried consequences that its prudent authors would wish to avoid. Jacques Lacan's reading of *Totem and Taboo* argued that Freud linked "the apparition of the signifier of the Father, as author of the Law, to death, or rather to the murder of the Father, thus demonstrating that if this murder is the fruitful moment of the debt through which the subject binds himself for life to the Law, the symbolic Father, insofar as he signifies the Law, is actually the dead Father."[173]

Stuart Schneiderman assisted in understanding Lacan's concept of the dead father in the Oedipal complex with these words:

> Once the first father was murdered, he became identified with the Law and this Law was far more ferocious and inhibiting than the real father had been. [Lacan's] critique of the Freudian Oedipus complex states that the privilege accorded to the act of murder was actually a wish to revive and resuscitate the father, who was father, who occupied the paternal function fully, only insofar as he was dead.[174]

It was not enough in the detention center's orgy of politico-familial violence simply to murder the Father, simply to execute the thousands of ritual victims posed in his symbolic stead, because doing so slides the "Father" signifier into what Lacan called the "Name-of-the-Father," the Law. As the Law the dead father becomes a transcendental omnipresence (from which, as the truism has it, one cannot hide) "far more ferocious and inhibiting than the real father" (or Enemy).[175] By denominating the mythic, dead Oedipal Father *le Nom-du-Père*, Lacan called into play related connotations that speak directly to the theme. The French *nom*, meaning "name," is homonymic with *non*, meaning "no." The Name-of-the-Father is thus overlaid on the No-of-the-Father, the Law that forbids, beginning with the *no* prohibiting incest with the Mother and continuing by extension into all laws.[176] "Violence is thus even more sacrilegious when it offends the law of the mother/country than when it wounds the father and mother."[177] The word "sacrilegious" here is far from gratuitous because Lacan's designation "Name-of-the-Father" linked the symbolic Father with the transcendental paternal authority of Christian canon ("In the Name of the Father, and of the Son") who ultimately, and most significantly in the Oedipal context, is *one* with the Son.[178]

When the Father was symbolically murdered in the detention centers, the ritual had to incorporate a mechanism to protect its authors from the greater threat of the Name-of-the-Father, which simple execution would bring to bear against the Junta. Torture surfaced as the ideal compromise to satisfy conflicting demands of killing the Father and at once preventing his death, preventing his return as the Name-of-the-Father, for it enacted a mock execution that carefully protected the victim's life while it destroyed his body and his subjectivity. If the Father's presence had to be preserved to ensure the Name-of-the-Father's absence, then that presence would be a castrated one maintained by prolonged destruction. It would be a presence in which the Son implicitly asserted, borrowing a few words from Nietzsche, "I am already dead of my father."[179] "The military reminded us constantly that we were already dead," noted one survivor, "they called us 'the walking dead.' "[180] The symbolic order in which these ritual victims were obliged to be dead and alive was, as Lacan put it, "simultaneously non-being and insisting to be";[181] the ritual confined *desaparecidos* to the proper order.

The struggle against the Father (Enemy) assumed the form of *prolonged* torture rehearsed on the bodies of *multiple* victims precisely in order to focus Junta violence on the specific "fruitful moment" in which the Son dominated the Father and usurped his Power, in which the Son had his phallus empowered, but before the Father had died, passed to the status of Name-of-the-Father, and thus returned as the Law penalizing the Son for his transgression. The victim "is constantly suspended in the time of the Other." "What ultimately matters is not the truth but the hour of truth," the ritual timespan in which torture is efficacious.[182] The "dirty war" theater of operation was temporally fixed in this closure of the "fruitful moment" in which the Son usurped the phallus and exploited its power to dominate the Father and collect the spoils, but in which, at the same time, the life of the Father was guarded within confines that guaranteed his impotence and preempted his empowerment by default in death. "Procrastination is thus one of the essential dimensions of the tragedy";[183] in Junta torture the murder was forever imminent but forever postponed. Should the victim have begun to die under torture, there was an attending physician to "revive and resuscitate" him so that the process of his prolonged destruction could continue.

> The death of the victim solves nothing; the executioner is swindled. . . . And the torture itself must contrive to become ever more elaborate; the refinement of punishments, the inventive debauchery, constitutes—take a good look—enrichment ad infinitum of the intertwining ties between victim and executioner. Death is a stupid accident, bringing failure of the deeper scheme, for it severs, always unseasonably, always prematurely, those invisible bonds. The anguish inflicted must be endless for it to represent and attest to the longing for endless ties. . . . The absolute of possession demands the absolute of torture.[184]

"You're not going to be able to die," one victim was told in the La Perla detention center, "here you're going to stay alive as long as we want you to."[185]

XI

No grave sealed the *desaparecidos'* fate; these dead were never covered over. Their unresolved absence was imbued with a haunting vitality. Whereas torture as a prolongation of the Father's murder ritually prevented emergence of the Name-of-the-Father, the dead *desaparecidos'* empty graves returned the symbolic Father as a signifier (Law) with renewed vehemence, bringing his *no* to bear yet more forcefully (as the empty grave inaugurating Christianity well attests). The drama is not over, the elderly Oedipus stated in *Colonus,* "until I am dead, and you have buried me."[186] "Oedipus is . . . *not* buried—*not yet buried*—since the mystery (the riddle) of his mythic disparition is precisely such that Oedipus does die (or disappears) but *without leaving a corpse.*" For this reason the drama of Oedipus, like that of the *desaparecidos,* "has, in effect, *no end.*"[187]

A preoccupation with the bodiless grave was not new to Argentine history. One Buenos Aires social scientist recognized an Argentine "obsession with corpses and empty tombs," to which one might add—given the fanfare for La Recoleta, a Buenos Aires cemetery bordered by chic cafés and boutiques—the insistent social presence of graves in general.[188] Before *desaparecidos* were tallied so excessively that "there is not tomb enough and continent/to hide the slain," the exhumation of Evita Perón's body for reburial in a secret tomb in Milan rehearsed the "empty grave" theme.[189] General Pedro Aramburu, responsible for the emptying of the one grave and the secrecy of the other, was himself later executed by the Montoneros (who held a grudge in part over the transfer of Evita's remains), and his corpse "disappeared" a few years later. The Peronists responsible for the theft of Aramburu's corpse from its mausoleum in July 1974 held the dead general hostage, demanding the return of Evita's remains in exchange. The deal was finalized in November 1974, one empty grave settling accounts for another.[190] During the "dirty war" beginning in 1976, the theme then became central: "The 'empty' tomb was as much an element of this macabre scene as was the deliberate denial later on of identifiable tombs for the *desaparecidos.*"[191] Even the graves of the interred *desaparecidos* were emptied of subjects, of identities, and designated "NN" (from the Latin *non nominatus,* "not named").

The Crusades formally launched by Pope Urban II in November 1095 had as their central symbolic purpose the recapture of the risen Christ's empty grave in Jerusalem. "Enter upon the road to the Holy Sepulcher," Urban urged, "wrest that land from the wicked race and subject it to yourselves."[192] Earlier Byzantine counteroffensives sounded the same theme. In 972 and 974, for example, John Tziisces was intent on "delivering the Holy Sepulcher of Christ our God from the bondage of Muslims."[193] Likewise the holy "dirty warriors" sought to control the empty grave because it represented divine power (Name-of-the-Father), and sovereignty over it therefore empowered. Torture rituals could seal inside the empty grave what should not come out (Law) and draw forth from it what the Junta most desired. The Father/Son reversal function could multiply the grave, rehearse its emptying, reproduce it with the empty graves of surrogates in celebration of a dead God-made-Son.

"The naval of the world," as Urban put it, is controlled by whoever holds the Holy Sepulcher. Lesser parts of the globe were also controlled in association with graves, these occupied graves because humans rather than deities were interred in them. The Scynthians buried many of their significant dead on the frontiers of the territory, the graves "marking the limit" because "the primary function of a corpse honored in this way is to mount guard, to defend territory or ensure victory for it."[194] Graves were similarly used as border markers in various conquest agendas. Ferdinand and Isabella—to cite one notable example—were buried in Granada, to which they expanded the territory of Castile with the conclusion of the Reconquest in 1492. Drawing upon the same motif the 1203 Osma copy of the Beatus *mappaemundi* depicted Christ's apostles buried in the regions where, according to tradition, their evangelical work broadened the limits of Christendom. An enemy's desecration of graves that marked the limits, mounted guard, or stood as monuments to victory neutralized those functions and disempowered the grave. By "emptying" the graves of *desaparecidos*, the territory taken by the Enemy was likewise regained.

For the story of the *desaparecidos* to conclude, the graves must ultimately be filled. Forensic anthropology and organizations such as the Mothers of the Plaza de Mayo make their contributions toward that end, attempting to reconnect identities with anonymous bodies and to thereby fill in haunting voids.[195] Argentine President Carlos Saúl Menem approached the same problem in a more symbolic manner in late 1989, emptying the grave of Juan Manuel Rosas—over a hundred years after the caudillo's burial in England—in order to ceremoniously fill the dead dictator's "empty" spot in the pantheon in La Recoleta cemetery.[196] Menem freighted the already symbolically laden Rosas reburial (a gesture of "leaving resentment behind") by staging it as a preamble to the pardons he would subsequently extend to military officers for crimes related to the "dirty war" and its aftermath. Rosas was exhumed from his tomb of shame (that of burial in forced exile) and received by his compatriots as a national hero (via burial in La Recoleta), the poetics thus already set in motion when indicted and convicted military officers were accordingly retrieved from their "tomb" of shame (prison in some cases, probable incarceration in others) and exalted as the presidential pardon implied condonation of their offenses and the impropriety of the litigation imposed on them by the Alfonsín administration.[197] Linking the pardon with the "filling" of Rosas's "empty grave" further implied a more far-reaching symbolic maneuver because the pardon covered offenses in most cases related (in some directly, in others indirectly) to the *desaparecidos*, to the victims with empty graves. Rosas's attributes were split and distributed: The corpse finally at rest in its ("proper") grave was symbolically allocated by implication to the unburied *desaparecidos*, while the honor of national recognition associated with the corpse's repatriation and burial in La Recoleta was conferred upon the military. Menem's deployment of an "empty grave" strategy—exhuming a corpse from its grave at this specific moment and for this specific purpose, more than a century after burial—thus made a symbolic gesture to legitimate the military pardon (and the military violence) by "filling" the *desaparecidos'* empty graves vicariously, by putting the dead to rest at last, by foreclosing the cumulative story that will not end "until I am dead, and you have buried me."

"What are these rites, really, by which we fulfill our obligation to what is called the memory of the dead," Lacan asked, "if not the total mass intervention, from the heights of heaven to the depths of hell, of the entire play of the symbolic register."[198] We have not the Father but his Name, not a grave but a void emitting signs, not the *desaparecidos* but the signifier that represents them in the symbolic order of language making absence present. Psychoanalysts following Lacan have posited an intermediary between the prelinguistic Imaginary order and the Symbolic order instituted with the subject's acquisition of language: "The transition from the breast-filled mouth to word-filled mouth is achieved through experiences of 'empty mouth,'" a concept I have mentioned earlier in passing. "Learning to fill the void of the mouth with words constitutes an early paradigm of introjection. . . . First the empty mouth, then the absence of objects become words, and finally experiences with words themselves are converted into other words." Thus a chain of signification commences, departing from a lack—the "empty mouth"—that is filled. "Language, which makes up for . . . absence by *representing* presence, can be *understood* only within a 'community of empty mouths.'"[199] The *desaparecidos* and the Name-of-the-Father can be understood only within the context of "empty graves," lacks that are filled with "the absence of objects become words." As Lacan put it, "Just as what is rejected from the symbolic register reappears in the real, in the same way the hole in the real that results from loss sets the signifier in motion."[200]

The *desaparecidos* opened up a hole in the real, and it was this "empty grave" that mobilized the Law. A lack set the *picana*-phallus in motion to fill the hole where the Enemy should have been but was not, where the Father's power was voided, where his Name was missing. A symbolic debt thus accrued through a negative amortization: The more the Son (Junta) repaid the Father (Enemy) by "giving" him the phallus (*picana*), by filling his mouth with the object that at once emptied it, the more he owed the Law. The Son who murdered the Father was entrapped by his lineage into the structure of a debt peonage: He inherited a symbolic debt from the Father (for the empowerment of his phallus through murder), which he then owed with interest to the master signifier under whose authority he consequently fell, the Name-of-the-Father.

When the Name-of-the-Father modulated into the "dirty war's" Christian eschatology, the Junta again suffered the consequences of the reversal by which it became its own mimetic rival. The vicars of Christ (Junta) and the Antichrist were now indistinguishable, the latter "annihilated" only because it was incorporated into the former. "In his relation to God the Father," or, for my purposes here, the Name-of-the-Father, "Antichrist [Junta/Son] appears as a defiant and rebellious child, passionately concerned to frustrate the intentions of the father and even daring to usurp the father's place and to ape his authority."[201] If the Junta's usurpation of power and aping of the Father were to survive the Name-of-the-Father's transcendental authority, if it were to extend the symbolic struggle beyond the politico-familiar model and into the eschatology of "dirty war" myths, then it became incumbent on the torture rituals to provide a symbolic function by which the Junta rivaled and destroyed the Name-of-the-Father even while remaking itself in the image of *this* mimetic model. Such would imply an autoapotheosis, the symbolic transformation of the Junta into *deity*. "Enough of intermediaries," one of Ernesto Sábato's characters insists, "GOD, THE EXTERMINATOR."[202]

5

Sacrifice and the Surrogate Victim

¡Viva la patria! ¡Arriba los corazones![1]

I

ON DECEMBER 24, 1976, at the close of the first year of the "dirty war" and on the eve of the Son-God's rebirth into Christendom, de facto President Jorge Rafael Videla addressed a message to Argentina: "Sacrifice has been, without a doubt, the sign of the year that is ending. A shared and indispensable sacrifice that constitutes the beginning of the arduous journey toward the true reencounter of all Argentines; sacrifices . . . that permit us to assume the essential theme of the great Argentine family: that of national union."[2]

With these retrospective observations General Videla rhetorically consolidated the gains that he and the other members of the Junta forecast at the time of the March coup d'état. On that occasion the people of Argentina were made to understand that the Process of National Reorganization would begin by "establishing a just order" that "will exact from each one his personal quota of sacrifice."[3] Military discourse throughout the "dirty war" accordingly propagated the restoration of order in Argentina as a *process* dependent on the (coerced) cooperation of each citizen. The emphasis invariably stressed an external woe imposed on the nation, and the resultant necessity that Argentines subordinate their personal interest to elimination of the problem. What each citizen sacrificed, the Junta argued, recycled and returned with interest to the well-being of the population as a corporate whole. If during the "dirty war" the sacrifice was great and the payoff out of range, then the citizens had to trust that the "arduous journey" would lead finally to the happy resolution promised by the Junta.

As Admiral Massera explained the agenda to a youthful audience (the young a primary target of "dirty war" violence), "At this time the country can only offer you a creative adventure full of risks, inconveniences, and sacrifices."[4] In another passage, noteworthy for its interweaving of sacrificial motifs with the Myth of International Conspiracy, Massera implied that each Argentine's "personal quota" of sacrifice was a localization, a filtering-down of the *patria's* sacrifice as a geopolitical whole. He argued that the great world powers—the United States and the Soviet Union—knew what catastrophe would fall on mankind if they confronted one another directly. They therefore "opted to exercise their hostilities by supporting local conflicts, thus sacrificing less-powerful countries which—whether they like it or not—become martyr metaphors" of the cold war struggle.[5] In a domestic configuration analogous to the international one interpreted here by Massera, the Junta's conspicuous, hegemonic effort to eliminate the Enemy likewise displaced and localized the greater conflict onto less powerful bodies, onto "martyr metaphors" in the detention centers. "World War III" was battled out unilaterally, lopsidedly, at the torture table, rehearsing and preempting the imaginary conflagration of global (and, in related myths, cosmic) proportions in which Junta mythology contextualized its violence.[6]

Having narrativized the "dirty war" around the "sign" of sacrifice, Junta discourse reinforced the propriety of exacting a "personal quota" from each Argentine by positing the military, and above all the Junta itself, as paradigms of self-sacrifice for the *patria*. It is for this reason that the sacrifice propagated as the "sign" of the "dirty war's" inaugural year was qualified by General Videla as "shared": Each Argentine contributed his or her "personal quota," and the extraordinary outstanding balance required in the tally of accounts to neutralize "subversion" was provided by the military through—as General Videla put it—"an act of service that, with faith in God Our Lord, I offer to the Fatherland, to the army, and to all the Argentine people."[7]

Outside of "dirty war" mythology, however, it is difficult to justify the distribution of the heaviest sacrificial burden to the military because the "dirty war's" primary strategy—abduction, torture, execution—situated the Junta more readily in the role of sacrificial executioner than in the role of victim. How was the sacrifice "shared," finally, if the military's posture as victim was so dramatically overshadowed by its ritual function as *sacrificer*? Why did *sacrifice* emerge as the sign of the Process of National Reorganization, and to what extent was this trope, like others mobilizing Junta mythology, demetaphorized by "dirty war" rituals to realize the Junta's violent "reorganization"?

To find a satisfactory answer to these questions, the focus here must be broadened to gain a metacultural understanding of the sociopolitical functions of sacrifice. Whether the rituals are staged on a pyramid in pre-Columbian Tenochtitlán or in a detention center in contemporary Argentina, sacrifice is a symbolic drama by which authoritarian leaders effect an autoapotheosis through the sanctified destruction of ritually charged victims, thereby generating an illusion of politico-religious legitimacy. The Christian, "dirty war" mythology that the torture rituals enacted "legitimates social institutions by bestowing upon them an ultimately valid ontological status, that is, by locating them within a sacred and cosmic frame of reference."[8] This mythology's appropriation and mobilization of a symbolic complex sought to transform a de facto regime with totalitarian aspirations into a theocracy whose intrinsic legitimacy was presumed as an ontological matter of fact and was celebrated by the rituals that sustained it. The "dirty war" was cleansed in Junta mythology when the murder of innocent victims became purposeful and indispensable under a canopy of sacred symbols and within a ritual context that was felicitous to the Junta's end. In the Argentine detention center "sacrificial killing is the basic experience of the 'sacred,'" of "our way of being Christian." "*Homo religiosus* acts and attains self-awareness as *homo necans.*"[9]

II

Sacrifice is always compensatory, always in response to an actual or imaginary absence. Like the romantic-tragic Hero of "dirty war" mythology, and like the subject of Oedipal drama (Junta), the sacrificer is mobilized by a lack. In order for a ritual of sacrifice to be efficacious, the sacrificial offering that opens and is transferred through the channel of exchange between man and deity must be highly valuable to the community either intrinsically, because it has been symbolically made so through ritual, or both. A significant valuation of the offering is crucial because, beyond honoring, appeasing, or nourishing the deity, the sacrificer has in mind barter: The community strongly desires an absent entity or state of affairs, so the sacrificer barters with a highly valued commodity to entice an exchange of like or greater value. "It was believed that if the hunger of dangerous gods was satisfied" via human sacrifice, for example, then "starvation, mortality, illness, and violent manifestations of nature could be avoided."[10] "To this idea of giving we would add that something is always expected in return; sacrifices do not happen for nothing, but rather because they need to happen, even though this need might be only emotional or psychological. We believe that no sacrifice is disinterested."[11] The gift offered to the god thus confirms a relation with implied mutual obligations. The interest of the community initiates the arrangement, but the sacrificer denies and projects the initiating impetus onto the deity's will or needs (hunger, for example), thereby assuming the dominant position while feigning subordination. Sacrifice, like all ritual, departs from a rift in social life and proceeds toward a symbolic compensation by—to use the Junta's term—"reorganizing" the reality (and often the hierarchical relations) associated with the troublesome absence.

By way of example assume that a drought (lack of water) is killing the crops on which a given community depends. The leaders governing the community find themselves impotent before the apparently pitiless natural forces that have imposed the plight. For want of recourse within the realm of the Real (the lack of water thus compounded by a lack of recourse), the leaders in control of the community (but not of the drought) displace the problem onto symbolic ground and feign control by implementing a mythic solution to a real problem: sacrifice. As the causes of the drought shift from a natural to a supernatural register, the politico-religious leaders are more strategically positioned to effect a "solution" by barter. Because in real terms a sacrifice has no causal worth in catalyzing a crop-saving rainfall, the Real is left behind as the leaders introduce symbolic actions that are efficacious within the mythological system (which they can control) designed specifically to deny impotence, invert it, and have it masquerade as power.

Similarly in the Argentine case the Junta displaced social, political, and economic problems onto mytho-military grounds, waging the "dirty war" in the detention centers—as the leaders perplexed by the drought resorted to sacrifice at their altars—to act out the compensatory theatrics by which impotence before a problem is recast as power. That displacement onto symbolic ground was disavowed as such and marketed as efficient, appropriate action to a population that was stunned by terror and proselytized with myths sanctioning the "dirty" tactics of ritual murder. Torture in the detention centers, like torture at the sacrificial altar, transformed a political disadvantage into politico-religious power through the symbolization and the exploitation of innocent victims.

Water (order in Argentina) was lacking, a (social-political-economic) solution was lacking, and the leaders in power had to *do something* to perpetuate the aura of competence that sustained their governance. When sacrifice (torture/execution in the detention centers) emerged as the solution, the transformation of impotence into power was effected through a mimetic identification and a projection: As representatives of the community that was *victimized* by the gods (through drought or "subversion"), the leaders symbolically reversed the roles of the scheme and usurped the position of omnipotence by projecting their status as the-one-victimized onto an Other, onto a surrogate (the sacrificial victim, the *desaparecido*). This scapegoat, this *desaparecido* freighted with the projection, was then duly destroyed in a drama of spectacular atrocity as the leaders flaunted their (symbolic) management of the problem before the populace.

Once sacrifice was instituted, once the Symbolic displaced the Real, the leaders who generated terror and disseminated the illusion of omnipotence could then deny the absurdity of their violence on grounds that were highly in their favor, often—as is clear in the "dirty war"—by appeal to a hodgepodge of politico-religious mythology that guaranteed the ontological and eschatological necessity of atrocity. When sacrifice failed to bring rain or when the torture and execution of *desaparecidos* repressed and aggravated political, social, and economic problems rather than solving them, the leaders who displaced the problem onto symbolic grounds and who commanded the illusion of omnipotence could then deal with dissent under the aegis of the new paradigm they had installed, via the same symbolic displacement and terror, not infrequently by projecting the blame back onto the "sinful" community and upscaling the number of sacrifices. "Thanks to its theatrical, mimetic character and the deep impression that its sacred solemnity can impart, ritual is self-perpetuating."[12] The sacrificial ritual itself thus becomes—despite the myths propagating it as a religious or quasi-religious act undertaken on behalf of the community's well-being—the field of a political struggle.[13] "In a centralized State sacrifice, with its function of regulating and managing violence, becomes a means of manipulation and of obtaining political power through control of ideology and of supernatural forces."[14]

The "god" to whom the sacrifice is purportedly offered tends to disappear as the foreground is dominated by the sacrificers who appropriate his function and as the scapegoating aspects of the ritual overshadow the honorific and reverential aspects. Sacrificial rituals in the Argentine detention centers were not offered *to* anything (other than the Junta itself), their emphasis rather placed on "reorganizing" social reality, generating power, and absenting evil, "sin," "subversion," and other pollutants whose "disappearance" endeavored to purify and unify "the great Argentine family." Indeed the *desaparecidos* were "victims of the same rigid and absolutely incomprehensible logic . . . as those whose hearts were pulled out to enable the sun to continue on its course," if "the same logic" is understood to be a mytho-logical system that endowed ritualized political violence with eschatological necessity. In the symbolic order where "dirty war" violence was elaborated, sacrificial torture rituals dominated the political struggle as the Junta elected "whatever is necessary to prevent the disappearance of a system" because loss of the Natural Order "would be equivalent to something like the end of the world."[15] One disappearance thus replaced the Junta's fear of another. The *desaparecidos* were sacrificed to service the belief that their absence restored the presence of "Western and Christian civilization."

Referring specifically to Aztec rituals,[16] Yototl González Torres concluded that "sacrifice was one of the most extreme forms of exploitation; through ritual murder of a human being diverse benefits, which ultimately fell back upon the state, were pursued."[17] Predominant among the benefits of ritualized murder in "dirty war" Argentina as much as in pre-Columbian Mesoamerica were material gains (spoils of war, tribute, slaves) and, more importantly, the "spoils" of abstract commodities—power, legitimacy, hegemony, apotheosis. These abstract commodities ascended purified from the bloody spectacle to the politico-religious leaders as its direct beneficiaries, providing them "the vital force they thought necessary to carry out their work."[18] The more the Junta sacrificed, the more it was empowered to sacrifice; the ritual perpetuated not only itself but also its numinous authors.

The cybernetic architecture of ceremonial cities designed as stages for sacrifice in Aztec society—great temples so constructed that a man standing at the base was unable to see the top, making the sacrificial victim's ascent seemingly rise into the sky[19]—then signaled a more general political agenda based on the theatrics of spectacular violence as I discussed them in Chapter 2. A number of colonial chronicles, notably the related texts of Tezozomoc and Fray Diego Durán, made specific reference to the political function of sacrificial rituals claiming religious justification. The Aztecs invited the chieftains of what they called the "Enemies of the House" in order "to apply diplomatic pressure upon a people they had failed to defeat in war."[20] Failure on the battlefield was "reorganized" at the altar. The often apologetic account of Alfredo López Austin was similarly unambiguous on the point: Actual as well as potential Aztec enemies were invited "to the most ostentatious and cruel ceremonies so they could return to their towns fearful and forewarned of the fate they would face in the case they were defeated."[21] As Durán recorded the spectacle, "The strangers sat down in the decorated boxes and awaited the ceremony, which had been unknown till this time. . . . The lords from the provinces who had come to observe the sacrifice were shocked and bewildered by what they had seen and they returned to their homes filled with astonishment and fright."[22]

The dissemination of terror facilitating expansion of the Aztec empire also served an internal function of repression that—in direct analogy to the function of spectacular violence in Argentina—was guaranteed by a public obliged to witness the rituals reinforcing its own subjugation. Tezozomoc observed in the Aztec case that "the chiefs and lords were invited to attend human sacrifices, under the penalty of themselves being sacrificed if they were absent from the ceremonies!"[23] As discussed in Chapter 2 the Junta similarly demanded the attendance of its population at all social levels, thereby consolidating the implied audience of participant-observers that the efficacy of its power-generating spectacle required. In both the Aztec and the Argentine cases, what Laurette Séjourné termed the "sanctification of violence" resulting in "sacred terror" reaped the political rewards of coercion, domination, and power, along with the social and military benefits that were simultaneously generated.[24] The transcendental justification of ritual murder combined with terror to silence interpretations questioning the propriety of a government that was founded on this violent centerpiece, as prolific as it was bloody.

Aztec and Argentine models of authoritarianism based on sacrifice both also claimed legitimate title to the victims' property. Whether the war was "flowered," as in the Aztec case, or "dirty," as in the Argentine, the spoils of war—including the market and prestige value of human lives—figured prominently among the factors motivating the troops. As Durán described the Mesoamerican affair, Aztec soldiers returned from operations "happy with the quantities of plunder and riches they brought, and the joy that going to war gave them was so great that soldiers could not be found in the cities, desiring war and going to it most willfully."[25]

In Argentina, similarly, the looting of "dirty war" victims' homes was instituted for the material gain of the task forces and their superiors. Causality was often inverted—the desire to loot preceding a victim's "subversion"—because the attractiveness of "spoils" in itself often proved sufficient cause to instigate the abduction, torture, extortion, and, in some cases, "disappearance" of Argentines from wealthy families.[26]

The spoils of greatest value and prestige among the Aztecs were captured prisoners delivered to the State for its sacrificial rituals.[27] In conventional warfare captors brought their prisoners to the priests who carried out the sacrifice (the State often buying the victims), after which "the bodies were laid by the skull rack, and each warrior identified the one that he had captured." The postsacrificial corpse, exhausted of its ritual potency insofar as the State was concerned, was then returned to the captor, who ate it and hung the bones in his home as a sign of prestige.[28] An emphasis on the acquisition of bodies was yet more pronounced in the Aztec empire's "flower wars," which had as their purpose not defense against or conquest of an enemy, but rather the capture of prisoners for the sacrificial rituals on which the society's political theology depended. In his *Historia de los yndios mexicanos*, Juan de Tovar explained the affair directly: "In reality wars were waged for no reason other than to bring back people . . . to be sacrificed."[29] As the result of an agreement reached between the Tlaxcala, Cholula, and Huexotzinco on the one hand and the Aztecs on the other, "flower wars" were staged battles fought on prearranged occasions.[30] In Argentina, where most victims were inimical not intrinsically but precisely because Junta mythology constructed their enmity, the "staged" war—a roundup staged as war—*created* the adversary it was purporting to eliminate in order likewise to generate a constant supply of ritual victims. (Penal retribution for real or mythic crimes also made its contribution to the body count: In Argentina all crimes of "subversion" were punished by torture rituals, just as in Aztec society "practically every crime that in modern jurisprudence constitutes a felony was made capital and often punished by sacrifice.")[31] The "dirty" war shared with the "flower" war and with conventional

Aztec warfare this need to bring the enemy back alive in order to destroy him ceremoniously. "Thus, even when he could as easily have been killed, an enemy was wounded so that he could not defend himself and . . . was dragged from the battleground."[32] In Argentina the need to protect the enemy's "aliveness"—here under the veil of the need to interrogate—was explicitly expressed during confrontations with Montonero guerrillas. Like the Mesoamerican warriors who "reportedly preferred being cut to pieces" to being captured and sacrificed, the Montoneros ingested cyanide tablets when their capture seemed imminent.[33] Rather than permit these suicides and tally the deaths as statistics in the Junta's favor, the task forces systematically checked the Montoneros' mouths and, when necessary, pumped their stomachs in order to bring the Enemy to the detention center alive. In Argentina—here unlike Mesoamerica—preservation of the victim's vitality was then extended as an abiding concern into the torture rituals themselves, which reaped their benefits from a *protracted destruction*.

Sacrificial rituals in Argentina, to summarize, signify within a mythological system that disavowed the absurdity of ritual violence (torture) as the efficacious means of remedying some social deficiency. By inverting total impotence into totalitarian domination and by projecting victimization onto a surrogate, torture in the Argentine detention centers dramatized a mythic solution to a real problem. The analogous function of human sacrifice in pre-Columbian civilization further indicates that leaders implementing violent rituals did so mimetically, by themselves adopting and exercising the role of victimizer rather than victim. The gods created lacks that victimized the community, and following suit the sacrificers usurped and exercised the same privilege themselves, creating lacks (*desaparecidos*, absences) by victimizing scapegoats destroyed in their and the community's stead. When these surrogate victims were culled from the community (as was the case in Argentina) rather than imported, the victims' identities were manipulated—some ties to the community severed, others strengthened—in order to satisfy the complex and competing functions that the ritual assigned to the *desaparecidos*.

III

By virtue of a "strange propensity to seize upon surrogate victims," as René Girard phrased it, societies practicing human sacrifice "actually conspire with the enemy [god] and at the right moment toss him a morsel that will satisfy his raging hunger."[34] The dynamics of such "conspiring with the enemy" were discussed earlier in their relation to identification with the aggressor. By resorting to violent symbolic gestures in an attempt to rectify a lack of power, the sacrificer (the Son in the Oedipal configuration, the Junta) "transforms himself from the person threatened into the person who makes the threat."[35] Consolidating the sacrificial model with the Oedipal drama as these pertain to torture/execution in the Argentine detention centers, one may posit the following: The Son/ Sacrificer (Junta), victimized by a lack (ultimately of power-phallus), mimed the behavior of the Father/Deity (Enemy) who caused and represented the threatening deficiency.[36] In acting out the reaction formation of his denied impotence, the Son/Sacrificer mimed his aggressor by victimizing a surrogate Other, a scapegoat, a *desaparecido* who, as I will discuss in greater detail momentarily, was elaborated to represent the deity being symbolically deposed and destroyed. By usurping the functions of the phallus proper to the Father/Deity, the Son/Sacrificer remade himself in the image of the Other he wished to displace and appropriated the symbolics of omnipotence, now on a transcendental scale. The deification of these ritual symbolics further enabled the Son/Sacrificer (Junta) to propagate his usurpation of power through the ritual murder of surrogates as an "indispensable" act of eschatological importance, while at the same time he could maintain his image as victim rather than victimizer, as messiah sacrificing himself on the community's behalf.

Because the Son/Sacrificer's mimetic rivalry engages with a transcendental paternal construct beyond the mundane Father, sacrificial rituals ultimately posed the Junta in a symbolic struggle against what I have been calling, following Jacques Lacan, the Name-of-the-Father. The sacrificial victim, the overdetermined *desaparecido*, was a surrogate representing first the Oedipal Father but then also the murdered Father's menacing absence, his symbolic presence, the function that the Father fulfilled as the Law insofar as he was dead. In this final phase of mimetic rivalry, anticipating the empty grave beyond the "fruitful moment" that keeps alive as it kills, the Junta's ritual protected its authors' gains by symbolically subordinating the Name-of-the-Father, the Law (or, in "dirty war" parlance, the Natural Order) that it purported to defend.

Human sacrifice among the Aztecs was not conducted in response to a specific lack (the drought of my original example), but rather was instituted as the politico-religious centerpiece to which all social structures and meanings ultimately referred.[37] Like the spectacles of public execution in eighteenth-century Europe, and like torture/execution in the Argentine detention centers, it served as the locus from which a political mythology was sustained, rather than as an occasional, unpleasant necessity that the regime pardoned itself for in light of the common good. In Aztec cosmology humankind was recreated by the god Quetzalcoatl "to carry out a perfectly concrete enterprise, an enterprise in which the gods themselves had failed: that is, to prevent the sun from being extinguished."[38] Here the gods—constructs, keep in mind, with no empirical reality outside of the fictions that created them—summoned man to sustain their metonymic representation (the sun) and to do so precisely because the gods themselves were unequal to the task. The hierarchical relation of a powerful paternal god to its dependent human "children" was thereby inverted as the enfeebled deities consigned their survival to the humans they created. Humans, that is to say, invented the gods by transcendentalizing a paternal construct, then effected a vertical reversal by subordinating the Father apotheosized into this mock-omnipotent form. "Starting from the model of sacrifice being normatively an offering from a filial dependent to a parental divinity," Meyer Fortes summarized, "it is almost as if the dependent worshipper is by this means enabled to redefine himself as the dominant quasi-paternal sustainer of the divinity's existence."[39]

The roles of Father and Son, as at the Argentine torture table, were reversed. Gods were created as man's creators and incontestable, inherent superiors, but then man—as author of the fiction and ritual—reserved the corresponding privileges of authorship to subordinate these deities *in the same act by which he worshiped them* (sacrifice).

The sacrificer also reserved another right: to exploit his fictive theological construct in order to endow acts of atrocity with ontological necessity. A god as the beneficiary of sacrifice is dubious at best. As Walter Burkert observed in regard to Greek cult practice, sacrifice "is objectionable, and was already felt to be so early on, because it so clearly and directly benefits man."[40] The Aztecs constructed a pantheon of deities and patterns of worship in such a way as to render sacrifice—to borrow Videla's adjective—"indispensable" (lest the sun should be extinguished); while in this-worldly terms the spectacle—invented by man, along with its cosmological accoutrements, *for* man—performed admirably in empowering the leaders of an authoritarian politico-religious regime. The regime's need to sacrifice human beings preceded the mytho-logical rationale called forth to sanctify it, and the benefits gravitated not to the deities but to the State. In the Aztec case the sociopolitical motivation was underscored from the start: According to the Codex Telleriano-Remensis, the first human sacrificial victims in Mesoamerica were the Tzinacantepeca who rebelled against Mexico in 1483.[41]

The "dirty war" mythology elaborated by the Junta worked within its respective sociolect to create "a system in which everything, including the gods [or, in Oedipal terms, Name-of-the-Father], were subordinated to it."[42] Once the ritual of torture/execution-as-sacrifice was instituted and the "dirty war" mythology was set in motion, the Name-of-the-Father (which served, circularly, as in the Aztec case, to sanction the very rituals that deposed it) was subordinated to the Junta. This was first accomplished by implication in the Junta's constructs of enmity. As the discussion of binary oppositions in Chapter 3 revealed, a mechanism of polarization provided that the imaginary negative attributes vehemently projected onto the Enemy returned inverted to reciprocally reload the Junta with positive attributes. The depiction of "subversion" as metaphysical Evil, for example, returned from the inimical antithesis "reorganized," recharged, to reinforce the Junta's symbolic transcendence into the divine attribute of metaphysical Goodness.

The Junta then appealed to the special relation it presumed to hold with deity in order to advance its autoapotheosis and, as a by-product, to mystify its agenda of political atrocity with an air of otherworldly sanction. Just as the medieval transition from *corpus Christi mysticum* (mystical body of Christ) to *corpus Ecclesiae mysticum* (mystical body of the Church) initiated the secularization of a mystery reliant on heaven but governed on earth, dependent on deity but usurping its role for sociopolitical purposes, so too the Junta grounded its agenda in the divinity that it replaced.[43] "Only God has the right to give or take human life," a spokesman of Junta ideology recognized, "homicide is a great sin because it wrests from God what is His, it usurps His right." Once elaborated under the canopy of what the military called "our way of being Christian," however, the mythology's authors assigned themselves a privileged position before that mandate: "Only one possessing delegated divine right, the power to kill when it is essential to the common good, has the authority to judge over human life."[44] In the detention centers the theme was likewise echoed: "Only God gives and takes life. But God is busy elsewhere, and we're the ones who must undertake this task in Argentina."[45] The Junta exercised its autoapotheosis as sole possessor and delegate of the Law, rehearsing in ritual murder the power to judge and condemn as He does. A theme common in the history of "Western and Christian civilization" was thus replayed at the torture table: A vicar displaced the transcendental authority in which his legitimacy was grounded. "We are God" the torturers told their victims in the Argentine detention centers, "We are the law [Name-of-the-Father]."[46]

In sacrifices on the Christian model, such as those in Argentina, "man puts God to death in an action symbolic of man's attempt to supplant God."[47] Torture rituals remade the Junta first in the likeness of paternal authority through mimesis and peripeteia (Son-Father role reversal) and then repeated the same structure in a higher register where the transcendental paternal concept, the Name-of-the-Father, was dominated as the mundane Oedipal Father had been previously. Torture/execution as sacrifice thereby recapitulated a process of cosmic as well as national reorganization, with all benefits of the rearrangement gravitating toward the sacrificers, toward the Junta, which at this juncture coveted the roles of both the sacrificer and the god to whom the sacrifice was made.

Having subordinated the Father in his mundane and transcendental representations, and having destroyed the former during the "fruitful moment" of torture, acquisition of totalitarian hegemony on a cosmic scale now only required that the sacrificers symbolically annihilate the deity that they endeavored to replace. Argentine torture on the model of Christian sacrifice implied "a sort of revenge against God."[48] In both the Aztec and Argentine systems, elimination of the deity (or Name-of-the-Father) symbolically executed through sacrifice of a surrogate made to represent Him cleared the way for the politico-religious leaders' autoelevation to the deified position. A void was both created and filled by the same sacrificial ritual.

"It was not men who died" in many Aztec sacrifices "but gods—gods within a corporeal covering that made possible their ritual death on earth."[49] In Christian theology, similarly, God-made-man is sacrificed, God as *flesh* is nailed to the cross. The Aztec transformation of a sacrificial victim into a man-god often involved extended rituals refining the victim's representation of a specific deity. Vicarious sacrifice of the major Aztec deities, notably Tezcatlipoca, was not carried out until an entire year of rituals groomed the victim into the image of the god for whom he was surrogate.[50] Here, as in the Argentine detention center, the incompatibility of "fathering" the gods and executing them was reconciled as these competing functions collapsed into a palimpsest, into a single, overdetermined ritual, again stressing the resuscitation-in-destruction of torture's "fruitful moment." The aliveness of the deity, like that of the victim representing him at the torture table, was ceremoniously protected in order to prolong his destruction: The god was murdered and yet always again present when the ritual was reenacted.[51] At the Aztec altar and in the Argentine detention center, theomorphic surrogates provided that the deity could be annihilated and at once preserved so that ritual murder could self-perpetuate in His name.

The Junta engaged mimetically with the Name-of-the-Father by appropriating His function and vicariously dominating Him—to summarize in Oedipal terms—then turned the power of that appropriation against its source in an attempt to destroy a transcendental abstraction by destroying the body of a surrogate that embodied it. In the "dirty war" lexicon the denomination "*desaparecido*" served well for victims absent to themselves as they were made to represent the Other required by the rituals. The victims, bearing the symbolic burden as incarnations of the Law (Name-of-the-Father) being destroyed, "disappeared without a trace" as they were displaced by their symbolic functions. The *desaparecidos* were viewed in "dirty war" mythology as embodiments of ideology, of a discourse that was powerful to the degree that it was intangible, an invisible enemy that the torture rituals sought to concretize and symbolically eliminate by destroying the scapegoats made to incarnate it. "In the beginning was the Word [phallus-power/Law], and the Word was with God [Name-of-the-Father], and the Word was God [Law=Name-of-the-Father]."[52] That construction was troublesome to the Junta's agenda; there was nothing tangible to torture, no corporal sentience to exploit in accessing a discourse and effecting a transformation, no access to the phallus-power, and no means to effect the reversal by which the godly position could be usurped. But then "the Word was made flesh" (when it intersected with another signifier, the *picana*-phallus), and as flesh a Word can be nailed to a cross.

As established by biblical texts beginning with Genesis, the Word of God brings mortal flesh to life, and then, at death, leaves the body behind as the soul soars toward the Hereafter. New Testament accounts provided that the divine Word was made flesh in Christ, the new Adam, but in this case Word and flesh were inextricably bound as the man-god rose from His Passion with soul and body intact. Dead mortals, in the meantime, awaited the Second Coming for their bodies' resurrection and reunion with the Word. The Word in "dirty war" torture rituals, here the Word of the Junta as Name-of-the-Father, was similarly introduced into the victim (via the Word's concretization in the picana-phallus as signifier) who was "nonexistent" as a subject and then "brought to life," spasmodically by shock of the Word and symbolically as he was "born again" into the identities that the rituals assigned him. During his torture (the process of his dying), the Word was then drawn out as the victim was made to mouth Junta discourse, to release the life force imparted to him. Once the Junta's Word, like the soul, had departed from the body, once the victim had "confessed," he was "dead" as a ritual object. The desaparecido was then an inconsequential casualty of the Word he released, a monological Word that rejoined, glorified, and strengthened the Name-of-the-Father from which it originally emanated.

IV

The transformation of the torture ritual victim into a surrogate deity was explicitly phrased in a novel by the Argentine Elvira Orphée. There a torturer prefaced a session by explaining the theogonic affair to the victim: "We are going to make you Christ."[53] Popular perceptions also recorded that symbolic equation of the desaparecido and immolated deity. During the first weekly procession of the Mothers of the Plaza de Mayo, for example, each demonstrator wore a nail attached to her jacket, "to remember the sacrifice of Christ, nailed to the cross." The Mother of a desaparecido further explained that "we also have our Christ, and relive Mary's grief."[54]

The suffering of Christ Himself was developed in the New Testament as wholly vicarious, as necessary for effecting fallen man's redemption. Christians, in turn, are expected to share in the Lord's suffering if they wish to participate in His glory. In "dirty war" vernacular and in the detention center rituals generating it, the desaparecidos satisfied this requirement of suffering not only in the extreme but also in performance of an implied and obligatory expiation. The burden of "indispensable" sacrifice on the Christian model, along with the accompanying symbolics of deification, were imposed on the desaparecidos at the torture table. Suggestions of that imposition were already discernible before a victim's abduction, notably in the repressors' expression obejear or hacerle la oveja.[55] Derived from its (dubious) sonic similitude with the phrase Orden de Búsqueda, the search order "made one a sheep" through the preparatory investigations preceding abduction. "I send you forth as sheep," the sacrificial Lamb of God explained to his apostles, sheep for the slaughter.[56] If Christ was "a lamb slain from the foundation of the world," then the tortured *desaparecidos* were sheep slain from the foundation of the Junta's "reorganized" Argentina.[57]

More than victims of a foundation sacrifice, however, the *desapareci-dos* were agents of a vicarious atonement, representing Christ Himself and, like Christ, the embodiment in sacrifice of a sin ("subversion") that had to be expiated. In the ESMA detention center a torturer explained to a detained priest that "in a war the just sometimes pay for the sinners," precisely the function of Christ on the cross.[58] Another religious victim, crying and praying during a mock execution, was told by her torturers: "Shut up. This is what you get for going around with that bearded man, that queer," the descriptions referring to Christ, in whose symbolic stead the victim succumbed to her eroticized martyrdom.[59] Elsewhere, in a provincial detention center, a tortured priest was told "in comparison to the Argentine military, the Romans persecuting the first Christians didn't know anything,"[60] the statement again stressing the victim's Christianity in relation to his "sacrifice." On another occasion the Christ poetics were dramatized by the form of torture itself: "They crucified me," one victim related, "they crucified me and left me in that situation for 48 hours."[61]

With torture rituals the champions of "Western and Christian civilizations" thus rehearsed on their victims' bodies that "every tongue should confess that Jesus Christ is Lord," but this "to the glory of God the Father," the Junta.[62] The Son (Junta) symbolically murdered the Son (Christ) as he aspired to be, as Christ was, a Son transformed into a God (Name-of-the-Father). The idea of the crucifixion was

> reconciliation with God the Father, atonement for the crime committed against him; but the other side of the emotional relation showed itself in the fact that the son, who had taken the atonement on himself, became a god himself beside the father and, actually, in place of the father. Christianity, having arisen out of a father-religion, became a son-religion. It has not escaped the fate of having to get rid of the father.[63]

The detention centers' sacrifice of the *desaparecidos*-as-Christ "allows beneath the cover of the Son the representation of the Oedipal wishes (the death of the Father, or of God)."[64] The Name-of-the-Father that the Junta wished to displace was symbolically eliminated by sacrificing the Son. "In the sacrifice of Jesus, the sovereignty of a single God is put to death: the death of the supreme authority of the idealized father."[65] At the same time, a related ritual function exploited the Son-God symbolics by "freeing" divine attributes that were then absorbed to apotheosize the Junta's new paternal status. Each *desaparecido* at the torture table was "always bearing about in the body the dying of the Lord Jesus, that the life also of Jesus might be made manifest in body."[66] The victim was assigned the agony of Christ's Passion, while the divine "life" made manifest by the ritual was disencumbered and channeled toward the Junta.

In military discourse at high levels, the concept of *desaparecidos*-as-Christ also gained expression, perhaps nowhere as suggestively as in the following comment and gesture made by Admiral Massera. The occasion was an August 1977 visit that U.S. Assistant Secretary of State for Human Rights Patricia Derian paid Massera at ESMA. The conversation, as recounted by Derian during her testimony at the Junta members' trials in 1985, included the following:

> I told him that I had seen a rudimentary plan of the floor that was immediately below the one where we were meeting, and I said, "It's possible that downstairs they're torturing someone as we speak." Then something really astonishing happened: He smiled at me with an enormous smile, made a gesture of washing his hands, and said, "You remember what happened with Pontius Pilate."[67]

Christ was arrested and tried by Jewish authorities, found guilty of blasphemy, and turned over to the Romans on charges of sedition. Among those punishing Him we find no Christians. Whereas Pontius Pilate executed a political criminal whose apotheosis came later (largely by virtue of His execution and empty grave), the devoutly *Christian* Argentine military executed its own God *as such*. Junta mythology precluding rationality and dismissing the paradoxical execution of the same deity in whose Name it waged holy war was, in its method, reminiscent of the discourse scripted to participant-observers when Christ was sentenced to death. "What will ye then that I shall do unto him whom ye call the King of the Jews?" Pilate asked the crowd, "and they cried out again, Crucify him. Then Pilate said unto them, Why, what evil hath he done? And they cried out the more exceedingly, Crucify him."[68] The *why*, here as in the Argentine detention center, was short-circuited, was shouted down, having as its only response a more vehement reaffirmation of the necessity for violence.

The Junta's adverse relation with its deity was also reminiscent of the politico-religious confusion that Fyodor Dostoyevsky's Grand Inquisitor experienced when Christ baffled the clarity of a purge's sanctified correctness by arriving on the scene as a potential victim. A piece of Buenos Aires graffiti testified to a popular perception of that same theme: "If Jesus Christ returned to earth [Cardinal of Buenos Aires Juan] Aramburu would turn him in to the SIDE [Service of State Information]."[69] Because Christ did not return to earth, let alone to Buenos Aires, the political urgency of His destruction was facilitated, manifested, and repeatedly reenacted through surrogates, *desaparecidos*, symbolically freighted with His transcendental absence. The absence handily predisposed the ritual to construct a Christ appropriate for the detention centers' cross, a "reorganized" Christ, a Christ who was congruous with "our way of being Christian." Indeed the torturers forging such surrogates bombastically clarified Christian canon for priests whom they charged with misinterpreting it, and they often based a victim's "subversion" precisely on his "cunningly distorted interpretation of Christian doctrine."[70] "You have made a mistake," one priest was told, "which is having interpreted Christ's doctrine too literally." "Christ talks about the poor, but the poor in spirit. . . . In Argentina the poor in spirit are the rich, and you, from now on, should help the rich people more since they are the ones who are spiritually needy."[71]

In Aztec as well as Christian practice, the sacrifice of deities concluded with or was symbolically celebrated by ingestion of the murdered god's body.[72] When the Christian faithful take communion of the Host (from *hostia*, "a sacrificial victim") and when Aztec priests eat the raw flesh of sacrificial victims, they incorporate the attributes of divinity.[73] In Catholic belief the consecrated eucharist is not a representation of Christ's body but rather *is* that body or, as the Council of Trent put it, is "the same Christ contained and immolated in an unbloody manner, who, on the altar of the Cross, offered himself once in a bloody manner."[74] The regularly performed sacrificial ritual of Christianity, the mass, is not a repetition of the crucifixion but rather a distinct sacrifice in which the god is eaten by the faithful. As an early (fourth to sixth century) Easter hymn put it, we are "looking forward to the supper of the lamb . . . whose sacred body is roasted on the altar of the cross. . . . Now Christ's our passover, our sacrifical lamb; His flesh is offered up."[75]

As noted earlier in the discussion of *chupar*—a vernacular signifier denoting abduction and connoting absorption into the body of repression—incorporating the victim provides a corporal trope for the ingestion of attributes, in the present case those of deity. One early medieval religious tract stressed that if the eucharist "dwells in us so that we might remain members of his body in it, it is right that we are in it so that from it we might live and thus feed upon the flesh of the Word."[76] Here the concept of the Junta's "nourishment" by "the flesh of the Word" is echoed. Discourse was embodied in the victim (the Word made flesh) who dwelt in the Junta's *corpus mysticum*, with its "nutrients," its attributes, then drawn forth by the *corpus* "digesting" it. The "flesh of the Word," the Word made tangible and accessible through its incarnation in scapegoats, was ritually "eaten." When the deified *desaparecido* was *chupado*, as when the transubstantiated Christ of the eucharist was ingested by the faithful, a transfer of divine attributes from the victim to the Junta was registered.[77] The *chupados'* symbolic divinity was incorporated by the Son-become-Father (Junta) apotheosizing his status to that of the Name-of-the-Father, while—as the corporal trope implies—the body of repression that had extracted these nutrients from the *chupado* decomposed and expelled the balance.[78]

Ritual incorporation of a sacrificial victim's body—even if only symbolically, as in the "dirty war" case—was overdetermined by religious, sexual, and aggressive motivators. The religious component was clear enough: Communion with the eucharist brought the glory of the risen body of Christ inside the faithful (which had sexual implications of its own), making the communicant one with Christ and his *corpus mysticum*. As a nun describing communion in a convent setting explained it, "We are all one body because we are all partakers of that one bread."[79] The social-cohesion potential of that oneness was not without its political advantages, and was readily exploitable by regimes prepared to capitalize on the commensal group forged by theophagy. In the most fundamental terms, "it would be hard to find a simpler and more vivid image of human civilization, where man attempts to surround nature and put it inside his (social) body, than the sacramental meal."[80] Control of those permitted to "surround" or to commune with the deity—the priests of Aztec society, the Argentine military absorbing the deified *chupados*—could then be utilized to create a politico-religious elite with access to powers recognized by but inaccessible to the populace. If the nuance of concomitance is set aside, in Catholicism the body of Christ is distributed to the faithful while the blood is reserved for a sacerdotal elite with corresponding privileges. As it was worded in a seventeenth-century manual for the clergy, Catholic priests "are those who every day consecrate, eat and drink the body and blood of Christ, and they have such great power that they open and close the doors of heaven: They save whoever they want to save and they condemn whoever they do not."[81]

Lying just beneath the surface of these politico-religious aspects of ritual cannibalism are the sexual and aggressive impulses calling them into play. The victim whose deified corpse is ingested must, of course, first be killed and then mutilated literally or symbolically. "The imagery of cannibalism usually includes, not only images of torture and mutilation, but of what is technically known as *sparagmos* or the tearing apart of the sacrificial body, an image found in the myths of Osiris, Orpheus and Pentheus."[82]

Outside of those myths the ecstatic violence consolidating around ingestion of a deity or other highly symbolized victim interwove sexuality into the scheme in the Dionysian "raving on the mountains," in radical Christianity's voluptuous self-mortifications, in the European depictions of New World orgiastic cannibalism, in the sparagmos and omophagy accompanying sexual crimes, and in the sexual torture of deified *chupados* in the Argentine detention centers.[83] "Oh God," exclaimed one medieval brother, "to love you is to eat you."[84] The autoeroticism of torture—the victim as fetish in a masturbatory drama—then signals the similarly reflexive nature of cannibalism tropes, wherein incorporation of the Other masks a self-consumption. In a context dominated by the Word made flesh and a sacrificed Son ultimately indistinguishable from the Father and the *corpus mysticum*, the tropes must ultimately run full circle. The eater and the eaten are revealed as one and the same: "If then you are the Body of Christ and His members," Augustine wrote, "your mystery is laid on the Lord's table; you are receiving your own mystery." At the sacrificial banquet, finally, "the cannibals eat themselves."

V

The beneficiary of the *desaparecidos'* symbolic transformation into Christ was the Junta and not its victim. The rituals deified the *desaparecidos* only to charge their sacrifice with positive attributes channeled into the Junta's autoapotheosis. The Christ symbolics embodied by the victim in the Father/Son theomachy at the torture table were, as discussed earlier, split and distributed in the Junta's favor. The *desaparecidos* as Christ sacrificed by the Name-of-the-Father (Junta) imbued the Oedipal reversal with an otherworldly air as far as the ritual's authors were concerned, while the victims' "deification" amounted to another expression of their destruction, their reduction to the subordinated status of Son, "eaten" and expelled as "excrement."

Every surrogate refers to the absence it represents, for every substitution there is something that has been displaced. Complexes of overdeterminants overlap in symbolic configurations: the victim as Oedipal Father and then Name-of-the-Father being reduced to the position of Son; the victim as *pharmakós*, as the embodiment of defilement ("subversion"), purifying the community with his sacrifice; the victim as Christ, in whom these first two representations intersect, interact, and reinforce the ritual's metaphysics with divinity and "Western and Christian" tradition. A number of indices then contribute to recognition of the final constituent in this palimpsest of representation whose layers constitute the *desaparecido* as surrogate victim: the Junta itself. As anthropologists have long recognized, "what one sacrifices is always oneself."[85]

The Junta's insistence on self-sacrifice, which may be understood here as a *vicarious* self-sacrifice effected through the ritual murder of *desaparecidos*, was multiply registered as the rituals integrated the sacrificer (Junta) into the symbolics of the victim. In the detention centers the torturer destroyed the victim's subjectivity and then filled the void of the one who "disappeared" by constructing an object in his and the Junta's likeness. In "dirty war" mythology much the same was accomplished by inversion: The narrative took a tragic turn as the Hero (Junta) ultimately "disappeared" into the image of the antagonist, becoming its own Enemy—and thus implicitly, but necessarily, the object of its own aggression—as it became a terrorist eliminating terrorism. The symbolic drama of the Junta's vicarious self-destruction further accrued in quotas through the reflexive nature of the Junta's descriptions of its Enemy, claiming the Other as its target in terms more directly applicable to the Junta itself; through the inextricable bind of subject (Junta) and object ("subversive" *desaparecido*) evidenced in the *creation* of inimical constructs, projected and retrieved, with no empirical reality outside of the subject within which they were brought forth and then destroyed; through the sharing of transitory identities migrating between Junta and *desaparecido*—the Son represented by the Junta and then by its victim, the Father and Name-of-the-Father represented by the victim and then the Junta, while the Christian mystery underlying all ("I and the Father are one")[86] united

Father and Son inextricably, the One always the Other in these shifts and drifts of peripeteia; through ubiquitous mimesis, the constant ritual construction and destruction of identities and the interchangeability of roles; and through identification and incorporation, the *chupado* internalized via tropes of ritual cannibalism deified finally into a symbolic theophagy. The Junta's fusion with its victim was the logical conclusion of the hegemonic engulfment and conceptual destruction of all Other, all exteriority, that characterized the "dirty war" from the beginning. When all inimical representations were *chupado*, taken in, when one became the Enemy (terrorist) in order to eliminate the Enemy, when the usurpative Son *became* the Father he sought to destroy, then the detour of aggression through surrogates concluded finally at the source from which it departed, at oneself-as-other, leaving the *picana*-phallus, the signifier of the lack, with nowhere to turn but back toward the Junta that wielded it. In the "dirty war" the Junta refined "the art of transforming the death of the father (or his murder) into suicide, the result of which is massacre and even the concentration camp."[87]

The murder of the Father in the "dirty war" was in this perspective a "suicide" of the Son (Junta) by proxy through murder of the *desaparecidos* as Son/Christ. As Lacan observed, "For a sadistic fantasy to endure" (in Argentina it endured through the torture of thousands of victims), "the subject's interest in the person who suffers humiliation must obviously be due to the possibility of the subject being submitted to the same humiliation himself."[88] Christianity forges the bond of a sadomasochistic fantasy directly via the mystery construing God-the-Father as one with the humiliated Christ on the cross; the Father's "interest in the person who suffers humiliation" is so great that he integrates Himself into the horror he authors. The autoeroticism experienced by the torturer follows suit: Through a projected masochism, the torturer vicariously experiences the fate of his victims, his presence in this objectified Other then reiterated through the victim's function as a fetish, as part-object representation of the phallus that the torturer appropriates and holds to be his own. The torturer "humiliates" himself by humiliating the victim; his pathological sexuality, his masturbations aided by props and violent subjugation of the Other, can masquerade as holy, as necessary, as scientific, as refined pyrotechnics of national security only within the ritual context, the detention center, to which they are confined. Elsewhere the torturer must cover his face.[89]

When the torturer's dynamics are abstracted and elevated to the level of the Junta obsessed with "self-sacrifice" on the Christian model, the sadistic fantasy generating scapegoats likewise anticipates—engenders—the Junta's own "humiliation." As noted earlier the Junta's agenda of aggrandizement, empowerment, and apotheosis—tidied up by righteous discourse laced with vestiges of liturgy and a baroque mythology "naturalizing" atrocity—self-deconstructed in direct proportion to fulfillment of the "reorganization's" goals. The symmetry was inescapably inherent to the ritual: The more efficaciously the sacrificial ritual refined the Junta's symbolic presence in the victim it destroyed, the more the Junta self-destructed. As that vicarious suicide became gradually evident, as the Junta began to fall with its victims, it progressively withdrew from the Name-of-the-Father symbolics that it tortured (itself) to ascertain, while simultaneously reassuming (and again self-defeating in mimesis) the position it had assigned to its victims, that of the Son on the model of Christ. Select characteristics of Christ—denied to the *desaparecidos*—were stressed accordingly: the Junta as abnegate, self-sacrificing Messiah; the Junta as the persecuted just One accepting His grim lot resolutely for the salvation of the *corpus mysticum*. Junta mythology accepted the self-deconstructing ritual's destruction of its authors, but only on its own terms.

In referring to what he described as "that stroke of genius on the part of Christianity," Nietzsche observed that "God himself sacrifices himself for the guilt of mankind, God himself makes payment to himself, God as the only being who can redeem man from what has become unredeemable for man himself—the creditor sacrifices himself for the debtor."[90]

Whether stylized as Christ or as Nietzsche's "God himself" (ultimately one and the same),[91] the Junta was left with the roles of sacrificer *and* victim, first because its hegemonic, totalitarian tendencies conceptually annihilated all Other (including the third party to whom the sacrifice was ostensibly made) and then because its rituals symbolically united it with the *desaparecidos* that it destroyed. The Christian paradigm structuring the Junta's system was closed, the sacrificial economy functioned hermetically within the Junta as it does within God, and the exchange of abstract commodities was internal. God pays the debt to Himself by sacrificing Himself, the Junta did likewise, and—within the symbolic realm fusing the identities of victim and victimizer—both God and Junta could claim abnegate self-sacrifice for the redemption of others.

Once the perspective is distanced from the symbolic realm of "dirty war" mythology, however, a dimension unfavorable to the Junta's self-image is revealed. God-the-Father and Christ may be one, and the Junta may have been symbolically indistinguishable from its victim, but when the nails were hammered in or the *picana* applied, the mystery of unity was suddenly suspect. God-the-Father paid Himself the debt by nailing up the *Son*, then cashed in on *His own* immolation. The Junta was present in the surrogate insofar as his positive attributes could be usurped, but absent in the surrogate insofar as he was physically destroyed. In their pioneering monograph *Sacrifice and Its Functions*, Henri Hubert and Marcel Mauss specified that

> the sacrificer gives up something of himself but he does not give himself. Prudently, he sets himself aside. . . . If he involved himself in the rite to its very end, he would find death, not life. The victim takes his place. . . . The sacrificer remains protected: The gods take the victim instead of him. *The victim redeems him.*[92]

The Argentine military may have been "the flesh of the nation . . . intrinsically linked to the nation itself," but when the axe fell that link's elasticity was exploited.[93] The messianic Junta was redeemed, at least temporarily, by the victimized population on which its violent "salvation" was imposed.

Christ's unity with the *corpus mysticum* of the faithful is bound to His mission: to be the One (consolidating the Many) who begins the new age by sacrificing His life. But if Christ is executed and eaten, and if the Many are one body with His, then they, too, must share the same fate. There the "mystical" comes into play: In rational terms the scheme collapses (because all of the faithful are not executed and eaten) and thus resorts to figurative discourse: He died "once for all."[94] The death of the One is a metonymy representing the collective death of the *corpus mysticum*, so that the Many are "reborn" into the new age, into the Kingdom of Heaven. As Carolyn Bynum put it following Augustine and Hilary Poitiers, "We are all present in the sacrifice and Resurrection of the cross"; "Christ, in dying, digests and assimilates us, making us new flesh in his flesh."[95] Christ died for the sins of the Many, in their stead, so that they might *live*. "By dying," as the Catholic Encyclopedia mysteriously worded it, "He killed death."[96]

Now in Argentina the Junta, identified in its mythology as the vicar of Christ and as one body with the *corpus reipublicae mysticum*, also had a new age mission, its Process of National Reorganization conceived as "the final closing of a historical cycle and the opening of a new one." Rather than the One, the Junta, immolating itself for the Many, however, rather than the messiah's sacrifice metonymizing the death of the Many and thereby affording universal salvation while bearing the cost, precisely the inverse occurred: The Many (*desaparecidos*) were sacrificed representing the One (Junta), while the Junta claiming itself messiah collected the spoils.[97] The Junta owed all of its gains (power, apotheosis, "reorganization," hegemony, wealth) to its sacrifice of victims, and it was therefore dependent on the continuing presence of those victims, and on its own symbolic presence in those victims, to establish the channels through which the "transaction" of coveted attributes was made. Symbolic debt was accrued as the Junta's transformation into the Father and subsequently Name-of-the-Father was realized "at the expense" of the *desaparecidos*.[98]

VI

The word *sacrifice* is rooted in the Latin *sacrificium*, itself composed of *sacer* ("sacred") and *facere* ("to make"), the etymology denoting the ritual's function of making its victim sacred.[99] Essential to both the etymology and the practice of sacrifice is an inherent paradox: The object of sacrifice is made sacred only by destroying it, by making it absent. The circularity of the system was succinctly described by René Girard: "Because the victim is sacred, it is criminal to kill him—but the victim is sacred only because he is to be killed."[100] Resulting from that paradox are two problems for the sacrificer: the neutralization of guilt for the criminality of his or her murder and the construction of the victim's identity to maximize positive gains from the ritual while minimizing detrimental fallout onto the sacrificer and his or her community. Because the sacred sacrificial offering is made and unmade in the same "fruitful moment," the sacrificers have a vested interest in extending that moment to reap its benefits and to postpone the consequences following it. Both the Aztec rulers and the Argentine Junta prolonged the "fruitful moment" by ritualizing sacrifice in such a way that it infiltrated the politico-religious structure of their societies at all levels, and by sacrificing human beings in great quantities, creating a continuum of "moments." The Junta further exploited the elasticity of its "moment" by subjecting its victims to slow, protracted destruction, the execution always imminent but always post-poned. By each of these means the empowering instant of sacrifice was stretched into the mythic timelessness that made its politico-religious advantages, including terror, omnipresent rather than episodic.

While sacrifice makes its victim sacred in order to transfer that quality to the sacrificers, the efficiency of the ritual inversely loads the same victim with negative qualities of which the society in question wishes to be purged, these passing from the sacrificer and his or her community to the victim. A two-way channel is established between the sacrificer and the scapegoat, between the Junta and the *desaparecido*, with all of the positive attributes flowing toward the sacrificer and all of the negative attributes flowing toward the victim. In Aztec as well as Argentine practice, the victim, still serving as deity surrogate, "also had the function of concentrating the people's hate."[101] The construction of victims as scapegoats consolidating not only hate but also "subversion," guilt, disorder, contamination, evil, and other negative qualities of which the sacrificers and their community wish to be purged ranks among the predominant characteristics of "dirty war" violence. Like the expulsion of the *pharmakós* in Greek civilization and like the tragedy *Oedipus the King* itself, the torture and execution of *desaparecidos* in Argentina was a ritual of purification.

In Western antiquity sacrifices were increased during times of plague, this "conspiring with the enemy" a symbolic solution implemented by miming the death scourge and loading the scapegoats with the disease to be taken from this world.[102] "As, on top of all the other ills, the plague raged," Paulus Orosius wrote, "they turned to murder as a remedy. They sacrificed men as victims, and they brought to their altars adolescents who had not reached puberty as a way of seeking the enemy's mercy."[103] Aline Rousselle added to that observation this conclusion: "Everyone was insistent on the necessity of spilling blood, as it was the price that had to be paid for the survival of the community and the salvation of each individual."[104] J. P. Vernant similarly recognized that "sterility, disease and death are all felt to be the power of the same defilement, a *míasma* that has disrupted the whole of life's normal course. What must be done is find the criminal who is the city's defilement . . . and eliminate the ill by eliminating him."[105]

The Junta's treatment of "subversion" stylized as a disease, discussed in Chapter 3, closely paralleled the repressive measures taken by European authorities in an attempt to prevent the plague from spreading. I later described the illness, the pollution, being loaded onto the scapegoat styled as a "germ" duly engulfed and destroyed by military "antibodies." The discussion of a Peruvian folk cure noted much the same: A guinea pig externalized the patient's illness by absorbing it, and the *curandero* terminated the cure by "sacrificing" the animal that objectified the problem. As long as the ritual context sustaining Junta mythology prevailed, the torture/execution of the "subversive" in Argentina—like the destruction of the guinea pig, the sacrifice of plague scapegoats, and the expulsion of the Greek *pharmakós*—purified the social body as the externalized and isolated defilement "disappeared."

The *desaparecido* as sacrificial victim was closely associated with the defiled community in order for the purification ritual to be efficacious, but at the same time was isolated and separated from it—scapegoated— so that the community's cure could pose as the elimination of an evil rather than as violence directed against itself. As Walter Burkert aptly phrased it, "The aggression excited by fear is concentrated on some loathsome outsider; everyone feels relieved by the communal projection of the fury born of despair, as well as by the certainty of standing on the side of the just and the pure."[106] If the distance between the scapegoat and the community is too distended, then the victim will lack the characteristics required to attract and concentrate the negative attributes: The Junta's torture and execution of Pakistanis, for example, would not have served the ritual's purpose. If, on the other hand, the similitude between the victim and the community is too great (as it was in Argentina), then "'impure' violence will mingle with the 'sacred' violence of the rites, turning the latter into a scandalous accomplice in the process of pollution, even a kind of catalyst in the propagation of further impurity."[107]

In an attempt to distance the victims of ritualized atrocity from the Argentine population at large and thereby avoid these effects, Junta mythology depicted the "subversives" in tropes of separation and ostracism. The mythology construed the targets of violence as infiltrating external conspirators, as *apátridas* ("countryless"), as "antinational" beings, as the enemies of "Western and Christian civilization," as germs alien to the *corpus mysticum*. Separating Argentines from the population only to return them as aliens to the State's torture/execution rituals also appealed to a series of manipulative redefinitions designed to fabricate their guilt. The Process "reorganizing," among other things, what it meant to be Argentine regarded anyone even passively opposed to the Junta's agenda as a traitor, as a "subversive" who disowned the country's historical achievement and who was therefore being reciprocally disowned by the State.

In the Junta's politico-religious violence, as in all contexts of "sacred" murder, purification was accomplished by "dirty" means that were sanctified by appeal to the mythology sustaining the ritual. "Subversion" was a sin against the Natural Order, and due punishment was therefore the responsibility of the Junta's self-styled theocracy because "without justice, peace is dirty." The dirtiness was neutralized in kind by dirty means—abduction, torture, execution—because "the cleaning begins by punishing the guilty."[108] This strategy of washing a stain out *with blood*, this grim ritual ablution of a social body purified through sacrifice, accomplished its purge while simultaneously channeling the negative attributes of atrocity into their inversion: The "dirtiness" of the "war" purified rather than defiled its authors, "as if somebody who had fallen into mud would clean himself with mud."[109]

Girard's contention that sacrifice of scapegoats serves to protect the community from violence against itself was plainly illustrated by an Argentina embroiled in escalating internal terrorism from both left- and right-wing organizations in the years prior to the 1976 coup d'état. The function of the scapegoat, following Girard, was to control mimetic rivalry and reciprocal violence by concentrating the hostilities; the destruction of surrogate victims, of *desaparecidos*, was carried out in an official and "sacred" ritual terminating the mimesis that would otherwise become progressively more intense.[110] "The sacrifice serves to protect the entire community from *its own* violence; it prompts the entire community to choose victims outside of itself."[111] If in pre-1976 Argentina terrorism from the political Left and Right mimetically accelerated one another in an increasingly violent upward spiral, then the subsequent "dirty war" attempted to break that mimetic pattern—unconsciously, to be sure—by concentrating the violent impulses on scapegoats, on *desaparecidos*, and by then destroying them. A "final" killing was necessary, a "final solution" achieved through what Girard called a "mechanism of the surrogate victim." The Junta's "hostile polarization against a victim must empty the group of internal hostility, unifying it so tightly that a cultural rejuvenation can really occur."[112] Sacrifice, as General Videla put it, was what made "the reencounter of all Argentines" and "national union" possible. Julia Kristeva explained that "this violent act [sacrifice] puts an end to previous (semiotic, presymbolic) violence, and, by focusing violence on a victim, displaces it onto the symbolic order *at the very moment* this order is being founded."[113]

When the "fruitful moment" of sacrifice transfers the battle from the Real to the Symbolic order, it retroactively substantiates the scapegoat's culpability as it establishes and reestablishes the mythology in which (surrogate) violence as a solution to intracommunity violence is legitimated. Girard rightly stressed that recognition of the victim as surrogate, as scapegoat, must remain unconscious on the part of the sacrificer and that "the persecutors do not realize that they chose their victims for inadequate reasons, or perhaps for no reason at all, more or less at random." In the "dirty war" one could rather expect "the victim to be seen as guilty and therefore to *be* mythically guilty. We can expect the violence of the group to be condoned and justified. This violence will be presented as a legitimate defense against a fearsome monster, as the just punishment of a guilty criminal."[114] The myth's failure to satisfactorily establish culpability would render the destruction of the scapegoat, the *desaparecido*, no more than it was beyond the mythic context: a proliferation of State atrocity arbitrarily meted out to citizens. Burton Mack summarized Girard's position on the point:

> This displacement of guilt also accounts for the necessity of the delusion that determines religious mentality. To acknowledge the deed as arbitrary and the victim as surrogate would plunge the group back into the terror of reciprocal violence. Only by retaining a fictional or mythic account of the event can the community avoid the truth about itself, which would destroy it. The mythic account casts the victim as savior and the event of his death as sacrifice. Rituals of sacrifice are instituted to substitute for the real thing. Thus the circle closes.[115]

The circle closed around a *desaparecido*, a victim caught in the hermetic, lopsided mimesis of the sacrificer in his struggle against symbolic presences and of the populace desperate for a solution. Overdeterminants stacked the odds against the surrogate. "The as-if element in the ritual becomes mythic reality; conversely, the ritual confirms the reality of the myth." The *desaparecido* was guilty coming and going. "In this way, by mutually affirming each other, myth and ritual become a strong force in forming a cultural tradition," a Process of National Reorganization.[116]

Similarly, in psychoanalytical terms, the scapegoat's mythic guilt is reinforced by a projection that accompanies the Son/Sacrificer's identification with the Father/Victim perceived as an aggressor. The moment that the aggressor's threat is internalized, "the offense is externalized. This means that the mechanism of identification with the aggressor is supplemented by another defense measure, namely, the projection of guilt."[117] As the ritual functioning unimpeded would have it, the *desaparecido* was guilty and the sacrificer and the community were not, the latter two allotting themselves a measure of sacredness—beyond their absolution—for having done away with the evil.

Despite the ritual's prudent protection of its authors, however, something of the guilt for senseless crimes mythologically justified remains with the perpetrators and their community. Once the "dirty" job is done, "the shock felt in the act of killing is answered later by consolidation; guilt is followed by reparation, destruction by reconstruction."[118] Burkert recognized that the "shock" of killing highly charged prey or sacrificial victims is resolved by rituals that creatively channel it, in part by stressing—as the Argentine military always did—that the atrocity is performed on behalf of others. While the "common sense disinclination to believe the monstrous" can for a time appease the conscience of a population that explains surrogate victimage to itself in refrains such as the Argentine *Por algo será* ("It must be for something") and *Algo habrá[n] hecho* ("He/she/they must have done something"), the myth sustaining "sacred" execution will eventually lose its credibility, and the sacrificers (Junta) will then be viewed as murderers of innocent citizens. Once Junta mythology was irreparably shattered (following the campaign attempting to salvage it in the Falklands/Malvinas), a demonstration chant was unambiguous: "There were no errors / There were no excesses / All of the Process military men / Are murderers."[119] The inherent paradox of sacrificial rituals—that purification is effected by miming the violence that sacrifice seeks to foreclose, that one murder replaces another—finally caught up with the Junta. The truth of arbitrary, unjustifiable violence was veiled only barely, and the community sharing in the guilt of scapegoating—even if only by virtue of not lifting the veil—would finally ostracize the Junta it once received quite favorably, calling forth the postponed truth that what had posed as cure for the disease was ultimately a mystified manifestation of its cause.

Clinicians learn from recovered psychotic patients that during their illness "there was a normal person hidden who, like a detached spectator, watched the hubbub of illness go past him."[120] In normal subjects the disavowal of a truth or the mytho-logical distortion of a reality likewise entrenches but never eradicates the repressed material. "For to fail to recognize presupposes a recognition," particularly in systematic failures to recognize, "where it must obviously be admitted that what is denied is in some fashion recognized."[121] Before Lacan, Jean-Paul Sartre described this machinery of bad faith lucidly: "It follows first that the one to whom the lie is told and the one who lies are one and the same person, which means that I must know in my capacity as deceiver the truth which is hidden from me in my capacity as the one deceived. Better yet I must know the truth very exactly *in order* to conceal it more carefully."[122]

When the population fulfilling the spectacular functions of participant-observer feigns a role as uninformed, and when the repressors themselves sanction their barbarities with canon systematically distorted to suit their needs, guilt for the unjustifiably violent transgressions is accrued. If scapegoating is to serve its function of ending internal violence rather than aggravating or perpetuating it, then the rituals must provide for dissolution of this culpability or else yield to procedures beyond them that can. The gains will be consolidated only if the "dirty" means by which they were attained is processed out.

One noteworthy ritual mechanism satisfying this need for autoexpiation is found in the Greeks' annual *Bouphonia*. Unlike the Christians, whose theology required the murder of a scapegoat-god but at the same time projected the guilt for His death onto another scapegoat (the Jews) essential to Christian mythic economy, the Greeks recognized that the guilt was theirs and invented rituals to neutralize it internally. During the great *Bouphonia* festivals a bull representing Zeus, the *Father* of the gods, was sacrificed in a temple. After the sacrifice the priests who had executed the bull ran from the temple in a feigned panic, screaming out a formula that absolved them for having killed a god. Later, in a special chamber of the temple, a mock-legal trial took place during which "the water-carriers accused those who had ground the axe and the knife, the latter accused those who had passed the axe, and these in turn accused the man who had slain the bull."[123] This last official followed suit by accusing the knife itself, which he had used to slit the bull's throat. The knife, having no voice to defend itself, was convicted of murder and duly executed. The priests (like the *curandero* with his guinea pig) thereby cleansed themselves and their community by objectifying the guilt and destroying the object representing it. The killing (and eating) of the gods, the perpetuation of sacrificial rituals, could then continue without concern for contamination or reprisals.[124]

VII

After the fall of the Junta, a trial likewise addressed culpability for sacrificial rituals (abduction, torture, execution) of the "dirty war." During this trial the Junta members provided the discourse that the *Bouphonia's* knife might speak were it so enabled: We are, the Junta members argued, instruments of the community's will and needs; we are scapegoats; we are not guilty but have been assigned the guilt. The Junta's reference to itself as scapegoat was in one sense correct: Its coup d'état was welcomed, its remedy for "the problem of subversion" was applauded in many quarters and condoned in most, and its bearing of the greatest penal burden was laden not only with community revenge (against itself) but also with political factors that tended to focus penal wrath on the Junta members as figureheads.[125] A contrived polarization of civilian and military factions in the post–"dirty war" period likewise contributed to the (conditional) legitimacy of the Junta's self-image as scapegoat. As Alain Rouquié rightly observed, social reality contextualizing the Junta's assumption of power and much of its "dirty war" was hardly "a pitched battle between two factions, on one side the heroic civilians defending republican institutions and on the other officers, antidemocratic by nature, lusting for power."[126] Rather military coups d'état in Argentina since the 1930s have always been made possible by popular support and, as demonstrated following the Easter week revolt during Alfonsín's administration, could be forestalled by adequate public protest.

Civilian applause for the military and its "dirty war" has been increasingly expressed in the post-Alfonsín period. On June 10, 1989, just prior to Carlos Saúl Menem's assumption of office, three pages of signatures filled an advertisement in the Buenos Aires newspaper *La Nación*, calling for "recognition and solidarity with the totality of Armed, Security and Police Forces which defended the Nation in the war unleashed by subversive aggression." On the same date *La Nación* reported that five hundred Argentines celebrated flag day by visiting former Lieutenant Colonel Aldo Rico, incarcerated for rebellion under Alfonsín. Rico shook hands and signed autographs before the well-wishers dispersed, singing the national anthem.[127] The reappearance in 1990 of the Carapintadas as *civilian* symbols of national recovery, with a considerable following among "desperate people" who "turn to anything that offers hope," similarly signaled the volatility of popular civilian-military relations and the renewability of the myth that construes "dirty" violence as messianic rather than atrocious.[128] It is not "standing outside of the social order in some excited state of self-regard that makes a political leader numinous," Clifford Geertz observed, "but a deep, intimate involvement—affirming or abhoring, defensive or destructive—in the master fictions by which that order lives."[129]

Depending on the historical moment at which it is perceived, the military Junta "alternates between being a murderer and being a sacred person, so that the innocence of the community and the efficacy of the sacrifice can be alternately stressed. The basic contradiction, in both cases, is between the community's desire for salvation and its desire to repudiate the means by which salvation is attained."[130] As the Junta's trials in 1985 indicated, "whatever the motivation for the original sacrifice [of *desaparecidos*], or the apportionment of guilt, the pattern of this kind of myth and ritual is clear: After the sacrifice the slayer must be punished, the sacrificer becomes a victim in turn."[131] Once it fell out of grace and out of office, the Junta, like its victims previously, and like Oedipus, was assigned the role of the *pharmakós*; the public recognized—if only temporarily—the reversal by which the "cure" was revealed as the "disease." The restoration of order to Argentina accordingly required that the Junta itself "disappear."

> In the person of the ostracized one the city expels whatever is in it that is too high and that embodies the evil which can fall on it from above. In that of the *pharmakós*, it expels whatever is most vile and embodies the evil that threatens it from below. Through this double and complementary rejection . . . it takes the true measure of man as opposed on the one hand to the divine and the heroic, on the other to the bestial and the monstrous.[132]

"This is indeed what the *pharmakós* is," Vernant noted earlier, "the king's double, but reversed like the carnival kings crowned for the duration of the festival." When the carnival of "dirty war" violence concluded, "the counterking [Junta] is expelled or put to death, carrying away with him all the disorder that he embodied and from which he thereby purges the community."[133]

Although the Junta under litigation was correct in recognizing the scapegoat role that it had come to assume, and although it of course had a vested interest in championing a perception of itself as scapegoat, the Junta's *interpretation* of this status was untenable. Its argument was founded, in effect, on an incorrect premise: that the indisputablity of the Junta's *pharmakós* functions necessitated the indisputablity of its innocence. Junta mythology fused the one with the other, but by any demystified measure it was clear that those—or some of those—responsible for "dirty war" transgressions and those prosecuted for them in 1985 were one and the same, regardless of the symbolic functions loaded onto them afterward. The Junta was a scapegoat *and* guilty. Guilt in post-"dirty war" litigation—unlike guilt assigned to the *desaparecidos*—gravitated toward its proper object rather than toward an arbitrary surrogate.

René Girard recognized that "the judicial system and the institution of sacrifice share the same function," and that sacrificial rituals (scapegoating to put an end to internal violence) "assume essential roles in societies that lack a firm judicial system."[134] If a community can establish culpability through formal judicial proceedings rather than through projection onto a sacrificial surrogate, if a competition of interpretations can be stilled by a tribunal that exhausts all procedures of appeal by the force of public power, then nonviolent means can terminate a cycle of mimetic violence, with the cathartic and decontamination functions shifting accordingly from the violent sacrificial spectacle to the trial. The judicial proceedings must accomplish with the Word what the sacrificial rituals enact in deed: the irreversible assignment of guilt. In societies where judicial systems lack sufficient credence to arbitrate a conclusion to mimetic violence or in those—such as the Argentina of the Process of National Reorganization—where its autonomy is compromised or annulled as it is subordinated to autocracy, sacrificial violence will tend to displace the judiciary. As one Argentine proponent of "dirty war" ethics saw it, "A state of war does not mean a state of injustice. ['Dirty'] war is a juridical sanction, that is, a judicial act. Its end is to reestablish the justice compromised by disorder."[135]

With the restoration of constitutional governance under Raúl Alfonsín in 1983, the reinstated Argentine judiciary displaced sacrificial rituals as the means to close a cycle of violence.[136] The focus of the spectacle and the functions of the participant-observers witnessing it accordingly shifted from the violent one previously rehearsed in the detention centers to the drama played out in the courtroom. When Prosecutor Julio César Strassera completed his closing statement at the Junta's trials, as I noted in Chapter 2, "the courtroom burst into an ovation," the resonating applause and the bravos creating an ambience like that of "the Colón Theatre on its best nights."[137] The defendants—now the show itself rather than the producers—exploited this state of affairs with scapegoat discourse protesting the "deplorable spectacle."[138] In response the participant-observers all the more vehemently guaranteed the truth of the crime and celebrated the righteousness of its punishment.

But not all of them. The fragility of Argentina's judicial system and its ineffectiveness in foreclosing internal violence through the irreversible assignment of guilt was underscored by dissent from powerful military and civilian sectors during the Alfonsín administration and again, most dramatically, by executive acts promulgated by Alfonsín's successor. On October 7, 1989, President Menem pardoned more than two hundred members of the military who were convicted or awaiting trial for crimes committed during the "dirty war," for participation in the three military uprisings against the Alfonsín administration, and for mismanagement of the Falklands/Malvinas war. Following this presidential pardon only seven of the most centrally responsible and symbolically important "dirty war" criminals remained incarcerated, among them former Junta members Videla, Massera, and Viola, as well as former police chief Ramón Camps. On December 29, 1990, Menem disregarded considerable domestic and international protest and extended a second pardon freeing these prisoners. Although he propagated the pardons as acts of national reconciliation, his mooting of the tribunal's "final word" enfeebled the judiciary's credibility as a peaceful alternative to atrocity on the sacrificial model. Beyond endorsing impunity for "dirty war" repression and dismantling Alfonsín's gains on human rights terrain, Menem's pardon reestablished the context in which military violence claims credibility as "a judicial act."

In the Alfonsín years prior to the pardon, the shift from sacrificial rituals to judicial proceedings was in military mythology already disavowed and rewoven back into the sanctification of violence. Driven progressively deeper into the reaction formation of Christian martyrdom fortified by its new status as the object of prosecution, the Junta entrenched itself in insistence on military self-sacrifice, not—of course—a symbolic one realized through torture of surrogate victims but rather a literal self-sacrifice that was quantifiable in the deaths and hardships suffered, on the model of Christ, in order to carry out the "great task" with which He entrusted His vicars. Military discourse formalizing this mythological reading on the eve of the commanders' probable incarceration consolidated all of its abstractions into a mission: "Sacrifice, which is the extremity of love, demands that one give his life to enact the Truth."[139]

On an occasion no less resonant than Resurrection Saturday, Juan Aramburu, cardinal of Buenos Aires, preached the example of Christ to the former commanders facing prosecution, stressing His voluntary and generous self-sacrifice on the cross in order to expiate the sins of mankind.[140] When that perception of self-sacrifice extended into the trials themselves, the Christian gloss similarly prevailed. Before the court "dirty war" mythology rendered the Junta members martyrs in the image of Christ, persecuted scapegoats left with little alternative but to accept the cross to which they had been unjustly sentenced. This posture, formalized by counsel, was as dangerous as it was quaint; it granted the military not only martyrs around whom to rally but also an implied share of pardon and apotheosis that—however ludicrous—accumulated a retroactive, mythological substantiation along with a civilian following to guaranty its "truth." In the interpretation of Major Julio Santiago Canteros, conviction and imprisonment was the Junta members' "glorious martyrdom of sacrificing their freedom after having realized, in fulfillment of their obligations, the assurance of freedom for us."[141] The defense counsel for General Galtieri expressed a similar opinion by inferring his client's affinity to Jesus Christ: "The crucifix that, thanks be to God, hangs in the courtroom above the judges' heads is there to represent the indignity that He suffered. It is nothing other than the image of the most notable victim of human justice. Let us be careful—I say—not to fall crudely in this [error] during the task [sentencing] that approaches."[142]

Among the defendants themselves General Videla most notably performed the role of self-sacrificial martyrdom, refusing to recognize the jurisdiction of the court and, like Christ, opting to place himself completely at its mercy. "As a Christian," Videla explained, "I am obligated to forgive any type of offense made against me."[143] In lieu of a statement before the court, Videla clarified the terms of his martyrdom in a written document:

> I have not appointed a defense attorney, I have not made a declaration before the Court, I have not brought forth evidence, I have not in any way approved of a trial in which the gravest transgressions have been committed. . . . Your Honors of this Court: You are not my natural judges. And for that reason you lack jurisdiction and legal authority to judge me.[144]

The tribunal lacked jurisdiction first because Videla did not recognize civilian appeal of his court-martial, and then because the judge of sacred violence, though "natural," is a transcendentalized construct circularly sanctioning the rituals that call it into being. Whether the victim is a *desaparecido* or the Junta itself, the rigor of Christianity convenes a supernatural tribunal during sacrifice as a judicial act. "Tomorrow the cross," in words we can imagine for General Videla, "but not the gallows."[145]

Notes

A NOTE ON METHOD

1. Linda Orr, "The Revenge of Literature: A History of History," *New Literary History* 12 (Autumn 1986): 1–22, is a useful synopsis of the issue, as are: Hayden White, "The Question of Narrative in Contemporary Historical Theory," in his *The Content of Form: Narrative Discourse and Historical Understanding* (Baltimore, Md.: Johns Hopkins University Press, 1987), and Lionel Gossman, "History and Literature: Reproduction or Signification," in R. H. Canary and H. Kozicki, eds., *The Writing of History: Literary Form and Historical Understanding* (Madison: University of Wisconsin Press, 1981). A revealing etymological history of the word *fact* was included in the third chapter of John Lukacs, *Historical Consciousness* (New York: Schocken Books, 1985).

2. Louis O. Mink developed this point lucidly, "revealing an incompatibility between our implicit presupposition of what historical narratives are about and our conscious belief that the formal structure of a narrative is constructed rather than discovered." See his "Narrative Form as a Cognitive Instrument," in R. H. Canary and H. Kozicki, eds. *The Writing of History: Literary Form and Historical Understanding* (Madison: University of Wisconsin Press, 1981), as well as the useful bibliography in the same collection. In Richard Rorty, *Philosophy and the Mirror of Nature* (Princeton, N.J.: Princeton University Press, 1980), "problems of justification within normal discourse" were understood as "practices adopted for various historical reasons and as the achievement of objective truth, where 'objective truth' is no more than and no less than the best idea we currently have about how to explain what is going on."

3. Edward Said, *The World, the Text and the Critic* (Cambridge, Mass.: Harvard University Press, 1983), 178. Nietzsche was the most explicit of the three: "It is precisely facts which don't exist, only *interpretations*," he wrote, in *The Portable Nietzsche*, ed. and trans. Walter Kaufmann (New York: Penguin Books, 1977), 458. See also the similar passage in section 481 of Nietzsche's *The Will to Power*, trans. Walter Kaufmann and R. J. Hollingdale (New York: Random

House, 1967), 267. Others with an affinity for this position included Søren Kierkegaard, for whom "truth is subjectivity," in *Concluding Unscientific Postscript*, trans. David F. Swenson and Walter Lowrie (Princeton, N.J.: Princeton University Press, 1968), and Jean-Paul Sartre, who summed up the issue succinctly with: "Will and perception are inseparable," in *The War Diaries*, trans. Quintin Hoare (New York: Pantheon Books, 1984), 39. More recently Michel Foucault wrote that "for history in its classical form, the discontinuous was both the given and the unthinkable: The raw material of history, which presented itself in the form of dispersed events—decisions, accidents, initiatives, discoveries . . . had to be rearranged, reduced, effaced in order to reveal the continuity of the events,"in *The Archaeology of Knowledge*, trans. A. M. Sheridan Smith (New York: Pantheon Books, 1972), 8. In the same vein Frederic Jameson added that interpretation is "an essentially allegorical act, which consists in rewriting a given text in terms of a particular interpretive master code," in *The Political Unconscious* (Ithaca, N.Y.: Cornell University Press, 1981), 10. Similarly Walter Burkert noted that "in the humanities we are usually dealing with chance selections of data, especially in all fields of history, and even more, that our data are already interpretations, acquiring their meaning in a preconceived system," in Robert G. Hamerton-Kelly, ed., *Violent Origins* (Stanford, Calif.: Stanford University Press, 1987), 149. From the viewpoint of structural anthropology, Claude Lévi-Strauss concurred: "Every civilization tends to overestimate the objective orientation of its thought and this tendency is never absent," in *The Savage Mind*, trans. George Weidenfeld and Nicolson Ltd. (Chicago, Ill.: University of Chicago Press, 1966), 3. In the perspective of intertextuality, Roland Barthes stressed that "this 'I' which approaches the text is already itself a plurality of other texts, of codes which are infinite" or which can no longer be traced to their origins, in *S/Z*, trans. Richard Miller (New York: Hill and Wang, 1974), 10. Vincent B. Leitch summarized Martin Heidegger's position, noting that "existence is textualized through and through—from beginning to end," and he aphoristically synthesized the poststructuralist position with these words: "History is substitution, signifier, figure, difference, text, fiction," in *Deconstructive Criticism: An Advanced Introduction* (New York: Columbia University Press, 1983), 70 and 58, respectively.

        4. Hayden White, "The Value of Narrativity in the Representation of Reality," in W.J.T. Mitchell, ed., *On Narrative* (Chicago, Ill.: University of Chicago Press, 1981), 3. That essay was also included, along with other useful works, in White's *The Content of Form*. The paragraph that follows in the text draws on arguments that White posited in various works. In addition to those cited above and "The Narrativization of Real Events," also in Mitchell, *On Narrative*, see White's *Metahistory: The Historical Imagination in Nineteenth-Century Europe* (Baltimore, Md.: Johns Hopkins University Press, 1973), and

"The Historical Text as Literary Artifact," in Canary and Kozicki, *The Writing of History*.

5. Gérard Genette, *Narrative Discourse: An Essay in Method*, trans. Jane Lewin (Ithaca, N.Y.: Cornell University Press, 1980), 25. "Psychoanalysis is the 'talking cure,'" positing the same issue on other ground, "but symptoms join in the conversation, too" because a symptom "*is a statement in a metalanguage about an object language*." See Jacques Lacan/Anthony Wilden, *The Language of the Self: The Function of Language in Psychoanalysis* (Baltimore, Md.: Johns Hopkins University Press, 1968), 236 and 309. (This book was first published under Wilden's name and then under Lacan's; in subsequent references to this work, both authors' names will be used—Lacan/Wilden.) The relation of Genette's "totality" to a master paradigm was suggested as Michel Foucault described "a sort of great, uniform text which has never before been articulated, and which reveals for the first time what men 'really meant' not only in their words and texts, their discourses and their writings, but also in the institutions, practices, techniques, and objects that they produced. In relation to this implicit, sovereign, communal 'meaning,' statements appear in superabundant proliferation, since it is to that meaning alone that they all refer and to it alone that they owe their truth." See Foucault, *The Archaeology of Knowledge*, 106.

6. Tzvetan Todorov, *Introduction to Poetics*, trans. Richard Howard (Sussex, England: Harvester Press, 1981), 71.

7. The quoted passage is from Roland Barthes, "Textual Analysis of a Tale by Edgar Allan Poe," in *The Semiotic Challenge*, trans. Richard Howard (New York: Hill and Wang, 1988), 288.

8. Michael Riffaterre, *Semiotics of Poetry* (Bloomington: Indiana University Press, 1978), 5–6.

9. Wolfgang Iser, *The Implied Reader: Patterns of Communication in Prose Fiction from Bunyan to Beckett* (Baltimore, Md.: Johns Hopkins University Press, 1974), 278.

10. The quoted poetry is from James Wright, *This Journey* (New York: Random House, 1982), 16. Wright was particularly adept at this type of enjambment; a passage earlier in his canon read: "Suddenly I realize / That if I stepped out of my body I would break / Into blossom." See his *The Branch Will Not Break* (Middletown, Conn.: Wesleyan University Press, 1963), 57.

11. Sophocles, *The Three Theban Plays*, trans. Robert Fagles, intro. and notes by Bernard Knox (New York: Penguin Books, 1984), 211.

12. Lacan/Wilden, *Language of the Self*, xii.

13. Jacques Derrida, *Dissemination*, trans. Barbara Johnson (Chicago, Ill.: University of Chicago Press, 1981), 63. For discussion see Said, *The World*, 184, and Josué V. Harari, ed., *Textual Strategies: Perspectives in Post-Structuralist Criticism* (Ithaca, N.Y.: Cornell University Press, 1979), 69.

14. Lacan/Wilden, *The Language of the Self*, 241.

15. Friedrich Nietzsche, *Beyond Good and Evil: Prelude to a Philosophy of the Future*, trans. with a commentary by Walter Kaufmann (New York: Vintage Books, 1966), 31 and 229, respectively. E. M. Cioran clearly pursued the Nietzschean position: "What is surprising if style should be simultaneously a mask and an admission?" See his *The Temptation to Exist*, trans. Richard Howard (New York: Quadrangle, 1976), 135.

16. Christopher Norris, *Derrida* (Cambridge, Mass.: Harvard University Press, 1987), 15. For a discussion of the relation to Jacques Lacan's "floating signifier," see Leitch, *Deconstructive Criticism*, 10–16.

17. Norris, *Derrida*, 60.

18. Ibid., 19.

19. Outstanding among these in the "dirty war" case were constructions from the repressors' vernacular lexicon, traces of a medieval paradigm, and the discursive function of symbolic actions, as I will demonstrate in subsequent chapters.

20. Said, *The World*, 188. "I wanted to track down in the decorative display of *what-goes-without-saying*," Roland Barthes wrote in a statement characteristic of early poststructuralism, "the ideological abuse which, in my view, is hidden there." Roland Barthes, *Mythologies*, trans. Annette Lavers (New York: Hill and Wang, 1972), 11. As Lacan reminded us the fact that something is obvious is no reason to overlook or dismiss it. In literary theory Todorov added that what "might seem a simple process of presentation on the level of discourse is transformed into a thematic element on the level of fiction," in his *Introduction to Poetics*, 57.

21. Cited in Sartre, *War Diaries*, 40; "human reality" translates Heidegger's concept *Dasein*. See also Sartre's *Being and Nothingness: An Essay on Phenomenological Ontology*, trans. Hazel E. Barnes (New York: Philosophical Library, n.d.), 218, where the discussion departed from "the world is human." As I will discuss, the Argentine Junta viewed reality as a divine rather than human construct. Within the Junta's essentially theocentric, medieval mentality, "hope was restored to the world because the world was God's discourse to man." See Umberto Eco, *Art and Beauty in the Middle Ages*, trans. Hugh Bredin (New Haven, Conn.: Yale University Press, 1986), 54, and section 3 of this introduction.

22. Lacan/Wilden, *The Language of the Self*, 31; on p. 35 Lacan noted that "the symptom itself is structured like a Language, because the symptom is a Language from which the Word must be liberated." Lacan also added: "There is no error which does not present and promulgate itself as truth." See his *The Seminars of Jacques Lacan*, book 1, ed. Jacques-Alain Miller, trans. John Forrester (New York: W. W. Norton, 1988), 263. Also recall Gregory Bateson's dictum, "All behavior is communication."

23. Jonathan Culler summarized the Derridean position regarding all texts in "Issues in Contemporary American Critical Debate,"in Ira Konigsberg, ed., *American Criticism in the Poststructuralist Age* (Ann Arbor: University of Michigan Press, 1981), 4. A text "anticipates any deconstruction the critic can achieve," with the critic bringing to the surface what "is always thematized in the text in the form of meta-linguistic statements"; see J. Hillis Miller, "Deconstructing the Deconstructors," *Diacritics* 5, no. 2 (Summer 1975): 31.

24. When the narration of events is highly mythologized, as it was in the "dirty war" case, a definitive "true" version (such as the one proposed by hypocrisy arguments) never preempts, moots, or supersedes all others (such as the military's). Rather I will "define the myth as consisting of all its versions" and build toward an understanding from that basis. See Claude Lévi-Strauss, *Structural Anthropology*, trans. Claire Jacobson and Brooke Grundfest Schoepf (New York: Basic Books, 1963), 217.

25. Jacques Derrida, *Writing and Difference*, trans. Alan Bass (Chicago, Ill.: University of Chicago Press, 1978), 278.

26. Lévi-Strauss, *Structural Anthropology*, 201.

27. See Anthony Wilden, *System and Structure* (London: Tavistock Publications, 1972), 31–34.

28. Burkert, in Hamerton-Kelly, *Violent Origins*, 150.

29. Ibid.

30. Ibid., 153. See also Walter Burkert, *Homo Necans*, trans. Peter Bing (Berkeley: University of California Press, 1983), 23, where ritual communication "is reciprocal and is strengthened by the reactions of each side."

31. Lacan/Wilden, *The Language of the Self*, 17.

32. See J. L. Austin, "Performative Utterances," in his *Philosophical Papers* (London: Oxford University Press, 1961) and his *How to Do Things with Words* (Cambridge, Mass.: Harvard University Press, 1962). The theory of illocutionary statements was further developed in John R. Searle, ed., *Speech Acts: An Essay in the Philosophy of Language* (London: Cambridge University Press, 1969), and in essays collected by Searle in *The Philosophy of Language* (London: Oxford University Press, 1971).

33. Barthes, *Semiotic Challenge*, 292.

34. Julia Kristeva, *Revolution in Poetic Language*, trans. Margaret Waller (New York: Columbia University Press, 1984), 59–60. For essential background on the concept of intertextuality, see Tzvetan Todorov, *Mikhail Bakhtin: The Dialogical Principle*, trans. Wlad Godzich (Minneapolis: University of Minnesota Press, 1984).

35. Bakhtin's words, cited in ibid., 48. See also Todorov, *Introduction to Poetics*, 23–24.

36. In "The Agency of the Letter in the Unconscious," Lacan argued that "what the psychoanalytic experience discovers in the unconscious is the whole

structure of language." See his *Écrits*, trans. Alan Sheridan (New York: W. W. Norton, 1977), 147.

37. Ibid., 72, and Lacan/Wilden, *The Language of the Self*, 20, respectively.

38. Jacques Lacan, *Écrits* (Paris: Editions du Seuil, 1966), 688–689; translation from introduction to Jacques Derrida, *Of Grammatology*, trans. and intro. by Gayatri Chakravorty Spivak (Baltimore, Md.: Johns Hopkins University Press, 1976), lxii.

39. Crusading piety sanctioning slaughter of conquered infidels was apparent, to cite one example, in the writings of chaplain Raymond of Aguilers, who noted the following in regard to the 1099 capture of Jerusalem: "For some of them, the easiest way, had their heads cut off; others were shot at with arrows and fell from the towers; some indeed were harshly tortured and were flaming with fire. In the streets and square, there were piles of heads and hands and feet. . . . They rode in blood up to the knees and the bits of the horses by the just and wonderful judgements of God." Cited in T.S.R. Boase, *Death in the Middle Ages: Mortality, Judgement and Remembrance* (New York: McGraw Hill, 1972), 15.

40. See John Leddy Phelan, *The Millennial Kingdom of the Franciscans in the New World* (Berkeley: University of California Press, 1970), 13. The theme was also developed forcefully in Alain Milhou, *Colón y su mentalidad mesiánica* (Valladolid, Spain: La Casa-Museo Colón, 1983).

41. Phelan, *The Millennial Kingdom*, 14. Also see pp. 44–46. See also Ernst H. Kantorowicz, "The Problem of Medieval World Unity," in Stanley Pargellis, ed., *The Quest for Political Unity in World History* (Washington, D.C.: U. S. Government Printing Office, 1944), 31–37.

42. The incorporation of the *corpus mysticum* into medieval political agendas was elucidated in Ernst H. Kantorowicz, *The King's Two Bodies: A Study in Mediaeval Political Theology* (Princeton, N.J.: Princeton University Press, 1957).

43. Eco, *Art and Beauty*, 53. See also Jacques Le Goff, *Medieval Civilization, 400–1500*, trans. Julia Barrow (New York: Basil Blackwell, 1989), 330–331.

44. Emilio E. Massera, *El camino a la democracia* (Buenos Aires: El Cid Editores, 1979), 102. On another occasion Massera explained in a national broadcast that "God wanted me to intervene decisively in incidents of the highest importance." See ibid., 129. The December 2, 1986, Argentine federal court conviction of Ramón Camps on charges related to human rights violations made specific reference to Camps's "sacrilegious pretension of having acted under divine guidance." See Bradley Graham, "Argentine Ex-Police Chief Convicted of 'Tormenting' 73," *Washington Post*, December 3, 1986.

45. General Juan Manuel Bayón, in a 1977 document from a course for high-ranking army officials, cited in Enrique Vázquez, *PRN / La Ultima: Origen, apogeo y caída de la dictadura militar* (Buenos Aires: Editorial Universitaria de Buenos Aires, 1985), 83.

46. Lieutenant Colonel Hugo I. Pascarelli, in an address on the occasion of the one hundred fiftieth anniversary of the first artillery group; de facto president Jorge Rafael Videla was in the audience. Cited in Emilio F. Mignone, *Iglesia y dictadura* (Buenos Aires: Ediciones del Pensamiento Nacional, 1986), 190.

47. See Frederick H. Russell, *Just War in the Middle Ages* (Cambridge: Cambridge University Press, 1979), 292. During the trials following the "dirty war," defense attorneys for Leopoldo Galtieri cited Augustine and Francisco de Vitoria in arguing that "wars must be and are just when they are initiated to redress offenses." See "'La distinción entre guerras sucias y limpias, no ha existido jamás,'" *El Diario del Juicio* 22 (October 22, 1985).

48. See Frank Bottomley, *Attitudes to the Body in Western Christendom* (London: Lepus Books, 1979), 161.

CHAPTER 1

1. *Nazi Conspiracy and Aggression*, vol. 7, Document L-90 (Washington, D.C.: Office of the United States Chief of Counsel for Prosecution of Axis Criminality, 1946), 871–873.

2. As I will discuss later there were three military Juntas in Argentina between 1976 and 1983. For the sake of discursive efficiency and unless otherwise specified in context, the word "Junta" will be used throughout this study to represent the de facto regime conceptually as a single governing entity, in the same way that "crown" is sometimes used to represent a monarchy or "the government" to denote successive administrations as a continuum.

3. Organization of American States, Inter-American Commission on Human Rights, *Report on the Situation of Human Rights in Argentina* (Washington, D.C.: OAS, 1980), 54. The Inter-American Commission on Human Rights will hereafter be referred to as the "OAS Commission."

4. Emilio E. Massera, *El camino a la democracia* (Buenos Aires: El Cid Editores, 1979), 62.

5. Thomas E. Skidmore and Peter H. Smith suggested that the clandestine nature of violent repression in Argentina may have been derived in part from the Argentine military's study of how the Brazilian security forces were criticized for mistreating political prisoners during the early 1970s. "The Brazilian mistake, according to the Argentines, was to place suspects under official arrest, thus leaving a legal trail." See their *Modern Latin America* (New York: Oxford University Press, 1984), 107.

6. When one detention center survivor asked a guard if she was going to be killed, he responded "that they were killing everyone, because if you send subversives to prison they go back to the same thing [subversion] when they are

freed." See the testimony of Miriam Lewin de García in *El Diario del Juicio* 21 (October 15, 1985): 413.

7. Terrorism under Rosas was distinct from "dirty war" repression in that it "was not popular, spontaneous, or indiscriminate. . . . Terror was not anarchic. Nor was it a delegated power, fashioned and applied by subordinates," as it was to a large extent after the 1976 coup. But beyond these fundamental differences in central control, specified targeting of victims, and delegation (even if by default) to subordinates, in the regimes of both Rosas and the post–1976 military dictatorship terror was predominant in "the distinctive style of the regime." For a summary of the issue regarding Rosas, see "The Terror," in John Lynch, *Argentine Dictator: Juan Manuel de Rosas, 1829–1852* (Oxford: Clarendon Press, 1981), in particular pp. 209–210.

8. See Carlos H. Waisman, *Reversal of Development in Argentina: Postwar Counterrevolutionary Policies and Their Structural Consequences* (Princeton, N.J.: Princeton University Press, 1987), 221–225. For background see Roberto P. Korzeniewicz, "Labor Unrest in Argentina, 1887–1907," *Latin American Research Review* 24, no. 3 (1989): 71.

9. Frederick M. Nunn, *Yesterday's Soldiers: European Military Professionalism in South America, 1890–1940* (Lincoln: University of Nebraska Press, 1983), 127. On p. 130 Nunn added that in the military Argentines "were more Prussian than the Prussians themselves." See pp. 170–171 for a brief summary of the professionalized military's entrance into Argentine politics in the 1930s. Alain Rouquié's remarks on p. 80 of *The Military and the State*, trans. Paul E. Sigmund (Berkeley: University of California Press, 1987), address Uriburu's Prussianism.

See also Robert A. Potash, *The Army and Politics in Argentina, 1928 to 1945*, vol. 1 (Stanford, Calif.: Stanford University Press, 1969), 3–5. Robert Wesson, ed., *The Latin American Military Institution* (New York: Praeger, 1986), 95–98 and 150–153, provided a succinct overview of Fascist influence on the Argentine military. In *Argentine Diary: The Inside Story of the Coming of Fascism* (New York: Random House, 1944), Ray Josephs gave an informal, day-by-day view into Fascist influences in Argentina between June 1943 and January 1944.

10. As General Galtieri put it, "The first World War was a confrontation of armies, the second of nations, and the third of ideologies." Cited in *Nunca más: Informe de la Comisión Nacional Sobre la Desaparición de Personas* (Buenos Aires and Barcelona: EUDEBA/Seix Barral, 1985), 474/443. The quoted passage, as well as the Junta's concept of "World War III," will be discussed later.

Above, as in all further citations from *Nunca más*, the first page number refers to the original Spanish-language edition and the second to the English translation published in New York by Farrar, Straus and Giroux in 1986. Passages from *Nunca más* cited in the text are in my translation, sometimes based on translations in the 1986 volume.

11. In reference to the military of the "dirty war" that would follow, Jacobo Timerman noted: "The ideology motivating the Argentine military stems more from a notion of the world they [sic] reject than from a world they would like to attain." See his *Prisoner Without a Name, Cell Without a Number*, trans. Toby Talbot (New York: Vintage Books, 1982), 94.

12. From a 1909 police report cited in Waisman, *Reversal of Development*, 216. For a succinct discussion of labor immigration in its relation to the rise of nationalism and right-wing repression between the two world wars, see Juan A. Oddone, "Regionalismo y nacionalismo," in Leopoldo Zea, ed., *América Latina en sus ideas* (Mexico City: Siglo Veintiuno Editores/UNESCO, 1986), 229-235.

13. The "ideological border" concept was very much in evidence during the later "dirty war" as well. Admiral Massera argued that the struggle was "against a strange and cruel power, against an invasion that crossed the moral borders of our conscience." Massera, *El camino*, 58.

14. The quoted words are from a presentation Onganía made at West Point on September 6, 1964, during the fifth Conference of American Armies. See Alain Rouquié, *Poder militar y sociedad política en la Argentina*, vol. 2 (Buenos Aires: Emecé, 1982), 231.

15. Alejandro A. Lanusse, *Mi testimonio* (Buenos Aires: Laserre Editores, 1977), 23. The text noted that such measures were "considered ridiculous by public opinion." Lanusse lifted the ban on Peronist parties in 1972 and called for the 1973 elections.

16. The quoted phrase is from Rouquié, *Poder militar*, 234. See also p. 259, where Rouquié described Onganía's fervent Catholicism. The gravest crisis, Admiral Massera asserted, was "the MORAL CRISIS." He added: "We must understand that our problem is not a simple choice between styles of government or economic formulas, between civilians and the military, between workers and owners. It is a choice between decadence and grandeur, between immorality and morality." Emilio E. Massera, *El país que queremos* (Buenos Aires: Editorial FEPA, 1981), 86.

17. General Galtieri, president of Argentina at the time of the Falklands/Malvinas war, ordered the invasion in part to enhance the viability of his presidential candidacy in Argentina's imminent return to democracy. See Adolfo Gilly, "Las Malvinas, una guerra del capital," in Alberto J. Pla et al., *La década trágica: Ocho ensayos sobre la crisis argentina* (Buenos Aires: Editorial Tierra del Fuego, 1984), 189.

18. See Rouquié, *Poder militar*, 284-285.

19. Clifford Geertz, "Centers, Kings, and Charisma: Reflections on the Symbolics of Power," in Sean Wilentz, ed., *Rites of Power: Symbolism, Ritual and Politics Since the Middle Ages* (Philadelphia: University of Pennsylvania Press, 1985), 31. Psychoanalysis has long recognized that "under interdictory systems, transgression is bound up with prohibition." See Serge Viderman, "Subject-

Object Relation and the Problem of Desire," in Serge Lebovici and Daniel Widlöcher, eds., *Psychoanalysis in France* (New York: International Universities Press, 1980), 196.

20. Waisman, *Reversal of Development*, 233. For an opposing view see Peter Waldmann, "Anomia social y violencia," in Alain Rouquié, ed., *Argentina hoy* (Mexico City: Siglo XXI, 1982), 220.

21. The Montoneros viewed the abduction as a reprisal for the 1956 execution of General Juan José Valle and twenty-six of his associates, who were summarily shot by the Aramburu administration after staging a minor pro-Perón military uprising. The Montoneros also held a grudge against Aramburu for the exhumation of Evita Perón's remains and their transfer to a secret tomb in Milan, and they demanded information on the body's whereabouts. For the date of Aramburu's assassination, the terrorists chose the historically charged first anniversary of the *Cordobazo*. Onganía was removed from office ten days later. For details on the *Aramburazo*, see Richard Gillespie, *Soldiers of Perón: Argentina's Montoneros* (Oxford: Clarendon Press, 1982), 89–99.

22. The quoted passage is from a Montonero communiqué released at the time of the so-called *Aramburazo*. See ibid., 90.

23. For further details see the OAS Commission, *Report*, 23n, and Grant Wardlaw, *Political Terrorism: Theory, Tactics, and Counter-Measures* (Cambridge: Cambridge University Press, 1982), 72. The latter placed the Argentine events in international context.

24. For details see Justo Escobar and Sebastián Velázquez, *Examen de la violencia argentina* (Mexico City: Fondo de Cultura Económica, 1975).

25. David Rock, *Argentina 1516–1982* (Berkeley: University of California Press, 1985), 355. "Vanish without a trace" is also the translation for a phrase used by Sophocles in *Oedipus the King* to describe the fate of both Laius (Oedipus's father) and Oedipus himself. That observation will gain greater significance in Chapter 4.

26. Amnesty International, *"Disappearances": A Workbook* (New York: Amnesty International USA, 1981), 7–8.

27. Alejandro M. Garro and Henry Dahl, "Legal Accountability for Human Rights Violations in Argentina: One Step Forward and Two Steps Backward," *Human Rights Law Journal* 8 (1987): 287n–288n.

28. For a succinct and useful summary of the context in which Perón's nationalist messianism signified, see Oddone, "Regionalismo y nacionalismo," 229–233.

29. *La novela de Perón* by Tomás Eloy Martínez dealt specifically with the day of Perón's return. The novel is available in English: *The Perón Novel*, trans. Asa Zatz (New York: Pantheon, 1988).

30. Gillespie, *Soldiers of Peron*, 144. For a discussion of fascism's influence on the younger Peron, see Waisman, *Reversal of Development*, 243-245. The depiction of subversion as "germs" is discussed in depth in Chapter 4.

31. Gillespie, *Soldiers of Peron*, 150. Osvaldo Soriano's novella *No habrá más penas ni olvido* (Barcelona: Seix Barral, 1980) dealt precisely with the confusion generated by Perón's shifts and inconsistencies. On p. 10 in his prologue, Soriano described those baffling politics: "Perón utilized a curious strategy of government: He disqualified as 'infiltrators' those whom the whole country recognized as Peronists . . . and he blessed as Peronists many of the outsiders who had contributed to his fall in 1955 and fought against him until shortly before his return."

32. For a discussion of the Montoneros' return to clandestine operations, see the chapter entitled "Return to Arms" in Gillespie, *Soldiers of Peron*.

López Rega's nickname "El Brujo" was well earned. He was the author of books on the occult—one of which he claimed to have coauthored with the Archangel Gabriel—and was notorious for otherworldly stunts such as his attempt to transfer Evita's soul into the body of Isabel Perón.

33. *El Libro de El Diario del Juicio* (Buenos Aires: Editorial Perfil, 1985), 245. The statistic is from Rock, *Argentina*, 363.

34. For a concise discussion of the impact of Perón's populist politics on inflation, see Donald C. Hodges, *Argentina, 1943-1976* (Albuquerque: University of New Mexico Press, 1976), 170. Inflation for the period between March 1975 and March 1976 increased to 566.3 percent.

35. Ibid., 182.

36. Garro and Dahl, "Legal Accountability," 289. Acting President Italo A. Luder signed the decree while Isabel Perón was on extended leave that year.

37. Ibid.

38. For a brief discussion of the factions within the military, see Rock, *Argentina*, 369-370 and 373-374. A more comprehensive, journalistic account was included in John Simpson and Jana Bennett, *The Disappeared and the Mothers of the Plaza* (New York: Saint Martin's Press, 1985).

39. Hodges, *Argentina*, 182.

40. In almost seven years of military rule, there were three Juntas. The members of the first Junta were General Jorge Rafael Videla, commander of the army; Admiral Emilio Eduardo Massera, commander of the navy; and Brigadier General Orlando Ramón Agosti, commander of the air force. Members of the second and third Juntas, likewise commanders of their respective armed forces, were General Roberto Eduardo Viola (army); Admiral Armando Lambruschini (navy); Brigadier General Omar Domingo Rubens Graffigna (air force); and General Leopoldo Galtieri (army); Admiral Jorge Isaac Anaya (navy); Brigadier General Basilio Arturo Lami Dozo (air force).

41. Originally published in Buenos Aires newspapers on April 5, 1976. The translation is modified slightly from Brian Loveman and Thomas M. Davies, Jr., eds., *The Politics of Antipolitics: The Military in Latin America* (Lincoln: University of Nebraska Press, 1978), 178–180. At the time of the September 6, 1930, coup d'état, Lieutenant Colonel Enrique Rottjer made much the same argument, calling the military intervention a "sacrifice" that the officer corps made on behalf of the people, adding his hope that such a move would never again need to be taken. The army, he continued, represented the people and transcended its normal mission because the military was "flesh of the nation . . . intrinsically linked to the nation itself" and as such "could not remain indifferent to the situation." Nunn, *Yesterday's Soldiers*, 261. Similarly Onganía's 1966 remarks at the time of his coup d'état paralleled those of Videla very closely; see Loveman and Davies, eds., *The Politics of Antipolitics*, 174–176.

42. Cited in several sources, among them Amnesty International, *"Disappearances": A Workbook*, 9; the Argentine Commission for Human Rights publication *Argentina: Proceso al genocidio* (Madrid: Elías Querejeta Ediciones, 1977), 22; and Daniel Frontalini and María Cristina Caiati, *El mito de la guerra sucia* (Buenos Aires: Centro de Estudios Legales y Sociales, 1984), 25.

43. From a radio announcement made by the Junta on taking control of Argentina; translation from Loveman and Davies, eds., *The Politics of Antipolitics*, 177.

44. Ibid.

45. Quoted phrase is from a speech by Lieutenant Colonel Jorge Edward Goleri, given on the occasion of an April 1976 book burning. Cited in Frontalini and Caiati, *El mito*, 90.

46. OAS Commission, *Report*, 19.

47. Cited in *Nunca más*, 342/333. In a press conference General Viola added: "Subversion is all action—clandestine or visible, insidious or violent—that seeks the alteration or the destruction of the people's moral criteria and form of life, with the end of seizing power and imposing a new form based upon a different scale of values." Quoted in Frontalini and Caiati, *El mito*, 75. General Guillermo Suárez Masón corroborated: "Facing the advance of a *total* action on the part of Marxism it is essential to have an integral response from the State. It would be absurd to suppose that we have won the war against subversion because we have eliminated its armed threat." Quoted in ibid., 19. And Admiral Massera stated, "One must understand that subversives are not only the terrorists groups of whatever ideology, but subversives are also the ideological saboteurs, and those who with easy solutions incite a new postponement of our destiny." Massera, *El camino*, 22. For additional examples see Andrés Avellaneda, *Censura, autoritarismo y cultura: Argentina 1960–1983*, vol. 1 (Buenos Aires: Centro Editor de América Latina, 1986), 137.

48. General Luciano Benjamín Menéndez, cited in Avellaneda, *Censura*, 27.

49. Marcial Castro Castillo, *Fuerzas armadas: Etica y represión* (Buenos Aires: Editorial Nuevo Orden, 1979), 88 (italics are from the original) and 90, respectively.

50. Cited in Argentine Commission for Human Rights, *Argentina: Proceso al genocidio*, 13. A version varying slightly (due to translation from the English original in *The Guardian*, May 6, 1977) but identical in meaning appeared in Enrique Vázquez, *PRN/La Ultima: Origen, apogeo y caída de la dictadura militar* (Buenos Aires: EUDEBA, 1985), 73. Ramón Camps later attempted to disclaim this statement in an interview published in Madrid on January 27, 1983.

51. Massera, *El camino*, 101, and Avellaneda, *Censura*, 28–29.

52. Carapintada Aldo Rico later offered the same argument. See Jorge Grecco and Gustavo González, *Argentina: El ejercito que tenemos* (Buenos Aires: Editorial Sudamericana, 1990), 138. The legal resort here was to article 34 (3) of the Argentine Criminal Code, which provides that a person who "causes a wrong to avoid a greater wrong that was imminent and in which he was not involved" is exempt from punishment. See Garro and Dahl, "Legal Accountability," 325.

53. *El Libro de El Diario del Juicio*, 314.

54. Similarly Jean-Paul Sartre recognized, in reference to the Holocaust, that "it is not the Jewish character that provokes anti-Semitism, but, rather, that it is the anti-Semite who creates the Jew." See his *Anti-Semite and Jew* (New York: Schocken Books, 1965), 143. Earlier, referring to the Spanish in the sixteenth century, Gonzalo Fernández de Oviedo noted, "If they did not have foreign enemies, they would look for enemies amongst themselves." Cited in Américo Castro, *Aspectos del vivir hispanico* (Madrid: Alianza Editorial, 1987), 37. The title of Argentine Carlos Gambetta's book, *Todos somos subversivos* ("We Are All Subversives"), well captured the idea as far as the "dirty war" was concerned.

55. *El Libro de El Diario del Juicio*, 256. This matter will be dealt with specifically in the following chapter.

56. "The presence of the guerrillas had simply provided the military with a convenient pretext for extirpating all those whom it had viewed as imperilling the dominance of its ultra-right Catholic nationalism and *laissez-faire* economic program." Mark Osiel, "The Making of Human Rights Policy in Argentina: The Impact of Ideas and Interests on a Legal Conflict," in *Journal of Latin American Studies* 135 (1986): 167. The mythological and psychodynamic implications of "extirpation" will be explored in subsequent chapters.

57. See ibid., 145. The count of *desaparecidos* documented by CONADEP is 8,960, but the actual number of "dirty war" victims is believed to be significantly higher. The 12,000 figure is a scholarly estimate based on the extant evidence. The figure used by many human rights groups in Argentina is 30,000. On a per capita basis, to situate the Argentine Junta's repression in the context of that experienced under other recent Latin American dictatorships, for each person who "disappeared" or died in official custody in Brazil, 10 died in Uruguay and

over 300 died in Argentina. See Alfred Stepan, *Rethinking Military Politics: Brazil and the Southern Cone* (Princeton, N.J.: Princeton University Press, 1988), 69–70. Stepan's per capita statistics were based on the official CONADEP count; if the 12,000 figure is reasonable, they therefore underrepresented the number of victims in relation to the total Argentine population.

58. Rock, *Argentina*, 367.

59. The quoted passage is from Osiel, "Making of Human Rights Policy," 139. The statistics are from *Nunca más*, 296.

60. In the 1977 Directive 504 General Videla specified "normalization of the industrial, educational and religious environments" as priorities. The religious concern is analyzed in subsequent chapters. See "La orden secreta de Videla," *El Diario del Juicio* 28 (December 3, 1985).

61. From March 1976 Junta proclamations; Loveman and Davies, eds., *The Politics of Antipolitics*, 177–178.

62. Oscar Troncoso, "El proceso de reorganización nacional/2: Cronología y documentación (De abril de 1977 a junio de 1978)," in Daniel Rodríguez Lamas et al., eds., *Presidencias y golpes militares del siglo XX* (Buenos Aires: Biblioteca Política Argentina, Centro Editor de América Latina, 1985), 58.

63. *Conozcamos a nuestro enemigo: Subversión en el ámbito educativo* (Buenos Aires: Ministerio de Cultura y Educación, 1978), 5.

64. Massera, *El camino*, 90. The admiral added that he was "truly persuaded that the young people's misappropriation of thought and instability of values are the most destructive consequences of the so-called security crisis which defines our times."

65. Francisco Carcavallo, quoted in Avellaneda, *Censura*, 138. Also see pp. 24–25 for other similar expressions.

66. Massera, *El país*, 79.

67. Cited phrase from Avellaneda, *Censura*, 24.

68. Osiel, "Making of Human Rights Policy," 173.

69. *Nunca más*, 329–331/318–319. For details see María Seoane and Hector Ruíz Nuñez, *La noche de los lápices* (Buenos Aires: Editorial Contrapunto, 1986). Another "night of pencils"–type roundup was also described in Noemí Ulla and Hugo Echave, *Después de la noche: Diálogo con Graciela Fernández Meijide* (Buenos Aires: Editorial Contrapunto, 1986), 14–27.

70. *Nunca más*, 327/316. Parents in search of "disappeared" children were frequently admonished by security personnel for having failed to raise their children properly and to adequately oversee the activities of their wayward offspring.

71. Testimony presented by Graciela Susana Geuna to the United Nations, dated March 6, 1984; in CELS files. Citations are from pp. 28 and 53, respectively.

72. The quoted passages are from *Conozcamos a nuestro enemigo*, 59.

73. *Nunca más*, 294/285.

74. Wealth in mythopoetic romance often is expressed in its ideal forms, power and wisdom; the former in particular was a commodity central to "dirty war" myths and rituals, as I will discuss in later chapters.

75. Adolfo Gilly identified "the violent restructuring of the country's economy" as the primary objective of the 1976 coup and the subsequent repression. See his "Las Malvinas," 203; see also Gilly's "Argentina después de la dictadura," in Alberto J. Pla et al., *La década trágica: Ocho ensayos sobre la crisis argentina* (Buenos Aires: Editorial Tierra del Fuego, 1984), particularly pp. 229-232. The Montoneros referred to the coup similarly (though in politicized rhetoric) as one sponsored by "the oligarchy, the imperialist monopolies, and the upper strata of the national bourgeoisie." Gillespie, *Soldiers of Perón*, 232. For an overview of the Junta's economic policy, see Waisman, *Reversal of Development*, 280-286, and Rock, *Argentina*, 367-373. The final report of the Mar del Plata delegation to CONADEP (an unpublished document) stated on p. 4 that the repression was a means "to demolish all types of organized opposition" against "transformation of the national economic structure," so that the Junta could establish an economy of "financial speculation" after "delivery of the fundamental sources of production into foreign hands."

76. *Nunca más*, 296/368.

77. Cited in ibid., 375/369. By the end of September 1976, wages were at 50 percent of their 1974 level. Directive No. 504/77 issued in April 1977 by General Roberto Eduardo Viola, then head of the First Army Corps, concerned the industrial front of the antisubversive campaign. See Garro and Dahl, "Legal Accountability," 327. In more bombastic rhetoric Admiral Massera explained that "the government knows that man does not live by bread alone" and for that reason "is going to induce the reeducation of all sectors involved in production." Massera, *El camino*, 45.

78. For details see Hodges, *Argentina*, 183. For a succinct summary of the role of unions in Argentine political history, see Lisbeth Haas, "Argentina," in Gerald Michael Greenfield and Sheldon L. Maram, eds., *Latin American Labor Organizations* (New York: Greenwood Press, 1987), 1-24.

79. *Nunca más*, 64/61.

80. *El Libro de El Diario del Juicio*, 250. The victim was doubly damned, once by acrohomonymy and again by his "subversive" profession.

81. Ibid.

82. OAS Commission, *Report*, 14-15.

83. Ibid., 12-20 and 29; and Garro and Dahl, "Legal Accountability," 291-294.

84. See Garro and Dahl, "Legal Accountability," 290.

85. Ibid., 290 and 393. Heleen F.P. Ietswaart pointed out that Argentine legal discourse "combines formalism and pomposity with shallow rhetoric and a low level of verisimilitude in a typical way that finds hardly any parallel, even in

Latin American countries that are otherwise comparable, such as Brazil and Chile. Argentine official discourse liberally uses phrases . . . which would be wholly ridiculous and unacceptable elsewhere." See Ietswaart, "The Discourse of Summary Justice and the Discourse of Popular Justice," in Richard Abel, ed., *The Politics of Informal Justice*, vol. 2 (New York: Academic Press, 1982), 176.

86. Garro and Dahl, "Legal Accountability," 298.

87. Denial as a performative speech act was also required in a "disappearance," as will be clarified later.

88. *Nunca más*, 17/11. The theatrics of "dirty war" violence will be the specific concern of Chapter 2.

89. Ibid., 18/12–13.

90. Quoted passage from Enrique Dahl and Alejandro M. Garro, trans., "Argentina: National Appeals Court (Criminal Division) Judgement on Human Rights Violations by Former Military Leaders," *International Legal Materials* 26 (1987): 334.

91. *Nunca más*, 22/17.

92. Signatures and identification documents were also forged to withdraw funds from *desaparecidos'* bank accounts. Rank was apparently respected in the distribution of these and other spoils: "The non-commissioned officers, who were the lowest on the distribution scale, expressed great resentment towards officers" who benefited disproportionately from the "dirty" tasks assigned to their subordinates. See Amnesty International, *Testimony on Secret Detention Camps in Argentina* (London: Amnesty International, 1980), 29.

93. *Nunca más*, 303/289. See also OAS Commission, *Report*, 59–65. For details and cases of infants treated as "spoils of war," see Julio E. Nosiglia, *Botín de guerra* (Buenos Aires: Tierra Fértil, 1985). Luis Puenzo's 1985 film *The Official Story* dramatized the circumstance of one such adoption. In recent years the Mothers and Grandmothers of the Plaza De Mayo have dedicated themselves to searching for the children of *desaparecidos* and attempting to return them to their natural families.

94. See James Given, "The Inquisitors of Languedoc and the Medieval Technology of Power," *American Historical Review* 94, no. 2 (April 1989): 352.

95. According to *Webster's*, this is defined as: 1) "the getting of sexual pleasure from dominating, mistreating or hurting one's partner, 2) the getting of pleasure from inflicting physical or psychological pain on others."

96. See, for example, *Nunca más*, 176/159, 283/273, and 320–321/308–309.

97. One testimony related that the five-year-old daughter of "disappeared" parents committed suicide by gunshot shortly after having witnessed a session in which her father was tortured. Ibid., 320/307–308.

98. See, for example, ibid., 188/171.

99. See, for example, ibid., 317/305.

100. See OAS Commission, *Report*, 107, for a description of "the machine."

101. See *Nunca más*, 217/202–203.

102. *El Diario del Juicio* 3 (June 11, 1985): 63.

103. *Nunca más*, 211/196–197.

104. OAS Commission, *Report*, 80.

105. In 1977–1979 these Montoneros became "directly and incredibly, 'political advisers' to the Navy Chief" Massera, who was expressing presidential ambitions in the populist mode as his tenure on the military Junta drew to a close. See Gillespie, *Soldiers of Perón*, 248, and Americas Watch, *Truth and Partial Justice in Argentina* (New York: Americas Watch, 1987), 45. The Montonero leaders' "feigned" compliance recalls Lévi-Strauss's haunting question: "To what extent has the hero become the dupe of his own impersonation?" See his *Structural Anthropology* (New York: Basic Books, 1963), 174. Miguel Bonasso's novel *Recuerdo de la muerte* (Mexico City: Ediciones Era, 1984) dealt specifically with these Montoneros and provided an implied response: On p. 134 he wrote, "This business of simulating has its problems; one knows how it begins but not how it will end. . . . [The Montonero character feigning compliance] vaguely remembered a film about someone pretending to be mad; he was put in a lunatic asylum and wound up totally out of his mind." Lisandro Raúl Cubas, one of the prisoners selected for "recuperation," remarked, "Every once in a while one had to reflect on what was being feigned and what wasn't. In my personal case, I could only put my ideas in order well after my liberation." Testimony in APDH files, 10.

106. Americas Watch, *Truth and Partial Justice*, 44.

107. OAS Commission, *Report*, 80.

108. A harvest of Junta denials as reiterated during the 1985 trials is available in the following articles from *El Diario del Juicio* 15 (September 3, 1985): "Videla: 'La responsibilidad no era de la Junta Militar'"; "Massera: 'Pudo haberse retenido a algún hombre'"; "Agosti: 'No recuerdo haber recibido denuncia alguna.'" *El Diario del Juicio* 16 (September 10, 1985) included: "Lambruschini: 'Todos eran derivados a la justicia,'" and "Galtieri: 'No hubo centros ocultos de detención.'"

109. Ulla and Echave, *Después de la noche*, 28.

110. Based on her meetings with Junta members, Patricia Derian, Under Secretary of State for Human Rights during the Carter administration, observed that responses to her questions seemed to follow a formula. First there was denial that there was any problem, followed by a heated discussion that concluded with a concession but also with a projection of blame onto Communists, terrorists, and others. See *El Diario del Juicio* 9 (July 23, 1985): 193.

111. Diana R. Kordon and Lucila I. Edelman, eds., *Efectos psicológicos de la represión política* (Buenos Aires: Sudamericana-Planeta, 1986), 44. See also pp. 31 and 34, regarding the assumption of guilt by parents of *desaparecidos* and the State's propaganda campaign to foster it.

112. Garro and Dahl, "Legal Accountability," 294. The authors noted that between 1976 and 1979 there were 5,487 writs of habeas corpus filed. Despite the futility of the gesture as described in the text, General Videla testified before the Supreme Council that "all habeas corpus writs . . . were responded to" during his presidency. See "Videla," in *El Diario del Juicio* 15 (September 15, 1985).

113. General Tomás Sánchez de Bustamante, quoted in Garro and Dahl, "Legal Accountability," 294.

114. For an autobiographical account of Timerman's ordeal, see Jacobo Timerman, *Prisoner Without a Name, Cell Without a Number*, trans. Toby Talbot (New York: Vintage Books, 1982). General Ramón J.A. Camps responded with a book of his own, *Caso Timerman: Punto final* (Buenos Aires: Tribuna Abierta, 1982).

115. Garro and Dahl, "Legal Accountability," 296.

116. OAS Commission, *Report*, 120. According to excerpts in the *New York Times* on September 17, 1979, Viola stated that "like all wars, this one has left tremendous wounds that only time can heal . . . there are the dead, the wounded, the jailed, and those who are absent forever. Don't ask for explanations where there are none."

117. *Nunca más*, 55/52; see also pp. 56/53 for additional passages of official denial.

118. Hannah Arendt, *The Origins of Totalitarianism* (New York: Meridian Books, 1958), 437.

119. OAS Commission, *Report*, 31–33. See also *Nunca más*, 342–343/334.

120. *Observaciones y comentarios críticos del gobierno argentino* (Buenos Aires: Círculo Militar, 1980), 68. Other contradictions abound; see, for example, OAS Commission, *Report*, 88–89. The word *negativa*, translated as "negative," also connotes denial and the refusal to respond.

121. The slogan's pun is lost in translation; "derechos humanos" is the Spanish equivalent of "human rights." The passage literally translates as "(We) Argentines are straight [i.e., forthright] and human."

122. *Observaciones y comentarios*, 5. The dictatorship also published its response to the OAS findings in *La Nación* on May 8, 1980. A paid advertisement sponsored by a right-wing civilian organization affiliated with the military was published in Buenos Aires newspapers on the third day of the OAS Commission's on-site observation. It consisted primarily of a "list of honor" of military personnel who "died at the hands of those who attacked and attack from behind and who now seek refuge in international bureaucracy and the OAS." *Clarín* (September 9, 1979): 14.

123. *El Libro de El Diario del Juicio*, 245.

124. See Garro and Dahl, "Legal Accountability," 300.

125. See OAS Commission, *Report*, 126–128.

126. For the first see ibid., 119; for the second, Emilio F. Mignone, *Iglesia y dictadura* (Buenos Aires: Ediciones del Pensamiento Nacional, 1986), 66.

127. Troncoso, *El proceso*, 15.

128. From the periodical *Gente*; cited, as are the two quoted passages in the preceding sentence, in Horacio Verbitsky, *La última batalla de la tercera guerra mundial* (Buenos Aires: Editorial Legasa, 1984), 153.

129. Roberto L. Esteso and Alberto Spagnolo, "La 'malvinación' de la política," in Alberto J. Pla et al., *La década trágica: Ocho ensayos sobre la crisis argentina* (Buenos Aires: Editorial Tierra del Fuego, 1984), 105. Prior to the Falklands/Malvinas crisis, the Argentine military government attempted in 1978 to instigate a conflict with Chile over another minor territorial issue. The conflict was thwarted by international pressure.

130. Until March 23, when the initial orders for the invasion were given, the mission remained undisclosed even to top-ranking military officers. See Alejandro Dabat, "El derrumbe de la dictadura," in Alberto J. Pla et al., *La década trágica: Ocho ensayos sobre la crisis argentina* (Buenos Aires: Editorial Tierra del Fuego, 1984), 137.

131. Gilly, "Las Malvinas," 190. For interviews with Argentine soldiers who fought in the Falkland/Malvinas, see Daniel Kon, *Los chicos de la guerra* (Buenos Aires: Editorial Galerna, 1982). Studies of the war include O. R. Cardoso et al., *Malvinas: La trama secreta* (Buenos Aires: Sudamericana/Planeta, 1983) and Fritz L. Hoffman and Olga Mingo Hoffman, *Sovereignty in Dispute: The Falklands/Malvinas, 1493–1982* (Boulder, Colo.: Westview Press, 1984).

132. *Argentina, 1983* (Buenos Aires: CISEA/Centro Editor de America Latina, 1984), 162 and 161, respectively. For the complete text of the Final Document in the context of domestic and international response to it, see pp. 151–163.

133. Ibid., 162.

134. Ibid., 151 and 162.

135. Ibid., 378. Many political prisoners who had spent years in detention declined the Junta's amnesty offer immediately. As Claude Bremond observed in a separate context, "Pardon is always conditional, for it retroactively transforms the injury inflicted into a service obtained and demands a proportional service in exchange." "The Logic of Narrative Possibilities," *New Literary History* 11, no. 3 (Spring 1980): 405.

136. *Argentina, 1983*, 440. For the complete text of the National Pacification law, see pp. 440–442.

137. Ibid., 569. On the same day as the mentioned decree, Alfonsín issued another decree ordering the arrest and prosecution of high-ranking Montoneros. For a discussion of the constitutionality of the repeal of the military government's amnesty law, see Dahl and Garro, "Argentina: National Appeals Court," 319, and Amnesty International, *Argentina: The Military Juntas and Human*

Rights: Report of the Trial of the Former Junta Members, 1985 (London: Amnesty International, 1987) 10–11.

138. For details on the creation and organization of CONADEP, see *Nunca más*, 443–456/428–441. Members of CONADEP became major targets of attack by right-wing paramilitary groups affiliated with the security forces. In three Argentine cities the homes of CONADEP delegates were bombed. The commission's president, Ernesto Sábato, related to me in a private conversation that threats to him included one that drew heavily on a central metaphor of his novels *Sobre héroes y tumbas* and *Abaddón: El exterminador*. "We're not going to kill him [Sábato]," an anonymous caller told Sábato's wife, "we're going to gouge out his eyes and cut off his hands."

139. *Nunca Más: The Report of the Argentine National Commission on the Disappeared*, with an introduction by Ronald Dworkin (New York: Farrar, Straus and Giroux, in association with Index on Censorship, 1986). CONADEP also produced a television documentary by the same title.

140. The quoted passages are from Tulio Halperin Donghi, "Argentina's Unmastered Past," *Latin American Research Review* 23, no. 2 (1988): 15.

141. Ibid.

142. See Americas Watch, *Truth and Partial Justice*, 18–19.

143. Dahl and Garro, "Argentina: National Appeals Court," 325.

144. The trials opened on April 22, 1985, and concluded on December 9, 1985.

145. Martin Anderson, "Life Sentences Asked for 5 Argentine Officers," *Washington Post*, September 19, 1985.

146. *El Libro de El Diario del Juicio*, 351.

147. *El Diario del Juicio* 28 (December 3, 1985): 7. In a letter to the Buenos Aires police, Ramón Camps similarly explained how subversion falsified the military's reality. See "El general Camps cursó una carta a la policía bonaerense," *La Prensa*, July 5, 1986.

148. *El Libro de El Diario del Juicio*, 262–263.

149. Ibid., 265.

150. Ibid., 251.

151. For specifics see Amnesty International, *Argentina: The Military Juntas and Human Rights*, 46–53; Dahl and Garro, "Argentina: National Appeals Court," 326; and Americas Watch, *Truth and Partial Justice*, 36.

152. For details see Dahl and Garro, "Argentina: National Appeals Court," 327. Agosti was released in 1989 after serving a three-and-a-half-year term.

The convicted Junta leaders' accommodations in the military prison of Magdalena were plush. Rather than in cells the former commanders were housed in luxuriously appointed four-bedroom/two-bathroom bungalows with gardens.

Each prisoner had a cook and a valet assigned to him. After reviewing photographs taken secretly with a telephoto lens, one journalist observed that the incarcerated Junta leaders "indeed looked indistinguishable from bankers or businessmen on vacation." See Amos Elon, "Letter from Argentina," *The New Yorker* (July 21, 1986): 78–79. The laxity with which military authorities interpreted incarceration for Junta members has other implications as well: In 1989 Emilio Massera—ostensibly serving a life sentence—was photographed at large in Buenos Aires.

153. Garro and Dahl, *Legal Accountability*, 336.

154. Quoted words are Alfonsín's. *Washington Post* April 20, 1987.

155. The remaining two-thirds were against retired officers, police, or former civilian operatives. Garro and Dahl, "Legal Accountability," 337.

156. Ibid., 339. The only exceptions specified by the law were rape, misappropriation of real property through extortion, and abduction and misrepresentation of the identity of children.

157. Ibid., 339–342.

158. Rico cited the "spiritual and intellectual corruption" pervading the army as the enemy of his crusade. Chris Kline, "Argentina's Vexing Military Problem," *The Times of Latin America*, July 26, 1989: 7.

159. The speech is appended to Carlos J. Moneta et al., *La reforma militar* (Buenos Aires: Editorial Legasa, 1985), 232. Alfonsín made similar comments in a January 24, 1989, speech delivered to the nation following a leftist terrorist attack against the Third Army Infantry Regiment in La Tablada.

160. For a summary of the rebellion, see Eugene Robinson, "Mutiny Underlines Argentine Impasse," *Washington Post*, December 8, 1988.

161. Cited in Kline, "Argentina's Vexing Military Problem," 6.

162. In addition to the nine hundred mutinous troops, more than four thousand others in twenty units—ranging in size from company to regimental strength—openly refused to take part in any attack on the rebels.

163. Seineldín, however, contends that the conditions of his capitulation included a tacit official promise that a blanket military pardon would be granted.

164. Public pressure resulting from economic crisis forced Alfonsín to transfer the presidency in July rather than December of 1989.

165. The remaining prisoners, including Junta members Videla, Viola, and Massera, were freed by a second presidential pardon in December 1990. The significance of these pardons will be discussed in Chapter 5.

166. Shirley Christian, "Army's Rambo, Ousted, Is Storming the Hustings," *New York Times*, April 5, 1990. Menem ousted Rico from the army in 1989.

167. Quoted phrase from Ernesto Barreiro, "If Menem Falters in Argentina . . . ," *New York Times*, March 23, 1990: A34.

CHAPTER 2

1. Walter Burkert, *Greek Religion: Archaic and Classical*, trans. John Raffan (Oxford: Basil Blackwell, 1985), 166. See also Lewis Richard Farnell, *The Cults of the Greek States*, vol. 5 (Oxford: Clarendon Press, 1909), 127.

2. On p. 867 the *Standard Dictionary of Folklore and Mythology*, vol. 2, refers to the festivals of Dionysus as "unrestrained orgies in which victims were torn to pieces and devoured raw, men in states of ecstasy emasculated themselves, and intercourse was promiscuous."

3. The most obvious mythological example "would be that Dionysus, the god of wine, was himself killed and dismembered as wine for sacramental drinking." Burkert, *Greek Religion*, 238. Burkert also pointed out on p. 162 that in the blessed state of frenzy both votary and god were called by the same name, Bacchus.

4. Quoted phrase is from ibid., 58.
Hyperbolic depiction of the phallus was apparent in the eternal erection of Priapus, son of Dionysus and Aphrodite. Phallic symbols were worn by the players in early Greek comedy, and comedy itself was an outgrowth of songs denoted "phallic" by virtue of their direction to Phales, a fertility god closely associated with Dionysus. In satyr plays, too, phalluses were donned by the players, as were the skins of goats that had been sacrificed to the gods. Goat sacrifice similarly recalls the etymology of *tragedy*, composed as it is of the Greek words *tragos* ("goat") and *ode* ("song"); tragedy as a "goat song" registers Dionysus's transformation by Zeus into a kid, which occasioned the sacrifice of goats to Dionysus in cult observation.

5. Sophocles, *The Three Theban Plays*, trans. Robert Fagles, intro. and notes by Bernard Knox (New York: Penguin Books, 1984), 25.

6. Friedrich Nietzsche, *On the Genealogy of Morals and Ecce Homo*, trans. Walter Kaufmann (New York: Vintage, 1969), 67. See also pp. 65–72.

7. Ibid., 66.

8. Torture by dog attack was also used, though not prominently, in the "dirty war"; see *Nunca más: Informe de la Comisión Nacional Sobre la Desaparición de Personas* (Buenos Aires and Barcelona: EUDEBA/Seix Barral, 1985), 183/166. Page numbers following the slash refer to the English-language edition of *Nunca más* published in New York by Farrar, Straus and Giroux in 1986.

9. Bartolomé de las Casas, *Brevísima relación de la destrucción de las Indias*, ed. André Saint-Lu (Madrid: Ediciones Cátedra, 1984), 77.

10. Hernán Cortés, *Cartas de relación de la conquista de México* (Mexico City: Espasa-Calpe Mexicana, 1985), 45.

11. Nietzsche, *Genealogy*, 66.

12. Michel Foucault, *Discipline and Punish: The Birth of the Prison*, trans. Alan Sheridan (New York: Vintage Books, 1979), 8.

13. *Nunca más*, 7/1. The CONADEP report frequently employed similar language stressing the dramatic and tragic nature of the "dirty war," including, on p. 11/6, a reference to "the most terrible drama that the Nation has suffered in its history," which made Argentines "tragically famous."

14. See *Nunca más*, 8/3, 16–25/10–20. See also the discussion of abductions in Chapter 1.

15. *Nunca más*, 17/11. One or two somber men in suits, with concealed pistols, could obviously have carried out an abduction more efficiently.

16. Ibid., 17/11.

17. Ibid., 377/371. Several other instances of executions staged as shoot-outs or escape attempts were mentioned in the testimonies; see, for example, ibid., 36/31.

18. Ibid., 69/67. For a summary of alleged armed confrontations cited by the prosecution during the 1985 trials, see Amnesty International, *Argentina: The Military Juntas and Human Rights: Report of the Trial of the Former Junta Members, 1985* (London: Amnesty International, 1987), 26–27.

19. Other types of overt theatrics abounded in the "dirty war." For information on mock executions, see *Nunca más*, 38/33, 45/41, 46/42, 64/62, 155/143, 194/178, and 348/339. On changes of identity, see ibid., 142/132–33 and 135–136/128–129, and Emilio F. Mignone, *Iglesia y dictadura* (Buenos Aires: Ediciones del Pensamiento Nacional, 1986), 121. On camouflaging theaters of sound and odor, see *Nunca más*, 196/180 and 175/158, respectively. On fictitious confessions and other statements extorted from prisoners, see ibid., 139/131, and *El Libro de El Diario del Juicio*, (Buenos Aires: Editorial Perfil, 1985), 267.

20. Foucault, *Discipline*, 47.

21. Ibid., 57.

22. *Nunca más*, 16/10.

23. Foucault, *Discipline*, 12.

24. Ibid. Penal spectacles were also popular in the Americas. See, for example, the execution of revolutionary Tupac Amaru in John Hemming, *The Conquest of the Incas* (New York: Harcourt, Brace and Jovanovich, 1970), 446–449. Spectacle was also prominent during the wars of independence, the extravagant bloodiness of the hordes riding behind the Spanish General José Tomás Boves a noteworthy case in point. When Boves was succeeded after his death by General Tomás Morales, an appreciation for the poetics of atrocity was heightened further. Morales, for example, captured one patriot, savagely murdered him, fried his head in oil, and sent the head to Caracas to be displayed in a birdcage. See Indalecio Liévano Aguirre, *Bolívar* (Madrid: Ediciones Cultural Hispánica del Instituto de Cooperación Iberoamericana, 1983), 112.

25. Foucault, *Discipline*, 34.

26. Ibid., 49.

27. In the Americas the *guardamigo* or *pie de amigo* was an "iron instrument . . . placed beneath the chin of prisoners taken out to be shamed, to prevent them from lowering their heads to hide their faces." See Constancio Bernaldo de Quirós, *La picota en América* (Havana: Jesús Montero, Editor, 1948), 86. Compare this with the expression "to save face."

28. Michel de Certeau, *Heterologies: Discourse on the Other*, trans. Brian Massumi (Minneapolis: University of Minnesota Press, 1986), 186. See also Foucault, *Discipline*, 44.

29. Poisoners, the sacrilegious, parricides, sodomites, and incendiaries were burned at the stake in Europe. See Michel Ragon, *The Space of Death*, trans. Alan Sheridan (Charlottesville: University of Virginia Press, 1983), 185. Regarding the saw see Robert Held, *Inquisition/Inquisición: A Bilingual Guide to the Exhibition of Torture Instruments from the Middle Ages to the Industrial Era* (Florence: Qua D'Arno, 1985), 46–49; the "breast ripper" was discussed on p. 136. Held also noted, on p. 136, that expanding oral, rectal, and vaginal pears were also closely connected symbolically to the offenses that they punished, reserved for heretical preachers, passive male homosexuals, and women guilty of sexual union "with Satan or his familiars," respectively. In addition to these direct symbolic connections, the relation between crime and punishment was often mediated by obliging the condemned to wear insignias representing their offenses. In modern Latin America an expression of crime/punishment poetics was clear in Guatemalan torture under Jorge Ubico, where a head-shrinking skullcap was used "to pry loose secrets and crush improper thoughts." See Richard Immerman, *The CIA in Guatemala* (Austin: University of Texas Press, 1982), 199.

30. See Ruth Richardson, *Death, Dissection and the Destitute* (London: Routledge and Kegan Paul, 1987), 19.

31. Foucault, *Discipline*, 45. Bernaldo de Quirós noted one such instance, the 1745 punishment of a slave who killed his master: "And with the same hatchet that killed the master they cut off his two hands (alive) and nailed them to the gallows." See Bernaldo de Quirós, *La picota*, 103.

32. Bernaldo de Quirós observed that garrotting was the "intermediary between the gallows and the knife." Ibid., 109.

33. See Felipe Guamán Poma de Ayala, *Nueva crónica y buen gobierno*, ed. John V. Murra and Rolena Adorno, trans. Jorge L. Urioste (Mexico City: Siglo XXI, 1980), 363. According to the Myth of Incarrí, the head of the Incarrí (Inca plus the Spanish word *rey*, or "king") was being held in the governmental palace in Lima or, in some versions, in Madrid. It had no power because it was separated from its body. If it were freed and could reunite with its body (in some versions it grew a body, downward toward the feet, while in captivity), then it would again engage in battle with the Catholic God and—if successful—would free the

Indians from subjugation. See Manuel Burga, *Nacimiento de una utopía: Muerte y resurrección de los Incas* (Lima: Instituto de Apoyo Agrario, 1988) and Juan M. Ossio A., *Ideología mesiánica del mundo andino* (Lima: Ignacio Prado Pastor, 1973).

34. See Hemming, *The Conquest of the Incas*, 449.

35. The partially excavated Aztec Templo Mayor is visible today behind the cathedral and beside the major colonial edifices of Mexico City's main square (*zócalo*). Hernán Cortés's decision to rebuild Tenochtitlán was intended to associate the city's prestige with Spanish governance and to prevent its ruins from becoming monuments to Aztec grandeur. Earlier in the conquest of Mexico, Christian sanctuaries were established on the sites of native temples. In 1538 Charles V instructed the Mexican episcopate to use the stones from destroyed native temples to build churches. See Robert Ricard, *The Spiritual Conquest of Mexico*, trans. Lesley Byrd Simpson (Berkeley: University of California Press, 1966), 36 and 38.

36. Like the *picana*, other instruments of torture throughout history seem to have particularly potent symbolic value. One vivid example is the "Iron Maiden" of Nuremberg, an anthropomorphic container into which a victim was placed and then pierced by spikes when the maiden's doors were closed. For details see Held, *Inquisition/Inquisición*, 25–27. For creative treatment of the maiden theme, see Frank Graziano, ed., *Alejandra Pizarnik: A Profile* (Durango, Colo.: Logbridge-Rhodes, 1987), 99.

37. Foucault, *Discipline*, 12, and French legislation cited in Held, *Inquisition/Inquisición*, 30. Joseph-Ignace Guillotin first promoted the National Assembly legislation requiring that all executions be carried out by the instrument that now bears his name.

38. Foucault, *Discipline*, 13.

39. Ragon, *The Space of Death*, 187, and Jules Michelet, cited in Ragon on p. 190. "How had I failed to recognize that nothing was more important than an execution," Camus's Meursault asked himself, "that, viewed from one angle, it's the only thing that can genuinely interest a man?" Albert Camus, *The Stranger*, trans. Stuart Gilbert (New York: Vintage Books, 1946), 138.

40. Fernando de Montesinos, *Auto de la fe celebrado en Lima a 23 de enero de 1639* (Lima: Pedro de Cabrera, 1639), 22. The author also noted, on p. 26, that "the balcony of the Most Excellent wife of the Viceroy was very well adorned." For a second example see Hemming, *The Conquest of the Incas*, 448–449, regarding mass attendance at Tupac Amaru's execution.

41. Ragon, *The Space of Death*, 182.

42. Camus, *The Stranger*, 141.

43. Foucault, *Discipline*, 58. The guillotine later came to assume the spectacular function previously held by other execution devices, notably during the French Revolution. See also Ragon, *The Space of Death*, 188–189.

44. Foucault, *Discipline*, 9.

45. Ibid. This shift of theatrical focus from spectacular punishment to judicial proceedings will be of more specific concern in Chapter 5. For the moment I might mention one illustration from what prosecutor Julio César Strassera referred to as the 1985 trials' "seventeen dramatic weeks," in *El Libro de El Diario del Juicio*, 243. When Strassera closed his remarks with the freighted slogan *nunca más*, "The courtroom burst into an ovation. . . . The applause was deafening, echoing a thousand times off the walls, and there were even several *bravos* directed to the prosecutors. All of this gave the courtroom the feeling of the Colón Theatre on its best nights." See Alberto Amato, "Lo que nunca debió pasar," *El Diario del Juicio* 18 (September 24, 1985).

46. Foucault, *Discipline*, 15. Ragon observed: "This taste for the execution-spectacle was to last a long time, the last public execution taking place in France in June 1939, in the presence of ladies and gentlemen in evening dress." Ragon, *The Space of Death*, 190.

47. Jon Nordheimer, "Bundy Is Put to Death in Florida After Admitting Trail of Killings," *New York Times*, January 25, 1989.

48. "Death Row's Macabre Death Watch," *Washington Post*, April 8, 1990.

49. The three preceding quotations in the text are from John G. Leyden, "Death in the Hot Seat: A Century of Executions," *Washington Post*, August 5, 1990.

50. Foucault, *Discipline*, 17.

51. The quoted phrase is borrowed from Ernesto Sábato's novel *Abaddón: El exterminador* (Barcelona: Seix Barral, 1982), 37.

52. One survivor referred to the *desaparecidos'* "transfer" (execution) as "dying being dead or like never dying." *Nunca más*, 184/167.

53. T. J. Scheff, *Catharsis in Healing, Ritual and Drama* (Berkeley: University of California Press, 1979), 153. See also pp. 162–163 regarding manipulation of levels of awareness in "Dionysian dramas" that cause a state of shock rather than catharsis.

54. The first two quoted passages are from *Nunca más*, 9/3–4. The last quoted passage is from Hannah Arendt, *The Origins of Totalitarianism* (New York: Meridian Books, 1960), 378.

55. M.F.C. Bourdillon, "Introduction," in Bourdillon and Meyer Fortes, eds., *Sacrifice* (London: Academic Press, 1980), 14. See also Robert G. Hamerton-Kelly, ed., *Violent Origins: Walter Burkert, René Girard and Jonathan Z. Smith on Ritual Killing and Cultural Formation* (Stanford, Calif.: Stanford University Press, 1987), 18 and 154.

56. Elaine Scarry, *The Body in Pain: The Making and Unmaking of the World* (New York: Oxford University Press, 1985), 13–14.

57. Ibid., 28 and 27, respectively.

58. Ibid., 27.

59. See Serge Viderman, "The Subject-Object Relation and the Problem of Desire," in Serge Lebovici and Daniel Widlöcher, eds., *Psychoanalysis in France* (New York: International Universities Press, 1980), 189. The first torture sessions in the Argentine detention centers were intended to "soften up" the victim. *Nunca más*, 63/60.

60. From *Der Weg der SS*, issued by the SS Hauptamt-Schulungsamt, in Arendt, *The Origins of Totalitarianism*, 340n.

61. Emilio E. Massera, *El camino a la democracia* (Buenos Aires: El Cid Editores, 1979), 45.

62. A participant-observer function parallel to the public role as the audience of abstracted power spectacles was discernible in the dictatorship's press releases regarding confrontations between the armed forces and "terrorists." After analyzing such texts published by the Argentine government, Heleen Ietswaart concluded that "the 'public' pervades the discourse in a striking fashion," its role as audience-guarantor made apparent in the following passage: "The people [as depicted in the military press releases] perform a number of crucial roles: They are approving witnesses to the events, they cooperate by informing the security forces about 'suspect happenings' and generally assisting them, and they serve as the audience for a moral and political lecture about 'subversion' and their role in the struggle against it." Heleen F.P. Ietswaart, "The Discourse of Summary Justice and the Discourse of Popular Justice," in Richard Abel, ed., *The Politics of Informal Justice*, vol. 2 (New York: Academic Press, 1982), 176.

63. Foucault, *Discipline*, 27.

64. Kenneth Macgowan and William Melnitz, with Gordon Armstrong, *Golden Age of the Theatre* (Englewood Cliffs, N.J.: Prentice-Hall, 1979), 22.

65. Sophocles, *The Three Theban Plays*, 20.

66. "We are all guilty, in one form or another," President Alfonsín observed in reference to the "dirty war." Cited in Horacio Verbitsky, *Civiles y militares: Memoria secreta de la transición* (Buenos Aires: Editorial Contrapunto, 1987), 137.

67. Arendt, *The Origins of Totalitarianism*, 435 and 437, respectively. But, as Clifford Geertz pointed out, "Common sense is not what the mind cleared of cant spontaneously apprehends; it is what the mind filled with presuppositions . . . concludes." See "Common Sense as a Cultural System," in his *Local Knowledge* (New York: Basic Books, 1983), 84.

68. Laws promulgated by the Junta made the enforcement of silence clear: "It is forbidden to inform, comment or make any reference to subjects which relate to subversive activity. . . . This includes information relating to abductions and disappearances." See Lawyers Committee for International Human Rights, *Violations of Human Rights in Argentina: 1976–1979* (New York: LCIHR, 1979), 51. In reference to prisoners taken from the detention centers on "intelligence" missions to identify other "subversives," Graciela Susana Geuna's testimony

noted: "It was evident . . . that the prisoner was in rags, with an appearance very different from that of the men who 'accompanied' him. There were even some prisoners who were taken out on the streets barefooted or with black eyes from the beatings they had gotten, but the people who passed by pretended not to see anything, obviously for their own safety." Geuna, CELS, 16.

69. Arendt, *The Origins of Totalitarianism*, 435.

70. The defense mechanism known as "identification with the aggressor," developed by Anna Freud in the 1930s, will be discussed in greater detail in Chapters 4 and 5.

71. *Nunca más*, 9/4. Arendt pointed out how during World War II "common sense reacted to the horrors of Buchenwald and Auschwitz with the plausible argument: 'What crime must these people have committed that such things were done to them!' " Arendt, *The Origins of Totalitarianism*, 446. See also Julia Braun de Dunayevich and Janine Puget, "State Terrorism and Psychoanalysis," *International Journal of Mental Health* 18, no. 1 (1989): 98–112.

72. Wayne C. Booth studied this as a discursive technique in *The Rhetoric of Fiction* (Chicago: University of Chicago Press, 1961). Scheff discussed how "the sharing of private information between members of a group promotes a strong, primitive sense of inclusion," relating this to theatrical settings where information is manipulated to generate a desired response in the audience as participant-observer. Scheff, *Catharsis in Healing*, 156–157.

73. One of the characters in Miguel Bonasso's novel *Recuerdo de la muerte* (Mexico City: Ediciones Era, 1984) remarked, on p. 305, that in order to "protect their siesta, their ravioles, their soccer game" the middle-class citizens were "capable of not hearing screams, of not seeing the Falcons, of denying what their senses are telling them" because "the immigrants' *don't get involved* was firmly rooted."

74. Testimony of Luis Armando Rebura, videotape 5 of the 1985 trial proceedings, APDH. In his introduction to Sophocles's Theban plays, Bernard Knox cited an apt passage from Anatole France's *Penguin Island*: "So as not to limit human freedom, I hereby assume ignorance of what I know, I wind tightly over my eyes the veils which I have seen through, and in my blind clairvoyance, I allow myself to be surprised by what I have foreseen." Sophocles, *The Three Theban Plays*, 147.

75. Scarry, *The Body in Pain*, 28. One of the Argentine detention centers was housed in a radio broadcast station.

76. *Nunca más*, 62/60.

77. Scarry, *The Body in Pain*, 61.

78. Geuna, CELS, 16.

79. Jacobo Timerman, *Prisoner Without a Name, Cell Without a Number*, trans. Toby Talbot (New York: Alfred A. Knopf, 1981), 39.

80. In the ESMA detention center the room where prisoners worked—called the *pecera* (fishbowl or fishtank)—also suggested poetics of observation from outside. The testimony of one survivor noted that the *pecera*—where prisoners conducted modest intelligence tasks—was constructed of "dividing panels with windows that made it possible to see from the inside out and from the outside in." *El Diario del Juicio* 21 (October 15, 1989): 414. In another context the *pecera* anticipates the ESMA prisoners' fate as "fish food."

81. In the repressors' vernacular *perejil* was equivalent to "idiot" or "retard." It literally translates to the English "parsley," though familar use of the plural *perejiles* signifies "buttons and bows, trimmings, fripperies" and "extra titles, handles (to one's name)." The familiar usage, particularly through the implied gaudiness, again registers a vernacular suggestion of flaunting the "secret."

82. de Certeau, *Heterologies*, 41.

83. Emilio E. Massera, *El país que queremos* (Buenos Aires: Editorial FEPA, 1981), 53.

84. *Nunca más*, 167/152. A November 1977 document presented to the Junta by the Argentine Episcopal Conference stated: "There is a kind of underlying conviction at many levels of society that the exercizing of power is arbitrary, that there are inadequate possibilities for defense, that the citizens find themselves without recourse before an omnipotent, police-like authority." Mignone, *Iglesia y dictadura*, 68.

85. Tulio Halperin Donghi, "Argentina's Unmastered Past," *Latin American Research Review* 23, no. 2, (1988): 13. Juan E. Corradi's essay "The Culture of Fear in Civil Society," in Monica Peralta-Ramos and Carlos H. Waisman, eds., *From Military Rule to Liberal Democracy in Argentina* (Boulder, Colo.: Westview Press, 1986), 113–129, well summarized the proceedings of a 1981–1982 Social Science Research Council seminar on the "culture of fear."

86. Arendt, *The Origins of Totalitarianism*, 475.

87. Foucault, *Discipline*, 214.

88. Michel Foucault, *Microfísica del poder*, ed. and trans. Julia Varela and Fernando Alvarez-Uria (Madrid: Las Ediciones de La Piqueta, 1979), 88. Foucault's description of the Panopticon's function parallels very closely the long-term aspirations of the Argentina Junta's Process of National Reorganization: "Although it [the Panopticon] arranges power, although it is intended to make it more economic and effective, it does so not for power itself, nor for the immediate salvation of a threatened society: Its aim is to strengthen the social forces—to increase production, to develop the economy, spread education, raise the level of public morality." Foucault, *Discipline*, 207–208.

89. Jeremy Bentham first published *Panopticon; or The Inspection House* (London: T. Payne, 1791) in 1781. The work's lengthy subtitle is revealing: *The Idea of a New Principle of Construction applicable to any Sort of Establishment, in which Persons of any description are to be kept under Inspection: and in particular*

to Penitentiary-Houses, Prisons, Manufacturies, Houses of Industry, Mad-Houses, Work Houses, Lazarettos, Poor-Houses, Hospitals, and Schools.

90. Foucault, Discipline, 201.

91. Arendt, The Origins of Totalitarianism, 430.

92. Ibid., 31.

93. Foucault, Discipline, 214.

94. Translation modified slightly from Brian Loveman and Thomas M. Davies, Jr., eds., The Politics of Antipolitics: The Military in Latin America (Lincoln: University of Nebraska Press, 1978), 177.

95. Francis Barker, The Tremulous Private Body: Essays on Subjugation (London: Methuen, 1984), 26.

96. Scheff, Catharsis in Healing, 138–139.

97. Jacques Le Goff, Medieval Civilization: 400–1500, trans. Julia Barrow (New York: Basil Blackwell, 1989), 177.

98. Scarry, The Body in Pain, 46.

99. Ibid., 36.

100. See Viderman, "The Subject-Object Relation," 189.

101. A particularly chilling example is found in Nunca más, 65/62: "'Julian the Turk' began to shout and swear at us and 'chain' us all. The scene was Dantesque, since we were handcuffed and blindfolded and had no idea where the blows were coming from. We fell one on top of the other, screaming with pain and horror. I could tell that other people were also hitting and kicking us; they pulled us up by the hair when we fell down." Salted water was then thrown on the victims to burn the wounds.

102. Ibid., 60–61/57–58.

103. In Paraguay "laboratory" was the vernacular signifier for the torture room annexed to the Department of Police Investigations. See Amnesty International, Torture in the Eighties (New York: Amnesty International, 1984), 169.

104. Nunca más, 36/30 and 45/40–41; Organization of American States, Inter-American Commission on Human Rights, Report on the Situation of Human Rights in Argentina (Washington, D.C.: OAS, 1980), 83. The Inter-American Commission on Human Rights will hereafter be referred to as the OAS Commission.

105. Nunca más, 60/57, 131/124, 132/125–126.

106. Ibid., 60/57. Total disorientation is also well illustrated by another prisoner who reported, on p. 194/178, that he had lost a toe "under circumstances I can't remember."

107. Scarry, The Body in Pain, 41.

108. Ibid.

109. Ibid., 40.

110. See Yi-Fu Tuan, Space and Place: The Perspective of Experience (Minneapolis: University of Minnesota Press, 1977), 34–35.

111. Scarry, *The Body in Pain*, 45.

112. Supervision of torture by physicians was already well established in the Middle Ages. See Philippe Ariès, *The Hour of Our Death*, trans. Helen Weaver (New York: Vintage, 1982), 353. One noteworthy case in "dirty war" Argentina was that of Dr. Jorge Antonio Berges, a former police doctor arrested in 1985 for participation in torture at four detention centers.

See Carlos Martínez Moreno's novel *El color que el infierno me escondiera* (Mexico City: Editorial Nueva Imagen, 1981), 25, for a fictional depiction of the "clinical asepsis" of torture.

113. The fact that many of the mentioned institutions (and their names) existed prior to their conversion into detention centers after March 1976 is irrelevant to my argument for three related reasons. First, my intent is to postpone the moment of reference from word to world, to explore texts as such prior to recontextualizing them socially and historically. Second, whether or not the names of these institutions existed beforehand, they were incorporated into the vernacular lexicon as intertexts and must therefore be treated as integral to "dirty war" discourse rather than as alien texts within it. And finally, names often precede the events that occasion their interpretation. One thinks immediately of the names of saints, or of Christopher (from *Christum ferens*, "carrier of Christ") Columbus, whose name after his first voyage was widely interpreted to stress his role in bringing Christianity to the New World.

114. *El Libro de El Diario del Juicio*, 256.

115. *Nunca más*, 319/307–308. Recalling the "projection" of the abstract spectacle discussed earlier, the following observation regarding tragedy is very suggestive in the present context: "In the movie, where darkness permits a more erotically oriented audience, the plot usually moves toward an act which, like death in Greek tragedy, takes place off stage, and is symbolized by a closing embrace." See Northrop Frye, *Anatomy of Criticism* (Princeton, N.J.: Princeton University Press, 1973), 164.

116. Tuan, *Space and Place*, 35.

117. Ibid., 37. See also Richard M. Griffith, "Anthropodology: Man A-Foot," in Stuart F. Spicker, ed., *The Philosophy of the Body* (Chicago, Ill.: Quadrangle Books, 1970), 277–278.

118. René Girard, *The Scapegoat*, trans. Yvonne Freccero (Baltimore, Md.: Johns Hopkins University Press, 1986), 13. Myths generated during such crises add their contribution as—in Lévi-Strauss's phrase—"machines for suppression of time." See Edmund Leach, *Claude Lévi-Strauss* (New York: Viking Press, 1970), 125.

119. Scarry, *The Body in Pain*, 41. See *Nunca más*, 63/60–61.

120. Ibid., 44/39–40; *El Libro de El Diario del Juicio*, 66, and testimony of Lila Pastoriza, APDH files, 15, respectively. In his *Survival in Auschwitz*, trans. Stuart Woolf (New York: Collier Books, 1961), 121, Primo Levi noted: "Do you

know how one says 'never' in camp [Auschwitz] slang? 'Morgen früh,' tomorrow morning." When intense pain obliterates perception of time, the sufferer may perceive the agony as of greater or lesser duration than it was as measured linearly. The Koran, II:261, relates the story of a man made to die for a hundred years and then revived by God, who asked: "How long have you been here?" The victim replied: "A day, or part of a day."

121. *El Diario del Juicio* 3 (June 11, 1985): 63.

122. That experience parallels a contrast in textual temporality: "There is a 'problem of time' because two temporalities are found juxtaposed: that of the universe represented and that of the discourse representing it." See Tzvetan Todorov, *Introduction to Poetics*, trans. Richard Howard (Sussex: Harvester Press, 1981), 29.

123. Jacqueline de Romilly, *Time in Greek Tragedy* (Ithaca, N.Y.: Cornell University Press, 1968), 31.

124. Jean-Paul Sartre, *Being and Nothingness: An Essay on Phenomenological Ontology*, trans. Hazel E. Barnes (New York: Philosophical Library, n.d.), 59.

125. Ibid.

126. *Nunca más*, 19/13-14. Rebelling military forces under Alfonsín painted their faces black and were known—and are known presently on the political scene—as the *Carapintadas* (painted or made-up faces).

127. Testimony of Graciela Susana Geuna, CELS, 15.

128. Isidoro J. Ruíz Moreno described how the task forces were subjected to the same treatment—beginning with abduction—that they would later inflict on their victims. See his *Comandos en acción: El ejército en las Malvinas* (Buenos Aires: Emecé, 1986), 41-42.

The Geuna testimony noted that a Sergeant Díaz "participated in a course given by the Third Corps in which they tortured one another; for the occasion they took some La Perla prisoners and made them read 'communist' discourses to enrage the torturers even more." Geuna, CELS, 60.

For a passage from the military history of unquestioning obedience, see Ricardo Rodríguez Molas, *Historia de la tortura y el orden represivo en la Argentina* (Buenos Aires: Editorial Universitaria de Buenos Aires, 1984), 84-85.

A journalistic account of the "dirty war" noted that by 1976 six hundred Argentine officers had graduated from the U.S. Army School of the Americas (Fort Gulick) in the Canal Zone, where the "methods and theory of torture were an important feature of the course" and where the students themselves were tortured. See John Simpson and Jana Bennett, *The Disappeared and the Mothers of the Plaza* (New York: St. Martin's Press, 1985), 54.

129. For coercion of repressive forces at higher levels, see *Nunca más*, 254-255. The sexuality of torture will be discussed in Chapter 4, and the eschatology of the "dirty war" in Chapter 3.

130. Edward Peters, *Torture* (London: Basil Blackwell, 1985), 183-184.

131. OAS Commission, *Report*, 78.

132. Freud developed the mechanisms of identification in their relation to the group in *Group Psychology and Analysis of the Ego, Standard Edition*, ed. James Strachey, vol. 18 (London: Hogarth Press, 1953). For discussion see Jacques Lacan/Anthony Wilden, *The Language of the Self: The Function of Language in Psychoanalysis* (Baltimore, Md.: Johns Hopkins University Press, 1968), 170–171. For a word on the military clergy's support of the normalization of repressive violence, see Mignone, *Iglesia y dictadura*, 33.

133. The Geuna testimony noted that Capitan Jorge Exequiel Acosta "slept at the La Perla camp, in a car, La Perla became his home" Geuna, CELS, 51. Another task force member noted of the ESMA detention center: "We practically lived there." See Raúl David Vilariño, "Vilariño acusa otra vez," *La Semana*, año 6, no. 378 (January 3, 1984), 60. For a discussion of how "it is impossible to adopt fully a deviant life-style and identity without also assuming the symbolic pattern associated with them," see Bruce Jackson, "Deviance as Success: The Double Inversion of Stigmatized Roles," in Barbara A. Babcock, ed., *The Reversible World: Symbolic Inversion in Art and Society* (Ithaca, N.Y.: Cornell University Press, 1978). The quoted passage is from p. 264.

134. The testimony of Lisandro Raúl Cubas related that Admiral Massera "personally tortured the prisoners." With his direct involvement Massera sought to "fortify the 'blood pact' and the 'esprit de corps' of his subordinates." Cubas, APDH, 86.

135. Timerman, *Prisoner Without a Name*, 39. "There is a shift from a shame-guilt status in which the individual [torturer] must cope with the consequences of his 'problem,' to an occupational status in which the individual copes with the needs of his stigma." See Jackson, "Deviance as Success," 266.

136. Geuna, CELS, 17.

137. Timerman, *Prisoner Without a Name*, 40. Referrring to a Nazi guard in the Warsaw ghetto, Chaim A. Kaplan—a prisoner there before his execution in Treblinka—wrote: "In his stupid face you can read the conviction that the whole world was created entirely for his benefit." See his *Scroll of Agony: The Warsaw Diary of Chaim A. Kaplan*, ed. and trans. Abraham I. Katsh (New York: Collier Books, 1973), 244.

138. Peters, *Torture*, 183–184.

139. As will be discussed in Chapters 4 and 5, detention center victims were destroyed in a ritualistic reenactment of the torturers' own destruction, their roles entangled in psychosexual structures and in the dynamics of vicarious sacrifice.

140. *El Libro de El Diario del Juicio*, 256.

141. René Girard in Hamerton-Kelly, *Violent Origins*, 78–79.

142. The quoted passages are from Claude Lévi-Strauss, *Structural Anthropology*, trans. Claire Jacobson and Brooke Grundfest Schoepf (New York: Basic Books, 1963), 173–174.

143. Franz Kafka, *The Penal Colony: Stories and Short Pieces*, trans. Willa and Edwin Muir (New York: Schocken Books, 1961), 198.

144. Scarry, *The Body in Pain*, 59.

145. Cited in Michel de Montaigne, "Of Cannibals," in *Selected Essays by Montaigne*, ed. and intro. Blanchard Bates (New York: Modern Library, 1949), 85. "It is not enough," it was argued during the heyday of torture as a public spectacle, "that wrongdoers are justly punished. They must if possible judge and condemn themselves" Foucault, *Discipline*, 38.

146. Alexandre Kojève, *Introduction to the Reading of Hegel*, ed. Allan Blood, trans. James H. Nichols, Jr. (New York: Basic Books, 1969), 8. The same author observed that "to desire the Desire of another is in the final analysis to desire that the value that I am or that I 'represent' be the value desired by the other: I want him to 'recognize' my value as his value. I want him to 'recognize' me as an autonomous value" (7). Analogously in Greek legends animals often offered themselves for sacrifice. The animal was sprinkled with water and told to shake itself, "for the animal's movement is taken to signify a 'willing nod,' a 'yes' to the sacrifical act." See Walter Burkert, *Homo Necans: The Anthropology of Ancient Greek Sacrificial Ritual and Myth*, trans. Peter Bing (Berkeley: University of California Press, 1983), 4. For an excellent example of a victim subordinating his discourse to the executioner's, see Hemming, *The Conquest of the Incas*, 448–449.

147. See Arendt, *The Origins of Totalitarianism*, 352–353 regarding the Soviet police victims; see Kaplan, *Scroll of Agony*, regarding the Warsaw ghetto, notably p. 74: "We have begun to look upon ourselves as 'inferior beings.'"

148. Arendt, *The Origins of Totalitarianism*, 452.

149. *Nunca más*, 55/52. Julio Cortázar quoted the following definition of "disappearance" offered by Niall MacDermot, secretary general of the International Commission of Jurists: "It is the denial of a person's right to exist, to have an identity. It turns a person into a nonperson." See Cortázar's *Argentina: Años de alambradas culturales*, ed. Saúl Yurkievich (Barcelona: Muchnik Editores, 1984), 140.

150. *Nunca más*, 31/25. *Chupar*, literally "to suck," was the word used in the repressor's vernacular to signify abduction. The absorption and incorporation of the victim into the body of repression as implied by *chupar* will be addressed specifically in Chapters 4 and 5.

151. *Nunca más*, 182/164. On p. 443 of *The Origins of Totalitarianism*, Arendt stressed that "the real horror of the concentration and extermination camps lies in the fact that the inmates, even if they happen to keep alive, are

more effectively cut off from the world than if they had died, because terror enforces oblivion."

152. OAS Commission, *Report*, 77.

153. *Nunca más*, 30/23.

154. Cited in Diana R. Kordon and Lucila I. Edelman, eds., *Efectos psicológicos de la represión política* (Buenos Aires: Sudamericana/Planeta, 1987), 94 and 98, respectively. *Cantar* ("to sing") was vernacular for giving information under torture.

155. Testimony of Lisandro Raúl Cubas, APDH, 9.

156. *Nunca más*, 60/57.

157. Ibid., 53/50.

158. Geuna, CELS, 6; and Kordon and Edelman, *Efectos psicológicos*, 94, respectively. See also *El Diario del Juicio* 3 (June 11, 1985): 65, where one prisoner explained "I was already dead," and another said, on p. 63, "I didn't know if I was dead or not dead." Under Charles Manson's sexual domination members of the "family" would similarly "die to themselves." One member remarked, "I became Charlie. . . . There was nothing left of me any more." See Charles Lindholm, *Charisma* (New York: Basil Blackwell, 1990), 132.

159. Scarry, *The Body in Pain*, 48.

160. Ibid., 49.

161. Appended to Henry Charles Lea, *Torture*, intro. Edward Peters (Philadelphia: University of Pennsylvania Press, 1973), 167.

162. From Sebastian Guazzini, *Tractatus ad Defensam*, appended to Henry Charles Lea, *Torture*, intro. Edward Peters (Philadelphia: University of Pennsylvania Press, 1973), 190.

163. From St. Augustine's *The City of God*, book 19, ch. 6, appended to Henry Charles Lea, *Torture*, intro. Edward Peters (Philadelphia: University of Pennsylvania Press, 1972), 179.

164. Appended to Lea, *Torture*, 202–206. For a survey of other perceptions contributing to the decline of torture, see pp. 149–164. See also Rodríguez Molas, *Historia de la tortura*, 15–20.

165. Quoted passage cited in Kordon and Edelman, *Efectos psicológicos*, 98.

166. From the trial testimony of Alberto Barret Viedma, 1985 trial videotape 3, APDH.

167. *Nunca más*, 47/43. One Roman victim promised to confess if his torture was stopped and then kept his word by asking: "Tell me what it is you wish me to say." See Lea, *Torture*, 22.

168. *Nunca más*, 192/176.

169. See Scarry, *The Body in Pain*, 28.

170. *Nunca más*, 399/390

171. Beccaria, cited in Lea, *Torture*, 207.

172. Foucault, *Discipline*, 41.

173. Testimony of Lila Pastoriza, APDH, 15.

174. El Diario del Juicio 3 (June 11, 1985): 65.

175. François Hartog, The Mirror of Herodotus: The Representation of the Other in the Writing of History, trans. Janet Lloyd (Berkeley: University of California Press, 1988), 128.

176. Cited in Scarry, The Body in Pain, 41–42. Similarly the Bolshevik purges conformed to this circular structure with no exits; see Arendt, The Origins of Totalitarianism, 473.

177. Beccaria, cited in Lea, Torture, 207.

178. Final Report of the Mar del Plata delegation to CONADEP (an unpublished document), 11.

179. Scarry, The Body in Pain, 28–29.

180. Quoted phrase is from de Certeau, Heterologies, 41.

181. Nunca más, 61/58. Timerman noted that "the silence was part of the terror." Prisoner Without a Name, 35. Adolfo Aristarain's film Tiempo de Revancha ("Time for Revenge") provided a moving metaphorical depiction of a protagonist's discourse crushed, replaced by the State's, and followed by self-enforced silence.

182. Viderman, "The Subject-Object Relation," 195 and 194, respectively. Compare with Kojève, Introduction to the Reading of Hegel, 14: The desaparecido "exhausted" of ritual worth "is no longer anything more than an unconscious thing, from which the living man turns away in indifference, since he can no longer expect anything from it for himself."

183. Nunca más, 232/218.

184. Robert Cox, "Argentina's Domestic Miracle," The New Republic, March 19, 1984: 23. During the heyday of spectacular execution in Europe, the criminals' corpses were similarly treated, "left to rot at the foot of the gibbet. Indeed, the enclosure around the gibbet was used as a rubbish dump, and the bodies of the executed criminals were gradually covered up." Ragon, The Space of Death, 183.

185. The Aguarunas are one of four subgroups or "tribes" of the Jivaroan language family. For a discussion of the tsantsa rituals, see Michael Brown, Una paz incierta: Comunidades aguarunas frente al impacto de la carretera marginal (Lima: CAAAP, 1984), 30–32. A transcription of the entire tsantsa ceremony in Spanish translation is provided in Tsantsa: La celebración de la cabeza reducida (Peru: Mundo Shuar, 1980).

186. The ritual worthlessness of the neutralized shrunken heads was reinterpreted in economic terms after the Amazon basin was exploited by white explorers and settlers. The Aguarunas then found in their trash an item for trade, as the tsantsas made their way to the tourist market in cities of the Andean republics.

CHAPTER 3

1. *Nunca más: Informe de la Comisión Nacional Sobre la Desaparición de Personas* (Buenos Aires and Barcelona: EUDEBA/Seix Barral, 1985), 172/155–156. Page numbers after the slash refer to the English-language edition of *Nunca más*, published in New York by Farrar, Straus and Giroux in 1986. Security forces in Haiti under François Duvalier were known as *Tontons macoutes*, referring—in the Creole spoken by Haitian masses—to a dreaded mythological figure of the same name who kidnapped children. The verb *cachar* (suggested by "La Cacha") literally means "to smash, to break in pieces," and in Argentine usage it also signifies "to scoff at, deride, ridicule," all functions of the detention center. (In Peruvian slang *cachar* means "to fuck.")

2. Stuart Schneiderman, *Jacques Lacan: The Death of an Intellectual Hero* (Cambridge, Mass.: Harvard University Press, 1983), 160.

3. The cited passages are from Elisa Marroco, "Un grito que no cesa," in the Buenos Aires monthly *Madres de la Plaza de Mayo*, año 4, no. 38 (January 1988): 14–15. See also Diana R. Kordon and Lucila I. Edelman, eds., *Efectos psicológicos de la represión política* (Buenos Aires: Sudamericana/Planeta, 1987), 130.

4. For the refrain and the CONADEP statement, see *Nunca más*, 15/9 and 235/222, respectively. The Hannah Arendt passage is from her *The Origins of Totalitarianism* (New York: Meridian Books, 1960), 437.

5. Roland Barthes, *Mythologies*, trans. Annette Lavers (New York: Hill and Wang, 1978), 133. Regarding this death-in-disappearance, one victim's testimony stated: "It was like dying without disappearing, or disappearing without dying. A death in which the person dying had no participation: It was like dying without struggling, like dying being dead or like never dying." *Nunca más*, 184/167. See Chapter 2 for a discussion of the *desaparecidos* as transmitters of Junta discourse. Regarding the symbolics of "transmission," recall that the "La Cacha" detention center was housed in a radio station.

6. "This is because the Other is a scandal which threatens his [the Junta's] essence," Barthes wrote. *Mythologies*, 151. As I will discuss later in this volume, binary opposition with the Other also guarantees that essence.

7. Cited in Ricardo Rodríguez Molas, *Historia de la tortura y el orden represivo en la Argentina* (Buenos Aires: Editorial Universitaria de Buenos Aires, 1984), 22.

8. In Miller's introduction to his *Arthur Miller's Collected Plays* (New York: Viking, 1957), 39.

9. Claude Lévi-Strauss, *Structural Anthropology*, trans. Claire Jacobson and Brooke Grundfest Schoepf (New York: Basic Books, 1963), 230.

10. Barthes, *Mythologies*, 142 and 143, respectively.

11. See Clifford Geertz, "Centers, Kings and Charisma: Reflections on the Symbolics of Power," in Sean Wilentz, ed., *Rites of Power and Politics Since the Middle Ages* (Philadelphia: University of Pennsylvania Press, 1985). Wilentz's comments on p. 4 of the same volume are also useful.

12. Rodríguez Molas, *Historia de la tortura*, 71, and Alain Rouquié, *Poder militar y sociedad política en la Argentina*, vol. 2 (Buenos Aires: Emecé, 1982), 31, respectively. The latter statement was made at the Círculo Militar in Buenos Aires in 1943. Compare this with General Videla's Christmas message to the soldiers in Tucumán, where Videla expressed his desire "for peace to reign again in our Army" (rather than in "our Nation"). The trend persists in Carapintada ideology, where "the Argentine Army is anterior to the Nation itself." See Raúl Jassen, *Seineldín: El ejército traicionado, la patria vencida* (Buenos Aires: Editorial Verum et Militia, 1989), 177.

13. Ernst H. Kantorowicz, "The Problem of Medieval World Unity," in Stanley Pargellis, ed., *The Quest for Political Unity in World History* (Washington, D.C.: U.S. Printing Office, 1944), 33.

14. See Frank Bottomley, *Attitudes to the Body in Western Christendom* (London: Lepus Books, 1979), 90.

15. An observation made in the twelfth century by Hugh of St. Victor, cited in Umberto Eco, *Art and Beauty in the Middle Ages*, trans. Hugh Bredin (New Haven, Conn.: Yale University Press, 1986), 57.

16. See Carl L. Becker, *The Heavenly City of the Eighteenth-Century Philosophers* (New Haven, Conn.: Yale University Press, 1968), particularly pp. 33–74. The cited passages are on p. 53.

17. Fray Miguel de Arcos in Lewis Hanke, ed., *Cuerpo de documentos del siglo XVI* (Mexico City: Fondo de Cultura Económica, 1943), 3.

18. Marcial Castro Castillo, *Fuerzas armadas: Etica y represión* (Buenos Aires: Editorial Nuevo Orden, 1979), 13 and 15, respectively. See also the same work's first appendix, on pp. 181–185, for Castro Castillo's development of the Natural Order concept.

19. Ibid., 25.

20. Ibid., 30.

21. Ibid., 82.

22. Frederick H. Russell, *The Just War in the Middle Ages* (Cambridge: Cambridge University Press, 1979), 16.

23. Castro Castillo, *Fuerzas armadas*, 36. (Italics here and in all further citations are in the original.) Similarly the Judeo-Christian tradition must account for the "Wrath of God" in positive terms: "Not that God is wicked, but that Wrath is the countenance of Holiness for sinful man." See Paul Ricoeur, *The Symbolism of Evil*, trans. Emerson Buchanan (Boston, Mass.: Beacon Press, 1967), 63. Medieval precedents for the religious justification of violence are plentiful. In 1062–1064, for example, Alexander II granted a plenary indul-

gence—forgiveness of *all* sins—to those who fought against the Muslims. (Among the Muslims themselves, notably in the Asassin sect, a specific religious doctrine was developed to justify the murder of religious and political adversaries who were considered "unrighteous.") Later, during the conquest of Mexico, Bernal Díaz made reference to the papal *Bulas de Cruzada* by which a soldier could gain dispensation for sins committed during warfare.

24. Russell, *The Just War,* 17.

25. Jonathan Riley-Smith, "Crusading as an Act of Love," *History* 65, no. 214 (June 1980): 186. See Castro Castillo, *Fuerzas armadas,* 36, in regard to divine authority.

26. Castro Castillo, *Fuerzas armadas,* 58.

27. Both passages from ibid., 109.

28. Russell, *The Just War,* 19, following Augustine.

29. Francisco de Vitoria, *Reflecciones sobre los Indios y el derecho de guerra* (Madrid: Espasa-Calpe, 1975), 122. On p. 120 he wrote, "It is legitimate in war to do whatever is necessary to defend the common good."

30. Castro Castillo, *Fuerzas armadas,* 85.

31. The phrase was used by Lieutenant Colonel Hugo I. Pascarelli; cited in Emilio F. Mignone, *Iglesia y dictadura* (Buenos Aires: Ediciones del Pensamiento Nacional, 1986), 190.

32. Maire Jaanus Kurrik, *Literature and Negation* (New York: Columbia University Press, 1979), 246. Victims were encouraged to participate in this negation. One man, who was tortured and had lost three sons, was asked by General Galtieri "to forget everything that happened and not to hate the army" and was also counseled to "always remember the colors of our flag 'that covers the sky above our Fatherland.'" In another case a torture victim whose status was legalized arrived at the Mendoza Prison in serious need of medical attention. He was given an aspirin to help him "forget what had happened and look toward the future." The two cases are from *Nunca más,* 199/184 and 212/197, respectively.

33. Jacobo Timerman, *Prisoner Without a Name, Cell Without a Number,* trans. Toby Talbot (New York: Vintage Books, 1982), 12–13.

34. For the strikingly similar Christian discourse of Ambrose in the fourth century, see Peter Brown, *The Body and Society* (New York: Columbia University Press, 1988), 347.

35. Umberto Eco, "James Bond: Una combinatoria narrativa," in *Análisis estructural del relato* (Mexico City: Premia Editora, 1982), 99. In the following chapter I will discuss the role of fetishes in torture during the "dirty war."

36. Alexandre Kojève, *Introduction to the Reading of Hegel,* ed. Allan Bloom, trans. James H. Nichols, Jr. (New York: Basic Books, 1969), 29.

37. Peter Stallybrass and Allon White, *The Politics and Poetics of Transgression* (Ithaca, N.Y.: Cornell University Press, 1986), 5. The psychosexual relation between the Junta and its enemy will be explored in the next chapter.

38. Kojève, *Introduction to the Reading of Hegel*, 15.

39. Serge Viderman, "The Subject-Object Relation and the Problem of Desire," in Serge Lebovici and Daniel Widlöcher, eds., *Psychoanalysis in France* (New York: International Universities Press, 1980), 184, 185, 203, and 186, respectively. Lacan recognized, as I will indicate in the next chapter, that "the relations of the master and the slave are essentially reversible." See Jacques Lacan, *The Seminar of Jacques Lacan*, book 2, ed. Jacques-Alain Miller, trans. Sylvana Tomaselli (New York: W. W. Norton, 1988), 263.

40. Jean-Paul Sartre, *Anti-Semite and Jew*, trans. George J. Becker (New York: Schocken Books, 1965), 17. In Christendom this sleight-of-hand dates back to Augustine, who dealt with the troubling presence of evil in God's universe by placing it in the service of its antithesis: Because evil highlights what is good, it serves a purpose in the grand scheme of the infinitely beneficent God. For a discussion, following Hegel and Nietzsche, of the antithetical basis of religion (or, for our purposes, religious politics), see Kenneth Burke, "A Dramatistic View of the Origins of Language and Postscripts on the Negative," in his *Language as Symbolic Action: Essays on Life, Literature, and Method* (Berkeley: University of California Press, 1968).

41. Emilio de Ipola, "La bemba," in his *Ideología y discurso populista* (Mexico City: Folios Ediciones, 1982), 196. See Castro Castillo, *Fuerzas armadas*, 20, for an outstanding example of constructing an inimical stereotype.

42. Joseph Campbell, *The Hero with a Thousand Faces* (Princeton, N.J.: Bollingen Series/Princeton University Press, 1968), 136.

43. Cited in Mignone, *Iglesia y dictadura*, 40.

44. The quoted passage is from Russell, *The Just War*, 17. Lewis Hanke's *Aristotle and the American Indians* (Bloomington: Indiana University Press, 1975) explored this theme and competing Spanish interpretations of it.

45. Quoted in J. H. Parry, *The Establishment of the European Hegemony, 1415–1715* (New York: Harper & Row, 1961), 168. One defense counselor during the 1985 trials cited Vitoria in a just war argument during his closing statement. An Augustinian friar also expressed the common "immaturity" theme in a trope: "All these Indians are like nestlings whose wings have not yet grown enough to allow them to fly themselves." Quoted in Lyle N. McAlister, *Spain and Portugal in the New World, 1492–1700* (Minneapolis: University of Minnesota Press, 1984), 172.

46. John Leedy Phelan, *The Millennial Kingdom of the Franciscans in the New World* (Berkeley: University of California Press, 1970), 65, and Juan Ginés de Sepúlveda, *Democrates alter de justis belli causis apud Indos*, trans. in Frederick Pike, ed., *Latin American History: Select Problems* (New York: Harcourt, Brace

and World, 1969), 47, respectively. Sepúlveda also saw fit "to subdue by force of arms, if no other means be possible, those who by their natural condition ought to obey others, but who refuse to accept their domination." For Sepúlveda's position in the context of an overview of early modern Spanish just war doctrine, see Silvio Zavala, *New Viewpoints on the Spanish Colonization of America* (Philadelphia: University of Pennsylvania Press, 1943), 38–48.

47. Phelan, *The Millennial Kingdom,* 66. For a discussion of this, see pp. 59–68.

48. Homik Bhabha, "The Other Question . . . : The Stereotype and Colonial Discourse," in *Screen* 24, no. 6 (1983): 18.

49. This mythological wisdom gained public expression in the refrains reviewed in the previous chapter: The military knew the "something" that made sense of the confused social reality.

50. Juan E. Corradi, "The Culture of Fear in Civil Society," in Monica Peralta-Ramos and Carlos H. Waisman, eds., *From Military Rule to Liberal Democracy in Argentina* (Boulder, Colo.: Westview Press, 1986), 119.

51. Emilio E. Massera, *El camino a la democracia* (Buenos Aires: El Cid Editores, 1979), 44; and Massera, cited in Oscar Troncoso, "El proceso de reorganización nacional/2: Cronología y documentación (De abril de 1977 a junio de 1978)" in Daniel Rodríguez Lamas et al., eds., *Presidencias y golpes militares del siglo XX* (Buenos Aires: Biblioteca Política Argentina, Centro Editor de América Latina, 1985), 103, respectively.

52. Between his escape and his subsequent recapture and execution, Horacio Domingo Maggio reported: "When we had to urinate they brought us a bucket and gave us two or three seconds to finish; it was obviously impossible to do that so we wound up wetting our mattresses, for which we were then beaten."Maggio, APDH, 1.

53. See Elaine Scarry, *The Body in Pain: The Making and Unmaking of the World* (New York: Oxford University Press, 1985), 4.

54. E. W. Straus, *Phenomenological Psychology* (New York: Basic Books, 1966), 143. Note also that the Spanish word *peón,* originally denoting a foot soldier, came in colonial Latin America to signify natives working the *hacendados'* lands. The term is also interesting in contradistinction to *caballero* ("gentleman"), which has its root in *caballo* ("horse"): In military hierarchy being on one's own feet was of less rank than being mounted on a beast of burden.

55. Yi-Fu Tuan, *Space and Place: The Perspective of Experience* (Minneapolis: University of Minnesota Press, 1977), 43. The psychoanalysis of dream symbolism corroborates this: "The right-handed path always means the path of righteousness and the left-hand one that of crime." Wilhelm Stekel, cited in Sigmund Freud, *The Interpretation of Dreams,* trans. James Strachey (New York: Avon Books, 1965), 393. In early Christianity "Jesus was popularly believed to have been born through the right side of the Virgin." Norman Cohn, *The Pursuit of*

the Millennium (New York: Oxford University Press, 1970), 43. Ritual process and altar symbolism in some Peruvian *curandero* healing expresses "a movement from left to right, from negative, harmful forces to positive, curative powers." See Donald Joralemon, "The Role of Hallucinogenic Drugs and Sensory Stimuli in Peruvian Ritual Healing," *Culture, Medicine and Psychiatry* 8, no. 4 (December 1984): 401. Anticipating the discussion in the following chapter, I will note here that the name "Laius"—that of Oedipus's father—means "left-sided."

56. In a sixth-century mosaic, San Apollinare Nuovo, Ravenna. Reproduced in Jeffrey Burton Russell, *Lucifer: The Devil in the Middle Ages* (Ithaca, N.Y.: Cornell University Press, 1984), 24.

57. The italicized passage is one of Lacan's descriptions of the psychoanalytical myth. Cited in Shoshana Felman, "Beyond Oedipus: The Specimen Story of Psychoanalysis," *MLN* 98, no. 5 (1983): 1044.

58. Bhabha, "The Other Question," 35.

59. Claude Lévi-Strauss, cited in Jacques Lacan/Anthony Wilden, *The Language of the Self: The Function of Language in Psychoanalysis* (Baltimore, Md.: Johns Hopkins University Press, 1968), 250.

60. Northrop Frye, *Anatomy of Criticism* (Princeton, N.J.: Princeton University Press, 1973), 207. I am drawing also from p. 187.

61. Frye also termed these protagonist and antagonist; Vladimir Propp used Hero and Villain. I employ "Hero" because it seems most accurate as an expression of the Junta's self-perception and also suits the present mythological context. "Enemy" was chosen for consistency in this concept's development through this chapter as it relates to the others. The use of these terms will be collective, archetypal—the many soldiers are one Hero, the many "subversives" one Enemy.

62. In Robert G. Hamerton-Kelly, ed., *Violent Origins: Walter Burkert, René Girard and Jonathan Z. Smith on Ritual Killing and Cultural Formation* (Stanford, Calif.: Stanford University Press, 1987), 108.

63. Claude Bremond, "The Logic of Narrative Possibilities," *New Literary History* 11, no. 3 (Spring 1980): 392.

64. Frye, *Anatomy of Criticism*, 195.

65. From the March 25, 1976, statement made by the military Junta on taking control of Argentina. Translation from Brian Loveman and Thomas M. Davies, Jr., eds., *The Politics of Antipolitics: The Military in Latin America* (Lincoln: University of Nebraska Press, 1978), 176.

66. From March 25, 1976, Junta statement; translation from Loveman and Davies, *The Politics of Antipolitics*, 176.

67. From an April 5, 1976, speech by de facto president Videla; translation from Loveman and Davies, *The Politics of Antipolitics*, 178. Compare this with II Corinthians 5:17, "The old has passed away, behold the new has come." The coming of Christ, of course, was believed to initiate the New Age.

68. Quoted passages from the March 25, 1976, Junta statement; translation from Loveman and Davies, *The Politics of Antipolitics*, 177.

69. Quoted passages from the above-cited Junta and Videla statements; translations from Loveman and Davies, *The Politics of Antipolitics*, 176–179.

70. First two passages are from the above-mentioned Videla speech; translation from Loveman and Davies, *The Politics of Antipolitics*, 179–180, and the third is from Videla, cited in Ramón J.A. Camps, *Caso Timerman: Punto final* (Buenos Aires: Tribuna Abierta, 1982), 25.

71. The first three quotes are from Videla, cited in Troncoso, "El proceso de reorganización nacional," 82, and the last is from Massera, *El camino*, 51.

72. Timerman, *Prisoner Without a Name*, 101; for discussion of the World War III concept, see also pp. 102–103. The Junta's world war ideation was also expressed internationally. Cordell Hull remarked that the threat of a third world war would come from the "pampas," and Vice President Henry Wallace commented in January 1944 that "the next war will come via that country [Argentina]." See Cynthia Brown, *With Friends Like These* (New York: Pantheon, 1985), 93 and 251, respectively.

73. In a 1977 press conference and a 1979 lecture by Videla at the University of Buenos Aires. See Horacio Verbitsky, *La última batalla de la tercera guerra mundial* (Buenos Aires: Editorial Legasa, 1984), 20.

74. Emilio E. Massera, *El país que queremos* (Buenos Aires: Editorial FEPA, 1981), 43. For the cold war ideology behind this doctrine, see Richard Immerman, *The CIA in Guatemala* (Austin: University of Texas Press, 1982), 101–104.

75. From a didactic pamphlet for teachers entitled *Conozcamos a nuestro enemigo: Subversión en el ámbito educativo* (Buenos Aires: Ministerio de Cultura y Educación, 1978), 12–13.

76. Massera, *El camino*, 51.

77. Massera passage from ibid., 150. The Videla quotation is excerpted from a 1978 speech appended to Neil Larson, "Sport as Civil Society: The Argentine Junta Plays Championship Soccer," in Neil Larson, ed., *The Discourse of Power: Culture, Hegemony, and the Authoritarian State* (Minneapolis: Institute for the Study of Ideologies and Literature, 1983), 125.

78. Paraphrasing Rubens Graffigna, as cited in Verbitsky, *Ultima batalla*, 31.

79. Larsen, *The Discourse of Power*, 117.

80. Cited in Daniel Frontalini and María Cristina Caiati, *El mito de la guerra sucia* (Buenos Aires: Centro de Estudios Legales y Sociales, 1984), 11. See also p. 41.

81. General Galtieri's comments, cited in *Nunca más*, 474/443.

82. Massera, *El camino*, 48. On p. 58 much the same was argued: "Man's soul has become the battleground."

83. Ibid., 50. Orlando Agosti concurred, "The West is for us a process of development more than a geographical location," as did Omar Graffigna, "More

than a geographical dimension, the West is a spiritual location." Both passages cited in Andrés Avellaneda, Censura, autoritarismo y cultura: Argentina 1960–1983, vol. 1 (Buenos Aires: Centro Editor de América Latina, 1986), 31. The liberation of the "Western" concept from geopolitical reference was handy in pragmatic terms: Argentine relations with the Soviet Union improved after 1976. Subordination of the Junta's "Western and Christian" agenda to export interests was most evident in Argentina's response to the grain embargo decreed by Jimmy Carter following the Soviet invasion of Afghanistan. Rather than allying itself in the embargo with the "West" on whose behalf it was purportedly fighting the "dirty war," the Junta exploited the opportunity to expand its grain sales to the Soviets (at an embargo premium) and to strengthen diplomatic ties with Moscow. See Aldo César Vacs, Discreet Partners: Argentina and the Soviet Union Since 1917, trans. Michael Joyce (Pittsburgh, Pa.: University of Pittsburgh Press, 1984).

84. Cited in Horacio Verbitsky, Civiles y militares: Memoria secreta de la transición (Buenos Aires: Editorial Contrapunto, 1987), 115. Compare this with Minister of Economy Martínez de Hoz's words: "There was no visible or identifiable enemy" Cited in Frontalini and Caiati, El mito, 34.

85. Cited passages are from the episcopate affiliated with the military; cited in Mignone, Iglesia y dictadura, 65 and 124, respectively.

86. Camps, Caso Timerman, 21.

87. Paraphrased in Verbitsky, Ultima batalla, 15.

88. Cited phrases are from General Nicolaides, in Frontalini and Caiati, El mito, 78. René Girard observed that mythologically justified "violence will be presented as a legitimate defense against a fearsome monster." Cited in Hamerton-Kelly, Violent Origins, 179.

89. For a review of the pre-Christian political use of holy war myths beginning with the Persian empire of Cyrus the Great (500 BC), see Joseph Campbell, "The Historical Development of Mythology," in Henry A. Murray, ed., Myth and Mythmaking (Boston: Beacon Press, 1960), 26.

90. Massera, El país, 44.

91. Kantorowicz, "The Problem of Medieval World Unity," 33. The phrase cited in the next sentence is from the same source.

92. Cited in Phelan, The Millennial Kingdom, 120.

93. Quoted passage from Colonel Horacio José Vermal, paraphrased in Verbitsky, Ultima batalla, 16.

94. Cohn, Pursuit of the Millennium, 35. Calamities inspiring millennial prophecies included the onslaught of the Mongols, the fall of the Holy Land, the Black Death, and the Great Schism.

95. Cited passages from a 1977 course document for high-ranking army officers, in Enrique Vázquez, PRN/La Ultima: Origen, apogeo y caída de la dictadura militar (Buenos Aires: EUDEBA, 1985), 83.

96. Castro Castillo, Fuerzas armadas, 93.

97. Cited in Verbitsky, *Civiles y militares*, 114.

98. Ramón Agosti, paraphrased in Verbitsky, *Ultima batalla*, 16. The reference was to the Virgin Mary, appointed earlier in the century as an honorary general in the Argentine army. The Virgin is also prominent in Carapintada ideology.

99. Quoted passages are from a lecture by Alberto Baldrich to the Círculo Militar on July 26, 1940. Cited in Frederick M. Nunn, *Yesterday's Soldiers: European Military Professionalism in South America, 1890–1940* (Lincoln: University of Nebraska Press, 1983), 262.

100. Monsignor Victorio Bonamín, cited in Avellaneda, *Censura*, 133.

101. Frye, *Anatomy of Criticism*, 187.

102. Cited in *Nunca más*, 342/333; see Chapter 1 for a discussion of this.

103. Castro Castillo, *Fuerzas armadas*, 120.

104. Russell, *The Just War*, 20.

105. In 1977 both Patricia Derian (the assistant secretary of state for human rights under Jimmy Carter) and Cyrus Vance visited President Videla on separate occasions, Vance presenting the Junta with a list of 7,500 political prisoners and *desaparecidos*. These visits were motivated, in part, by the testimony of Argentine human rights violation victims before the House Subcommittee of Human Rights hearings held in September 1976. The Humphrey-Kennedy Act (later repealed by the Reagan administration) followed in 1978, prohibiting all military sales, aid, loans, or training to Argentina.

106. From a statement by Rubén Jacinto Chamorro, then director of the ESMA detention center, in Frontalini and Caiati, *El mito*, 23. See similar example in *Nunca más*, 349/340.

107. Russell, *The Just War*, 20.

108. Final report of the Mar del Plata delegation to CONADEP, 7.

109. Quoted passage from Organization of American States, Inter-American Commission on Human Rights, *Report on the Situation of Human Rights in Argentina* (Washington, D.C.: OAS, 1980), 78. See Girard, cited in Hamerton-Kelly, *Violent Origins*, 91. The reversal of roles in what Girard termed "generative scapegoating" will be discussed in greater detail later.

110. Castro Castillo, *Fuerzas armadas*, 121. Detention center torture rituals celebrated this belief, one of them "a kind of ceremony in which a great number of very excited people participated, shouting all at once. They spoke of God and said that the prisoners were the enemies of God." *Nunca más*, 152/141.

111. Roland Barthes, "Day by Day with Roland Barthes," in Marshall Blonsky, ed., *On Signs* (Baltimore, Md.: Johns Hopkins University Press, 1985), 110.

112. Castro Castillo, *Fuerzas armadas*, 84.

113. Ibid., 120.

114. Revelation 13:13.

115. Massera, *El camino*, 101.

116. Ibid., 15.

117. Ibid., 17.

118. Massera, *El país*, 111.

119. Acts 10:38; Mark 5:8–9, respectively. Similarly in fifteenth-century Europe the widespread scofula (a disease of the lymph glands) was believed to be curable by the touch of a king's hands.

120. Romans 5:19.

121. Massera, *El país*, 71.

122. One of the torturers in the La Perla detention center had as his code name "the Priest"; torture and interrogation under him were referred to as "taking one's confession." See *Nunca más*, 43/38.

123. See Frank Bottomley, *Attitudes to the Body in Western Christendom* (London: Lepus Books, 1979), 161. In the Middle Ages this scapegoating function in which evils were consolidated in an enemy also appealed to a temporal manipulation. The medievals held that "what is fundamental for humanity is contemporary"; "the crusaders at the end of the eleventh century did not believe that they were going to punish the descendants of Christ's executioners, but rather those executioners themselves." Jacques Le Goff, cited in Alain Milhou, *Colón y su mentalidad mesiánica* (Valladolid, Spain: La Casa-Museo de Colón, 1983), 179–180.

124. Pope Boniface VIII's bull *Unam sanctam* read, in part, "Urged by faith we are bound to believe in one holy Church . . . which represents one mystical body, the head of which is Christ, and the head of Christ is God." See Ernst H. Kantorowicz, *The King's Two Bodies: A Study in Mediaeval Political Theology* (Princeton, N.J.: Princeton University Press, 1957), 194. My discussion of the *corpus mysticum* follows Kantorowicz, pp. 193–232.

125. Cited in ibid., 200. Rupert of Deutz similarly stated, "To the one and only Son of God and Son of Man, as if to its head, all the members of the body are joined." See Carolyn Walker Bynum, *Holy Feast and Holy Fast: The Religious Significance of Food to Medieval Women* (Berkeley: University of California Press, 1987), 62.

126. Lucas de Penna, cited in Kantorowicz, *The King's Two Bodies*, 203.

127. Hermann of Schilditz, cited in ibid.

128. Ibid., 199.

129. Ibid., 208. The passage is clearly a secularization of the Christian model: "The City of God, that social body whose head is Christ, forms the New Adam, the sum of redeemed and recreated humanity and makes up a cosmic 'perfect man.'" Bottomley, *Attitudes to the Body*, 96, summarizing Augustine.

130. Kantorowicz, *The King's Two Bodies*, 210. Frye summarized the literature of the *corpus mysticum* that "has organized most political theory from Plato to our own day." Cited are John Milton ("A Commonwealth ought to be but one as a huge Christian personage") and Thomas Hobbes (whose *Leviathan* was

originally published with a frontispiece "depicting a number of mannikins inside the body of a single giant"), among others. See Frye, *Anatomy of Criticism*, 142–143. See also "The Body of the King" section in François Hartog, *The Mirror of Herodotus*, trans. Janet Lloyd (Berkeley: University of California Press, 1988).

131. Michel Foucault, *Discipline and Punish: Birth of the Prison*, trans. Alan Sheridan (New York: Vintage Books, 1979), 48. The equation of a population with its leader is not unusual in violent agendas of the modern era. A succinct expression of this surfaced at the great Nazi party rally of 1934: "Adolf Hitler is Germany, and Germany is Adolf Hitler." See Charles Lindholm, *Charisma* (New York: Basil Blackwell, 1990), 101.

132. Robert Held, *Inquisition/Inquisición: A Bilingual Guide to the Exhibition of Torture Instruments from the Middle Ages to the Industrial Era* (Florence: Qua D'Arno, 1985), 126.

133. Castro Castillo, *Fuerzas armadas*, 124.

134. Foucault, *Discipline*, 216.

135. Cited in Rudolph Binion, *Hitler Among the Germans* (New York: Elsevier, 1976), 1 and 24, respectively. For the continuation of the trope in its relation to anti-Semitism in Argentina, see Timerman, *Prisoner Without a Name*, 76, where Zionists extracted "blood and money" from Argentina. The poison variation of destruction-from-within was also evident in the "dirty war." Having murdered three priests, for example, a task force painted the walls with an explanation: "This is what they get for poisoning the minds of our youth." *Nunca más*, 356/349.

136. Binion, *Hitler Among the Germans*, 24 and 25, respectively.

137. See Immerman, *The CIA in Guatemala*, 113 and 117.

138. For the rhetoric of U.S. proponents of invasion of Cuba, see Richard E. Welch, Jr., *Response to Revolution* (Chapel Hill: University of North Carolina Press, 1985).

139. In post–"dirty war" Argentina, body/illness tropes have also been used in political rhetoric addressing another perennial "internal enemy"—the economy. Peronist president Carlos Saúl Menem, for example, was inaugurated in 1989 while the monthly inflation rate was over 100 percent; he referred to his austerity plan as "major surgery without anesthesia."

140. Massera, *El país*, 77.

141. Massera, *El camino*, 17. See also p. 22, where Massera discussed a "convalescence" to "recuperate national health," and p. 76, where similar tropes were used. On p. 101 Massera added: "This coagulation of ethics is, in reality, the most corrosive virus."

142. Cited in Frontalini and Caiati, *El mito*, 21. The same argument was made in a June 27, 1976, blessing by Monsignor Pío Laghi; see Verbitsky, *Civiles y militares*, 113, and Avellaneda, *Censura*, 138. See also Castro Castillo, *Fuerzas armadas*, 80 and 138, where the "medicinal" function of punishment was

discussed. See Robert A. Potash, *The Army and Politics in Argentina, 1928 to 1945*, vol. 1 (Stanford, Calif.: Stanford University Press, 1969), 38, for a military self-perception as the "innards" of Argentina.

Compare with U.S. Assistant Secretary of State John Moors Cabot's use of the same trope in the 1950s: "We should not assume that the anti-bodies which exist in the Latin American body politic will always repel an intrusion of the Communist virus." In Immerman, *The Cia in Guatemala*, 132. Guatemalan President Romero Lucas García, who came to power in 1978, told his citizens that State terror generated by death squads should be thought of as a kind of "allergy" that they must "learn to live with." Ibid., 201.

143. Cited in Vázquez, PRN, 85.

144. For discussion of the prefix *anti*, see Chapter 1. On at least two occasions Massera adapted the antibody trope to the war of ideologies: The people were susceptible to "subversive" ideas because there were insufficient "intelligence antibodies" for adequate "natural resistance." Massera, *El camino*, 85; see also p. 121.

145. Guzzetti was referring specifically to the nonofficial right-wing paramilitary forces, such as the Triple A. Because these groups were closely associated with the governmental repressive forces, I include them in the archetypal Hero metonymically representing the repressive forces as a whole.

146. Sartre, *Anti-Semite*, 28.

147. Luke 13:32.

148. Recall Massera's comparison of "subversion" to "plagues that scourged the world" in previous centuries. Massera, *El camino*, 17.

149. Foucault, *Discipline*, 195–199. In the Middle Ages pogroms were directed against lepers when epidemics broke out; the lepers were accused of having caused or spread them by poisoning wells. Compare this with the "subversives," who similarly "poisoned" Argentina from within.

150. Jacques Derrida, *Dissemination*, trans. Barbara Johnson (Chicago, Ill.: University of Chicago Press, 1981), 98. Derrida's discussion of the *pharmakon*, which means both "remedy" and "poison," will be discussed more directly in the following chapter.

151. Roland Barthes, *A Barthes Reader*, ed. and intro. by Susan Sontag (New York: Hill and Wang, 1982), 379. "Speech is irreversible: A word cannot be *retracted*, except precisely by saying that one retracts it. To cross out is here to add: If I want to erase what I have just said, I cannot do it without showing the eraser itself."

152. See Derrida, *Dissemination*, 100.

153. Castro Castillo, *Fuerzas armadas*, 26. But on p. 167 he wrote, "An infected limb cannot be amputated if it can be cured with antibiotics." The surgery trope, borrowed from Aquinas (see Russell, *The Just War*, 260), is used frequently in military discourse. In Chile, for example, one Admiral remarked,

"We are the nation's surgeons. When a patient has cancer in his leg, it [the leg] is eradicated and the patient is saved. We are eradicating Marxism. . . . We are conducting a surgical operation. . . . Our work is humanitarian." Cited in Robinson Rojas Sandford, *The Murder of Allende*, trans. Andrée Conrad (New York: Harper and Row, 1976), 193.

154. See Carlos Arturo Molina Loza, "Don Hermógenes Miranda: Un curandero llamado Pato Pinto." *Anthropologica* 2, no. 2 (1984): 335–386. In the above-mentioned Biblical parable from Mark 5, the "unclean spirit" is similarly directed into a herd of swine, which then jumps off a cliff. For the means by which folk treatments of illness—like Guzzetti's metaphor—express "essentially the restoration of the balance of power," see Meredith B. McGuire, "Words of Power: Personal Empowerment and Healing," *Culture, Medicine and Psychiatry* 7 (1983): 221–240.

155. In the proclamation made at the time of the March 1976 coup, the Junta remarked: "We will continue fighting, without quarter, all forms and subversion, both open and clandestine, and will eradicate all forms of demagoguery." Translation from Loveman and Davies, *The Politics of Antipolitics*, 177.

156. *Lupus*, the Latin word meaning wolf, is also apt for other obvious reasons and calls to mind Freud's use of the dictum *Homo homini lupus* ("Man is a wolf to man") in his *Civilization and Its Discontents*, trans. James Strachey (New York: Norton, 1962), 58.

157. Among psychiatric stress-inducing treatments, one thinks immediately of the paradigm—electroconvulsive shock therapy—in its relation to torture by *picana*.

158. *Peripeteia* ("reversal") is "a change of the [Hero's] situation into its opposite." As Bernard Knox pointed out the ambiguity of the word *prattomenon* in Aristotle's definition allows for a second interpretation, "a change of the action into its opposite." "Surely," Knox continued, "the phrase has both meanings." See his *Oedipus at Thebes* (New Haven, Conn.: Yale University Press: 1957), 31–32.

159. Girard in Hamerton-Kelly, *Violent Origins*, 91 and 86, respectively.

160. For Propp's definition of "function," see his *Morphology of the Folktale*, rev. and ed. Louis A. Wagner (Austin: University of Texas Press, 1968), 19–24.

161. Frye, *Anatomy of Criticism*, 136.

162. For discussion of the Kojève passage, see Lacan/Wilden, *The Language of the Self*, 193.

163. Kojève, *Introduction to the Reading of Hegel*, 4.

164. Frye, *Anatomy of Criticism*, 141.

165. The word *Christ* is the Greek translation of the Hebrew word signifying "messiah."

166. Barthes, *Mythologies*, 143.

167. Jacques Lacan, cited in Charles E. Scott, "The Pathology of the Father's Rule: Lacan and the Symbolic Order," *Thought: A Review of Culture and Idea* 61 (1986): 118.

168. General Juan Manuel Bayón, cited in Vázquez, *PRN*, 85.

169. From the Junta proclamation at the time of the March 1976, coup; translation from Loveman and Davies, *The Politics of Antipolitics*, 177.

170. By a conservative rendering the Juntas violated Articles 3, 5, 8, and 9 of the Universal Declaration of Human Rights.

171. Viderman, "The Subject-Object Relation," 197.

172. The magical object with which the Hero realized the goal of his quest similarly took the form of weapons ("objects possessing a magical property, such as cudgels, swords, guslas, balls, and many others") in many of the folktales analyzed in Propp's morphology. See Propp, *Morphology of the Folktale*, 43–50.

173. Scarry, *The Body in Pain*, 56.

174. José A. Martínez de Hoz, minister of economy, and General Albano Harguindeguy, cited in Frontalini and Caiati, *El mito*, 34 and 35, respectively. Compare this with Hitler's similarly mimetic response to an imaginary enemy: "The Jews are being fought by us with the same means as they employed against us"; "You can only fight one poison with another." See Binion, *Hitler Among the Germans*, 25–26.

175. Further mythological elaboration insulated the Junta from this recognition, as was evident in the trials, and reinforced the righteousness of its quest. Elements of the romantic myth thus persist because the Junta never came to the tragic recognition that its own actions generated its self-destruction rather than the happy ending it felt its heroism deserved. The military quest must therefore continue—as Carapintada discourse and gesture exemplify—inspired to action by this new obstacle.

176. Lévi-Strauss, *Structural Anthropology*, 224.

177. Frye, *Anatomy of Criticism*, 209.

178. It is for this reason, among others, that the Junta best described itself by describing its Enemy, as I will discuss in the following chapter. Hitler, similarly, often described himself when describing "the Jew."

179. Troncoso, "El proceso de reorganización nacional," 42.

180. Such was the case in Nazi Germany as well, where the war effort emerged as almost a pretext to legitimate and escalate the primary agenda of the extermination camps. As Arendt put it, "These camps are the true central institution of totalitarian organizational power." Arendt, *The Origins of Totalitarianism*, 438.

181. Walter Burkert, *Homo Necans: The Anthropology of Ancient Greek Sacrificial Ritual and Myth*, trans. Peter Bing (Berkeley: University of California Press, 1983), 27–28.

182. Bernadette Bucher, *Icon and Conquest: A Structural Analysis of the Illustrations of de Bry's Great Voyages*, trans. Basia Miller Gulati (Chicago, Ill.: Chicago University Press, 1981), 164.

CHAPTER 4

1. See Aline Rousselle, *Porneia: On Desire and the Body in Antiquity*, trans. Felicia Pheasant (New York: Basil Blackwell, 1988), 1. The Macarius tale may be read in English in *Palladius: The Lausiac History*, trans. Robert T. Meyer (Westminister, Md.: Newman Press, 1965), 59.

2. In another legend the Sages of Palestine captured sexual desire. They were first inclined to execute it, but instead they maimed it "for if you kill it, the world itself goes down." See Peter Brown, *The Body and Society* (New York: Columbia University Press, 1988), 62.

3. Rousselle, *Porneia*, 1. Regarding castration see pp. 107–128. Themes of sexual desire in relation to religiosity are dealt with throughout the Brown book. See also Jacques Le Goff, *The Medieval Imagination*, trans. Arthur Goldhammer (Chicago, Ill.: University of Chicago Press, 1988), 94. Matthew 19:12 referred to young males who "have made themselves eunuchs for the kingdom of heaven."

4. Edmund G. Gardner, *The Dialogues of St. Gregory* (London: Philip Lee Warner, Publisher to the Medici Society, 1911), 55. The four books of the *Dialogues*, written in 593 (following the fall of Rome, when the End was thought to be imminent), were among the most popular reading of the Middle Ages.

5. For a discussion of the St. Benedict events, see Frank Bottomley, *Attitudes to the Body in Western Christendom* (London: Lepus Books, 1979), 103–104. A number of medieval religious tales depicted men crawling through thorns to overcome temptation, and in one case Christ appeared to a lustful youth after he castigated himself by walking through a thornbush. See Frederic C. Tubach, *Index Exemplorum: A Handbook of Medieval Religious Tales* (Helsinki: Suomalainen Tiedeakatemia Akademia Scientiarum Fennica, 1969), entries 4835 and 4840. Elsewhere Gregory of Nyssa referred to Macrina as "an earth virgin of thorns and thistles." Brown, *The Body and Society*, 279.

6. In the Bottomley translation of the passage, it reads "growing nearby" rather than "to grow hard by."

7. The pious believe that the descendants of these roses may still be seen in the garden of the monastery of the *Sagro Sepco*. See Gardner, *The Dialogues of St. Gregory*, 263.

8. Rosa de Lima (1586–1617) was canonized in 1671, during the papacy of Clement IX.

9. Philippe Ariès, *The Hour of Our Death*, trans. Helen Weaver (New York: Vintage, 1982), 393. The fusion of sexuality, violence, and religion was depicted

during the sixteenth century artistically as well as ascetically: Albrecht Dürer's *Fourth Horseman of the Apocalypse* was mounted on a beast with disproportionately large genitals, Nicklaus Manuel had a woman guide Death's hand into her vagina, and so on. See ibid., 370–373.

10. Jacinto de Parra, *Rosa laureada entre los santos* . . . (Madrid: Impressor Eclesiástico de la Real Corona de Castilla, 1670), 2.

11. In Juan Meléndez, *Tesoros verdaderos de la Yndias*, vol. 2 (Rome: Imprenta de Nicolas Angel Tinassio, 1681), 230. Mallarmé's phrase "I love the horror of being virgin" is particularly resonant in this context.

12. See ibid., 200.

13. Juan Meléndez, *Festiva pompa, culto religioso, veneración reverente* . . . (Lima, 1671), 48–49. Much the same is expressed in Meléndez, *Tesoros*, 269.

14. Meléndez, *Tesoros*, 332 and 333, respectively.

15. Ibid., 250.

16. Marcial Castro Castillo, *Fuerzas armadas: Etica y represión* (Buenos Aires: Editorial Nuevo Orden, 1979), 78.

17. Ramón J.A. Camps, *Caso Timerman: Punto final* (Buenos Aires: Tribuna Abierta, 1982), 21.

18. *Nunca más: Informe de la Comisión Nacional Sobre la Desaparición de Personas* (Buenos Aires and Barcelona: EUDEBA/Seix Barral, 1985), 347/338 and 348/339, respectively. Page numbers after the slash refer to the English-language edition of *Nunca más*, published in New York by Farrar, Straus and Giroux in 1986. Carapintada ideology continued in this vein; Aldo Rico's "Operation Dignity," for example, was described as "an act of profound love." See Raúl Jassen, *Seineldín: El ejército traicionado, la patria vencida* (Buenos Aires: Editorial Verum et Militia, 1989), 178.

19. Frederick H. Russell, *The Just War in the Middle Ages* (Cambridge: Cambridge University Press, 1979), 17. See also pp. 214–215.

20. Ibid., 261. "Charity" here follows the theological use of *caritas, charitei* to signify Chrisitian love. See Jonathan Riley-Smith, "Crusading as an Act of Love," *History* 65, no. 214 (June 1980): 177. Compare this with Monsignor Pío Laghi: In the "dirty war" "the thought of Thomas Aquinas is applicable; he teaches that under such circumstances love of the Fatherland is considered equal to love of God." Cited in Andrés Avellaneda, *Censura, autoritarismo y cultura: Argentina 1960–1983*, vol. 1 (Buenos Aires: Centro Editor de América Latina, 1986), 139.

21. Brown, *The Body and Society*, 109.

22. As Jung put it, "The word 'love' includes every kind of morbid sexual abomination as well as every kind of greed that has ever degraded man to the level of a beast or a machine." Cited in Rosemary Gordon, "Narcissism and the Self—Who Am I That I Love?" *Journal of Analytical Psychology* 25 (1980): 247.

23. See Michel Foucault, "Sexuality and Solitude," in Marshall Blonsky, ed., *On Signs* (Baltimore, Md.: Johns Hopkins University Press, 1985), 370.

24. Cited in Brown, *The Body and Society*, 17.

25. Cited in Hannah Arendt, *The Origins of Totalitarianism* (New York: Meridian Books, 1960), 454n. Laboratory experiments have shown that rapists similarly experience "substantial arousal to nonsexual violence." See Vernon L. Quinsey et al., "Sexual Arousal to Nonsexual Violence and Sadomasochistic Themes Among Rapists and Non-Sex-Offenders," *Journal of Consulting and Clinical Psychology* 5, no. 4 (1984): 651–657.

26. From an annotated listing of sexually motivated murders appended to Deborah Cameron and Elizabeth Frazer, *The Lust to Kill* (New York: New York University Press, 1987), 170–174.

27. The two quoted passages in the preceding sentences are from Jacobo Timerman, *Prisoner Without a Name, Cell Without a Number*, trans. Toby Talbot (New York: Vintage Books, 1982), 157 and 17, respectively. See also p. 14. After the "dirty war" Amos Elon reported that "the [Alfonsín] Presidential assistant who declined to be identified by name said that his countrymen were fascinated with the 'eroticism of violence.'" See Elon, "Letter from Argentina," *The New Yorker* (July 21, 1986): 80.

28. Cited in Ricardo Rodríguez Molas, *Historia de la tortura y el orden represivo en la Argentina* (Buenos Aires: Editorial Universitaria de Buenos Aires, 1984), 149. Rodríguez Molas mentioned other instances of pre-"dirty war" torture with patent sexual content, among them two cases—one involving a male, one a female—in which objects were inserted in the anus and another case in which several torturers combined the use of the *picana* with feeling the victim's breasts and inserting fingers in her vagina.

29. For examples of the sexual organization of torture with the *picana*, see *Nunca más*, 28/22, 35/29–30, 39/34, 43/38–39, 46/42, 49/45, 331/321, 345/336, and 419/415.

30. Raúl Vilariño, "Vilariño acusa otra vez," *La semana*, año 6, no. 378 (January 3, 1984): 66.

31. Undercover reconnaissance missions into the domiciles of "subversives" were known as "technical penetrations," the two key concepts at play here on another level. See *Nunca más*, 258/247.

32. At least as far as the torturer is concerned, E. M. Cioran's contention that "the moans of the victim parallel the moans of ecstasy" was amply evidenced in the Argentine detention centers. See his *A Short History of Decay*, trans. Richard Howard (London: Basil Blackwell, 1975), 3. For an introduction to sadomasochism as "a planned ritual or theatrical production," see Thomas S. Weinberg, "Sadomasochism in the United States: A Review of the Recent Sociological Literature," *Journal of Sex Research* 23, no. 1 (February 1987): 50–69.

33. Quoted phrase from Sigmund Freud, *Three Essays on the Theory of Sexuality*, Standard Edition, ed. James Strachey, vol. 7 (London: Hogarth Press, 1953), 157.

34. Testimony of Graciela Susana Geuna, CELS, 50.

35. *El Diario del Juicio* 15 (September 3, 1985): 340.

36. The two examples are from *Nunca más*, 37/32 and 30/23, respectively. In the former passage reference was also made to a torturer called "Death with a feminine voice."

37. Ibid., 191/174–175, 211/196, and 67/65–66, respectively. See also pp. 52/49, 155/143, 212/197, and 346/337. For consent to rape as a condition of a prisoner's liberation, see p. 50/46.

38. *El Diario del Juicio* 21 (October 15, 1985): no pp.

39. Other phallic objects were used but less frequently. One survivor testified that a police club was inserted in her vagina. *Nunca más*, 49/45.

40. For examples of insertion in the vagina, see ibid., 49/45, 155/143, and 212/197. "Sodomies" with the *picana* are included in the examples listed in note 29.

41. The punitive/sexual function of the *picana's* "discharge" is reminiscent of the role that lightning often played in medieval religious tales. A priest was struck by lightning, for example, after making love to his mistress; another priest was saved from lightning by the Virgin; a woman who accused a saint of raping her was struck by lightning; the tree under which an eloping scribe and nun planned to have intercourse was struck by lightning; and so on. See Tubach, *Index Exemplorum*, entries 3043, 3044, 3046, and 3495.

42. A practical joke designed to terrorize *Buenos Aires Herald* editor James Neilson in 1980 registered one such expression. Neilson's wife received a letter ostensibly from a woman ("Susana") confessing to an affair with Neilson and expressing the sexual pleasure she enjoyed with him. The terror commenced when it became clear that "Susana" was one of the vernacular names for the bedframe to which the victims of *picana* torture were bound. See John Simpson and Jana Bennett, *The Disappeared and the Mothers of the Plaza* (New York: St. Martin's Press, 1985), 239.

43. Walter Burkert, *Homo Necans: The Anthropology of Ancient Greek Sacrificial Ritual and Myth*, trans. Peter Bing (Berkeley: University of California Press, 1983), 59.

44. C. Laurin, cited in J. Laplanche and J. -B. Pontalis, *The Language of Psycho-Analysis*, trans. Donald Nicholson-Smith (New York: W. W. Norton, 1973), 312. Burkert followed Detlev Fehling in pointing out, on p. 558, that "among some primates, the male delimits his territory by facing outward and displaying his erect phallus."

45. Lévi-Strauss, cited in Roman Jakobson's chapter, "Dear Claude, Cher Maitre," in Blonsky, *On Signs*, 185.

46. Ibid.

47. "Phallus" in its present psychoanalytic usage refers (unless the text indicates otherwise) not to the male genitalia and its actual or potential severance from the body but rather to a signifier and its functions in what Jacques Lacan called the Symbolic order.

48. Jacques Lacan/Anthony Wilden, *The Language of the Self: The Function of Language in Psychoanalysis* (Baltimore, Md.: Johns Hopkins University Press, 1968), 188.

49. Constancio Bernaldo de Quirós, *La picota en América* (Havana: Jesús Montero/Biblioteca Jurídica, 1948), 31. *Picotas* were also placed in other strategic locations within a municipality; see p. 17.

50. Bernardo de Vargas Machuca, *Milicia y descripción de las Indias* (Madrid: Pedro Madrigal, 1599), 105–106. For discussion see Richard M. Morse, "The Urban Development of Colonial Spanish America," in Leslie Bethell, ed., *The Cambridge History of Latin America*, vol. 2 (Cambridge: Cambridge University Press, 1984), 75–76, and María Antonia Duran Montero, *Fundación de ciudades en el Perú durante el siglo XVI* (Seville: Escuela de Estudios Hispano-Americanos, 1978), 68–70. For description of a similar procedure enacting Pizarro's foundation of Cuzco, see John Hemming, *The Conquest of the Incas* (New York: Harcourt, Brace and Jovanovich, 1970), 142–143 and corresponding note. See also p. 314, where the Inca Titu Cusi was alleged to have performed *picota* rituals in ratifying the treaty of Acobamba. For other examples of town foundations involving the *picota*, see Bernaldo de Quirós, *La picota en América*, 58–59, 62–63, 67, 69, and 70.

51. Quoted passages from Rodríguez Molas, *Historia de la tortura*, 36–37, and Bernaldo de Quirós, *La picota en América*, 17, respectively.

52. Bernaldo de Quirós, *La picota en América*, 83.

53. Ibid., 127.

54. Quoted passage from the definition of *picota* given in Martín Alonso, *Enciclopedia del idioma*, tomo 3 (Madrid: Aguilar, 1958), 3263. Compare this with the adventurous etymology provided in Sebastian Covarruvias Orozco in *Tesoro de la lengua castellana, o española* (Madrid: Luis Sánches, impressor del Rey N.S., 1611), 587.

55. Rodolfo Lenz, *Diccionario etimológico* (Santiago: Universidad de Chile, 1980), 581–582. The etymology cites a bit of verse, describing how the "lazy oxen" are obliged to move by the *picana*. The *picana's* original meaning has been displaced by the torture-related usage.

56. Figurative uses cited in the text are from *Collins Spanish-English/English-Spanish Dictionary*, 2d ed. (London: Collins, 1988), 514. Also suggestive in the present context are other significations of *picar*: to cut into pieces; to burn the mouth (thus the adjective *picante*); and to irritate or offend.

57. Fray Antonio de la Calancha, *Crónica moralizada del orden de San Agustín en el Perú, con sucesos egemplares en esta monarquía,* tomo 1 (Barcelona: Pedro Lacavalleria, 1638), 825. In iconographic depiction the pole extending from the head of the impaled priest curiously resembles the *capirote*—a kind of elongated dunce cap—worn by Inquisition penitents, though in the present case it is surrounded by a halo.

58. In the iconography Ortiz, like Christ, is simultaneously pierced diagonally through the chest by a lance. The illustration is tipped into Calancha, between pp. 782 and 783. Other accounts report a less glorious impalement: Martin de Morua wrote, "They then made a deep, narrow hole and placed him in it, head down with his feet upwards, and placed a palm spear in his caecum [*sic*]." See Hemming, *The Conquest of the Incas,* 418–419.

59. Michael Alexander, ed., *Discovering the New World: Based on the Works of Theodore de Bry* (New York: Harper and Row, 1976), 24. De Bry's *Grands Voyages,* published in Frankfurt in 1591, is one of the earliest and most important European graphic depictions of the Americas.

The narrative accompanying another of de Bry's illustrations on p. 31 explained that the "Florida" natives "never left the place of battle without piercing the mutilated corpses of their enemies right through the anus with an arrow. During this task a protective force always surrounded them." This practice is particularly significant in the context of power generated through "sodomy" with the *picana.*

60. Laplanche and Pontalis, *The Language of Psycho-Analysis,* 313.

61. Already in the cultures of Old Europe, several millennia before the birth of Christ, "magical power was obviously attributed to phallic objects and conferred an appropriate benefit." See Marija Gimbutas, *The Gods and Goddesses of Old Europe, 7000 to 3500 BC: Myth, Legends and Cult Images* (Berkeley: University of California Press, 1974), 220.

62. Lacan, cited in Anthony Wilden, *System and Structure* (London: Tavistock Publications, 1972), 284. For Lacan's conception of the phallus, see "The Signification of the Phallus," in Jacques Lacan, *Écrits: A Selection,* trans. Alan Sheridan (New York: W. W. Norton, 1977). See also: Lacan/Wilden, *The Language of the Self,* 186–188 and 304–305; and Wilden's "Critique of Phallocentrism" in his *System and Structure.*

In establishing the phallus as the signifier in which language is joined to desire in the Symbolic order, as "the privileged signifier of that mark in which the role of the logos is joined with the advent of desire," Lacan cited the Sanskrit noun *lakshana,* which means both "signifier" and "phallus." See his *Écrits,* 287, and Lacan/Wilden, *The Language of the Self,* 188 and 151–152. In Greco-Roman tradition a similar union of the phallus and the word was provided by the most significant phallic figure in Western culture, the god Hermes, who was also "messenger of the gods" and "the giver of discourse." See John P. Muller and

William J. Richardson, *Lacan and Language: A Reader's Guide to "Écrits"* (New York: International Universities Press, 1982), 349–350.

63. Guy Rosolato, cited in John T. Irwin, "The Dead Father in Faulkner," in Robert Con Davis, ed., *The Fictional Father: Lacanian Readings of the Text* (Amherst: University of Massachusetts Press, 1981), 164.

64. Francis Barker, *The Tremulous Private Body: Essays on Subjection* (London: Methuen, 1984), 105.

65. See Michael Clark, *Jacques Lacan: An Annotated Bibliography* (New York: Garland Publishing, 1988), 53.

66. Lacan/Wilden, *The Language of the Self*, 187, and Victor Smirnoff, "The Fetishistic Transaction," in Serge Lebovici and Daniel Widlöcher, eds., *Psychoanalysis in France* (New York: International Universities Press, 1980), 305–306, respectively. The latter wrote: "Thus the fetish lies somewhere between the phallus, to which it is linked by metonymy, and the subject."

67. For torture as a "making present" of the *desaparecidos*, see Chapter 3. Freud adopted the term "fetish" by analogy to the objects "in which savages believe that their gods are embodied." The deistic qualities of the *desaparecidos* as fetishes from which the "gods" were released through eroticized torture rituals will be discussed in the following chapter. See Freud, *Three Essays on the Theory of Sexuality*, 153.

68. Lacan/Wilden, *The Language of the Self*, 187.

69. Lacan explained: "If the desire of the mother is the phallus, the child wishes to be the phallus in order to satisfy that desire." *Écrits*, 289.

70. Josué V. Harari, summarizing the position of Michel Foucault in his introduction to Harari, ed., *Textual Strategies: Perspectives in Post-Structuralist Criticism* (Ithaca, N.Y.: Cornell University Press, 1979), 42. Foucault followed psychoanalysis in observing "that speech is not merely the medium which manifests—or dissembles—desire; it is also the object of desire." See his book *The Archaeology of Knowledge*, trans. A. M. Sheridan Smith (New York: Pantheon Books, 1972), 216.

71. Matthew 5:27–30.

72. Bruno Bettelheim, *Symbolic Wounds: Puberty Rites and the Envious Male* (New York: Collier Books, 1954), 90.

73. Burkert, *Homo Necans*, 68. A paradigm of the phallic power was then paraded; on p. 69 he noted: "A single phallus was set up for worship and carried through the city as if in a triumph."

74. Richard M. Fried, *Nightmare in Red: The McCarthy Era in Perspective* (New York: Oxford University Press, 1990), 120.

75. See the Guatemalan entry in Amnesty International, *Torture in the Eighties* (New York: Amnesty International, 1984). Regarding Argentina, see the testimony of Raúl David Vilariño in *La Semana*, January 5, 1984.

76. Brown, *The Body and Society*, 416.

77. Tubach, *Index Exemplorum*, entry 2518.

78. Ibid., entries 674, 773, 1303, 1801, 2268, 2302, and 2071, respectively. The symbolic relation between a crime and its punishment is sometimes paralleled by a relation between the punishment and later interpretations of it. In cases like St. Bartholomew's, for example, the punishment established symbolics that then modulated forward into construction of the martyr's saintly function. Precisely because his skin was flayed, Bartholomew became the patron saint of hide tanners and shoemakers. For other variations of the symbolic relation between crime and punishment (one of which, entry 5395, generated evidence: Wounds bled in the presence of murderers), see ibid., entries 2234, 3448, 4697, and 4904. See also Brown, *The Body and Society*, 20, where a woman's desire of another man during intercourse with her husband results in a child resembling that man.

79. Michel Foucault, *Discipline and Punish: The Birth of the Prison*, trans. Alan Sheridan (New York: Vintage Books, 1979), 55 and 45, respectively.

80. While torture by electric shock is used by repressive regimes throughout the world, the *picana* is prevalent only in Argentina and three bordering countries: Uruguay, Paraguay, and Bolivia. The Syrian "Black Slave" ("an apparatus which when switched on inserts a heated metal skewer into the anus") is the only contemporary form of torture that rivals the explicitness of the *picana's* sexuality. See Amnesty International, *Torture in the Eighties*, 243.

81. Franz Kafka, *The Penal Colony: Stories and Short Pieces*, trans. Willa and Edwin Muir (New York: Schocken Books, 1961), 197. The thematics of Kafka's Harrow allude to passages in Jeremiah 17:1 ("The sin of Judah is written with a pen of iron; with a point of diamond it is engraved in their hearts") and Jeremiah 31:33 ("I will put my law in their inward parts and write it in their hearts"). See Rudolph Binion, *Soundings Psychohistorical and Psycholiterary* (New York: Elsevier, 1981), 14, and *After Christianity: Christian Survivals in Post-Christian Culture* (Durango, Colo.: Logbridge-Rhodes, 1986), 88.

82. *Nunca más*, 37/32.

83. Michel de Certeau, *Heterologies: Discourse on the Other*, trans. Brian Massumi (Minneapolis: University of Minnesota Press, 1986), 162.

84. Nicolas Abraham and Maria Torok, "Introjection-Incorporation: Mourning or Melancholia," in Serge Lebovici and Daniel Widlöcher, eds., *Psychoanalysis in France* (New York: International Universities Press, 1980), 6–7.

85. As the Spanish maxim has it, *Con sangre la letra entra*.

86. See Abraham and Torok, "Introjection-Incorporation," 6–7.

87. Edward S. Casey and J. Melvin Woody, "Hegel, Heidegger, Lacan: The Dialectic of Desire," in Joseph H. Smith and William Kerrigan, eds., *Interpreting Lacan* (New Haven, Conn.: Yale University Press, 1983), 110. The authors were closely following Lacan, who added that "the eclipse of the subject" is "closely

bound up with the *Spaltung* or splitting that [the subject] suffers from its subordination to language." Lacan, *Écrits*, 313.

88. Quoted passage from Sophocles, *The Three Theban Plays*, trans. Robert Fagles, intro. and notes by Bernard Knox (New York: Penguin Books, 1984), 239.

89. Timerman, *Prisoner Without a Name*, 82–83.

90. *El Libro de El Diario del Juicio* (Buenos Aires: Editorial Perfil, 1985), 23. The phrase is untranslatable. Very literally it reads, "I eat it [the penis] up doubled over and my mother is the daughter of a whore." As mentioned in the text, *hijo/a de puta* signifies figuratively as an insult.

91. Jacques Derrida, *Dissemination*, trans. Barbara Johnson (Chicago, Ill.: University of Chicago Press, 1981), 124.

92. Sigmund Freud, "Dostoevsky and Parricide," in his *Character and Culture*, trans. James Strachey (New York: Collier Books, 1963), 202.

93. The phrase "that dangerous supplement" was used by Jean-Jacques Rousseau to describe masturbation. In "Plato's Pharmacy" (see particularly p. 110 in *Dissemination*) and in the chapter titled after Rousseau's phrase in *Of Grammatology*, Derrida departed from the two meanings of the French word *supplément* ("addition" and "replacement") to describe writing, masturbation, and the *pharmakon* as simultaneously secondary and compensatory on the one hand and on the other substitutive and usurpative.

94. Noemí Ulla and Hugo Echave, *Después de la noche: Diálogo con Graciela Fernández Meijide* (Buenos Aires: Editorial Contrapunto, 1986), 66. One survivor testified that a torturer said to a woman "more or less paternally something like 'I can't bear the suffering of a woman'; then he put a pistol to her chest and proceeded to rape her." Testimony of Armando Rodolfo Fertitta, APDH, 2.

Amos Elon commented: "The 'conquest' of women is considered by men here [in Argentina] to be a duty, and it often implies humiliation and the deliberate inflicting of pain. But though men conquer and humiliate women as lovers, they adore and worship mothers. The relative immunity enjoyed during the years of the *proceso* by the group called Mothers of the Plaza de Mayo may be a case in point." Elon, "Letter from Argentina," 80.

95. Ulla and Echave, *Después de la noche*, 68. Other repressors had similar nicknames, perhaps the most notorious being the pseudonym "Gustavo Niño" (*niño*, meaning boy) that Alfredo Astiz used in the "technical penetration" of the Mothers of the Plaza de Mayo. See *Nunca más*, 135/127–128.

96. Testimony of Norma Susan Burgos, APDH, 4.

97. The mythology of the "dirty war" supported the Junta's position as Son. The antagonists of a messianic Hero's quest are often depicted as sinister figures (the "monster of Marxism") that are paternal in origin. "Stated in direct terms: The work of the hero is to slay the tenacious aspect of the father (dragon, tester, ogre king)." See Joseph Campbell, *The Hero with a Thousand Faces* (Princeton, N.J.: Bollingen Series/Princeton University Press, 1968), 352. At least one of

those archetypes already embodied the father imago: "The hero was a man who by himself had slain the father—the father who still appeared in the myth as a totemistic monster." See Sigmund Freud, *Group Psychology and the Analysis of the Ego*, trans. James Strachey (London: Hogarth Press, 1948), 113. For a succinct review of Oedipal-type myths, see Clyde Kluckhohn, "Recurrent Themes in Myths and Mythmaking," in Henry A. Murray, ed., *Myth and Mythmaking* (Boston: Beacon Press, 1968), 53.

98. For discussion of "lifting" the power from the torture victim's body, see Chapter 3.

99. Final report of the Mar del Plata delegation to CONADEP (an unpublished document), 9.

100. Both passages from Serge Viderman, "The Subject-Object Relation and the Problem of Desire," in Serge Lebrovici and Daniel Widlöcher, eds., *Psychoanalysis in France* (New York: International Universities Press, 1980), 186. This "impotence" was demonstrable in the simplest terms by the regime's illegitimacy: The Junta had no de jure power.

101. See Chapter 1 for statistics. Massera made reference to "the university youth subject to a castration almost without precedent" Emilio E. Massera, *El país que queremos* (Buenos Aires: Editorial FEPA, 1981), 53.

102. "The boy enters the Oedipal complex by a half-fraternal rivalry with his father"; see Lacan/Wilden, *The Language of the Self*, 271.

103. Emilio E. Massera, *El camino a la democracia* (Buenos Aires: El Cid Editores, 1979), 116. The two most charismatic and popular leaders in Argentine history, Juan Perón and Hipólito Yrigoyen, were both strongly paternal figures, and both were reelected to the presidency in their old age, as waning Symbolic fathers.

104. "In the first case one's father is what one would like to *be*, and in the second he is what one would like to *have*." See Freud, *Group Psychology*, 62.

105. Cited in Bernard Knox's notes to Sophocles, *The Three Theban Plays*," 140. In *Oedipus the King* the Mother's identity is split between a woman and her deformed representation in the Sphinx. Oedipus solves the riddle of a female monster, the Sphinx, and receives his mother (Jocasta) in reward. As a result the Sphinx commits suicide, as Jocasta will do later when Oedipus has solved the "riddle" that reveals him as her son. See Richard Caldwell, *The Origin of the Gods: A Psychoanalytic Study of Greek Theogonic Myth* (New York: Oxford University Press, 1989), 33 and 65.

106. Massera, *El país*, 53.

107. Cited in Diana R. Kordon and Lucia I. Edelman, eds., *Efectos psicológicos de la represión política* (Buenos Aires: Sudamericana/Planeta, 1987), 129.

108. Cited in Ernst H. Kantorowicz, *The King's Two Bodies: A Study in Mediaeval Political Theology* (Princeton, N.J.: Princeton University Press, 1957), 213.

109. John Mandeville, *The Travels of Sir John Mandeville*, trans. C.W.R.D. Moseley (New York: Penguin Books, 1983), 43.

110. Revelation 21:9 and 21:2.

111. In the context of feminized place names, note that a cherished concept of the Junta—*La Patria* ("fatherland")—has masculine denotations etymologically (rooting in *pater*, or father) but is a "feminine" word (terminating in *a* and carrying the feminine article).

Regarding Bolívar, in one trope Europe was styled as a kind of hag, "hunched over under the weight of years," but the New World was given fair-maiden qualities. See Simón Bolívar, *Doctrina de Libertador*, ed. Manuel Pérez Vila (Caracas: Biblioteca Ayacucho, 1979), 173. Compare this with the metaphor used by Admiral Massera, after noting the need for Argentina to wake from its "historic siesta": If "we always have to dance with the ugliest girl maybe it's because we always arrive late to the ball." Massera, *El camino*, 113.

112. Insofar as a battle for the phallus-as-Word at the torture table is concerned, "being-there is always a property of paternal speech. And the site of a fatherland." Derrida, *Dissemination*, 146.

113. "Lacan's *moi* corresponds to the internalization of the other through identification." Lacan/Wilden, *The Language of the Self*, 160.

114. Laplanche and Pontalis, *The Language of Psycho-Analysis*, 208.

115. Lacan/Wilden, *The Language of the Self*, 161.

116. Freud, cited in Jean Laplanche, *Life and Death in Psychoanalysis*, trans. Jeffrey Mehlman (Baltimore, Md.: Johns Hopkins University Press, 1976), 91.

117. *El Libro de El Diario del Juicio*, 247. For another example see Massera, *El país que queremos*, 54.

118. Massera, *El camino*, 49.

119. *Argentina, 1983* (Buenos Aires: Centro Editor de America Latina, 1984), 151. During the 1985 trials the prosecution cited directives defining subversion that similarly functioned as the Junta's projective self-definition. The objective of subversion, the de facto regime explained, was "to take power, not through the legal system as the result of the election process, but rather outside of the legal system."

120. Geuna, CELS, 56; see also p. 53.

121. *El Diario del Juicio*, 21 (October 15, 1985). The statement was made by task force personnel to the testifier when she expressed surprise that they were young ("about 20 to 22 years old") and "dressed like students."

122. The former quotation is from Daniel Frontalini and María Cristina Caiati, *El mito de la guerra sucia* (Buenos Aires: Editorial CELS, 1984), 78; the latter is from a 1977 War College text cited in Enrique Vázquez, *PRN/ La Ultima: Origen, apogeo y caída de la dictadura militar* (Buenos Aires: EUDEBA, 1985), 85.

123. Cited in Vázquez, *PRN/La Ultima*, 71. The Nazi-like denomination "Third Republic" recalls that, in the same way, "the Nazis started with the fiction of conspiracy and modeled themselves, more or less consciously, after the example of the secret society of the Elders of Zion." Arendt, *The Origins of Totalitarianism*, 378.

124. General Ramón Camps, from a 1983 interview reprinted in *Argentina, 1983*, 63. See also pp. 440–442 for the wording of the October 1983 Law of National Pacification.

125. From the Camps interview, *Argentina, 1983*, 63.

126. José Martínez de Hoz and General Albano Harguindeguy, respectively, cited in Frontalini and Caiati, *El mito*, 34 and 35.

127. *El Libro de El Diario del Juicio*, 319. See also *El Diario del Juicio* 18 (September 24, 1985), in which Moreno Ocampo made a similar remark. In the context of mimesis and reversal of roles, note that the Montoneros began with a position of right-wing Catholic authoritarian integralism and ended up waging an armed struggle as left-wing terrorists.

128. See *Nunca más*, 7/1 and 481/449.

129. Massera, *El camino*, 49.

130. See Chapter 1 for discussion.

131. See Grant Wardlaw, *Political Terrorism: Theory, Tactics, and Counter-Measures* (Cambridge: Cambridge University Press, 1982), 155.

132. Later, according to Simpson and Bennett, Chamorro and Bazán were believed to be living together while the former was naval attaché to the Argentine embassy in South Africa. The same authors added: "Supposedly, another Montonero woman, tortured at ESMA, married one of her torturers; they were believed to have made their way to Mexico City, where they began a new life" Simpson and Bennett, *The Disappeared*, 397.

Liliana Cavani's 1973 film *The Night Porter* treated the same theme: An ex-prisoner had an affair with the Nazi who had previously tortured her. *The Night Porter* was banned in Argentina under the Junta.

133. Speech delivered in Buenos Aires on January 24, 1989. From p. 3 of the translated transcription in files of Americas Watch, Washington, D.C.

134. Abraham and Torok, "Introjection-Incorporation," 5. On p. 10 they added, "We should like to make clear that it is not simply a matter of going back to the literal sense of words but of using them in such a way—in speech or in action—that their 'figurativeness' is thereby destroyed."

135. The anonymous woodcut, "New World Scene" (ca. 1505), is reproduced in Gloria Gilda Deak, *Picturing America*, vol. 1 (Princeton, N.J.: Princeton University Press, 1988), plate 4. A discussion of the image is included on p. 5 of vol. 2.

136. See Jean-Paul Duviols, *L'Amérique espagnole vue et rêvée* (Paris: Editions Promodis, 1985), 102–103.

137. Bernadette Bucher, *Icon and Conquest: A Structural Analysis of the Illustrations of de Bry's "Great Voyages,"* trans. Basia Miller Gulati (Chicago, Ill.: University of Chicago Press, 1981), 50.

138. Ibid.

139. Compare this with Freud: "Identification [with the father] is ambivalent from the very first; it can turn into an expression of tenderness as easily as into a wish for someone's removal. It behaves like a derivative of the first *oral* phase of the organisation of the libido, in which the object that we long for and prize is assimilated by eating and is in that way annihilated as such." Freud compared this to the "devouring affection" that some cannibals have for their enemies. See Freud, *Group Psychology*, 61–62.

140. Laplanche and Pontalis, *The Language of Psycho-Analysis*, 212.

141. The quoted phrase is from the Junta proclamation at the time of the coup; translation from Brian Loveman and Thomas M. Davies, Jr., eds., *The Politics of Antipolitics: The Military in Latin America* (Lincoln: University of Nebraska Press, 1978), 177. The centrality of the liturgical year in the medieval outlook on life is evidenced to some degree in contemporary Argentina, where major events of the "dirty war" and post-"dirty war" periods often coincide with significant days in the Christian calendar. Videla's 1975 statement of warning to the Perón administration, his Tucumán sermon to the soldiers fighting the ERP, his speech proclaiming sacrifice as the "sign of the year," and the later (under Alfonsín) "full stop" law virtually ending litigation for "dirty war" crimes were all closely associated with Christmas (the day the Son is born). In 1987 the military uprisings took place during Easter week. One rebellion was quelled on the afternoon of Good Friday (Son on the cross), another then breaking out and lasting until Alfonsín negotiated its conclusion on Easter Sunday (when He has risen and is incorporated back into the Father). Alfonsín then returned to the Plaza de Mayo to report the surrender of the rebels with these words: "Compatriots, Happy Easter." For a word on the liturgical calendar in medieval life, see Jacques LeGoff, *Medieval Civilization, 400–1500*, trans. Julia Barrow (New York: Basil Blackwell, 1989), 180.

142. Monica Rector, "The Code and Message of Carnival: 'Escolas-de-Samba,'" in Thomas A. Sebeok, ed., *Carnival!* (New York: Mouton Publishers, 1984), 39.

143. Ibid.

144. Ibid.

145. John A. Hardon, *Modern Catholic Dictionary* (Garden City, N.Y.: Doubleday, 1980), 83.

146. Translation excerpted from Loveman and Davies, *The Politics of Antipolitics* 178–180.

147. Mikhail Bakhtin, *Rabelais and His World*, trans. Helene Iswolsky (Cambridge, Mass.: MIT Press, 1968), 7.

148. For a definition see the introduction to Barbara A. Babcock, ed., *The Reversible World: Symbolic Inversion in Art and Society* (Ithaca, N.Y.: Cornell University Press, 1978), especially pp. 14–15.

149. See Bahktin, *Rabelais*, 109.

150. V. V. Ivanov, "The Semiotic Theory of Carnival as the Inversion of Bipolar Opposites," in Thomas A. Sebeok, ed., *Carnival!* (New York: Mouton Publishers, 1984), 11.

151. These are listed in the "Subversives" column of the tabulation of binary oppositions in Chapter 3.

152. Foucault, *Discipline*, 29. On p. 124 of Harold Bloom, ed., *Sophocles' "Oedipus Rex"* (New York: Chelsea House, 1988), Vernant noted that Oedipus, "the paradigm of the double man, the reversed man . . . is embodied in the reversal that transforms the divine king into the scapegoat."

153. The reversal of sex roles is also common to Carnival, as manifest notably in transvestism.

154. From anthropologist Peter Rigby's work, cited in Bucher, *Icon and Conquest*, 168.

155. Ivanov, "The Semiotic Theory," 14.

156. See Peter Stallybrass and Allon White, *The Politics and Poetics of Transgression* (Ithaca, N.Y.: Cornell University Press, 1986), 17. The quoted passage is from Bahktin, *Rabelais*, 81.

157. Anna Freud, *The Ego and the Mechanisms of Defense*, trans. Cecil Baines (New York: International Universities Press, 1966), 113.

158. René Girard, *Violence and the Sacred*, trans. Patrick Gregory (Baltimore, Md.: Johns Hopkins University Press, 1977), 145.

159. Viderman, "The Subject-Object Relation," 195.

160. Burkert concurred: "In human ritual . . . the aggressive gesture can become so important that its object is unessential." Burkert, *Homo Necans*, 41.

161. For an anecdotal, quasi-comic depiction of mimesis in the detention centers, see Timerman, *Prisoner Without a Name*, 5.

162. Djelal Kadir, *Questing Fictions: Latin American Family Romance* (Minneapolis: University of Minnesota Press, 1986), 86.

163. See Martha Noel Evans, "Introduction to Jacques Lacan's Lecture: The Neurotic's Individual Myth." *The Psychoanalytic Quarterly* 48 (1979): 399.

164. Stuart Schneiderman, "Saying of Hamlet," *Sub-stance* 8 (1974): 79. Lacan once followed Jean Cocteau, punning that "the mirror should reflect a little more before returning our image to us."

165. From Bernard Knox's notes to Sophocles, *The Three Theban Plays*, 131.

166. Ibid., 179 and 180.

167. J. P. Vernant, "Ambiguity and Reversal: On the Enigmatic Structure of *Oedipus Rex*," in Harold Bloom, *Sophocles' "Oedipus Rex*," 111.

168. For discussion see the "Plato's Pharmacy" section in Derrida, *Dissemination*. Quoted passage is from p. 110.

169. Foucault, *Discipline*, 47.

170. See Lacan/Wilden, *The Language of the Self*, 271.

171. Sigmund Freud, "Thoughts on War and Death," in *Collected Papers*, vol. 4, trans. Joan Riviere (New York: Basic Books, 1959), 314.

172. Schneiderman, "Saying of Hamlet," 77.

173. Lacan, cited in Lacan/Wilden, *The Language of the Self*, 270; the same passage in a different translation is in Lacan, *Écrits*, 199. See also Lacan/Wilden, *The Language of the Self*, 41 ("It is in the *name of the father* that we must recognize the support of the Symbolic function which, from the dawn of history, has identified his person with the figure of the law") and 270–271. Freud's *Totem and Taboo* is cited but not without recognition, as Lévi-Strauss put it, that its argument rides on a "vicious circle deriving the social state from events which presuppose it"; I shall not dwell on it. See Lévi-Strauss, *The Elementary Structure of Kinship* (Boston, Mass.: Beacon Press, 1969), 491. For René Girard's revision of *Totem and Taboo*, see his *Violence and the Sacred*, 193–222.

Compare this with Freud, in "Thoughts on War and Death," 311: "Beside the corpse of the beloved were generated not only the idea of the soul, the belief in immortality, and a great part of man's deep-rooted sense of guilt, but also the earliest inkling of ethical law." See also the dream of the dead father related in "Two Principles of Mental Functioning," trans. James Strachey, *Standard Edition*, vol. 12 (London: Hogarth Press, 1962), 225: *"His father was alive once more and he was talking to him."*

174. Stuart Schneiderman, *Jacques Lacan: The Death of an Intellectual Hero* (Cambridge, Mass.: Harvard University Press, 1983), 54. See Lacan, *Écrits*, 217 (it is the *dead* Father who "constitutes the law of the signifier"), 199, and 310. See also Stuart Schneiderman, ed. and trans., *Returning to Freud: Clinical Psychoanalysis in the School of Lacan* (New Haven, Conn.: Yale University Press, 1980), 7: "The death of the father . . . is not the end of the father but rather the beginning of his Law." Frederic Jameson summarized: "The very cornerstone of Freud's conception of the psyche, the Oedipus complex, is transliterated by Lacan into a linguistic phenomenon which he designates as the discovery by the subject of the Name-of-the-Father, and which consists . . . in the transformation of an Imaginary relationship to that particular imago which is the physical parent into the new and menacing abstraction of the Law." See his "Imaginary and Symbolic in Lacan: Marxism, Psychoanalytic Criticism, and the Problem of the Subject," *Yale French Studies* 55/56 (1977): 359. François Hartog noted that "when the king dies, he becomes perhaps even more of a king than when he was alive" in his *The Mirror of Herodotus*, trans. Janet Lloyd (Berkeley: University of California Press, 1988), 201.

175. The Name-of-the-Father's return also assumes symbolic depictions, such as—in the case of *Oedipus the King*—the plague. In a few medieval tales as well, "a ghost who had been mocked sent the plague as punishment." Tubach, *Index Exemplorum*, entry 3817. Derrida noted that "in the personification of the Laws in the *Crito*, Socrates is called upon to accept both death and the law *at once.*" Derrida, *Dissemination*, 123.

176. Compare this with Freud: "What no human soul desires there is no need to prohibit; it is automatically excluded." Freud, "Thoughts on War and Death," 312. This point is developed following Frazer in *Totem and Taboo*.

177. Derrida, *Dissemination*, 123.

178. Lacan argued that "the attribution of procreation to the father can only be the effect of a pure signifier, of a recognition, not of a real father, but of what religion has taught us to refer to as the Name-of-the-Father." Lacan, *Écrits*, 199.

179. Friedrich Nietzsche, *On the Genealogy of Morals and Ecce Homo*, trans. Walter Kaufmann (New York: Vintage Books, 1969), 222. Nietzsche made this remark not long before he went insane and distributed letters signed "Dionysus" and "The Crucified One." Elsewhere Derrida noted that "Socrates thus takes voice from the father; he is the father's spokesman. And Plato writes *from out of his death.*" Derrida, *Dissemination*, 148.

180. Geuna, CELS, 6.

181. Jacques Lacan, *The Seminar of Jacques Lacan*, book 2, ed. Jacques-Alain Miller, trans. Sylvana Tomaselli (New York: W. W. Norton, 1988), 326. On p. 232 Lacan noted that the Oedipus of *Colonus* "lives a life which is dead."

182. Jacques Lacan, "Desire and the Interpretation of Desire in *Hamlet*," trans. James Hulbert, *Yale French Studies* 55/56 (1977): 17 and 16, respectively.

183. Ibid., 24.

184. Viderman, "The Subject-Object Relation," 190.

185. Geuna, CELS, 6.

186. The version cited in the text conforms to that used in Lacan translations and in Felman (see next note). Fagles's translation of the line in question from *Oedipus at Colonus* reads: "When I am dead, and you have put my body in the grave." Sophocles, *The Three Theban Plays*, 319.

187. Shoshana Felman, "Beyond Oedipus: The Specimen Story of Psychoanalysis," *MLN* 98, no. 5 (1983): 1037.

Approaching the myth from another perspective, "empty grave" thematics further echo Oedipal dynamics: The *desaparecidos*-as-phallus are denied a place inside the Mother/earth, the consecrated ground of the *patria*. As Jung recognized, the phallus "buried in the earth like a corpse, is at the same time inseminator of the earth." See C. G. Jung, *Symbols of Transformation: Prelude to a Case of Schizophrenia*, trans. R.F.C. Hull (Harper Torchbooks/Bollingen Library, 1956), 436.

188. Quoted passage from Elizabeth Helin, cited in Elon, "Letter from Argentina," 81. "Empty grave" themes were also prominent in many medieval tales. For examples from Pope Gregory's *Dialogues*, see Gardner, *The Dialogues of St. Gregory*, 86 and 248.

189. Quoted passage from *Hamlet*, act 4, scene 4. Evita Perón's body was stolen from its grave after Juan Perón was deposed by the 1955 military coup d'état.

190. Following the "dirty war," during the Alfonsín administration, anonymous terrorists in 1987 consolidated "empty grave" and fragmented-body themes by opening the tomb of Juan Perón, amputating the hands from the corpse, and demanding $8 million in ransom for their return.

191. Elon, "Letter from Argentina," 81. For a specific "empty grave" example, see the "Science and the 'Disappeared'" section in Eric Stover and Elena O. Nightingale, eds., *The Breaking of Bodies and Minds* (New York: W. H. Freeman, 1985).

192. F. E. Peters, *Jerusalem* (Princeton, N.J.: Princeton University Press, 1985), 281–282.

193. From a letter dated 975, quoted in ibid., 243.

194. Hartog, *Mirror of Herodotus*, 135–136. Compare this with the empowering function of Oedipus's grave.

195. Through the work of Clyde Snow and Argentine forensic anthropologists, many of the NN graves have been opened in an attempt to identify skeletal remains and then properly rebury them. See Christopher Joyce and Eric Stover, *Witness from the Grave* (New York: Little, Brown, 1991).

196. See Shirley Christian, "Argentines Honor a Warlord of Old," *New York Times*, October 2, 1989. During his dictatorship Rosas himself established a precedent by having the bones of General Juan Facundo Quiroga exhumed, cleaned with alcohol, perfumed, and reburied in La Recoleta. See Judith Laikin Elkin, "Recoleta: Civilization and Barbarism in Argentina," *Michigan Quarterly Review* (Spring 1988): 221–239.

197. The implied exaltation was in some cases explicit and even flaunted. Menem, for example, received one of those who had been pardoned, Carapintada Mohamed Alí Seineldín, at his suburban presidential residence. See Shirley Christian, "Pardoned Argentine Officers out of Jail," *New York Times*, October 10, 1989.

198. Lacan, "Desire," 38.

199. All quoted passages in this paragraph are from Abraham and Torok, "Introjection-Incorporation," 6–7.

200. Lacan, "Desire," 38. Stuart Schneiderman observed: "The empty grave is also a subject; so the human subject is always split between a mark and a void." Schneiderman, *Jacques Lacan*, 7.

201. Norman Cohen, *The Pursuit of the Millennium* (New York: Oxford University Press, 1970), 85–86.

202. Ernesto Sábato, *Abaddón: El exterminador* (Barcelona: Seix Barral, 1982), 410. A long tradition of existential literature pursues the theme of God-as-exterminator. For discussion see the "Born Guilty" chapter in Rudolph Binion, *After Christianity: Christian Survivals in Post-Christian Culture* (Durango, Colo.: Logbridge-Rhodes, 1986), 69–94.

CHAPTER 5

1. These are the concluding words of a manifesto circulated among the members of a secret army lodge, headed by Juan Domingo Perón, around the time of Perón's June 1943 coup d'état. The paragraph immediately preceding the cited passage read: "Ours will be a generation sacrificed on the altar of the highest good, that of the Argentine nation, which will later shine with unparalleled brilliance for the greater good of the continent and all humanity." From Colonel Juan V. Oroña, *La logia militar que derrocó a Castillo* (Buenos Aires, 1966), 111; translation from Joseph S. Tulchin, *Problems in Latin American History: The Modern Period* (New York: Harper and Row, 1973), 308.

2. Oscar Troncoso, "El proceso de reorganización nacional/1 (De marzo de 1976 a marzo de 1977)," in Daniel Rodríguez Lamas et al., *Presidencias y golpes militares del siglo XX* (Buenos Aires: Biblioteca Política Argentina, Centro Editor de América Latina, 1985), 88.

3. Translation of the coup d'état proclamations are from Brian Loveman and Thomas M. Davies, Jr., *The Politics of Antipolitics: The Military in Latin America* (Lincoln: University of Nebraska Press, 1978), 178–179. Similarly the proclamations asserted: "We trust that both workers and businessmen will be conscious of the sacrifices required in these early days" and "the task before us is both arduous and pressing. It will not be free of sacrifices." Loveman and Davies, *The Politics of Antipolitics*, 180 and 177, respectively.

4. Emilio E. Massera, *El camino a la democracia* (Buenos Aires: El Cid Editores, 1979), 51.

5. Emilio E. Massera, *El país que queremos* (Buenos Aires: Editorial FEPA, 1981), 38.

6. For discussion see Chapter 3.

7. *El Diario del Juicio* 25 (November 12, 1985).

8. Cited in Suzanne Campbell-Jones, "Ritual in Performance and Interpretation: The Mass in a Convent Setting," in M.F.C. Bourdillon and Meyer Fortes, eds., *Sacrifice* (London: Academic Press, 1980), 100.

9. Walter Burkert, *Homo Necans: The Anthropology of Ancient Greek Sacrificial Ritual and Myth*, trans. Peter Bing (Berkeley: University of California Press,

1983), 3. Religious man acts and attains self-awareness as a man who kills, and Burkert also reminded his readers that those "who turn to religion for salvation from this 'so-called evil' of aggression are confronted with murder at the very core of Christianity—the death of God's innocent son." He followed this with precedents from the Old Testament, concluding that "blood and violence lurk fascinatingly at the very heart of religion." Burkert, *Homo Necans*, 1–2.

10. Alfredo López Austin, *The Human Body and Ideology: Concepts of the Ancient Nahuas*, vol. 1, trans. Thelma Ortiz de Montellano and Bernard Ortiz de Montellano (Salt Lake City: University of Utah Press, 1988), 377.

11. Yototl González Torres, *El sacrificio humano entre los mexicas* (Mexico City: Fondo de Cultura Económica, 1985), 26.

12. Burkert, *Homo Necans*, 29.

13. For a discussion of sacrifice "as being, mostly, about *power*, or *powers*," see J.H.M Beattie, "On Understanding Sacrifice," in M.F.C. Bourdillon and Meyer Fortes, eds., *Sacrifice* (London: Academic Press, 1980), 37–39.

14. González Torres, *El sacrificio humano*, 36. See also Ross Hassig, *Aztec Warfare: Imperial Expansion and Political Control* (Norman: University of Oklahoma Press, 1988), 11, where Aztec "religion and ideology were manipulated in the service of the State."

15. These passages and the one in the previous sentence are from Laurette Séjourné's "Ensayo sobre el sacrificio humano," in *Cuadernos Americanos* 9, no. 5 (1950): 171. For a brief discussion of the "panic dread" resulting from the collapse of a militarized social system, see Sigmund Freud, *Group Psychology and the Analysis of the Ego*, trans. James Strachey (London: Hogarth Press, 1948), 46–51. René Girard noted: "When the religious framework of a society starts to totter, it is not exclusively or immediately the physical security of the society that is threatened; rather, the whole cultural foundation of the society is put in jeopardy. The institutions lose their vitality; the protective facade of the society gives way; social values are rapidly eroded, and the whole cultural structure seems on the verge of collapse." See Girard, *Violence and the Sacred*, trans. Patrick Gregory (Baltimore, Md.: Johns Hopkins University Press, 1977), 49.

16. "Aztec" will be used rather than "Mexica" to avoid confusion among nonspecialists.

17. González Torres, *El sacrificio humano*, 254.

18. López Austin, *The Human Body*, 251. González Torres similarly addressed "regeneration through sacrifice of human beings." *El sacrificio humano*, 100.

19. See Hernán Cortés, *Letters from Mexico*, trans. and ed. Anthony Pagden (New Haven, Conn.: Yale University Press, 1986), 472.

20. Ibid., 462.

21. López Austin, *The Human Body*, 380. The political function of sacrifice has been most forcefully developed in Laurette Séjourné's "Ensayo" and "Los

sacrificios humanos: ¿Religión o política?" in *Cuadernos Americanos* 17, no. 1 (1958).

Bernal Díaz, on the Cortés expedition conquering the Aztecs, described his captured fellow soldiers' demise in sacrificial rituals and then remarked: "I feared death more than ever." See Bernal Díaz del Castillo, *Historia de la conquista de Nueva España* (Mexico City: Editorial Porrúa, 1983), 372.

22. See Diego Durán, *The Aztecs*, trans. Doris Heyden and Fernando Horcasitas (New York: Orion Press, 1964), 109–113. A passage from the *Crónica Mexicayotl* is engraved on the wall in Mexico City's Museo de Antropología: "We will go out to establish ourselves and conquer all peoples of the universe; and for that reason I tell you in all truth that you will be the lords and kings of everything all over the world; and when you are kings you will have innumerable, interminable subjects who will pay you tribute."

23. Cited in Séjourné, "Ensayo," 166. Parents were sentenced to sacrifice for insubordination if they protested the authority's purchase of their children for sacrifice to the rain gods.

24. Quoted phrases from Séjourné, "Los sacrificios," 147. Nietzsche similarly referred to the Aztec's " 'deification' of cruelty."

25. Diego Durán, *Historia de las Indias de Nueva España*, vol. 1 (Mexico City: Editora Nacional, 1951), 192. One of the primary targets of the empire was the wealthy Tlaxcala, whose riches derived from an extensive mercantile network that the Aztecs sought to control.

26. See Chapter 1 for details regarding "spoils" of the "dirty war." There is notable medieval European precedent in Aquinas, who "supported the right of just warriors to retain their plunder without sin provided their pillaging was motivated by justice rather than cupidity." See Frederick H. Russell, *The Just War in the Middle Ages* (Cambridge: Cambridge University Press, 1979), 278. During the most active years (850–1250) of the Spanish Reconquest, "military action was most frequently a raid for booty, including slaves." Mark A. Burkholder and Lynan L. Johnson, *Colonial Latin America* (New York: Oxford University Press, 1990), 16.

27. In addition to the observations below, the concept of human life as a commodity was suggested in the "dirty war" by the adoption (or sale) of some *desaparecidas'* newborns to families affiliated with the repression. See Chapter 1 for discussion.

28. See Hassig, *Aztec Warfare*, 121.

29. The original Tovar manuscript is in the John Carter Brown Library, Providence, R.I. Cited passage from *Manuscrit Tovar: Origines et croyances des Indiens du Mexique*, Jacques Lafaye (Graz, Austria: Akademische Druck-und Verlagsanstalt, 1972), 93. Tovar added: "In these battles they intended more to capture than to kill because the entire idea was to bring men back alive to feed the idol." The wording is almost identical in Durán.

30. The staging of war, both "dirty" and "flower," was reinforced by other theatrics: "An appearance of open hostility was maintained for the benefit of the common people." Cortés, *Letters from Mexico*, 462.

31. Ibid., 464.

32. Hassig, *Aztec Warfare*, 114–115. The captives were then bound or placed in cages for transport.

33. Quoted passage from ibid., 115.

34. Girard, *Violence and the Sacred*, 4. Regarding the Aztecs López Austin added: "These ritual deaths originated in the concept of gods in need, starving, desirous of vital force. Man, dependent on divine gifts, must restore vigor to his benefactors by surrendering energy from the different components of his own organism." López Austin, *The Human Body*, 377.

35. Anna Freud, *The Ego and the Mechanisms of Defense*, trans. Cecil Baines (New York: International Universities Press, 1966), 113.

36. "Phalli and phallic symbols are a common, if not a universal, attribute of early deities." This observation was followed by a number of examples in R. Money-Kyrle, *The Meaning of Sacrifice* (London: Hogarth Press, 1930), 61. In the perspective of traditional psychoanalysis, the same author also noted, on p. 64, that "a god, like a king, is a substitute for a father. He is invented to still a need."

37. Most societies that practiced sacrifice did so only at moments of crisis, and the victims were relatively few. Only the Mexicas and a few other Mesoamerican peoples "sacrificed men in such huge quantities and with such frequency." González Torres, *El sacrificio humano*, 301.

38. Séjourné, "Ensayo," 168. As Tovar explained it the priests claimed the gods (sun) were "dying of hunger" and asked for war to provide sacrifical victims to feed them. Lafaye, *Manuscrit Tovar*, 93.

39. Bourdillon and Fortes, *Sacrifice*, xvi.

40. Burkert, *Homo Necans*, 7. Burkert continued: "Is the god 'to whom' the sacrifice is made any more than a transparent excuse for festive feasting? All he gets are the bones, the fat, and the gall bladders. Hesiod says that the crafty Prometheus, the friend of mankind, caused this to be so in order to deceive the gods, and the burning of the bones became a standard joke in Greek comedy."

41. Cortés, *Letters from Mexico*, 457. Prior to this occasion only birds and small animals were sacrificed. See also Séjourné, "Los sacrificios."

42. Séjourné, "Ensayo," 166. "The birth of the Sun appears in some legends as fertilization by the celestial Father, pregnancy of the terrestrial mother, and the birth of the luminous Sun." López Austin, *The Human Body*, 56. The sacrificers as Son thus generated a victimage to nourish themselves.

43. The *corpus mysticum* is discussed in Chapter 3. For details see Ernst H. Kantorowicz, *The King's Two Bodies: A Study in Mediaeval Political Theology* (Princeton, N.J.: Princeton University Press, 1957), 193–232.

44. Marcial Castro Castillo, *Fuerzas armadas: Etica y represión* (Buenos Aires: Editorial Nuevo Orden, 1979), 130.

45. Jacobo Timerman, *Prisoner Without a Name, Cell Without a Number,* trans. Toby Talbot (New York: Vintage Books, 1982), 31. "For there is no power but of God: The powers that be are ordained of God. Whosoever therefore resisteth the power, resisteth the ordinance of God." Romans 13:1–2; see also 13:4. Compare this with Money-Kyrle: "The voice of the avenger within the self is ventriloquized and heard as the voice of God." Money-Kyrle, *The Meaning of Sacrifice,* 205.

46. *Nunca más: Informe de la Comisión Nacional Sobre la Desaparición de Personas* (Buenos Aires and Barcelona: EUDEBA/Seix Barral, 1985), 31/24–25, see also 72/69; and Geuna, CELS, 20, see also 6 and 48. (In this and subsequent *Nunca más* citations, page numbers after the slash refer to the English-language edition of this work, published in New York by Farrar, Straus and Giroux in 1986.) A sign at one detention center read: "Welcome to Olympia of the Gods." *El Diario del Juicio* 5 (25 June 1985): 114. See also *Nunca más,* 163/149, where likewise El Olímpo was "thus named because it was 'the place of the gods.'" One can imagine "dirty war" torturers uttering words much the same as the following, addressed by Oedipus to the chorus "as if addressing the entire city of Thebes": "You pray to the gods? Let me grant your prayers." See Sophocles, *The Three Theban Plays,* trans. Robert Fagles (New York: Penguin Books, 1984), 171.

47. John T. Irwin, "The Dead Father in Faulkner," in Robert Con Davis, ed., *The Fictional Father: Lacanian Readings of the Text* (Amherst: University of Massachusetts Press, 1981), 168. He continued, "In Christianity, not only does God become man, and man put God to death, but as a result of that death, man now enjoys a privilege that formerly belonged only to the gods—immortality."

48. Guy Rosolato's phrase, cited in ibid.

49. López Austin, *The Human Body,* 376. The victims condemned to die in the arena of the Roman Empire's bloody *ludi* were also "sometimes dressed up as gods or other mythological figures." Aline Rouselle, *Porneia: On Desire and the Body in Antiquity,* trans. Felicia Pheasant (New York: Basil Blackwell, 1988), 128.

50. Book 2 of the Florentine Codex described this and many other examples. An English translation is available: Bernardino de Sahagún, *A History of Ancient Mexico,* trans. Fanny R. Bandelier (Glorieta, N.M.: Rio Grande Press, 1976). In Argentina the public was also expected to prepare for the "sacredness" of the ritual. Admiral Massera called for "an examination of conscience and reorganization of our attitudes" to participate in "an experience as truly natal as this one." Massera, *El camino,* 61.

51. See Burkert, *Homo Necans,* 76.

52. John 1:1. The related passage a few lines down in the text is from John 1:14.

53. Elvira Orphée, *La última conquista de El Angel* (Buenos Aires: Javier Vergara Editor, 1984), 60.

54. Jean-Pierre Bousquet, *Las locas de la Plaza de Mayo* (Buenos Aires: El Cid Editor, 1984), 47.

55. The cited task force vernacular is from *Nunca más*, 258/247. *Hacerle la obeja* was mistranslated in the English edition, where "'doing a sheep' to someone" should read "making one [turning one into] a sheep."

56. Matthew 10:16. Regarding pastor/sheep imagery in Christianity, Northrop Frye observed: "Perhaps the use of this particular convention is due to the fact that, being stupid, affectionate, gregarious, and easily stampeded, the societies formed by sheep are most like human ones." See Northrop Frye, *Anatomy of Criticism* (Princeton, N.J.: Princeton University Press, 1973), 143. For biblical passages on the essence of suffering, unjust suffering, persecution, and the joyful acceptance of these in Christ's name, see, for example, Matthew 5:10–12 and 10:24; John 15:19–21; 1 Peter 4:13–19; 2 Corinthians 1:4–7 and 4:9–11; and Timothy 2:10.

57. Quoted passage from Revelation 13:8. Also recall the well-known statement attributed to John the Baptist: "Behold the Lamb of God, who takes away the sins of the world." See also Genesis 22:8, where "God will provide himself a lamb for the burnt offering," the lamb, in rabbinic interpretation, being Isaac himself.

58. *Nunca más*, 355/356.

59. Ibid., 348/339. Since the Cuban revolution beards tend to be associated with communism. "Queer" is *puto* in the original.

60. *Nunca más*, 349/339–340.

61. *El Diario del Juicio* 29 (December 11, 1985): 530. Another instance of crucifixion, in this case upside down, was mentioned in John Simpson and Jana Bennett, *The Disappeared and the Mothers of the Plaza* (New York: St. Martin's Press, 1985), 19. In Aztec culture crosses were associated with the gods of rain, and—as chronicler Diego de Landa reported in his *Relación de las cosas de Yucatán*—after the conquest the victims sacrificed to these gods were in some cases crucified before their hearts were extracted. See Cortés, *Letters from Mexico*, 450.

62. Quoted passages from Philippians 2:11.

63. Sigmund Freud, *Moses and Monotheism*, *Standard Edition*, ed. James Strachey, vol. 23 (London: Hogarth Press, 1964), 136.

64. Guy Rosolato, cited in Irwin, "The Dead Father," 164–165.

65. Ibid., 165.

66. Cited passage from 2 Corinthians 4:10

67. *El Libro de El Diario del Juicio* (Buenos Aires: Editorial Perfil, 1985), 91. The English here is retranslated back from the Spanish transcription.

68. Mark 15:12–14.

69. Cited in Emilio F. Mignone, *Iglesia y dictadura* (Buenos Aires: Ediciones del Pensamiento Nacional, 1986), 154.

70. Cited in Daniel Frontalini and María Cristina Caiati, *El mito de la guerra sucia* (Buenos Aires: Centro de Estudios Legales y Sociales, 1984), 23. In the ESMA detention center a priest was told: "You're not a guerrilla, you're not involved in the violence, but you don't realize that when you go to live there [in an impoverished community] you unite with people, you unite with the poor, and uniting with the poor is subversion." Following the murder of a bishop, another repressor commented: "That communist priest *hijo de puta* had it coming." Mignone, *Iglesia y dictadura*, 192.

71. *Nunca más*, 349/340.

72. The Maenads' Dionysian ritual (the *oreibasia*, or "raving on the mountains") similarly culminated in the *sparagmos* (tearing apart) and omophagy (eating raw) of an animal or human victim.

73. In addition to ritual cannibalism, the Aztecs practiced *teoqualo* ("god-eating") in a form similar to Christian communion. A dough-like paste was made in the figure of the god Huitzilopochtli, then ritually divided and eaten.

In Christendom the powers of the God's body internalized through communion gained expression in a cycle of medieval religious folktales in which the faithful were granted favors through visions in which they dipped the bread they ate into Christ's wounds. See Frederic C. Tubach, *Index Exemplorum: A Handbook of Medieval Religious Tales* (Helsinki: Suomalainen Tiedeakatemia Akademia Scientiarum Fennica, 1969), entry 761. These practices had precedent in antiquity: "Having been covered in flour, the child would be slaughtered by a neophyte. All those present would then dip pieces of bread in his blood and eat them, according to Tertullian. Minucius Felix . . . says that the child was eaten by the whole community." See Rousselle, *Porneia*, 115.

74. Cited in Campbell-Jones, "Ritual in Performance," 95.

75. Carolyn Walker Bynum, *Holy Feast and Holy Fast: The Religious Significance of Food to Medieval Women* (Berkeley: University of California Press, 1987), 49. In the "dirty war" burning (and also torturing) the victim's bodies was often referred to as "having a barbeque" and "grilling."

76. From Paschasius Radbertus of Corbie, *The Lord's Body and Blood*, in George E. McCracken, ed. and trans., *Early Medieval Theology* (Philadelphia, Pa.: Westminster Press, 1957), 96.

77. In his novel *Recuerdo de la muerte* (Mexico City: Ediciones Era, 1984), on p. 312, Miguel Bonasso wrote of the Montoneros who were granted elite status as detainees serving in an advisory capacity to Admiral Massera, referring to Massera's "anthropophagy" in "'eating' his victims" to acquire their attributes. Popular expressions in Argentina just before the fall of the Junta treated the motif during a procession of some 40,000 protesters, in which a placard contributed this message: "The cannibals ate themselves and 27,000 men, women

and children." Cited in Horacio Verbitsky, *Civiles y militares: Memoria secreta de la transición* (Buenos Aires: Editorial Contrapunto, 1987), 37. The cannibal trope, which I shall return to, was borrowed from Argentine author Jorge Luis Borges. The 27,000 figure referred to some human rights groups' estimate of the number of *desaparecidos*.

78. "Born of Desire, action tends to satisfy it, and can do so only by the 'negation,' the destruction, or at least the transformation, of the desired object: To satisfy hunger, for example, the food must be destroyed or, in any case, transformed." Alexandre Kojève, *Introduction to the Reading of Hegel*, ed. Allan Bloom, trans. James H. Nichols, Jr. (New York: Basic Books, 1969), 4. Although the etymology does not sustain the relation, it is interesting to note that in Spanish the concepts of scatology and eschatology are represented by the same word, *escatología*.

79. Campbell-Jones, "Ritual in Performance," 99. One textual foundation for these beliefs is in 1 Corinthians 10:17: "Because the bread is one, we though many, are one body, all of us who partake of the one bread."

80. Frye, *Anatomy of Criticism*, 143. Bynum broadens the image: Eating in the late Middle Ages was "an occasion for union with one's fellows and one's God, a commensality given particular intensity by the prototypical meal, the eucharist, which seemed to hover in the background of any banquet." Bynum, *Holy Feast*, 3.

81. Ivan Pérez Bocanegra, *Ritual formulario, e institución de curas, para administrar a los naturales de este Reyno . . .* (Lima: Geronymo de Contreras, 1631), 420.

82. Frye, *Anatomy of Criticism*, 148. Similarly Dionysus (the god of wine) was himself killed and dismembered to serve as wine for sacramental drinking. On p. 222 Frye referred further to "the disappearance of the hero, a theme which often takes the form of *sparagmos* or tearing to pieces."

83. A symbolic *sparagmos* is registered in Argentine torture: "What does a man feel [when tortured with the *picana*]? . . . When electric shocks are applied, all that a man feels is that they're ripping apart his flesh." See Timerman, *Prisoner Without a Name*, 33. Recall that one of the figurative meanings of *picar* (at the root of *picana*) is "to cut into small pieces." More literally the knife was sometimes used in addition to or instead of the *picana*: The body of one victim, for example, "was lacerated all over. The boy showed the most horrible signs of torture, which had practically cut him to pieces." *Nunca más*, 309/318.

84. Cited in Bynum, *Holy Feast*, 66.

85. Evans-Pritchard, cited in Beattie, "On Understanding Sacrifice," 34. Beattie noted on p. 30 that the sacrificial offering represents "(probably among other things) the person or persons who are making the sacrifice or upon whose behalf the sacrifice is being made." Evans-Pritchard also recorded the sacrificial words of the Shilluk divine king: "The flesh of this animal is as my flesh, and its

blood is the same as my blood." See Campbell-Jones, "Ritual in Performance," 99. Jung observed, "What I sacrifice is my own selfish claim, and by doing this I give up myself. Every sacrifice is therefore, to a greater or lesser degree, a self-sacrifice." See C. G. Jung, *Psychology and Religion: West and East*, trans. R.F.C. Hull (New York: Pantheon Books, 1958), 261. Reflecting on the Book of Job, David Bakan noted: "The child who may be killed by the father is ambiguously both someone else and the father himself"; "A confounding of self and other is present from the beginning of sacrifice. One gives up what one loves—'giving up' being ambiguously intransitive and transitive." See David Bakan, *Disease, Pain and Sacrifice: Toward a Psychology of Suffering* (Chicago, Ill.: University of Chicago Press, 1968), 119 and 124, respectively.

86. John 10:30.

87. Daniel Sibony, "*Hamlet*: A Writing-Effect," *Yale French Studies* 55/56 (1977): 88. Money-Kyrle noted: "Direct expiation is vengeance against the self. . . . Vicarious expiation, on the other hand, is vengeance against the self by proxy"; "The desire for punishment is nothing more than the destructive impulse of an inverted hate, and the sense of guilt is simply the fear of this hate. The voice of the avenger within the self is ventriloquized and heard as the voice of God. And this voice is persistent and allows no rest until in despair its hearer turns and rends himself, or finds someone else to injure in his place." Money-Kyrle, *The Meaning of Sacrifice*, 205.

88. Jacques Lacan, "Desire and the Interpretation of Desire in *Hamlet*," trans. James Hulbert, *Yale French Studies* 55/56 (1977): 16.

89. Like the detention center, the space in which the Aztec "flower wars" took place was sacred and assumed special significance. Hassig, *Aztec Warfare*, 10. For a lucid discussion of penal contexts in which deviance can be legitimately enacted, see Bruce Jackson, "Deviance as Success: The Double Inversion of Stigmatized Roles," in Barbara A. Babcock, ed., *The Reversible World: Symbolic Inversion in Art and Society* (Ithaca, N.Y.: Cornell University Press, 1978), 258–275.

90. Friedrich Nietzsche, *On the Genealogy of Morals and Ecce Homo*, trans. Walter Kaufmann (New York: Vintage Books, 1969), 92.

91. See Horacio Verbitsky, *La última batalla de la tercera guerra mundial* (Buenos Aires: Editorial Legasa, 1984), 47, where Junta member Ramón Agosti made reference to the Junta in holy trinity terms as "three military powers exercizing the indivisible political power of the Nation, embodied in the Military Junta."

92. Henri Hubert and Marcel Mauss, *Sacrifice: Its Nature and Function*, trans. W. D. Halls (Chicago, Ill.: University of Chicago Press, 1964), 98. Simon O. Lesser's discussion of audience response to tragedy in *Fiction and the Unconscious* (Boston: Beacon Hill, 1957), 238–268, is useful in understanding how the population at large also "sacrifices itself" through the *desaparecidos* as scapegoats.

Lesser described how a tragedy's audience vicariously but emotionally participates in the drama via identification with the characters. At some point after the hero's reversal of fortunes, however, the audience disengages to avoid even vicarious participation in the hero's destruction.

93. Lieutenant Colonel Enrique Rottjer made this statement at the time of the September 6, 1930, coup d'état; cited in Frederick M. Nunn, *Yesterday's Soldiers: European Military Professionalism in South America, 1890–1940* (Lincoln: University of Nebraska Press, 1983), 261. In Carapintada ideology "the soldier must be for the citizens the very incarnation of the contents of National Being." See Raúl Jassen, *Seineldín: El ejército traicionado, la patria vencida* (Buenos Aires: Editorial Verum et Militar, 1989), 180.

Jacques Derrida observed that "the pharmaceutical operation must . . . *exclude itself from itself,*" an observation that is particularly relevant in light of the germ/antibody trope discussed in Chapter 3. See his *Dissemination,* trans. Barbara Johnson (Chicago, Ill.: University of Chicago Press, 1981), 128.

94. Hebrews 2:9.

95. Bynum, *Holy Feast,* 31. On p. 54 she wrote, "Christ 'digested' Christians, binding them to his body—i.e., the church."

96. "Jesus Christ, III" *Catholic Encyclopedia,* vol. 7 (New York: McGraw Hill, 1967), 931. Compare this with Chapter 3, where the Junta killing subversives stylized as death is discussed.

97. This relation of the Many (*desaparecidos*) killed for the One (Junta) was illustrated at a more fundamental level by the detention centers' economics of retribution: "If a soldier, worker or member of the public died, four of us [prisoners] would be killed; if on the other hand the victim were a junior officer, the payment would increase, and so on up the scale until it reached Videla himself. In that case we would all be shot without hesitation." *Nunca más,* 205/ 190.

98. See Jacques Lacan/Anthony Wilden, *The Language of the Self: The Function of Language in Psychoanalysis* (Baltimore, Md.: Johns Hopkins University Press, 1968), 304. Concerning the Aztecs López Austin wrote: "The vocabulary in use indicates that in reality it was a kind of business transaction: Sacrifice to the gods was called *nextlahualiztli,* literally an 'act of payment.'" López Austin, *The Human Body,* 74. Elsewhere Aeschylus referred to the Erinyes as "collectors of blood," "as though they were a kind of tax officials. The murderer must 'pay.'" J. P. Guépin, *The Tragic Paradox: Myth and Ritual in Greek Tragedy* (Amsterdam: A. M. Hakkert, 1968), 160. Mark 10:45 explains that Christ came "to give his life as ransom for many."

99. Guépin pointed out that *sacer* may also signify "cursed," the etymology thus carrying the sacred/cursed ambiguity of the sacrificial victim.

100. Girard, following Marcel Mauss, in *Violence and the Sacred,* 1. Blame for violence against the sacrosanct is sometimes projected onto the victims

themselves. Burkert noted that certain Greek myths transform Dionysus into a kid and that "because it was simpler to style the sacrificial animal an 'enemy of god,'" the goat was killed for Dionysus "because it gnaws at the vine." Burkert, *Homo Necans*, 77.

101. González Torres, *El sacrificio humano*, 304.

102. For a succinct catalog of examples, see René Girard, *To Double Business Bound* (Baltimore, Md.: Johns Hopkins University Press, 1988), 144.

103. Cited in Rousselle, *Porneia*, 127–128.

104. Ibid., 128.

105. J. P. Vernant, "Ambiguity and Reversal: On the Enigmatic Structure of *Oedipus Rex*," in Harold Bloom, ed., *Sophocles' "Oedipus Rex"* (New York: Chelsea House, 1988), 115.

106. Walter Burkert, *Greek Religion: Archaic and Classical*, trans. John Raffan (London: Basil Blackwell, 1985), 83.

107. Girard, *Violence and the Sacred*, 39.

108. Both passages from Castro Castillo, *Fuerzas armadas*, 82.

109. Heraclitus (recognizing that purification with blood in the Greek mode is troublesome), as cited in Guépin, *The Tragic Paradox*, 167.

110. For Girard's definition of "scapegoat," see his "Generative Scapegoating," in Robert G. Hamerton-Kelly, ed., *Violent Origins: Walter Burkert, René Girard and Jonathan Z. Smith on Ritual Killing and Cultural Formation* (Stanford, Calif.: Stanford University Press, 1987).

111. Girard, *Violence and the Sacred*, 8.

112. Girard, "Generative Scapegoating," 91.

113. Julia Kristeva, *Revolution in Poetic Language*, trans. Margaret Waller (New York: Columbia University Press, 1984), 75.

114. Girard, "Generative Scapegoating," 78–79. Elsewhere Girard similarly observed: "The sacrificial process requires a certain degree of *misunderstanding*. The celebrants do not and must not comprehend the true role of the sacrificial act." Girard, *Violence and the Sacred*, 7.

115. Hamerton-Kelly, *Violent Origins*, 9.

116. Burkert, *Homo Necans*, 34.

117. Anna Freud, *The Ego*, 118–119.

118. Burkert, *Homo Necans*, 38.

119. Cited in Verbitsky, *Civiles y militares*, 38. The rhythm and rhymes of the chant are lost in translation.

120. Sigmund Freud, *An Outline of Psycho-Analysis*, trans. James Strachey (New York: Norton, 1969), 59.

121. Lacan/Wilden, *The Language of the Self*, 96.

122. Jean-Paul Sartre, *Being and Nothingness: An Essay on Phenomenological Ontology*, trans. Hazel E. Barnes (New York: Philosophical Library, n.d.), 49.

123. Guépin, *The Tragic Paradox*, 33.

124. See Hyman Maccoby, *The Sacred Executioner* (London: Thames and Hudson, 1982), 8. Guépin noted, on p. 33, that "all partook of the meat" and that in related sacrificial rituals the Cretans "imitated the ravings of an unbalanced mind, in order that it might be believed [by Zeus] that the awful crime [the sacrifice] was committed not by guile but in madness." Burkert cited a Babylonian text concerning bull sacrifice that described a priest bending over the bull's severed head to explain, "This deed was done by all the gods; I did not do it." Burkert, *Homo Necans*, 11. Finally the blame is put on the sacrificial bull himself, "for the first step in the ceremony was to coax the bull to the vicinity of the altar on which lay some sacred barley-corns"; when the bull ate, "his death was then regarded as deserved for this sacrilege." Maccoby, *The Sacred Executioner*, 177.

125. For discussion of the politics, see Mark Osiel, "The Making of Human Rights Policy in Argentina: The Impact of Ideas and Interests on a Legal Conflict," in *Journal of Latin American Studies* 135 (1986), particularly pp. 148–159.

126. "Hegemonía militar, estado y dominación social," in Alain Rouquié, ed., *Argentina hoy* (Mexico City: Siglo XXI, 1982), 28.

127. "Vivas a Rico en Campo de Mayo," *La Nación*, June 10, 1989.

128. Quoted phrases were cited in Shirley Christian, "Army's Rambo, Ousted, Is Storming the Hustings," *New York Times*, April 5, 1990.

129. Clifford Geertz, "Centers, Kings, and Charisma: Reflections on the Symbolics of Power," in Sean Wilentz, ed., *Rites of Power: Symbolism, Ritual and Politics Since the Middle Ages* (Philadelphia: University of Pennsylvania Press, 1985), 33. In many agendas of political or social violence leaders emerge as exaggerated expressions of conscious or unconscious desires with considerable currency in their populations. "I know that everything you are, you are through me, and everything I am, I am through you alone," Adolf Hitler could assert, with Charles Manson behind him almost verbatim: "I am only what lives inside each and every one of you . . . I am only what you made me. I am a reflection of you." See Charles Lindhold, *Charisma* (New York: Basil Blackwell, 1990), 101 and 131. See also p. 7, where charisma was described as "*a relationship*, a mutual mingling of the inner selves of leader and follower."

130. Maccoby, *The Sacred Executioner*, 179.

131. Guépin, *The Tragic Paradox*, 62. The same author similarly observed on p. 5: "The killing is a necessary evil; it evokes feelings of guilt, which are evaded as much as possible by all kinds of religious precautions and artifices, but the guilt often breaks forth in the form of a talion: The sacrificer must be sacrificed in his turn."

132. Vernant, "Ambiguity and Reversal," 121–122.

133. Ibid., 119.

134. Girard, *Violence and the Sacred*, 23 and 18, respectively.

135. Castro Castillo, *Fuerzas armadas*, 132.

136. "Whether juridical or ritual processes of redress are invoked against mounting crisis, the result is an increase in what one might call social or plural *reflexivity*, the way in which a group tries to scrutinize, portray, understand, and then act on itself." See Victor Turner, *From Ritual to Theatre: The Human Seriousness of Play* (New York: Performing Arts Journal Publications, 1982), 75.

137. Alberto Amato, "Lo que nunca debió pasar," *El Diario del Juicio* (September 24, 1985).

138. General Videla in *El Diario del Juicio* 25 (November 12, 1985).

139. Cited in Enrique Vázquez, *PRN/La Ultima: Origen, apogeo y caída de la dictadura militar* (Buenos Aires: EUDEBA, 1985), 85. The sacrificial rhetoric continues in the 1990s. On the first anniversary of the La Tablada attack, army commander General Isidro Cáceres referred characteristically to the "dirty war" "in which the Armed Forces fully delivered themselves to sacrifices in order to overcome the scourge of subversion." Cited in *Boletín CELS*, 6, no. 19 (February/ March, 1990): 2.

140. See Verbitsky, *Civiles y militares*, 119.

141. "Situación del militar que exaltó a Videla," *La Razón*, January 18, 1986.

142. *El Diario del Juicio* 22 (October 22, 1985).

143. *El Diario del Juicio* 32 (December 31, 1985).

144. *El Diario del Juicio* 25 (November 12, 1985).

145. Quoted passage from Fyodor Dostoevsky, *The Brothers Karamazov*, trans. Constance Garnett (New York: Signet Classics, 1957), 592.

About the Book
and Author

A fascinating account of political repression in Argentina, this book takes as its thematic locus the intersection of religion, violence, and psychosexuality as they relate to the desire for power and to the myths and rituals manifesting that desire. Graziano's inquiry into the source of political violence is culturally grounded, focusing on psychological, historical, anthropological, and religious phenomena often dismissed as "insignificant peculiarities" in traditional investigations.

The author traces the messianic mythology ratifying the Junta's "dirty war" to the medieval Christian paradigm on which it is based, providing a historical and ideological context for understanding contemporary perceptions of torture and execution as necessary, holy acts. The study also explores the relation of Argentine political atrocity to rituals of human sacrifice in Aztec and other preindustrial cultures, to medieval and early-modern practices of torture, to eighteenth-century public executions in Europe, and to sexual murders. "Disappearance" and torture as political strategies, the social roles imposed by repressive regimes, and symbolic constructs of the "invisible enemy" are also treated in depth.

Divine Violence is based on analysis of victim testimony, formal and informal military discourse, trial transcripts, detention center vernacular, and torturer statements, substantiated by a vast multidisciplinary body of secondary literature. The result is a book that not only offers astonishing insights into state terror in Argentina but also elucidates the historical development of violent repression as a social rite and as a political practice in Western culture.

Frank Graziano is assistant professor of Spanish and Latin American studies at The American University. He has recently held fellowships from the John Carter Brown Library, The Johns Hopkins University, and the Fulbright Scholar Program. His many publications include studies of Alejandra Pizarnik, Felisberto Hernández, and Saint Rose of Lima.

Index

AAA. *See* Anti-Comunista Argentina
  (Argentine Anti-Communist
  Alliance)
Abductions, 36–37, 41, 95, 193, 251(n15)
  Enemy and, 142
  erroneous, 40, 102
  flaunting, 78
  guilt and, 91
  as incorporation, 176, 208–209
  mythology of, 52
  naturalization of, 112
  overacted, 80
  secret, 65, 255(n68)
  vernacular of, 262(n150)
  See also Disappearances
Absence
  Hero and, 138–140
  rectifying, 140–141
  sacrifice and, 193–194
  unresolved, 187
Absorption
  abduction and, 208–209
  vernacular of, 262(n150)
Abstract spectacles, 73–76, 153, 154
  implied audience for, 76, 78–81,
    255(n62)
  psychological effect of, 82, 84
  ritual efficacy of, 75
Acts and Statutes of the Process of
  National Reorganization, 34–35, 42
Adoptions
  forced, 37, 298(n27)
  See also Children

Aggressor, identification with, 76–77, 171–
  175, 180, 200, 220, 256(n70)
Agosti, Orlando Ramón, 239(n40),
  245(n108), 248(n142), 271(n83),
  304(n91)
  sentence for, 53
Aguarunas, 264(nn 185, 186)
  headshrinking rituals of, 105
Alfonsín, Raúl, 222, 224, 249(nn 159, 163),
  255(n66), 291(n141)
  amnesty and, 54, 58
  commission of inquiry of, ix
  inauguration of, 49–50
  La Tablada incident and, 175–176
  Montoneros and, 247(n137)
  Semana Santa uprisings and, 55–58,
    260(n126)
Amaru, Tupac: execution of, 69, 253(n40)
Amnesty, 54
  conditional, 42–43, 247(n135)
  rebelling for, 55–57, 58
  See also Pardon
Amnesty Law. *See* Law of National
  Pacification
Anaya, Jorge Isaac, 239(n40)
  sentence for, 53
Antibodies, 133, 136–137
Antichrist, 107, 127, 137, 145, 183, 190
  as death, 128
  Enemy as, 125
  infiltration by, 129
  See also Christ

311